Praise for *Reading Christian Apocrypha*

Nicklas and Spittler's *Reading Christian Apocrypha* invites us to consider a wide range of Christian texts as exactly that—texts that offer us profound insight into the history of Christian thought and practice. Shedding the boundaries of the canon as scholarly signposts, they powerfully demonstrate the value of Christian apocrypha for rigorous historiography, and the errors we make when we exclude these sources from our investigations of the past.

Meghan R. Henning, University of Dayton

In this wide-ranging and innovative study, Nicklas and Spittler say farewell to the notion that apocrypha are historically worthless and theologically often dangerous. Instead, they show the great contribution the apocrypha have made to the history of Christianity, from ancient Armenia to modern Auschwitz and from Ireland to India. Traveling apostles, baptizing women, and visionary knights are just some of the wonderful cast of characters in this fascinating book.

Jan N. Bremmer, University of Groningen

Tobias Nicklas and Jane E. Spittler have written a deeply insightful, engaging, and refreshingly original study of the Christian Apocrypha. Their superb book guides readers through key aspects of the apocryphal continent, demonstrating how essential it is to read apocryphal texts to truly grasp the complex dimensions of early and medieval Christianity. This compelling exploration of the Christian Apocrypha reshapes the field by introducing innovative methodological approaches—most notably, a fresh reading based on the French *lieux de mémoire* theory, which highlights how the construction of memory plays a vital role in shaping group identity. Combining scholarly excellence with remarkable accessibility, this is a must-read for anyone interested in the history of Christianity, biblical and New Testament studies, as well as ancient and medieval Christian literature.

Valentina Calzolari Bouvier, University of Geneva

READING CHRISTIAN APOCRYPHA

READING CHRISTIAN APOCRYPHA

TRADITION, INTERPRETATION, PRACTICE

TOBIAS NICKLAS
JANET E. SPITTLER

FORTRESS PRESS
Minneapolis

READING CHRISTIAN APOCRYPHA
Tradition, Interpretation, Practice

30 29 28 27 26 25 1 2 3 4 5 6 7 8 9

Library of Congress Control Number: 2025935083 (print)

Cover image: © The British Museum; One of a group of eight tiles at the British Museum associated with the parish church at Tring, Hertfordshire. England, c. 1320–1330.
Cover design: Laurie Ingram Art + Design.com

Print ISBN: 978-1-5064-8140-1
eBook ISBN: 978-1-5064-8141-8

CONTENTS

PREFACE

The following book is not intended as another "Introduction to Apocryphal Christian Literature," nor do we offer any new translations of apocryphal writings. Those who are interested in such introductions and translations can now make use of a wealth of excellent publications. In addition to a large number of books and articles, there is the fantastic website of NASSCAL (the North American Society for the Study of Christian Apocryphal Literature), which indexes an incredible number of writings and is constantly being updated with the latest research, including links to a wide range of online material, ranging from blog posts to digitized manuscripts.

We are also not interested in treating apocrypha as "sensational." In this book, no secrets are exposed, no hidden truths are brought to light. Our purpose is quite different, though—at least to us—no less exciting. We aim to illustrate how our understanding of the history of Christianity expands and changes when we take the testimony of apocryphal literature seriously. What do these works tell us about the development of early Christianity? about the various of forms of "lived religion"? about Christian ideas of time and space—indeed, of the world and its end? The idea here is not to replace the biblical canon with apocrypha. However, we believe that a canon—any canon—that is not in constant dialog with the world into which it is supposed to speak can become a dead, even dangerous object. Noncanonical works have always been part of this dialog—and continue to be to the present day.

To demonstrate this, we can only proceed with a series of examples, dismantling prejudices and opening up boundaries along the way. It is hardly necessary to say that this book is not the final word on the significance of apocrypha in the history of Christianity. To the contrary, it is an invitation to further study. We offer a wide array of hints and glimpses, rather than definitive analyses and conclusions. Trained as textualists, we work primarily with literature—but apocrypha are, of course, also represented in images, music, performance, architecture, etc. We concentrate largely on antiquity and late antiquity because this is where our expertise lies—but apocrypha were also produced and received throughout Middle Ages and beyond. In our selection of texts, we concentrate on writings from Europe, the Mediterranean region, and Western Asia—again, because these are the languages and traditions in which we were trained. The extent to which there is also exciting material produced in Latin America, Africa, Oceania or other parts of the world that can be meaningfully interpreted as "apocrypha" is still completely unexplored. We are certain that there are still huge treasures to be unearthed.

Before we embark on the actual reading journey, however, we would like to thank a number of people without whom this book would not have been possible. We have developed and discussed many of the ideas in this book between the two of us over the past few years. That's why we don't mark which of us contributed more in which chapter. Instead, we present this book as what it is: a joint effort in the truest sense of the word. It would, however, not have been possible without the larger network of all those who have been involved in the "Beyond Canon" project (DFG-KollegFOR 2770) at Universität Regensburg, Germany, since 2018. No one does truly good work on apocryphal Christian literature alone: the range of languages, geographical locations, and historical periods that a single tradition might span means that it is simply impossible for an individual human being to have all the requisite skills and expertise to do it justice. That's why we say that the study of Christian apocrypha is a "team sport." And we wouldn't have it any other way. It is impossible to say how many ideas we owe to the many conferences, seminars, and—perhaps most important of all—casual conversations over lunch or coffee that have taken place within the Beyond Canon Centre. This book is dedicated to those who make Beyond Canon a space in which we can think exciting and sometimes crazy things together.

Finally, we thank Carey Newman, who offered us the wonderful opportunity to publish with Fortress. This book would not have been possible without his patience and the competent support from him and the staff at the publishing house!

Tobias Nicklas and Janet E. Spittler
Regensburg and Charlottesville in December 2024

Introduction

Since the earliest forms of Christianity, the term *apocryphal* (Greek: "secret, hidden"), and thus also the works categorized as apocrypha,[1] has been burdened with prejudices that have made unbiased scholarly work with these texts and the traditions associated with them incredibly difficult. This burden persists even to the present day. The prejudicial notion that apocrypha are historically worthless and theologically deficient (if not heretical, even dangerous) is still prevalent not only among laypeople but also in academic circles. Even the literary value of apocryphal works is viewed as rather limited. At best, the study of such "inferior" texts testifies to a rather marginalized "popular religion" (German: *Volksfrömmigkeit*) that has very little to do with proper theology.

At the same time, apocryphal works fascinate. Just consider Dan Brown's *Da Vinci Code*, which centers on a conspiracy theory about an alleged child born of Jesus and Mary Magdalene that finds its basis, at least to some extent, in the interpretation of apocryphal writings such as the Gospel of Mary and the Gospel of Philip. The success of Brown's novel reveals an eagerness to search for the "true Jesus story" in hidden

1. For the moment, we are not thinking of the so-called OT Apocrypha (or, in Catholic parlance, "Deuterocanonical Writings" of the OT); rather, in this book we use *apocrypha* or *apocryphal works* to refer to noncanonical Christian literature. For more on OT Apocrypha, see, e.g., the contributions in the seminal volume by Gerbern S. Oegema, ed., *The Oxford Handbook of the Apocrypha* (Oxford University Press, 2021).

or suppressed traditions that is very much alive today.[2] And while the plot of Brown's novel is, from a scholarly perspective, preposterous, it is surely true that experts in the field are similarly drawn to the study of apocrypha at least in part for the potential of new discovery, of revealing previously unknown forms of early Christianity.

These two attitudes—that is, the *dismissal* of apocryphal works as historically and theologically inferior, if not heretical, and the *fascination* with such works as representing long-hidden or suppressed forms of Christianity—are perhaps two sides of the same coin. They represent, we think, similar assumptions about the nature of these works, while assigning opposite judgments about their value.

In essence, both these attitudes toward apocrypha are evident already in the testimonies of early Christian writers. In *Against Heresies* (*Haer.* 1.20.1), for example, Irenaeus of Lyons (ca. 130–205 CE) accuses his opponents of using "a vast quantity of apocryphal and forged writings . . . which they themselves have fabricated to prove their doctrines." Immediately afterward, he describes a story that probably goes back to the Infancy Gospel of Thomas, as a "fraud."[3] The testimony of Tertullian (ca. 150–220 CE) in *The Resurrection of the Flesh* (*Res.* 63) is little different: His opponents falsified "whether by pen or by interpretation" the truth by "smuggling in the secret teaching of apocryphal works, stories of blasphemy."[4] In this usage, which we also find in other early church authors, the term *apocryphal*, which, again, literally means "hidden" or "secret," is associated with writings that are described as forgeries, deception, heresy, or even blasphemy.

2. See also the stimulating discussion of this book by Bart D. Ehrman, *Truth and Fiction in "The Da Vinci Code": What We Really Know About Jesus, Mary Magdalene, and Constantine* (Oxford University Press, 2006); for the background of the plot see Umberto Eco, *Die Geschichte der legendären Länder und Städte*, 2nd ed. (Deutscher Taschenbuchverlag, 2016), 409–29.

3. Latin text in Irenaeus, *Epideixis. Darlegung der apostolischen Verkündigung. Adversus Haereses. Gegen die Häresien I*, ed. Norbert Brox, Fontes Christiani 8/1 (Herder, 1993).

4. Text: Tertullian, *Opera II*, CCSL 2:1012. Translation by Tobias Nicklas.

But even in ancient Christianity, the opposite attitude is also to be found: Some early Christian authors designated their own writings as apocryphal, though with a positive valence.[5] These works claim to contain hidden, that is, apocryphal wisdom and to reveal it to those who are worthy of it. This claim has an obvious appeal, no less in the ancient period than in the present. The best known of these writings is certainly the Gospel of Thomas, a collection of sayings of Jesus, the prologue of which reads:[6] "These are the secret [= "apocryphal"] sayings which the living Jesus spoke, and Didymus Judas Thomas wrote them down."[7] We find something very similar at the beginning of the Gospel of Judas,[8]

5. For more details see Tobias Nicklas, "'Apokryph gewordene Schriften'? Gedanken zum Apokryphenbegriff bei großkirchlichen Autoren und in einigen 'gnostischen' Texten," in *In Search of Truth: Augustine, Manichaeism and Other Gnosticism: Studies for Johannes van Oort at Sixty*, ed. Jacob Albert van den Berg et al., Nag Hammadi and Manichaean Studies 74 (Brill, 2011), 547–65.

6. See "e-Clavis Gospel of Thomas," North American Society for the Study of Christian Apocryphal Literature, accessed February 1, 2025, https://www.nasscal.com/e-clavis-christian-apocrypha/gospel-of-thomas/. J. Keith Elliott, *The Apocryphal New Testament* (Oxford University Press, 2009), 123–47, offers an English translation of this text. Jens Schröter and Hans-Gebhard Bethge, "Das Evangelium nach Thomas (Thomasevangelium [NHC II,2 p.32,10–51,28]) Oxyrhynchus Papyri I 1, IV 654 und IV 655 (P.Oxy. I 1, IV 654 und IV 655)," in *Antike christliche Apokryphen in deutscher Übersetzung*, ed. Christoph Markschies and Jens Schröter (Mohr Siebeck, 2012), 1:483–526, provide a good overview of introductory questions, and the most important questions concerning the composition of the work are also discussed in a convincing manner.

7. Simon Gathercole, trans., *The Gospel of Thomas: Introduction and Commentary*, TENTS 11 (Brill, 2014), 189.

8. See "e-Clavis Gospel of Judas," North American Society for the Study of Christian Apocryphal Literature, accessed February 1, 2025, https://www.nasscal.com/e-clavis-christian-apocrypha/gospel-of-judas/. For a more substantive introduction to this writing see, e.g., Gregor Wurst, "Das Judasevangelium (CT 3)," in Markschies and Schröter, *Antike christliche Apokryphen*, 1:1220–34; a commentary with an introduction and English translation (which is quoted here) is provided by Johanna Brankaer and Bas van Os, *The Gospel of Judas*, Oxford Early Christian Gospel Texts (Oxford University Press, 2019).

which describes itself as "the secret account of the pronouncement in which Jesus spoke with Judas Iscariot." Both the Gospel of Thomas and Gospel of Judas attract readers by claiming to offer something mysterious, that is, content that goes beyond what is found in other gospels that are broadly addressed to a general audience of Christians. They therefore claim authority without being or *wanting to become* canonical.

But perhaps such a statement about canon is anachronistic: It is true that some authors, beginning in the second half of the second century, already evince the outlines of collections of important Christian writings that were regarded as authoritative and used in various congregational contexts. This applies in particular to the widely but by no means unambiguously attested collection of the four Gospels but also to the first collections of the Pauline letters. We can only speak, however, of a well-defined canon, at the end of which was a stable corpus of catholic letters and the Apocalypse of John, from the middle of the fourth century onward.[9] Even then, however, we can assume neither that this canon was recognized in the same way everywhere nor that the books that made up such a canon were actually available and accessible in every Christian community.[10] Even less can we assume that every Christian community was in possession of a complete Bible in the modern sense. To the contrary: Possession of a complete Bible, even at the community

9. The usual overviews of the development of the NT canon fluctuate between the description of canonization through the editing of a "New Testament" book and the description of a complex multistage process in which various collections were created. The truth probably lies somewhere in between. A very well-balanced account that includes a wealth of material can be found, e.g., in Christoph Markschies, *Kaiserzeitliche christliche Theologie und ihre Institutionen: Prolegomena zu einer Geschichte der antiken christlichen Theologie* (Mohr Siebeck, 2007), 216–336; see also Markschies, "Haupteinleitung," in Markschies and Schröter, *Antike christliche Apokryphen*, 1:1–180; important innovative contributions also appear in the volume *New Perspectives on the Formation of the New Testament*, *EC* 7, no. 1 (2016): 1–152.

10. The testimony of catalogs of ancient Christian libraries is fascinating (see, e.g., Markschies, *Kaiserzeitliche christliche Theologie*, 298–330).

level, was probably the exception (if only for reasons of cost).[11] At the same time, writings that were *not* part of this canon continued to be used and recognized as authoritative at both local and regional levels.[12]

It is also evident that individual texts of the Bible—and the New Testament in particular—were not received solely (and perhaps not even primarily) as written texts. This is true of highly educated ancient interpreters of Scripture and more ordinary Christians. Instead, one could speak of a mental, virtual entity, a "Bible in the mind," that is, a combination of biblical stories, figures, thoughts, and motifs stored in the memory that could be activated, varied, and used for argumentative purposes in different ways depending on context.[13] The boundaries of such a Bible in the mind are more fluid than those of the written collection of texts known as the Bible. Take, as a quick example, the magi with their camels, who worship the Christ child at the stable in Bethlehem as a bright star with a long tail shines overhead. Does this scene come from the Bible, is it apocryphal, or does it perhaps merge various canonical

11. Helpful here, for example, is the data on Constantine's commission to produce fifty full Bibles for Constantinople in Theodore Cressy Skeat, "The Codex Sinaiticus, the Codex Vaticanus and Constantine," in *The Collected Biblical Writings of T.C. Skeat*, ed. J. Keith Elliott, NovTSup 113 (Brill, 2004), 193–237.

12. Good examples are the texts associated with the island of Cyprus and the apostle Barnabas, which played an important role in the ecclesiastical independence of Cyprus from the patriarchate in Antioch (on the Orontes) and which were certainly authoritative (in Cyprus!) but which never became part of a NT canon. For more on this, see Tobias Nicklas, "Barnabas Remembered: Apokryphe Barnabastexte und die Kirche Zyperns," in *Religion als Imagination: Phänomene des Menschseins in den Horizonten theologischer Lebensdeutung; Festschrift für Marco Frenschkowski*, ed. Lena Seehausen et al. (Evangelische Verlagsanstalt, 2020), 167–88.

13. This is one of the fundamental results of the Novum Testamentum Patristicum project: Andreas Merkt with Tobias Nicklas and Joseph Verheyden, "Das Novum Testamentum Patristicum (NTP): Ein Projekt zu Erforschung und Auslegung des Neuen Testaments in frühchristlicher und spätantiker Zeit," *EC* 6 (2015): 573–95. Tobias Nicklas is currently preparing a monograph in collaboration with Stefan Alkier and Christine Wenona Hoffmann, which will take a closer look at the phenomenon of the "Bible in the minds."

and extracanonical elements? For many readers of this book (as for most Christians through history), the scene is easy to call to mind and will feel utterly biblical. But is there a stable in the Matthean Bethlehem? And how many magi (or kings?) are present? Is it three? Is that detail in the biblical text, or does it have some other source? For some readers of this book (as indeed for the majority of Christians through history), calling the magi to mind includes recalling their names, though, like the number three, the names Caspar, Melchior, and Balthasar appear nowhere in the biblical text that recounts this scene.

If we truly want to understand early Christian writings, we must disentangle multiple threads that are easily confounded: The existence of a bound Bible is *not* the same thing as universal access to a single complete text, nor is the biblical text identical to the "Bible in the minds" of believers; the status of individual works as canonical or apocryphal does *not* always indicate authority claimed by or given to them, nor does that status correspond to the extent of their dissemination and use. Further, the status, dissemination, and usage of an individual work can change over time. A work such as the Protevangelium of James[14] was widely disseminated for centuries and formed the foundation of late antique and medieval devotion to Mary. In both Roman Catholic and Orthodox churches, motifs from the Protoevangelium continue

14. See "e-Clavis Protevangelium of James," North American Society for the Study of Christian Apocryphal Literature, accessed February 1, 2025, https://www.nasscal.com/e-clavis-christian-apocrypha/protevangelium-of-james/. Only in modern times was the title Protevangelium of James added to this writing. In antiquity, the title The Birth of Mary is the most well documented. The text was written in Syria or Alexandria toward the end of the second century. Basically, it describes the prehistory of the birth of first Mary and then Jesus, and places it in the history of Israel. An excellent English translation, with substantive introduction and notes, is Lily Vuong, *The Protevangelium of James*, Early Christian Apocrypha 8 (Cascade, 2019). Another easily accessible English translation is provided by Elliott, *Apocryphal New Testament*, 48–67; a good introduction in German can be found in Silvia Pellegrini, "Das Protevangelium des Jakobus," in Markschies and Schröter, *Antike christliche Apokryphen*, 1:903–29. Jan N. Bremmer et al., eds., *The Protevangelium of James*, Studies on Early Christian Apocrypha 16 (Peeters, 2020), offers an in-depth insight into the very current debate.

to form an important part of Marian tradition, particularly the pictorial program. The text, however, never claimed to be canonical in the modern sense. It seems that there was never any serious discussion about whether it could be included within the canon of the New Testament.[15] The Epistle of Jude, on the other hand, is generally recognized as canonical, but today there is hardly any context in which it is regularly used in pastoral work or authoritatively used as the basis of a theologically important argument. The aforementioned Gospel of Judas, which describes itself as apocryphal, makes the highest authoritative claim for itself, but its influence seems to have been quite minimal, being recognized and used by a very marginal group. The Tiburtine Sibyl, an apocalyptic text from the fourth century that continued to be copied and disseminated well into the Middle Ages, was at various moments in history widely disseminated and influential, particularly with respect to the end-time ideas of the medieval "Holy Roman Empire of the German Nation." Today, the work seems almost entirely forgotten.[16] A line in the "Dies Irae" portion of the requiem mass ("teste David cum Sibylla") is the most evident residue of the former great significance of this work, which once helped the Roman Empire (and its successors) to inscribe itself on world history. The Tiburtine Sibyl is just one example of an extracanonical apocalypse that, at particular moments and places in history, was maybe more influential than the canonical Revelation; several others could be cited. Just these few examples indicate how prejudices, assumptions, and the improper use of terms can result in misleading

15. See more specifically, however, the rich contribution by Thomas R. Karmann, "Apokryph oder doch geradezu kanonisch? Zur Rezeption des *Protevangelium Jacobi* im antiken Christentum," in Bremmer et al., *Protevangelium of James*, 1–48.

16. See "e-Clavis Tiburtine Sibyl," North American Society for the Study of Christian Apocryphal Literature, accessed February 1, 2025, https://www.nasscal.com/e-clavis-christian-apocrypha/tiburtine-sibyl/. A good introduction to this text (with an English translation and an extensive bibliography) can be found in Stephen J. Shoemaker, "The Tiburtine Sibyl," in *New Testament Apocrypha: More Noncanonical Scriptures*, ed. Tony Burke and Brent Landau (Eerdmans, 2016), 1:510–25.

and inaccurate reconstructions of the history of Christianity and of Christian literature.

But this brings us to a key problem in working with apocrypha: What do we actually understand the terms "New Testament apocrypha" or "Christian apocrypha" to mean? The answer is simultaneously simple and complicated. A provisional rule of thumb might rely on two notions: These are works that (1) did not become part of the canonical New Testament (or the Christian Bible consisting of the OT and NT) but (2) in some way resemble biblical, especially New Testament, texts and/or participate in the biblical narrative worlds.[17] Many apocryphal Christian works are similar in genre to the works we encounter in the New Testament: gospels and gospel-like texts, stories about the apostles and their disciples, epistolary literature, and apocalyptic writings. When we say that apocryphal works "participate in the biblical narrative worlds," we mean to include texts that feature plotlines and characters known from canonical narratives, including, of course, Jesus, Mary, and the apostles but also Old Testament figures such as Abraham, Moses, Esther, or Solomon. A useful, if imperfect, analogy is the way in which a newly produced Star Wars television series might participate in the narrative world of the original films.

This rule of thumb for defining "Christian apocrypha" can, of course, be criticized as too vague and/or too capacious. We would defend

17. Overviews of modern definitions of apocrypha are provided by Simon C. Mimouni, "Le concept d'apocryphité dans le christianisme ancien et médiéval: réflexions en guise d'introduction," in *Apocryphité. Histoire d'un concept transversal aux religions du livre; En hommage à P. Geoltrain*, ed. Simon C. Mimouni, BEHER 113 (Brepols, 2002), 8–12, as well as Markschies, "Haupteinleitung," 111–14, who himself proposes the following definition: "'Apocrypha' are Jewish and Christian texts that have become canonical or tell stories about figures from biblical writings that have become canonical or pass on the words of such figures or claim to have been written by a biblical figure. They have not become canonical, but in some cases they were not intended to be. In some cases, they were also a genuine expression of the religious of the religious life of the majority church and often had a profound influence on theology and the visual arts." English translation from the German by Jacob Cerone.

it by observing that a definition that is based solely or too closely on the genres of New Testament literature is in danger of regarding apocryphal writings merely as imitations of canonical texts and the genres they represent. In fact, precisely these erroneous conclusions have been drawn over and over again in the history of scholarship. Moreover, the overreliance on genre in a definition of Christian apocrypha is immediately suspect, inasmuch as these early Christian genres are hardly uniform: The various texts that were referred to by early Christians as gospels, for example, are extremely diverse.[18] What's more, individual apocryphal writings may in fact be as old as or older than their canonical counterparts. This applies to the Apocalypse of Peter, which could be one of the sources of 2 Peter, to the Gospel of Thomas, and to the Gospel of Marcion, which some scholars consider to be a prefiguration of the Gospel of Luke we possess today.[19] Regardless of our evaluation

18. See the wonderful variety of texts compiled in Markschies and Schröter, *Antike christliche Apokryphen*. The preface to the Oxford Early Christian Gospel Texts series is also very helpful; see Christopher Tuckett, "Series Preface," in Christopher Tuckett, *The Gospel of Mary*, Oxford Early Christian Gospel Texts (Oxford University Press, 2007), v–xi.

19. On the Apocalypse of Peter possibly being one of the sources of 2 Peter, see Wolfgang Grünstäudl, *Petrus Alexandrinus: Studien zum historischen und theologischen Ort des zweiten Petrusbriefes*, WUNT 2/353 (Mohr Siebeck, 2013), 165–81, as well as, following Grünstäudl with slight modifications, Jörg Frey, "Second Peter in New Perspective," in *2 Peter and the Apocalypse of Peter: Towards a New Perspective*, ed. Jörg Frey et al., BIS 174 (Brill, 2019), 15–23. We consider it unlikely that the Gospel of Thomas was written very early. The extent to which the canonical Gospel of Luke is really the source of the Gospel of Marcion text or an edited form of it is increasingly being discussed. An overview of various proposals can be found, for example, in Dieter T. Roth, "Marcion's Gospel and Luke: A History of Research in Current Debate," *JBL* 177 (2008): 513–27, as well as Daniel A. Smith, "Marcion's Gospel and the Synoptics: Proposals and Problems," in *Gospels and Gospel Traditions in the Second Century: Experiments in Reception*, ed. Jens Schröter et al., BZNW 235 (de Gruyter, 2020), 129–74. Especially important are the voices of Matthias Klinghardt, *Das älteste Evangelium und die Entstehung der kanonischen Evangelien*, Texte und Arbeiten zum neutestamentlichen Zeitalter 60.1–2 (Francke, 2015), and Markus Vinzent, *Christ's Torah: The Making of the New Testament in the Second Century* (Routledge, 2024).

of these individual hypotheses, it is clear that apocrypha should not be understood *per definitionem* as imitators of literature that has become canonical. In some cases, this may be true in either a direct or an indirect way, but there are no grounds for this as a general claim.

Another problem with the overreliance on genre in defining Christian apocrypha is that it excludes many works that have long been regarded as apocryphal as well as other works that have *not* always been understood as apocryphal but clearly should be. As an example of the former, the journeys through heaven and hell narrated in some apocryphal apocalypses—most prominently the Apocalypse of Paul,[20] also known as the Visio Pauli—find no generic parallel in the New Testament; they are quite distinct from canonical Revelation. That said, they have been categorized as apocryphal literature from the beginnings of modern scholarship. Similarly, many works that are regularly referred to as apocryphal gospels bear no true generic similarity to the New Testament Gospels; the Gospel of Thomas, for example, is a collection of only loosely connected sayings of Jesus, and works such as the Gospel of Judas and the so-called Gospel of Truth are in fact dialogues (e.g., with the risen Savior). Another example is the so-called Apostolic Memoirs, which emerged in the Church of Egypt in the sixth century; these are works that resemble and are related to the canonical Gospels, with the primary aim of creating new narrative origins for the miaphysite Church of Egypt after the Council of Chalcedon (451 CE).[21] On the threshold of antiquity and the Middle Ages, in turn, multiple Lives of Mary are attested, some of which recount a gospel narrative from

20. See "e-Clavis Apocalypse of Paul," North American Society for the Study of Christian Apocryphal Literature, accessed February 1, 2025, https://www.nasscal.com/e-clavis-christian-apocrypha/apocalypse-of-paul/. For an up-to-date discussion of introductory issues see Jan N. Bremmer, "The Apocalypse of Paul," in *Early New Testament Apocrypha*, ed. J. Christopher Edwards, Ancient Literature for New Testament Study 9 (Eerdmans, 2022), 427–45; for an English translation of one old form of the text see, e.g., Elliott, *Apocryphal New Testament*, 616–44.

21. For further information, see Alin Suciu, *The Berlin-Strasbourg Apocryphon: A Coptic Apostolic Memoire*, WUNT 370 (Mohr Siebeck, 2017), 70–138.

the perspective of the Virgin Mary.[22] Other texts, some of which are very old, can be understood as paraphrases or reenactments of older Jesus narratives.[23] Not yet mentioned are texts whose relationship to the genres present in the New Testament is even less pronounced: One could think of collections of miracle narratives (such as the Byzantine collection of Marian miracles at a spring in Constantinople), Armenian narrative wreaths around major figures from the Old Testament such as Adam, Abraham, and others, and an apocryphal world chronicle such as the Palaia Historica.[24]

Readers of this book may be getting nervous: The category "Christian apocrypha" seems to be growing exponentially! Capaciousness is not, to our minds, a problem in itself; or, at least, its effects are far less problematic than a restrictiveness that prevents scholars and other readers from drawing fruitful connections between writings that are indeed connected. Our aim is not to set a clear boundary for what can be understood as Christian apocrypha but to provide criteria for when it makes sense to speak of Christian apocrypha and when it does not. Our result

---

22. Perhaps the most well-known text in this group is Life of the Virgin, which has been (wrongly) attributed to Maximus the Confessor and is now transmitted in Georgian. See Stephen J. Shoemaker, *The Life of the Virgin: Maximus the Confessor* (Yale University Press, 2012).

23. Tobias Nicklas first coined the term *Neuinszenierung* (English "re-enactment") in connection with the creation of second-century gospels. However, it can also be applied to many phenomena beyond gospel literature in the narrower sense. See Tobias Nicklas, "Zwischen Redaktion und 'Neuinszenierung': Vom Umgang erzählender Evangelien des 2. Jahrhunderts mit ihren Vorlagen," in Schröter et al., *Gospels and Gospel Traditions*, 313.

24. For the Byzantine collection of Marian miracles at a spring in Constantinople, see text and introduction in Ann-Mary Talbot and Scott Fitzgerald Johnson, eds., *Miracle Tales from Byzantium*, Dumbarton Oaks Medieval Library (Harvard University Press, 2012), 203–97. For Armenian narrative wreaths around major figures from the OT such as Adam, Abraham, and others, we refer to the various text editions by Michael E. Stone. On the Palaia Historica, see English translation (plus introduction) in William Adler, "Palaea Historica ('The Old Testament History')," in Bauckham et al., *Old Testament Pseudepigrapha*, 1:585–672.

is a broad concept of Christian apocrypha that is formulated from an etic perspective, that is, from a contemporary, scholarly perspective *not rooted within any particular strand of Christianity.* In many cases, this also coincides with what was described as apocryphal from the perspective of early church authors, and sometimes also with the claim of the texts themselves (i.e., their emic perspective); for the further assessment of the texts, however, these old perspectives, which are prejudiced in various ways, should be set aside.

How, then, can we refine the rule of thumb (laid out above) for defining or, perhaps better, approximating Christian apocrypha? We can confirm the first notion as a clear first criterion: *Christian apocrypha are writings that are not included in the Christian Bible.*[25] We might sharpen the second notion as follows into a second criterion: *Christian apocrypha are writings for which the Christian Bible forms privileged intertexts.* In this book and elsewhere,[26] we submit that Christian apocrypha are works that cannot be adequately understood without recognizing their intertextual relationship to biblical writings and the narrative world they create. The first criterion is necessary but not sufficient; the second criterion is also necessary, but it is intended not so much to circumscribe the category as to aid interpreters in deciding whether it is useful to examine texts *as* Christian apocrypha. Rephrased, the second criterion claims that *in order to speak meaningfully of Christian (or NT) apocrypha, such works must bear significant intertextual links with works in the New Testament.* Of course, this does not mean that all biblical texts are privileged intertexts for every apocryphal text, nor that biblical texts are the *only* intertexts necessary for adequate interpretation. Quite to the contrary! The point, rather, is to approach Christian apocrypha as a literary universe—still expanding today—that ultimately revolves

25. Note that even this simple statement requires qualification: 3 Corinthians, for example, was part of the Armenian Christian Bible for centuries.

26. For more detail (although much more technical than what is presented here) see Tobias Nicklas, "Semiotik – Intertextualität – Apokryphität: Eine Annäherung an den Begriff 'christlicher Apokryphen,'" *Apocrypha* 17 (2006): 55–78.

around the Christian Bible, even as individual works are in the orbit of other literary fields.

One disadvantage of these criteria is that they identify apocryphal works in a way that is quite removed from what was understood by the term *apocryphal* in antiquity. But this disadvantage brings with itself the advantage of avoiding the associations and prejudices of the ancient usage. Of course, one could go a step further and dispense with the term *apocryphal* altogether—perhaps that really is the best way forward. If we were to do so, the more neutral term *parabiblical* would probably be appropriate—and we will indeed use *parabiblical* in many instances in this book alongside *apocryphal* and with the same meaning. But for pragmatic reasons—simply because the concept of apocryphal writings is deeply established in academic language—we will continue to use it, albeit in full recognition of its problems.

We have not yet brought into view the advantages of these criteria. Most significant is that certain artificial boundaries created by rigid categorization are removed, offering an unobstructed view of literary trajectories and allowing new questions—not yet posed in older research—to be asked. Further, that these criteria are ultimately literary (rather than theological) makes it possible to transcend multiple boundaries that have perhaps seemed sensible in the past but have also repeatedly obscured our view of how Christian literary cultures actually developed. As just one brief but highly significant example, consider the boundary between apocryphal and hagiographic literature, which was sharply drawn by earlier scholars such as Wilhelm Schneemelcher and still remains in many, if not most, academic circles.[27] The decisive criterion for differentiating hagiographical literature (i.e., texts about saints) from apocryphal literature has been their respective chronological classification: Texts that were written before the recognition of a New Testament canon were to be classified as apocryphal, whereas later writings were to be classified as hagiographical. But this is an artificial boundary that has in practice

27. See Wilhelm Schneemelcher, *Neutestamentliche Apokryphen*, 6th ed. (Mohr Siebeck, 1989), 1:50, where the author briefly looks at some hagiographers "because older traditions live on in them."

obfuscated our understanding of the long lives of apocryphal works, including their enduring and substantial role within Christian thought and practice.

Further advantages are as follows:

(1) We can break away from the preoccupation with the earliest apocryphal literature. Questions concerning the origins of Christianity and the historical Jesus have dominated much of the scholarship on Christian apocrypha. Our approach reverses direction, raising questions of the *development* of Christian thought in a wide range of cultural contexts and religious milieus, as successive generations of Christians construct their own identities and histories through the medium of apocryphal literature. The exploration of these issues reveals a diversity of voices—by no means marginal or marginalized—within important historical, social, and political discourses, often in new and exciting ways. And, to be blunt, these are questions in response to which Christian apocrypha can really say something unique, significant, and decisive.

(2) Similarly, we can break away from our near exclusive focus on the reconstruction of the "original" or "authorial" version of apocryphal works. It is surely right and good that earlier scholarly efforts were harnessed in this direction, and the fruits of that labor are valuable indeed. But in practice, the critical editions and their translations into modern languages tend to be understood as more secure than they are, despite the fact that in most cases they represent a text form that does not occur in any of the ancient and medieval witnesses. Further, and more to the point, the lively diversity of the actual transmission of these works is relegated to a textual apparatus (or worse: an introduction in Latin) that is easily overlooked. An example: Modern scholarship interprets the apocryphal Acts of John as an apostolic narrative from the second century, basing such study on the (in itself excellent) critical edition available to us today.[28] To be sure, scholarship that aims to interpret the

---

28. See "e-Clavis Acts of John," North American Society for the Study of Christian Apocryphal Literature, accessed February 1, 2025, https://www.nasscal.com/e-clavis-christian-apocrypha/acts-of-john/. Éric Junod and Jean-Daniel Kaestli, eds., *Acta Iohannis*, 2 vols., Corpus Christianorum, Series Apocryphorum

second-century work can proceed in no other way. Rarely, however, does such scholarship fully reckon (either in its method or in the strength of its conclusions) with the fact that this text, not just in detail but also in its entire sequential arrangement, *does not exist in a single manuscript.* That said, when we reorient our perspective, turning to what has survived in the (in most cases much later) manuscripts, we find not a single work but an entire library of interrelated Johannine apostle narratives, representing the varied thought and practice of more than a millennium of Christianity in diverse locations. Especially influential among the texts of this library were the Acts of John by Prochorus, a later form of the Acts of John extant in a large number of manuscripts, which provided the bulk of the source material for reconstructing the second-century text. Here, an analogy from archaeology is useful: The shift in perspective that we are proposing is similar to the mid-twentieth-century shift in archaeology away from the until-then common practice of prioritizing the oldest stratum of material (literally digging through and sometimes even destroying later strata) and toward current best practices that regard each layer as important in its own right and worthy of preservation. In essence, scholarship has excavated Prochorus for fragments of the second-century Acts of John, but, with that labor accomplished, has largely ignored or discarded it. Despite the significant impact this work had on centuries of Christian understanding of who John was, Prochorus is not be found (at least to our knowledge) in any of the usual handbooks on apocryphal literature until recently, no doubt due to exclusive focus on "early" apocryphal acts.[29] Johannine

1–2 (Brepols, 1983), offer what is still an outstanding text edition in the standard format. An easily accessible English translation of the text in its reconstructed form is provided by Elliott, *Apocryphal New Testament*, 303–49; on introductory questions, see also Harold W. Attridge, "Acts of John," in Edwards, *Early New Testament Apocrypha*, 216–33. Janet E. Spittler is currently preparing a detailed commentary on this text.

29. But now see Janet E. Spittler, "The Acts of John by Prochorus," in *New Testament Apocrypha: More Noncanonical Scriptures*, ed. Tony Burke (Eerdmans, 2023), 3:262–361.

apostle narratives provide a clear example that we will discuss in some detail below, but a similar situation is evident in the case of numerous apocryphal works, particularly apostle narratives.[30]

(3) A consequence of this shift in perspective from focusing on origins to focusing on forward trajectories is that one of the greatest challenges in producing an "original" version of a text—that is, the fluid nature of its transmission—becomes an enormous opportunity for learning more about the history of Christian thought and practice. It is certainly true that, in most instances, the text of canonical New Testament works is far more stable than that of apocryphal works. This basic observation is sometimes lobbed against Christian apocrypha as an accusation: These works are shifty, not to be trusted, in contrast with the canon, which is legitimized in part by its stability. But if we set aside such ideological arguments, it is clear that the very fluidity of apocryphal texts is an advantage—a feature, not a bug—that, with each iteration, adaptation, or translation of a work, offers us new insight into different forms of Christianity. Consider, for example, the Acts of Thomas: The standard collections of New Testament apocrypha offer a long form of the Acts of Thomas, comprising a narrative in thirteen acts that takes the apostle to India—a form of the narrative that survives in very few manuscripts.[31] Until quite recently, however, far more common, shorter forms of the narrative (found in liturgical manuscripts and read among

30. We deliberately speak of "apostle narratives" and not of "apostolic acts" because the genres of many of these texts hardly correspond to that of Luke's canonical Acts of the Apostles.

31. See "e-Clavis Acts of Thomas," North American Society for the Study of Christian Apocryphal Literature, accessed February 1, 2025, https://www.nasscal.com/e-clavis-christian-apocrypha/acts-of-thomas/. For an easily accessible English translation, see Elliott, *Apocryphal New Testament*, 439–511; on introductory questions, see also Harold W. Attridge, "Acts of Thomas," in Edwards, *Early New Testament Apocrypha*, 290–307. A project led by Israel Muñoz Gallarte and Ángel Narro is currently examining the rich textual tradition. Important preliminary work on this can be found in the volume by Israel Muñoz Gallarte and Lautaro Roig Lanzillotta, eds., *New Trends in the Research on the Apocryphal Acts of Thomas*, Studies on Early Christian Apocrypha 20 (Peeters, 2024).

legends of the saints) have been largely neglected.[32] But the Thomas that has been actually remembered and celebrated in the greater church certainly corresponds significantly more to what we encounter in these manuscripts than to what the oldest Acts of Thomas passes down to us. Or consider the library of Coptic texts discovered at Nag Hammadi: A debate has arisen as to whether these works should primarily be interpreted as texts from the second or third century (when they were likely first composed) or as representative of the clearly later monastic context in which their respective manuscripts were produced and used.[33] In most instances, we don't have to choose: The answer is both-and.

(4) The removal of temporal boundaries allows us to consider writings that have not yet been examined within the context of Christian apocrypha. As already noted, late antique and medieval texts and traditions can be understood as apocryphal (or parabiblical) according to our criteria.[34] In medieval literature, this includes significant works related to the veneration of Mary, the reception of old and the creation of new apocalypses, large sections of influential collections such as

---

32. By way of introduction, see Cosmin Pricop, "Thomas weitererzählt: Rezeption der apokryphen Thomasakten im Synaxarion des Thomas-Festes," in *The Apostles Peter, Paul, John, Thomas and Philip with Their Companions in Late Antiquity*, ed. Tobias Nicklas et al., Studies on Early Christian Apocrypha 17 (Peeters, 2021), 270–94; on the so-called minor Acts of Thomas (now dubbed the Acts of Thomas and His Wonderworking Skin), see "e-Clavis Acts of Thomas and His Wonderworking Skin," North American Society for the Study of Christian Apocryphal Literature, accessed February 1, 2025, https://www.nasscal.com/e-clavis-christian-apocrypha/acts-of-thomas-and-his-wonderworking-skin/.

33. The highly provocative work by Hugo Lundhaug, *Images of Rebirth: Cognitive Poetics and Transformational Soteriology in the Gospel of Philip and the Exegesis of the Soul*, Nag Hammadi and Manichaean Studies 73 (Brill, 2010), provided the impetus for this. On a broader basis, the same question is also discussed using a number of examples in the volume by Joseph Verheyden et al., eds., *Texts in Context: Essays on Dating and Contextualizing Christian Writings from the Second and Early Third Centuries*, BETL 319 (Peeters, 2021).

34. The original meaning of "hidden" or "secret" is of course no longer relevant in this case.

Jacob of Voragine's *Legenda Aurea*, and even aspects of the legend of the holy grail, which continues to fascinate to this day. But even quite modern Jesus literature (from Bulgakov's *The Master and Margarita* to Max Brod's *The Master* to Karel Čapek's *Apocryphal Tales*, and many more) is full of elements that allow us to compare it with phenomena found in apocrypha. In addition to new objects of study, this opens up possibilities for interdisciplinary cooperation far beyond the confines of theological and religious studies faculties.

(5) The removal of temporal boundaries also leads to the opening up of geographic boundaries: Countries, regions, and cultural areas in which the production of apocrypha began only after the fourth century gain new significance; this includes Armenia, Georgia, Ireland, Iceland, the areas where Church Slavic was in use, and many other places. Translations and text forms that, for scholars of Christian apocrypha, were formerly relegated to the footnotes as of little use for the reconstruction of "early" or "original" versions can take their rightful places as important witnesses to the long lives of these traditions. What is truly exciting—and has hardly been investigated to date—is what happens when the usual Western, Eurocentric perspective is abandoned. And the geographic boundaries might be widened even further: Are there writings and traditions that can usefully be described as apocryphal (or parabiblical) in parts of the world that Christianity reached *after* the Middle Ages, for example in Latin America or sub-Saharan Africa?

(6) For pragmatic reasons, as already indicated, we will largely retain the term "Christian apocrypha," while often speaking of parabiblica (which we understand as a synonym). "Christian apocrypha" is at least a more neutral term than "New Testament apocrypha,"[35] which continues to be used in recent publications and which, as we have already seen above, establishes too close a relationship between the emergence of the New Testament canon and the production of apocrypha. But even the attribute *Christian* is not entirely unproblematic. First of all,

35. Thus, for example, the outstanding volumes *New Testament Apocrypha: More Noncanonical Scriptures* edited by Tony Burke (as well as Brent Landau in the first volume).

for some of the very earliest apocryphal texts, the category "Christian" can be applied only as an etic category (i.e., a category applied to the texts from outside) since these texts did not adopt the term emically (i.e., within their own frame of reference).[36] In some cases, the categories "Christian" and "Jewish," which are generally considered entirely distinct today, are not differentiated.[37] Even where the term *Christian* clearly applies, it does not mean that such texts and traditions presuppose a stable system of beliefs or doctrine that is supported by a large organized church that defines what is to be understood as Christian or not Christian. When we speak of "Christian apocrypha," we must be aware that the category "Christian" is not neutral, objective, or innocent but rather can be (and still is) linked to discourses of power. What initially sounds like a purely theoretical problem is concretized the moment we attempt to decide whether the writings from Nag Hammadi, usually attributed to various "gnostic"[38] groups, should be considered part of the literary universe of Christian apocrypha. From the point of view of representatives of the dominant church, in such cases the term *Christian* could be applied to such writings only in a highly deficient manner; however, this hardly does justice to the significance of these texts for the study of apocrypha—or for many of the individuals who read and valued them in late antiquity. The same, however, is probably also true from the opposite perspective: The group that we assume to be behind a writing

36. Stefan Alkier, "Terminologien kollektiver Identitäten in der Apostelgeschichte des Lukas," in *Juden – Heiden – Christen? Religiöse Inklusion und Exklusion in Kleinasien bis Decius*, ed. Stefan Alkier and Hartmut Leppin, WUNT 400 (Mohr Siebeck, 2018), 301–32, shows this in a highly convincing way using the example of the canonical Acts of the Apostles.

37. One example is the aforementioned Ascension of Isaiah, an apocalypse probably from the not-too-late second century. For a detailed discussion of this text, see Meghan Henning and Tobias Nicklas, "Questions of Self-Designation in the *Ascension of Isaiah*," in *The Ascension of Isaiah*, ed. Jan N. Bremmer and Tobias Nicklas, Studies in Early Christian Apocrypha 11 (Peeters, 2016), 175–98.

38. That this concept has been seen as highly problematic and overburdened is now common knowledge in scholarly research. We deliberately use the term with quotation marks.

such as the Gospel of Judas, which has been preserved in Coptic in the Tchacos Codex, may have felt so sharply opposed to representatives of an apostolic-majority Christianity that held fast to the God of Israel that in this case too it is difficult to determine what we can understand by the attribute *Christian*.[39]

(7) More difficult—though perhaps not absolutely necessary—is the delimitation of writings that today are normally subsumed under the category of Old Testament pseudepigrapha.[40] The crucial question asked in connection with the categorization of many Old Testament pseudepigrapha has been whether the text is Jewish or Christian. In some cases, the answer is quite simple: A writing such as the Syriac Cave of Treasures, which is largely concerned with biblical prehistory and figures such as Noah or Abraham, also integrally contains a section dealing with the life of Jesus.[41] Despite its emphasis on Old Testament parallels, the text can therefore reasonably be described as a Christian apocryphon. It is more difficult to assess texts such as 5 and 6 Ezra, two apocalypses that are included in today's collections of Christian apocrypha as well as Old Testament pseudepigrapha: 5 Ezra, which has survived only in various combinations with the Jewish apocalypse 4 Ezra, offers such clear intertextual references to writings such as Revelation or the Gospel of

---

39. On this, see also the discussion in Tobias Nicklas, *Jews and Christians? Second Century "Christian" Perspectives on the "Parting of the Ways"* (Mohr Siebeck, 2014), 40–43. The additional criterion introduced above—that is, that it makes sense to speak of Christian apocrypha where the privileged biblical intertexts originate at least in part from the NT—can perhaps be supplemented by the idea that the corresponding texts obviously presuppose tradent groups in which Jesus of Nazareth plays a decisive role for their own religious frame of reference. This establishes a reference point but, at the same time, a not too sharp boundary to Manichaean and Islamic writings, in which Jesus of Nazareth can play an important role but in which he is not normally assigned the key role.

40. For very foundational thoughts on this, see James R. Davila, *The Provenance of the Pseudepigrapha: Jewish, Christian, or Other?*, JSJSup 105 (Brill, 2005).

41. An easily accessible English translation of this text with a detailed introduction can be found in Alexander Toepel, "The Cave of Treasures," in Bauckham et al., *Old Testament Pseudepigrapha*, 1:531–84.

Matthew that we can describe the text as "Christian" in a broad sense. But whether the designation *Christian* can also be meaningfully used with respect to this text as a category distinct from "Jewish" is a question that must remain unanswered.[42] On the other hand, 6 Ezra, also usually handed down in combination with 4 Ezra and 5 Ezra, offers only such vague indications that it is even more difficult to decide whether the text can be meaningfully described as "Christian."[43] Other difficulties arise in connection with the Ascension of Isaiah, an apocalyptic writing that may have been written in the first decades of the second century.[44] Large parts of this writing can be read as a Jewish text; however, the fact that there are also passages that clearly refer to Jesus (here called "the Beloved") and his disciples has led to the reconstruction of a Jewish *Grundschrift* of the Ascension of Isaiah, which was then later adapted by Christians. To this day, many editions of early Jewish literature contain introductions and translations of this alleged *Grundschrift*, the so-called Martydom of Isaiah.[45] This Martyrdom of Isaiah, however, is unlikely to have ever existed. It is purely a construct of research that could not imagine that a Christian writing could speak for long stretches of time about Old Testament figures without even mentioning Jesus. The problems multiply when we look at texts that, like the Testaments of the Twelve Patriarchs, were transmitted seemingly exclusively in Christian,

---

42. For more on this, see Veronika Hirschberger, *Ringen um Israel: Intertextuelle Perspektiven auf das 5. Buch Esra*, Studies on Early Christian Apocrypha 14 (Peeters, 2018).

43. Easily accessible English translations on these texts can be found in Theodor A. Bergren, "Fifth Ezra," as well as Bergen, "Sixth Ezra," in Bauckham et al., *Old Testament Pseudepigrapha*, 467–82, 483–97; on 6 Ezra, see also the monograph currently being written by Luigi Walt for the series Apocryphes.

44. For current discussions on this text, see especially the essays in Bremmer et al., *Ascension of Isaiah*.

45. E.g., Erling Hammershaimb, *Das Martyrium Jesajas*, JSHRZ 2 (Gerd Mohn, 1973), 15–34.

often monastic circles.[46] At what point do the changes made to a work during transmission go so far that it can or should be read *also* as a Christian apocryphon? The aim here is not to provide definitive answers to such questions but to show how important it is to keep the boundaries between different groups of parabiblical texts open. This is not to say that such boundaries are never important or meaningful; rather, we must always be ready to rethink or redraw boundaries, depending on the question or problem at hand.

(8) Perhaps one final observation can be added to all of this. In our contemporary context, the notion of canonical writings is closely associated with the medium of a firmly bound and widely accessible book, the "Bible"; further, many readers are likely familiar with lists of canonical books (perhaps even in song!), if not also lists of apocryphal books, as we find them again and again in the works of early church authors.[47] As a consequence, we usually assume a sharply drawn line between canonical and apocryphal material. On closer inspection, however, it is more appropriate to speak of a communication space between canonical and apocryphal traditions that can express themselves in different media.[48] Even at the level of the establishment of New Testament texts in manuscript form, it was possible for originally extracanonical material to enter the textual tradition: The famous pericope of the adulteress, usually recorded in John 7:53–8:11, is probably the most well-known example. More subtle is the fact that textual forms that can be traced back to the influence of the apocryphal Acts of Paul and Thecla can be found

46. The Leiden school around Marinus de Jonge in particular also held the view that the Testaments originated as Christian writings.

47. A good overview can be found, e.g., in Markschies, "Haupteinleitung," 115–46.

48. See more on these thoughts in Tobias Nicklas, "Denk- und Kommunikationsräume jenseits und diesseits des Kanons," in *Kindness, Courage, and Integrity in Biblical Texts and the Politics of Biblical Interpretation: Festschrift Reimund Bieringer*, ed. Marilou S. Ibita et al., BETL 333 (Peeters, 2023), 261–76.

in individual manuscripts of the Pastoral Epistles.[49] And even physical Bibles almost always comprise more than the texts of the canonical writings alone. They contain paratexts such as headings, introductions, editorial notes, and in many cases illustrations.[50] The latter in particular can introduce elements into the Bible that have no basis in the canonical text. If, for example, we imagine the seer of Revelation as an old man due to his depiction in images, then this has nothing to do with the text but with images that go back to apocryphal writings (such as the aforementioned Acts of John by Prochorus).[51] This situation—in which biblical literature exists not just on the page but in both the varied cultural memory[52] of Christian communities and in the "Bible in the minds" of individual interpreters—the enactment of New Testament narratives, themes, figures, and motifs begins to blur the lines between canonical and non- or extracanonical. How, for example, are paraphrases or contextually conditioned reenactments of Jesus narratives, as we find them not only in apocryphal gospels but also in early church literature, to be assessed? When is a figure to be understood as biblical or canonical? Is every Abraham, Job, or Solomon, every Sarah and Rebekah we find in early church literature, simply identical to the biblical figure? Or do some of the characterizations of such figures in parabiblical traditions differ so

49. For good examples of this, see Thomas J. Kraus, "Thecla and the *Acts of Thecla*: Searching for Traces in the Manuscript Tradition," in Nicklas et al., *Apostles Peter, Paul, John*, 118–50.

50. See the important work by Garrick V. Allen, *Words Are Not Enough: Paratexts, Manuscripts, and the Real New Testament* (Eerdmans, 2024).

51. Impressive examples can be seen in the interplay between text and illustration in the so-called Bamberg Apocalypse. On this, see Stephanie Hallinger and Tobias Nicklas, "Von der Illustration zum Text: Ein intermediales Spiel mit der Bamberger Apokalypse," in *Textforschung zur Septuaginta, zum Hebräerbrief und zur Apokalypse*, ed. Georg Gaebel und Matthias Geigenfeind (de Gruyter, 2024), 351–79.

52. On this term, see especially Jan Assmann, *Cultural Memory and Early Civilization: Writing, Remembrance, and Political Imagination* (Baylor University Press, 2011).

clearly from what characterizes the figure in the biblical writings that we can no longer say for sure—at least from today's perspective—whether the figure is biblical?[53]

A similar question arises immediately when we leave the world of written texts and examine the representations of narratives, figures, themes, and motifs in other media. In iconographic representations, it is very often possible to recognize which biblical scene or sequence of scenes is depicted: Again and again, canonical and noncanonical motifs are interwoven, but the visual media have their own vocabulary and canon, such that the attempt to interpret them merely as illustrations of textual traditions is a glaring mistake.[54] What's more, does the representation of a biblical text (or a combination of biblical texts) in other media such as liturgy, drama, and iconography even claim correspondence with what is written in the narratives of the canon? Or does the translation into another medium already signal a communication space beyond the canon, a communication space in which the canonical and apocryphal combine or overlap, depending on how you look at it?

A simple example can illustrate this idea:[55] One of the most popular motifs we find in the paintings of the catacombs but also on ancient Christian sarcophagi is the raising of Lazarus.[56] Of course, the entire highly complex sequence of scenes narrated in John 11:1–44 is not

53. For examples on this, see the special issue *Women in Biblical and Para-Biblical Jewish and Christian Literature* of *ETL* 96 (2020).

54. On this point, see Felicity Harley, "Visual Apocrypha: The Case of Mary and the Magi in Early Christian Rome," in *Apocryphal and Esoteric Sources in the Development of Christian and Jewish Traditions*, ed. Igor Dorfmann-Lazarev (Brill, 2021), 381–408.

55. The following example is also used in Nicklas, "Denk- und Kommunikationsräume."

56. Again, a very detailed and helpful treatment can be found in Jutta Dresken-Weiland, *Bild, Grab und Wort: Untersuchungen zu Jenseitsvorstellungen von Christen des 3. und 4. Jahrhunderts* (Schnell & Steiner, 2010), 213–33; see also the selected images there. But see also the discussion of the much later picture by Caravaggio offered by Stephanie Hallinger, "Der Raum zwischen 'kanonisch' und 'parabiblisch'.

depicted but only the actual moment of the resurrection, when Lazarus comes out of the tomb (John 11:44). Many depictions clearly show that Lazarus is still wrapped in linen bandages (see John 11:44), from which he must first be freed. In this respect, the corresponding images are very much in keeping with the text of the Gospel of John.[57] However, the image of Jesus is striking: He is often depicted with a long staff with which he points to the tomb and/or Lazarus. Iconographically, the inclusion of the staff allows the artist to establish the deep connection between Jesus the miracle worker and the resurrected man—and to make the miraculous action of the scene comprehensible in a static image. Perhaps the staff also simply represents Jesus's miracle-working word. At the same time, however, the change of medium forces us to reenact the scene in a new way: As it brings to mind a magical instrument, a kind of magic wand, it opens up the possibility of interpreting Jesus as an extraordinary miracle worker—greater than all magicians—a miracle worker for whom even death sets no insurmountable limits.[58]

Whether such an interpretation, which is certainly attractive to many people, fully corresponds to what the Lazarus scene in the Gospel of John expresses is certainly questionable. But one thing is clear: While the craftsmen or artists who depicted Lazarus in this way almost certainly assumed that they were simply depicting "the" Lazarus scene, if papyrologists of today were to discover a papyrus fragment that described Jesus taking a magic wand in his hand to raise Lazarus, we would celebrate the sensational discovery of a new apocryphon.[59] The

Caravaggios Auferweckung des Lazarus (1609)," *Zeitschrift für Neues Testament* 51 (2023): 107–29.

57. Of course, we are not assuming that the craftspeople in question consulted the text of the Gospel of John in each case but rather that they worked through predetermined pictorial programs.

58. Similarly in Dresken-Weiland, *Bild, Grab und Wort*, 232.

59. Even the healing of a leper, which we find in the "Unknown Gospel" on Papyrus Egerton 2, differs only in details from those in Mark 1:40–45 and par. Nevertheless, we naturally understand it as apocryphal. For additional information on this text, one of the oldest apocryphal gospel fragments of all (with an introduction, commentary,

point here is not about a petty decision as to whether such an image in the catacombs of Rome is canonical. In one sense, it certainly belonged to a kind of canon of regularly requested images that were used to decorate Christian tombs in a given time. The point is that, with respect to the New Testament canon, such images (and other material culture) are located in a space of communication both *within and without at the same time*. The significance of such observations for the study of apocryphal traditions in relation to canonical traditions has hardly been researched to date.[60] What is clear, however, is that even the concept of "canon," previously understood as strictly delineated, is significantly more fluid and porous than normally assumed.

The present volume is a part of the paradigm shift outlined above—a shift that has gained momentum in Christian apocrypha research circles over the past twenty years or so but has only just begun to reach the broader circles of New Testament scholarship. Our intended audiences include specialists in the field of New Testament and biblical studies, as well as students at different levels and interested laypeople. We do not aim simply to present the current state of research; unlike comparable books, we will not offer an introduction to Christian apocrypha, presenting basic information and commentary on various works that are particularly well-known or that we consider to be important. Such introductions already exist.[61] That said, where apocryphal works are

---

and English translation), see Tobias Nicklas, "The 'Unknown Gospel' on Papyrus Egerton 2 (+ Papyrus Cologne 255)," in *Gospel Fragments*, ed. Thomas J. Kraus et al., Oxford Early Christian Gospel Texts (Oxford University Press, 2009), 11–120, as well as (somewhat bolder in its reconstructions) Lorne R. Zelyck, *The Egerton Gospel (Egerton Papyrus 2 + Papyrus Köln VI 255). Introduction, Critical Edition, and Commentary*, TENTS 13 (Brill, 2019).

60. In addition to Nicklas, "Denk- und Kommunikationsräume," see also now Tobias Nicklas, "Neutestamentlicher Kanon und christliche Apokryphen. Trends, Themen und Thesen," *Zeitschrift für Neues Testament* 51 (2023): 20–21.

61. During the last two decades, among others, Hans-Josef Klauck, *Apocryphal Gospels* (Baylor University Press, 2004); Klauck, *The Apocryphal Acts of the Apostles* (Baylor University Press, 2008); Bart D. Ehrman and Zlatko Pleše, *The Apocryphal Gospels: Texts and Translations* (Oxford University Press, 2011); Markschies and Jens

mentioned for the first time, the footnotes will provide a brief introduction and suggestions for additional reading; wherever space allows, the texts under discussion will be quoted at length. The focus of this volume, however, is not the classical introductory questions of which Christian apocrypha originated when and where, which groups of followers of Jesus they represent, and what their basic content is. Instead, we are interested in the further question of why it is so exciting to read Christian apocrypha and so important to take these works seriously. In other words, our central question is: *How does reading Christian apocrypha contribute to a more robust understanding of Christianity in its diversity as an integral part of a complex world?* While we will surely venture beyond the boundaries of antiquity at certain points, our focus will be on ancient writings and traditions; this is a natural consequence of our own expertise, not a statement on the relative importance of individual works. But this book is also an acknowledgment of the *limits* of our own expertise; it is intended as an invitation to a wider community of scholars with expertise in different languages, literatures, histories, and cultures to join us on the proposed path.

The answer to our central question will be neither complete nor one-dimensional. It will move along the following lines:

Chapter 1 demonstrates how our understanding of the Jesus tradition changes as soon as we take seriously the wealth of material extant in Christian apocrypha. When we set aside questions about the historical Jesus, centering instead consideration of the contexts, mechanisms, and developments of the Jesus tradition, Christian apocrypha can play a decisive role.

Chapter 2 takes up apostle narratives (often referred to as the "apocryphal acts of the apostles"), which offer diverse depictions of the missionary activities of the apostles as they bring Christianity even to the "end of the earth." A particular focus is the interplay of canonical and

Schröter, *Antike christliche Apokryphen*; Jens Schröter, *Die apokryphen Evangelien* (C. H. Beck, 2020); Edwards, *Early New Testament Apocrypha*; and the fascinating volumes edited by Tony Burke (and in vol. 1 also Brent Landau): *More New Testament Apocrypha* (Eerdmans, 2016–2023); and many more.

noncanonical material. What we hope to convey is the enormous—and largely untapped—value of this particular genre of extracanonical literature for understanding the history of Christian thought and practice as it moves across time and space.

The question of whether the world is an ordered cosmos or ultimately incomprehensible chaos has preoccupied people since the beginning of history. Chapter 3 turns to various genres to examine the accounts given in Christian apocrypha of the structure of the world and the associated locations of the afterlife—heaven, paradise, hell, and purgatory—and the significance of these accounts in discourses on the order of the world.

Closely related to this is the central question of chapter 4: Where do we stand in the framework of time and history? How do we recognize the signs of the times that can help us to recognize our position in history? What awaits us in the coming age and at the end of the ages? And what does this have to do with the beginning of time? Here, too, we will see how the testimony of Christian apocrypha, partly in dialogue with historiographical and chronological literature, provides material that broadens and deepens the spectrum of Christian answers to these questions.

The first two chapters do not focus on the reconstructed past but rather on the memory of this past and its function. Chapter 5 takes as its basis the theory of *lieux de mémoire*, that is, "places of memory," that are important for the construction of a group's identity, which goes back to French historian and social scientist Pierre Nora. Here we use selected examples to show how indispensable Christian apocrypha are if one wants to create such a symbolic history of Christianity.

All of this leads to chapter 6, in which a single work—likely, of all the texts dealt with in this book, simultaneously the least familiar to readers and the most widely circulated in the history of Christianity—is used to reflect on the significance of Christian apocrypha as evidence of "lived religion."

We emphatically do *not* promise a comprehensive overview of apocryphal Christian literature. Instead, we hope to reveal how reading and working with Christian apocrypha dramatically expands our understanding of the history of Christianity—and with that a significant strand of human religious, artistic, philosophical, and interpretive expression. We imagine ourselves to be pulling back the corner of a curtain or just cracking open the lid of a box to reveal the countless treasures inside—because perhaps the single greatest difference between apocryphal and canonical Christian literature is that the New Testament contains just twenty-seven works, while Christian apocrypha comprises enough works to keep us and all the readers of this book very busy for the foreseeable future.

CHAPTER 1

Reading Christian Apocrypha and Understanding Jesus Anew?

Has the *true story* of Jesus been hidden in secret writings kept under lock and key for centuries by the Vatican? Have these writings been stigmatized, suppressed, or even destroyed because they threaten the power and authority of the church? Would the revelation of these hidden works force us to completely rewrite the story of Jesus? While, like most readers and moviegoers, we find thrillers such as Dan Brown's *Da Vinci Code* (or, even better, *Indiana Jones and the Last Crusade*) fun and exciting,[1] they have very little to do with reality. It is certainly true that there are still huge treasures of documents in the Vatican libraries (some of which are difficult to access), but the impatience of, say, a North American Byzantinist waiting for the digitization of a potentially important thirteenth-century manuscript of an eighth-century church history is hardly the stuff bestsellers are made of—even if this is exactly the kind of evidence used by contemporary scholars to rewrite Christian history in a more nuanced and accurate way.

To be absolutely clear, then, we do not believe that the Vatican or some other ancient, perhaps secret, organization is deliberately suppressing Jesus texts that bring to light unknown truths that would fundamentally change our understanding of Christianity, past or present.

1. See the fascinating discussion in Ehrman, *Truth and Fiction*.

But we cannot completely ignore the persistent appeal of this idea, which continually surfaces in the more and less skillful forgeries of allegedly ancient texts about Jesus. Works such as the Secret Gospel of Mark, the authenticity of which is at least disputed, or the Coptic Gospel of Jesus's Wife, which has been clearly proven to be a contemporary forgery,[2] have prompted many readers to entertain the notion that the Jesus they've received through Christian tradition is not the *real* Jesus. Neither can we ignore the fierce reactions that each new "discovery" provokes among those who would defend the absolute and exclusive truth of canonical accounts of Jesus's life. But these debates generally have more to do with contemporary ideology than with ancient accounts of Jesus. Thus, while in our view the supposed presence of homoeroticism in the Secret Gospel

2. For the first edition of the Secret Gospel of Mark, see Morton Smith, *Clement of Alexandria and a Secret Gospel of Mark* (Harvard University Press, 1973). Perhaps the most comprehensive study to date is Scott G. Brown, *Mark's Other Gospel: Rethinking Morton Smith's Controversial Discovery*, Studies in Christianity and Judaism 15 (Wilfried Laurier University Press, 2005); most recently, see Geoffrey Smith and Brent Landau, *The Secret Gospel of Mark: A Controversial Scholar, a Scandalous Gospel of Jesus, and the Fierce Debate over Its Authenticity* (Yale University Press, 2023). For a highly critical perspective, see Stephen Carlson, *The Gospel Hoax: Morton Smith's Invention of Secret Mark* (Baylor University Press, 2005); and Peter Jeffery, *The Secret Gospel of Mark Unveiled: Imagined Rituals of Sex, Death and Madness in a Biblical Forgery* (Yale University Press, 2007). Important on the current debate is Tony Burke, ed., *Ancient Gospel or Modern Forgery? The Secret Gospel of Mark in Debate* (Cascade, 2013), and Michael J. Kok, *The Gospel on the Margins: The Reception of Mark in the Second Century* (Fortress, 2015). An up-to-date bibliography can be found at "e-Clavis Secret Gospel of Mark," North American Society for the Study of Christian Apocryphal Literature, accessed February 1, 2025, https://www.nasscal.com/e-clavis-christian-apocrypha/secret-gospel-of-mark/. For a current bibliography and summary of the discussion on the Coptic Gospel of Jesus's Wife, which was largely conducted on internet platforms, see "e-Clavis Gospel of Jesus' Wife," North American Society for the Study of Christian Apocryphal Literature, accessed February 1, 2025, https://www.nasscal.com/e-clavis-christian-apocrypha/gospel-of-jesus-wife/. See also Janet E. Spittler, "Responses to Mark Goodacre, James McGrath, and Caroline Schroeder on the *Gospel of Jesus' Wife*," in *Fakes, Forgeries, and Fictions: Writing Ancient and Modern Apocrypha; Proceedings from the 2015 York University Christian Apocrypha Symposium*, ed. Tony Burke (Cascade, 2017), 349–73.

of Mark is very much in the eye of the beholder, arguments about the text's authenticity cannot be cleanly separated from the homophobia of many scholars who have entered the fray. Likewise, while we struggle to understand where the notion that Jesus had a wife could fit within a contemporary feminist agenda, both feminism and misogyny played clear roles in the way arguments for and against the authenticity of the Jesus's Wife fragment were presented and received.

But that is not all: In point of fact, *every* gospel[3]—whether apocryphal or canonical—assumes that it tells the truth or an important part of the truth about Jesus. Otherwise, it would make no sense to bring another Jesus story into the world. However, this notion of truth is not exhausted at the level of the historical. To the contrary, the most important truth claims of the gospels—New Testament or apocryphal—aim at an entirely different level. The Gospel of John, for example, summarizes this aim as follows: "But these [words] are written so that you may trust that Jesus is the Messiah, the Son of God, and that through trust you may have life in his name" (John 20:31). In other words, gospels are not exclusively or even primarily concerned with describing who Jesus once was historically but who Jesus is and what that means (in the present and future for the addressees of the text).[4] To this end, gospels tell us about Jesus's life, his teaching (before and after the resurrection), and his (past and lasting) ministry. Whether one wants to accept these truth claims is another matter—but one that applies to both canonical and apocryphal works.

If we attend, then, to truth claims beyond simply the historical—that is, if the story of Jesus is understood as the totality of how Christians

3. In the following, we understand the term *gospel* very broadly. This is because we share the opinion that a scientifically clear definition has not yet been successful. Moreover, the debate about the genre of the "gospels" focuses far too exclusively on the texts that found their way into the NT.

4. This, in turn, does not mean that the gospels are fundamentally uninterested in historical data. The evangelist Luke, for example, shows in his prologue (see Luke 1:1–4) how important research as a historian (in the sense of ancient historiography) is to him.

throughout history have thought of and depicted Jesus—then perhaps the inclusion of apocryphal works *does* force us to completely rewrite the story. This is surely the case with the story of the disputes about who Jesus really is. We will see that this is at least as interesting as the attempts to reconstruct a historical Jesus.

This chapter will proceed as follows: First, we will deal with the standard question of the significance of Christian apocrypha for the study of the historical Jesus. This point has been quite controversial; our own approach is one of skepticism.[5] We assume that most apocryphal works provide us with little material that can be evaluated as historically reliable with any degree of probability. What is interesting from a purely research-historical point of view, however, is that the (in our opinions largely failed) attempts of the so-called Third Quest to reconsider the value of apocryphal gospels for historical Jesus research had the effect of redirecting scholarly attention to some largely neglected, even forgotten, gospels and gospel fragments.[6]

Second, we are interested in the extent to which apocryphal Jesus narratives can tell us something about the mechanisms of the transmission of the "remembered Jesus."[7] We will see how Jesus narratives were

5. See also Tobias Nicklas, "Traditions About Jesus in Apocryphal Gospels (with the Exception of the Gospel of Thomas)," in *Handbook for the Study of the Historical Jesus*, ed. Tom Holmén and Stanley E. Porter (Brill, 2011), 2081–2118.

6. The works of John Dominic Crossan, *Four Other Gospels: Shadows on the Contours of the Canon* (HarperCollins, 1985); Crossan, *The Historical Jesus: The Life of a Mediterranean Jewish Peasant* (HarperCollins, 1991); Helmut Koester, *Ancient Christian Gospels: Their History and Development* (Trinity Press International, 1990), as well as the work of the controversial but influential Jesus Seminar led by Robert W. Funk, are important here. Note that even the history of research into the historical Jesus and its division into different phases is a political issue; we are simply adopting an established term here.

7. The significance of concepts of social memory for the understanding of ancient Christianity is increasingly—and highly controversially—discussed today. A helpful introduction is provided by Sandra Huebenthal, *Gedächtnistheorie und Neues Testament: Eine methodisch-hermeneutische Einführung* (Narr Francke Attempto, 2022).

not only edited and transmitted in a narrow sense but could also be reenacted in various contexts. With the term *reenactment*, we are wrestling with the fact that attempts to determine the literary relationship of apocryphal gospels to the canonical writings often produce highly controversial results. It is extraordinarily difficult to demonstrate conclusively that the author of a given apocryphal gospel had access to one or more of the canonical Gospels in written form; the same is true of conclusively demonstrating complete independence of traditions. However, if we consider that *to this day* biblical texts, even where they are readily accessible in written form, are not always simply read or read aloud but are retold in different ways depending on the context, and if we contemplate an audience for whom the concrete performance of the text has been designed, we can begin to conceive of the interplay between the dimension of writing a text and dimensions related to orality (in concrete contexts).[8] We refer to a Jesus narrative (as well as other narratives) as a reenactment of a text that is very probably older, if it is not clear whether the author of a later text "had a written model before him or whether he knew such a model only from oral tradition (for example by reading it aloud, but perhaps also through narratives that could already be based on a written model). This is particularly possible if a story has already become firmly established in the 'cultural memory' of a group, at least in decisive traits (due to various media)."[9] Other examples will show how the engagement with Scriptures of Israel (that is, the OT) allowed new motifs to be created in the second century and later that could be linked to the Jesus narratives, while in

8. This model is related to important aspects of a so-called second orality.

9. Nicklas, "Zwischen Redaktion und 'Neuinszenierung,'" 313. Nicklas has also used the concept in other contexts: See, e.g., Tobias Nicklas, "Eine neue alte Erzählung im Rahmen antiker Jesustraditionen: Reste eines Exorzismus auf P.Oxy. lxxvi 5072," *Annali di storia dell'esegesi* 29 (2012): 13–27 as well as Nicklas, "Second-Century Gospels as 'Re-enactments' of Earlier Writings: Examples from the *Gospel of Peter*," in *Studien zum Petrusevangelium*, WUNT 453 (Mohr Siebeck, 2020), 125–39.

other cases the Old Testament background of such motifs could also be forgotten.[10]

Third, we will finally show what it might mean to reconstruct the story of Jesus with the help of noncanonical material (at least in the fragmentary way in which this is possible today). The number of topics available is immense:[11] In what contexts and to what extent was Jesus interpreted as a miracle worker or parable teller, as a teacher of wisdom or an apocalyptic prophet? What significance was attached to his death, and how was his resurrection understood? What forms of non-Christian polemics against Jesus did Christ-followers have to deal with? What forms of Christology—including christological titles—are recognizable in the texts?[12]

Readers who are interested in these and similar questions but limit themselves to consideration of the canonical Gospels dramatically restrict their own perspectives and the accuracy and adequacy of any conclusions they might reach. What's more, broadening one's view to include the apocryphal *gospels* alone is also not sufficient. Here we are thinking not only of the so-called agrapha (i.e., noncanonical sayings of Jesus that occur outside the gospels and related material)[13] but also

10. On this topic more generally see Tobias Nicklas, "The Influence of Jewish Scriptures on Early Christian Apocrypha," in *The Oxford Handbook of Early Christian Apocrypha*, ed. Andrew Gregory and Christopher Tuckett (Oxford University Press, 2015), 141–52.

11. We will by no means be able to even touch on all of these questions in what follows. Moreover, the possibilities for describing such discourses go far beyond what has been outlined here.

12. Very helpful on this (with different emphases) is Jean-Daniel Dubois, *Jésus apocryphe* (Mame-Desclée, 2011), and Philip Jenkins, *The Many Faces of Christ: The Thousand-Year Studies of the Survival and Influence of the Lost Gospels* (Basic Books, 2015).

13. For a definition and discussion of the meaning of these sayings of the Lord see, e.g., Tobias Nicklas, "Zur Problematik der so genannten 'Agrapha.' Eine Thesenreihe," *RB* 113 (2006): 78–93. For a detailed overview of these texts, see Mauro Pesce, *Le parole dimenticate du Gesù* (Arnaldo Mondadori, 2004). For an overview of older and more recent collections of Agrapha, see "e-Clavis Agrapha of

of narratives and statements about Jesus in other genres. There are, for example, multiple Jesus narratives contained in apocryphal apostle narratives and other works, including the pseudo-Clementine novel. We will see that some of these even purport to be eyewitness accounts.[14] In addition, there are statements about Jesus in apocalypses or in genres that only emerged in late antiquity (such as writings about the life of Mary or the so-called Apostolic Memoirs from Egypt, which are related to the gospels but represent a genre of their own).[15] Further, paraphrases of Jesus narratives in genres that are normally completely ignored in connection with apocrypha have been almost completely overlooked; these genres include pilgrim narratives, chronicles, lives of the saints, homilies, early church treatises, and even ancient commentary literature.[16] To be sure, such sources are of little interest when one concen-

---

Jesus," North American Society for the Study of Christian Apocryphal Literature, accessed February 1, 2025, https://www.nasscal.com/e-clavis-christian-apocrypha/agrapha-of-jesus/.

14. In addition to the pericope in the Pseudo-Clementine homilies presented below, the scene in the Acts of Peter (Actus Vercellenses) in which Peter describes the transfiguration of Jesus from his own perspective should also be considered (see §10). On the significance of Jesus traditions and the reception of Jesus in apocryphal apostle narratives, see also Julia Snyder, "Acts of John, Acts of Peter, Acts of Thekla, Third Corinthians, and Martyrdom of Paul," in *The Reception of Jesus in the First Three Centuries*, vol. 2, *From Thomas to Tertullian: Christian Literary Receptions of Jesus in the Second and Third Centuries CE*, ed. Jens Schröter and Christine Jacobi (T&T Clark, 2020), 363–85.

15. For statements about Jesus in apocalypses, see, e.g., Nicklas, "Apocalypse of Peter"; Lillia Milbach-Schirr, "Second Esdras"; and Mark Grundeken, "Shepherd of Hermas," all in Schröter and Jacobi, *Reception of Jesus in the First Three Centuries*, 331–40, 341–52, and 353–60. On the lives of Mary, see, e.g., Shoemaker, *Life of the Virgin*, especially the introduction, 1–35; on the apostolic memoirs, e.g., see Suciu, *Berlin-Strasbourg Apocryphon*, 70–138.

16. On Jesus traditions in early church authors in general, see Riemer Roukema, "Jesus Tradition in Early Patristic Writings," in Holmén and Porter, *Handbook for the Study of the Historical Jesus*, 2119–47. Our approach, however, goes further than Roukema's; we are also interested in late texts and those that are clearly dependent on canonical representations.

trates exclusively on the question of the historical Jesus. However, they testify to the wealth of arguments about and memories of Jesus from antiquity to the present day. In this chapter we barely scratch the surface, offering just a few highlights intended to invite readers to discover, sift through, and examine additional material.

1. Apocryphal Gospels and the Question of the Historical Jesus

One prominent aspect of the so-called Third Quest for the historical Jesus was the inclusion of previously neglected source material.[17] This is not the place to provide a detailed history of research on the subject. Instead, we will briefly present a few gospels whose significance for the quest has been a matter of particularly intense debate.

1.1. Example 1: The Controversial Gospel of Thomas

The Gospel of Thomas is surely one of the most well-known apocryphal gospels—in large part *because of* its consideration as a potential source of information on the historical Jesus.[18] Unlike many other Jesus texts, this work does not offer a continuous narrative; rather, it is now divided into 114 logia, that is, sayings of Jesus, some of which are provided with

17. In the meantime, the search for new departures is also beginning here. Important in this vein is James Crossley and Chris Keith, eds., *The Next Quest for the Historical Jesus* (Eerdmans, 2024).

18. Very helpful overviews on the significance the Gospel of Thomas has for the inquiry into the historical Jesus are offered, for example, by Edwin K. Broadhead, "The Thomas-Jesus Connection," in Holmén and Porter, *Handbook for the Study of the Historical Jesus*, 2059–80; Stephen J. Patterson, "The Gospel of Thomas and Historical Jesus Research," in *Coptica – Gnostica – Manichaica: Mélanges offerts à Wolf-Peter Funk*, Bibliotheque Copte de Nag Hammadi Études 7 (Peeters, 2006), 663–84; Patterson, "The *Gospel of Thomas* and the Historical Jesus," in Gregory and Tuckett, *Oxford Handbook of Early Christian Apocrypha*, 233–49 (including the extensive bibliography); Gathercole, *Gospel of Thomas*, 176–84. Konrad Schwarz, "Gospel of Thomas," in Schröter and Jacobi, *Reception of Jesus in the First Three Centuries*, 2:265–79, places a clearer focus on processed Jesus traditions and the reception of Jesus.

a brief narrative framework or are part of a dialogue. The text is preserved today in (probably) three Greek fragments, which were found in Oxyrhynchus (Upper Egypt) toward the end of the nineteenth century (Papyri Oxyrhynchus I 1; IV 654; IV 655). A complete manuscript, however, is available only in Coptic. This was discovered in 1945 as part of the late antique Nag Hammadi library.[19] While about half of the logia have clear or at least vague parallels in the canonical Gospels (e.g., in their parable discourse of Jesus), the remaining logia offer otherwise unknown Jesus material.

The passages with known parallels include, for example, logion 9, which is reminiscent of the synoptic parable of the sower (see Mark 4:3–8; Matt 13:3–8; Luke 8:5–8; also Ps-Hippolytus, *Ref.* 5.8.28–29). Unlike the Synoptics, however, the Gospel of Thomas does not offer a subsequent allegorical interpretation of the parable: "Jesus said: Behold, the sower went forth and filled his hand and sowed. Some fell onto the path, and the birds came and gleaned them. Others fell onto rock and did not take root in the ground and produce ears upwards. And others fell into thorns. They choked the seed, and worms ate them. But others fell onto the good soil, and it yielded good fruit upwards. It brought sixty per measure and one hundred and twenty per measure" (Gos. Thom. 9).[20] This logion follows directly on from another parable that we do not know from the canonical Gospels but that in structure is certainly reminiscent of synoptic parables. "And he said: The man is like a wise fisherman, who cast his net into the sea. He pulled it from the sea full of fish. Among them the wise fisherman found a good, large fish. He cast all the little fish out i[n]to the sea, and he chose the large fish without being troubled. He who has ears to hear, let him hear" (Gos. Thom. 8).

Logion 54, in turn, recalls the beatitude of the poor from the Sermon on the Mount and the Sermon on the Plain (Matt 5:3; Luke 6:20) but is not linked to other beatitudes: "Blessed are the poor, for

19. For the introduction see, e.g., Schröter and Bethge, "Das Evangelium nach Thomas," 483–522, and Gathercole, *Gospel of Thomas*, 3–184.

20. Translations of the Gospel of Thomas follow Gathercole, *Gospel of Thomas*.

yours is the kingdom of heaven." Another beatitude follows, but only a few sayings later; this one is *not* found in the canonical Gospels. Logion 58 reads, "Jesus said: Blessed is the man who has labored and found life" (see also other beatitudes in logia 68–69, 79). Other passages, on the other hand, give the impression of having little to do with what we read in the canonical Gospels. Logion 85, for example, reads, "Jesus said: Adam came into being from a great power and a great wealth, but he did not become [wor]thy of you. For if he had been worthy [he would] not [have tas]ted death."[21]

A stark contrast to the canonical Gospels is that the Jesus of the Gospel of Thomas is hardly—if at all—portrayed as the Jewish prophet and miracle worker whose life ends on the cross and who is encountered as raised from the dead by God. Instead, he is presented in the prologue of the text as the "living Jesus," who speaks secret words, which in turn are written down by (Didymus) Judas Thomas.[22] The rest of the text is understood against this background: the secret words of Jesus, who is understood as a voice speaking into all times (as opposed to within a particular historical context). Understanding his teachings is a matter of life and death (logion 1). The exact character of this gospel and its portrayal of Jesus is therefore the subject of some debate: The reference to the "living Jesus" seems to indicate a relationship of Jesus to God, who is also referred to several times as "the living one" (logia 3, 37, 50). Whether the teachings of this Jesus are (at least partially) to be interpreted as "gnostic" is also unclear, inasmuch as the text lacks the clear creation and redemption myth that so many "gnostic" works contain, at least implicitly.[23]

---

21. The square brackets indicate lacunae in the manuscript.

22. The Greek tradition ("Judas Thomas," albeit reconstructed) and the Coptic tradition ("Didymus Judas Thomas") differ in the form of the name.

23. We deliberately put the term *gnostic* in quotation marks because its use is rightly contested today. However, since the term continues to be encountered at every turn in the history of research on the Gospel of Thomas, we believe it is impossible to avoid it completely. Even the suggestion of speaking about a "biblical demiurgical"

The very fact that it is a collection of—at least at first glance—seemingly unconnected sayings of Jesus[24] allows for other interpretations. It is plausible, for instance, that we are dealing here with a writing that describes Jesus as primarily a teacher of wisdom. Some of its thoughts appear to be influenced by popular philosophy of the time (with a focus on [Middle] Platonism).[25] This basic character of the work contributes to ongoing debates about its place in the history of early Christian literature: Does the fact that we are dealing here with a collection of Jesus's sayings, that is, a sayings collection, mean that the Gospel of Thomas represents an *older* form of Jesus tradition than the canonical Gospels (with their detailed narrative elements or elaborate discourses, such as those in the Gospel of John)? Can we conclude from this that the Gospel of Thomas is also older than the canonical Gospels, at least in essence? Was it written all at once, or is it the product of a series of editorial stages?[26] To what extent does the Coptic text available today also represent (or depart from) an "original" version of this gospel?

The answers to these questions vary. We think it is very likely that the bulk of this text belongs to the middle of the second century rather than the first century. But even this broad statement does not preclude the possibility that the text contains valuable material about the

---

text does not help here, because the Gospel of Thomas does not seem to differentiate between an upper deity and a demiurgic creator.

24. This does not mean that clusters of logia do not appear to be more closely linked from time to time.

25. On the significance of Middle Platonic thought for at least parts of the Gospel of Thomas, see Stephen J. Patterson, "Jesus Meets Plato: The Theology of the *Gospel of Thomas* and Middle Platonism," in *Das Thomasevangelium: Entstehung – Rezeption – Theologie*, ed. Jörg Frey et al., BZNW 157 (de Gruyter, 2008), 181–205; and (in more detail) Ivan Miroshnikov, *The Gospel of Thomas and Plato: A Study of the Impact of Platonism on the "Fifth Gospel,"* Nag Hammadi and Manichaean Studies 93 (Brill, 2018).

26. See, for example, the complex proposal by April DeConick, *Recovering the Original Gospel of Thomas: A History of the Gospel and Its Growth*, LNTS 286 (T&T Clark, 2005).

historical Jesus. After all, even if the overall composition of the text is rather late, it is quite possible that individual logia are very old at their core or have been handed down in a form that comes very close to their original form. In other words, for the passages that have parallels in the canonical Gospels, especially the Synoptics,[27] it is necessary to consider (1) whether they could be independent of the synoptic versions, or, in the case of dependence, (2) whether they provide an older version than that of the Synoptics. For the passages without such parallels, on the other hand, we need to consider how plausible it is that they go back to the historical Jesus. But the next question is: How do we set the criteria for determining this plausibility?[28] Should texts that are reminiscent of those from the Synoptics, such as the parable of the great fish from logion 8 quoted above, be considered likely candidates? Or do we then fall victim to circular reasoning?[29]

We regard it quite plausible, even probable, that the Gospel of Thomas contains historically valuable memories of Jesus in at least some logia—even as the identification of *specific* logia as belonging to an early stratum of tradition will always be controversial. But what truly excites us about the Gospel of Thomas is that it offers an alternative portrait of Jesus—one that differs substantially from the portrait found in the Synoptics. The Jesus whom we encounter in the Gospel of Mark, Gospel of Matthew, and Gospel of Luke—the apocalyptic proclaimer of God's reign, the healer, the exorcist, the interpreter of the Torah—recedes, and we are presented with a wise teacher who speaks beyond the ages. To this day, the discovery of the Gospel of Thomas represents a real

27. The question of the literary relationship between the Gospel of Thomas and the Gospel of John is even more difficult to answer than that between the Gospel of Thomas and the Synoptics. See Stephan Witetscheck, *Thomas und Johannes – Johannes und Thomas: Das Verhältnis der Logien des Thomasevangeliums zum Johannesevangelium*, Herders Biblische Studien 79 (Herder, 2015).

28. The earlier criterion of "dissimilarity," which can be traced back to Ernst Käsemann, can now be rejected as insufficient.

29. See also the intelligent argumentation of Patterson, "*Gospel of Thomas* and Historical Jesus," 236–37 (in conversation with older research).

challenge for historical Jesus research. It demonstrates that there is no such thing as a presupposition-free inquiry into the historical Jesus.

However, there is another important consequence of the fact that the Gospel of Thomas consists largely of narratively unconnected logia: It is fundamentally impossible to make this text the central starting point for a history of Jesus, in the basic sense of the word. To write *history*, it is necessary to have at least the beginnings of a *story* structure. So even if a single logion were proven beyond doubt to have been said by the historical Jesus, it would be historically meaningless without some contextualization. Consider, for example, logion 42 ("Jesus said: Be passers-by!") or 74 ("He said, Lord, there are many around the well, but there is no-one in the well"); we cannot begin to understand what these sentences mean and how they could fit into the message of a historical Jesus without the context of a story—a way to place them within the life of Jesus. Such a story, however, is initially provided only by the New Testament Gospels. How far we can trust this story is another matter. However, the form and content of many of the Gospel of Thomas's logia suggest that what they say is not entirely compatible with what the Synoptic Gospels provide as a narrative framework for the story of Jesus. The mystery remains.

1.2. Example 2: The Unknown Gospel on Papyrus Egerton 2

When Papyrus Egerton 2—consisting of a total of four fragments, two of which contain significant textual material—was first made public in 1935,[30] it was the oldest material evidence of early Christianity (though it was soon overtaken by the now-famous Papyrus 52, with the remains of the Gospel of John). The discovery of such an old fragment, which contained not a canonical text but apocryphal accounts of Jesus that were unknown to that point, was, of course, sensational: The discussion as to whether the Unknown Gospel on Papyrus Egerton 2 offered texts about Jesus that were independent of the canonical Gospels, and

30. First edition: *Fragments of an Unknown Gospel and Other Early Christian Papyri*, ed. H. Idris Bell and T. C. Skeat (Trustees, 1935), 1–41.

perhaps even represented the more original form (or even a source of the canonical Gospels) in those places where parallels to the canonical Gospels can be seen, was and still is the subject of vigorous debate.[31] In the meantime, an additional fragment, Papyrus Köln 255, which can be connected to fragment 1 of Papyrus Egerton 2, has not only provided additional textual material but has also called the early dating of the manuscript into question.[32] Today, it is generally agreed that the fragment was written at the turn of the third century, though a margin of uncertainty (plus or minus twenty-five years or so) must always be taken into account.[33] Regardless, Papyrus Egerton 2 plus Papyrus Köln 255 remain among the oldest surviving text fragments of early Christianity.

The surviving narrative, which is, of course, older than the actual manuscript, offers some extraordinarily interesting material. On fragment 1 verso + Papyrus Köln 255 verso, we find a dispute between Jesus, the *nomikoi* (a term that likely refers to scholars of the Torah), and the "leaders of the people,"[34] which (similar to John 5:39, 45–64; 9:29) deals with questions of scriptural hermeneutics; on fragment 1 recto and Papyrus Köln 255 recto, we find sections of a scene in which Jesus is arrested by the leaders and left to the crowd, who apparently want to stone him but do not succeed, alongside an account of the healing of a leper. On fragment 2 verso, we find remains of a difficult to reconstruct (miracle?) narrative by the River Jordan[35] and a confrontation between Jesus and a group of unidentifiable Jewish opponents, reminiscent of the

31. For a summary of the history of research, see Zelyck, *Egerton Gospel*, 5–8.

32. First edition: Matthias Gronewald, "Unbekanntes Evangelium oder Evangelienharmonie (Fragment aus dem 'Evangelium Egerton')," in *Kölner Papyri (P.Köln) 6*, ed. Klaus Maresch et al. (Westdeutscher Verlag, 1987), 136–45.

33. For a paleographical description and dating of the manuscript, see Nicklas, "'Unknown Gospel' on Papyrus Egerton 2," 13–22, and Zelyck, *Egerton Gospel*, 34–48.

34. Translations follow Nicklas, "Unknown Gospel," unless otherwise stated.

35. We will discuss this scene in more detail below.

beginning of the Nicodemus scene in the Gospel of John, which leads to a quotation from Isaiah 29:13 LXX (on fragment 2 recto).

Of course, it is not possible to reconstruct a reliable and complete narrative from these fragments, but outlines are nevertheless recognizable:[36] The Jesus of the Unknown Gospel is portrayed as a miracle worker and teacher who is in conflict with Jewish opponents over questions of the Torah and the correct interpretation of Scripture. The way he deals with the healed leper, his references to the Scriptures, and other details lead to the conclusion that the Unknown Gospel emphasized Jesus's Jewishness. But what the core of this Jesus's message was remains unclear. While there are no indications that suggest a childhood story or even postresurrection narratives,[37] one can at least conclude on the basis of what has been preserved that this narrative presupposes the violent death of Jesus. The extent to which this text is able to provide us with something new and significant about the historical Jesus is extremely difficult to determine. It hinges on whether and to what extent the narratives of this text are dependent on or independent of the narratives recounted in the canonical Gospels. The pattern that emerges when the usual literary comparisons are made is so peculiar that no clear solution to the puzzle emerges:[38] (1) The parallels to some passages of the Gospel of John, above all to John 5:39, 45–46, and 9:29 on fragment 1 verso, are so clear that they can only be explained with the help of literary dependence. What is unclear, however, is which version is the older, that of the apocryphal gospel or that of the Gospel of John? (2) The situation is different with the parallels to Synoptic Gospels. At least at first glance, the account of the healing of a leper seems like a clear parallel to Mark 1:40–44 (par. Matt 5:2–4 and Luke 5:12–16). However, the extent of verbatim

36. See also the discussion in Nicklas, "Unknown Gospel," 96–114, and Tobias Nicklas, "Egerton Gospel (P.Egerton 2)," in Schröter and Jacobi, *Reception of Jesus in the First Three Centuries*, 2:195–206.

37. Of course, it is not unlikely that the text may also have contained an Easter message of some kind.

38. For the following, see the corresponding considerations in Nicklas, "Unknown Gospel."

parallels with the three Synoptics is *not* so great as to indicate clear literary dependence; the three Synoptic versions are much closer to each other than the Unknown Gospel is to any of them. The Unknown Gospel also contains a motif that is *not* found in the other texts: The leper explains his illness by saying that he was traveling with other lepers and had even eaten with them. Jesus's final sentence that he should sin no more (also without parallel in the synoptic narratives, but see John 5:14; 8:11) may refer to this statement. These data points are usually seen as evidence that we have a late form of the narrative in the Unknown Gospel; this is contradicted by the fact that this narrative is shorter than any of the synoptic parallels (in other words, it cannot be understood as an expansion of a preexisting text).

One could cite additional details, but the basic pattern has been sketched. We therefore consider it very likely that the author of the Unknown Gospel knew the Gospel of John and appreciated it so much that he also interspersed non-Johannine material with Johannine-sounding verses. And while we assume that the author of the Gospel of John knew the Synoptic Gospels and freely adapted them, this does not mean that the author of the Unknown Gospel also knew the Synoptics (or a part of them) in their written version and that they were available to him when he wrote his text. That said, because of the form of the text, which, like the Synoptics, can be divided at least in part into distinct pericopes, and because of the fact that, given its dependence on the Gospel of John, it can only have been written as early as the middle of the second century,[39] we also conclude that the source from which the text draws its synoptic material is not completely independent of the Synoptic Gospels. The catchy story of the healing of a leper just mentioned is an example that might clarify what we mean: Once you have heard it several times, it is not necessary to have such a story in writing in order to be able to repeat it in outline; in other words, the account of the healing of the leper in the Unknown Gospel is probably a reenactment of the

39. We consider the Gospel of John to be dependent on the Synoptic Gospels and therefore tend to date it to the first quarter of the second century.

synoptic narratives (or one of them) in the sense mentioned above.[40] In this episode, then, the author of the Unknown Gospel is neither literarily dependent nor totally independent of the Synoptics. To return to the question raised in this section, the episode has no real value for research on the historical Jesus.

Similar conclusions can be drawn with respect to many other early apocryphal Jesus narratives. Narratives about the birth and childhood of Jesus (such as the Protevangelium of James or the Infancy Gospel of Thomas) are almost entirely occupied with answering theological and narrative questions raised by (and filling in gaps left by) the canonical Gospels;[41] thus they are of little use for historical Jesus studies. The same largely applies to most of the esoteric gospels in dialogue form (such as the Gospel of Mary or the Sophia of Jesus Christ), which are primarily interested in secret knowledge[42] and show little interest in the historical Jesus. The apocryphal Gospel of Peter (probably from the middle of the second century) offers a narrative of the passion and resurrection of Jesus. Here Jesus is referred to throughout as "the Lord." In all likelihood, this work adapts material from all four canonical Gospels in free form and therefore yields hardly any material for the enquiry.[43] It has been repeat-

40. See Nicklas, "Zwischen Redaktion und 'Neuinszenierung,'" 318–21, for a more detailed discussion of this argument. Helpful here is the fundamental observation by Carolyn Kellas, "The Healing of the Leper: The Accounts in the Synoptic Gospels and Papyrus Egerton 2, Papyrus Köln 255," *IBS* 16 (1994): 161–73, who comes to the conclusion that the text on Papyrus Egerton 2 repeats precisely those elements of the synoptic narrative that make it recognizable.

41. Thus, for example, the Infancy Gospel of Thomas provides an account of Jesus's childhood, answering an obvious question raised by the Gospel of Matthew and Gospel of Luke but not at all addressed in the former and only minimally addressed in the latter (in Luke 2:41–52), that is: If Jesus was miraculously *born* the Son of God, what would he have been like as a child?

42. Still crucial to the discussion of these writings is Judith Hartenstein, *Die zweite Lehre: Erscheinungen des Auferstandenen als Rahmenerzählungen frühchristlicher Dialoge*, TU 146 (Akademie, 1999).

43. Tobias Nicklas, "Das Petrusevangelium im Rahmen antiker Jesustraditionen," in Nicklas, *Studien zum Petrusevangelium*, WUNT 453 (Mohr Siebeck, 2020), 63–89.

edly discussed whether the fragmentary Greek text sometimes referred to as the Gospel of the Savior (preserved on Papyrus Oxyrhynchus 840, a miniature codex) provides material about the historical Jesus.[44] This text reports on a dispute between Jesus and a Pharisaic high priest (probably named Levi) over questions of inner and outer purity. However, the text contains terminology that hardly indicates composition in the early second century, as is often assumed, but rather a later date.[45] Other fragments are too small to allow a detailed examination. This certainly does not exhaust all the possibilities; overall, however, the value of apocryphal texts with regard to the question of the historical Jesus is clearly limited.

2. On the Transmission of Remembered Jesus Material

However, none of this means that the apocryphal gospels are uninteresting or insignificant. To the contrary, they all represent "frozen moments" of the remembered Jesus.[46] Like any form of memory, how-

---

44. On this text, see Michael J. Kruger, *The Gospel of the Savior: An Analysis of P.Oxy. 840 and Its Place in the Gospel Traditions of Early Christianity*, TENTS 1 (Brill, 2005), and Kruger, "Papyrus Oxyrhynchus 840," in Kraus et al., *Gospel Fragments*, 123–215, which favors a rather early dating. Joachim Jeremias, *Unbekannte Jesusworte*, 4th ed. (Mohn, 1965), 50–60, has probably been the most intense advocate of interpreting this text as a testimony to the historical Jesus. For more details on the history of research, see Elisabeth Hernitscheck, "Im trüben Wasser des 'Davidsteichs' – P.xy. 840 und die Suche nach seiner Provenienz," in *Shadowy Characters and Fragmentary Evidence. The Search for Early Christian Groups and Movements*, ed. Joseph Verheyden et al., WUNT 388 (Mohr Siebeck, 2017), 89–108.

45. Harald Buchinger with Elisabeth Hernitscheck, "P.Oxy. 840 and the Rites of Christian Initiation. Dating a Piece of Alleged Anti-sacramental Polemic," *EC* 5 (2014): 117–24, which draws on an impulse from Francois Bovon, "Fragment Oxyrhynchus 840. Fragment of a Lost Gospel. Witness of an Early Christian Controversy over Purity," *JBL* 119 (2000): 705–28.

46. Huebenthal, *Gedächtnistheorie und Neues Testament*, offers an excellent introduction to the use of various theories of social memory in work on early Christianity. Here we adopt the term "frozen moments" from Sandra Huebenthal, "'Frozen Moments'—Early Christianity Through the Lens of Social Memory Theory," in *Memory and Memories in Early Christianity*, ed. Simon Butticaz and Enrico Norelli, WUNT 398 (Mohr Siebeck, 2018), 17–43.

ever, acts of remembering Jesus are as much about the present as the past. In many cases, Jesus narratives function as "origin narratives"[47] by and for groups that understand their own identity with reference to Jesus; one might ask, then, what these narratives are designed to communicate to their intended audience. In other words, they should not be read as simple testimonies to the historical Jesus but as normative statements about Jesus. In many cases these narratives are intended to convey crucial information about the origins of the group of Christ-followers to whom they belong or to whom they are addressed. Looking more closely at how the same story, so to speak, could be remembered very differently in very different contexts testifies not only to the flexibility of the memory of even short episodes but also to their enduring utility. This can be illustrated by different examples:

(1) Particularly exciting things emerge when we leave the field of the apocryphal gospels in the narrower sense and turn to Jesus narratives embedded in apocryphal apostle narratives.[48] Some accounts of Jesus in these texts even present themselves as eyewitness accounts! Our example comes from the Pseudo-Clementine novel,[49] specifically the

47. In other words, identity-forming and identity-reflecting narratives that address the origins of a group or movement. I think it is no wonder that in three of the four canonical Gospels (Mark, Luke, and John) the word ἀρχή already appears in the first verses (and Matthew begins with the "book of Jesus's becoming" or even refers to it as such; see Matt 1:1).

48. The following section offers a slightly edited, significantly abridged version of Tobias Nicklas, "Apocryphal Jesus Stories in the *Pseudo-Clementine Homilies:* The Syrophoenician Woman (*Hom.* 2.19) and the Dispute with the Sadducees," in *In Search of Truth in the Pseudo-Clementine Homilies*, ed. Benjamin M. J. De Vos and Danny Praet, WUNT 496 (Mohr Siebeck, 2022), 131–44. For a detailed discussion of the text and a discussion of the relevant secondary literature, please refer to this article.

49. An excellent introduction to this is provided by F. Stanley Jones, "Introduction to the *Pseudo-Clementines*," in *Pseudoclementina Elchesaiticaque inter Judaeochristiana. Collected Studies*, OLA 203 (Peeters, 2012), 7–49.

Greek version of the Pseudo-Clementine Homilies.[50] In Homily 2, we read of a nocturnal dialogue between Clement, the protagonist, and Peter, the ideal apostle from the perspective of the text. As part of the conversation, Peter offers a version of the story about the request of a non-Israelite woman, which is also known from the Gospel of Mark and Gospel of Matthew (Mark 7:24–30; Matt 15:21–28; see Hom. 2.19).[51] This episode is embedded in the framework of his teaching on the true prophet, God's justice, and the immortality of souls and, more specifically, his narrative about the arch-antagonist Simon Magus. The relevant passage (Hom. 2.19.1–3) reads as follows:

There is among us a certain Justa, a Syrophoenician woman, a Canaanite by race, whose young daughter was afflicted by a terrible illness. She approached our lord shouting and supplicating that he might heal her daughter. After being petitioned also by us, he said, "It is not permitted to heal the Gentiles, because they are like dogs on account of their use of different foods and practices, while the royal table has been given the sons and daughters of Israel." When she heard this, she asked also to have a share, like a dog, of the crumbs that fell from the same table. Having changed what she was, by living like the sons and daughters of the kingdom, she obtained healing for her daughter, as she asked.[52]

All of this is very reminiscent of the aforementioned narrative from the Synoptic Gospels. If the Jesus traditions of the Pseudo-Clementines were independent of those of the Synoptics, this would even be an interesting parallel tradition for inquiring about the historical Jesus. A closer look at the text, however, shows above all how much this narrative *differs* from the two synoptic accounts. The narrative of the

50. Greek texts follow the edition by Bernhard Rehm, *Die Pseudoklementinen I: Homilien*, 3rd ed., GCS 42 (Akademie, 1992).

51. A detailed examination of this passage is also offered by Patricia Duncan, *Novel Hermeneutics in the Greek Pseudo-Clementine Romance*, WUNT 395 (Mohr Siebeck, 2017), 143–52, to whose observations we owe much (and certainly have little to add).

52. Translation: Duncan, *Novel Hermeneutics*, 144.

Pseudo-Clementines shows only very superficial verbal similarities with the versions of the Synoptics. The most obvious innovations are that the story is told from Peter's perspective and that the woman is given the name Justa (with her daughter later introduced as Bernice; Hom. 3.73.2; 4.4.1; 4.6.2). But these are not the most important differences. What is truly significant is that this form of the narrative leads to a conclusion almost the *opposite* of what the synoptic, especially the Matthean, version offers. Here we would underscore one central point. The most striking variation among all three versions of the narrative is that each is built around a distinctive saying of Jesus. The Jesus of the Gospel of Mark answers the woman directly with the words, "Let the children be fed first, for it is not fair to take the children's food and throw it to the (small) dogs" (Mark 7:27, adapted from NRSVue); the Gospel of Matthew instead offers a combination of two logia. First, Jesus addresses his disciples and speaks about his own mission: "I was sent only to the lost sheep of the house of Israel" (Matt 15:24; see also 10:6). This is combined with a short version of Mark 7:27: "It is not fair to take the children's food and throw it to the dogs." Nothing of this kind is found in the Homilies. Instead, Jesus draws an even sharper line between Israel and the nations than is implied in the Gospel of Matthew: "It is not permitted to heal the Gentiles, because they are like dogs on account of their use of different foods and practices, while the royal table has been given the sons and daughters of Israel."

Although this is reminiscent of the synoptic parallels, this statement does not share a single word in common with their logia; the attitude of demarcation expressed in the first part is extreme even in the context of Jewish discourse. The second part is even more interesting. While the synoptic parallels make only an implicit comparison between people from the nations and small, likely young, dogs, the Homilies explicitly compare people from the nations with adult dogs: Neither observe *kashrut*, that is, Jewish dietary restrictions. Finally, all of this is supplemented with a final, related image. Unlike in the synoptic parallels, we read not only of a table or the table of the "masters of the dogs" but of a royal table reserved only for the sons of Israel. Are we to think here of God's eschatological banquet with his people? Perhaps the background of this statement is the notion that the observance of *kashrut* as part of God's Torah means not only doing God's will and separating the children of Israel from the nations but also preparing them to take their place at the royal table (of God), where the observance of *kashrut* is required.

The point of Jesus's words in the Pseudo-Clementine narrative is therefore quite distinct from that of the Synoptics. For this reason, the conclusion of the narrative must also differ from that of the canonical accounts. According to these texts, the healing of the daughter occurs because Jesus crosses a boundary—the boundary between Israel and the nations. This is particularly exciting in the Gospel of Matthew because it is the woman's clever argument that convinces Jesus to reconsider his own mission. In the Pseudo-Clementines, the opposite is the case: The woman from the nations turns to a lifestyle that corresponds to that of the children of Israel: She "judaizes."[53] Only in this way is the healing of her daughter possible. Therefore, even if these episodes from the Homilies are literarily dependent on the canonical texts (most likely the version of the Gospel of Matthew), they deal with them very freely. Key motifs make the story clearly recognizable, but the narrative of the Pseudo-Clementines presents variations on multiple levels when compared to the texts of the Synoptics. Despite their own multiple differences, the two synoptic versions are closer to each other than the Homilies is to either of the two. This can be seen in the specific wording, in missing and additional motifs, and even in aspects of form and structure. The reenactment of the narrative for the new context means that it now has a new function and a new theological point. Although at first glance we might think we are looking at the same story, its message in

53. We usually find the term *judaize* unhelpful; here it is appropriate because, while the text actually differentiates between Jews and people from the nations, she remains a woman from the nations who behaves like a Jew.

the Pseudo-Clementines is diametrically opposed to that in the synoptic narratives.

(2) The practice of drawing connections between memories of events from the life of the earthly Jesus and passages from the writings of Israel invoked to interpret those events is a well-known aspect of early Christianity. It is not necessary to repeat here the various techniques developed for this purpose in the writings of early Christ-followers. Signs of it can already be found in the very oldest testimonies from the New Testament, such as the ancient profession of faith preserved in 1 Corinthians 15:3–5, in the way in which the passion narratives incorporate texts such as Psalm 22 and Psalm 69, in the fulfillment quotations from the Gospel of Matthew, in the use and further development of biblical figures to interpret Jesus, and much more.[54] Such highly creative theological developments are also recognizable in writings contemporary with and postdating the New Testament. While in some texts the awareness of the scriptural background of a motif seems to be lost, in others new motifs emerge from the reflection of Scripture.

One of the key Old Testament texts from which important motifs for the description of the crucifixion of Jesus developed, especially in the Gospel of Mark and Gospel of Matthew, is Psalm 22/21 LXX.[55] Not only does Jesus die with the words of the psalm on his lips, but other aspects of the narrative (such as the division of his clothes) also make it clear that the suffering of the crucified Jesus corresponds to that of the suffering righteous man from the psalm. The depiction of Jesus's crucifixion in the apocryphal Gospel of Peter, a fragmentarily

54. For a broader discussion see, e.g., Tobias Nicklas, "Frühchristliche Ansprüche auf die Schriften Israels," in *Scriptural Authority in Early Judaism and Ancient Christianity*, DCLS 16 (de Gruyter, 2013), 347–68.

55. For a detailed discussion, see Tobias Nicklas, "Die Gottverlassenheit des Gottessohns. Funktionen von Psalm 22/21 LXX in frühchristlichen Auseinandersetzungen mit der Passion Jesu," in *Aneignung durch Transformation: Festschrift für Michael Theobald*, ed. Wilfried Eisele et al., Herders Biblische Studien 74 (Herder, 2013), 395–415.

preserved passion-and-resurrection narrative whose core may date back to the middle of the second century, also speaks of Jesus's executioners (here the "Jews") raffling off Jesus's clothes among themselves (v. 12).[56] While the scene may still be reminiscent of Psalm 22:19, the last words from Jesus dying on the cross are so changed compared to both the Gospel of Mark and Gospel of Matthew that their background in Psalm 22 is no longer recognizable: "And the Lord cried out and said, 'My power, power, you have forsaken me.' And when he had said this, he was taken up" (Gos. Pet. 19).

The function of this saying has clearly changed. It is no longer a question of portraying Jesus as the suffering righteous one of the Psalter, perhaps with an emphasis on his Davidic background. Nor is it necessary to go so far as to justify this description of Jesus's death with a docetic Christology, as has been repeatedly attributed to the Gospel of Peter.[57] Perhaps it is simply a matter of answering an important question in connection with the crucifixion of Jesus: How is it possible that the "Lord," the "Son of God," suffers on the cross and is unable to save himself? The answer in this text seems to be that his power—possibly the miraculous power given to him by God—has left him.[58] And yet, he does not simply die like any other person but is "taken up" (by God?). The text thus describes a relationship that is also important for the other gospels. In the crucifixion, God and his power seem to have abandoned Jesus, and yet they are there in a decisive way. None of this, however, has anything to do with Psalm 22.

---

56. Edition: Thomas J. Kraus and Tobias Nicklas, eds., *Das Petrusevangelium und die Petrusapokalypse: Die griechischen Fragmente mit deutscher und englischer Übersetzung*, GCS NS 11 (de Gruyter, 2004), 3–77; and (including detailed introduction and commentary) Paul Foster, *The Gospel of Peter: Introduction, Critical Edition and Commentary*, TENTS 4 (Brill, 2010).

57. On this, see the detailed discussion in Foster, *Gospel of Peter*, 157–65.

58. This is the suggestion of Thomas Hieke, "Das Petrusevangelium vom Alten Testament her gelesen," in *Das Evangelium nach Petrus: Text, Kontexte, Intertexte*, ed. Thomas J. Kraus and Tobias Nicklas, TU 158 (de Gruyter, 2007), 105–7.

But the reverse, the emergence of new biblical motifs, is also possible. To illustrate this, we will present a text that is not normally found in the collections of apocryphal gospels: an excerpt from the anonymous Latin homily De duobus montibus Sina et Sion (On the Two Mountains Sinai and Zion).[59] We are not claiming that this is an apocryphal gospel or a gospel fragment. And yet, this text, a creative paraphrase of the passion story, is profitably considered in the context of apocryphal gospels, inasmuch as it contains a number of elements that are not found in the canonical texts. The homily is generally assigned to the Christian *Adversus Iudaeos* literature; that is, it belongs to a whole series of writings whose anti-Judaism we rightly find intolerable today.[60] In terms of religious history, however, it is of course still interesting. Due to its manuscript tradition, it was wrongly attributed to Cyprian of Carthage (d. 258 CE). In reality, it probably originates from North Africa (probably Carthage or the surrounding area) but was composed by an unknown author. Scholars have repeatedly considered whether the author might have been a converted Jew,[61] but this remains a matter of speculation. The basic thesis of this coarse anti-Jewish text, which was probably written in the first half of the third century, is that Mount Sinai and Mount Zion stand for the old and the new covenant:[62] Mount Sinai symbolizes

59. The following section is a heavily abridged and adapted version of Tobias Nicklas, "Eine 'Passionsgeschichte' in Ps-Cyprians De duobus montibus Sina et Sion," in *Humanitas* 76, supplement 1 (2021): 74–85. There you will also find a concrete discussion of the secondary literature and an examination of the details of the partly corrupt Latin text.

60. Edition: Clara Burini, ed., *Pseudo Cipriano. I Due Monti Sinai et Sion*, Biblia Patristica (Nardini, 1994). On the following introductory questions, see especially Anni Maria Laato, *Jews and Christians in De duobus montibus Sina et Sion. An Approach to Early Latin Adversus Iudaeos Literature* (Åbo Akademi University Press, 1998).

61. For example, Jean Daniélou *Les origines du christianisme latin*, Histoires des doctrines avaint Nicée 3 (Cerf, 1978), 47–59.

62. This is justified with a number of other oppositions that run through the text. For an overview of the text, see Laato, *Jews and Christians*, 19–22 (including the

the rejection of Israel, Mount Zion the election of a new people. Here we will briefly look at a passage that shows how *new* motifs developed from ongoing mining of scriptural texts could be linked to the passion of Jesus in the third century.

Important for understanding this passage is that in this text Jesus is crucified in a garden (§3.1.7–8), in contrast to the Gospel of John, in which he is buried in a garden and also meets Mary Magdalene there (John 19:41; 20:15). The following short scene follows two sections in which the names Sinai and Zion are interpreted. Paragraph 6 concludes from the (alleged) definition of "Sinai" as "eternal trial and hatred" (6.1.7) that God gave the Jews the law in order to test them, to overtax them with it, and thus to induce them to eternal hatred. The word "Zion," on the other hand, stands for "test of bitterness and spying" (6.1.8; see already 2.1.3; 7.1.5).[63] All of this is a preliminary reference to the passion of "the holy wood," which the text relates to the Wisdom of Solomon (see Wis 2:17–22, quoted in 7.1.9–15). The section quoted below is in turn introduced by a combination of Psalm 105:14 LXX (in the Latin version) and Song of Songs 1:6:

Behold, the Jewish tempters! Thus it is written: *And they tempted the Lord in a watery place* [Ps 105:14 LXX]. Indeed, the image explains the height of the wood, as Solomon says of him, *They set me up as a watch for the orchard* [Song 1:6], because he [= Jesus] hung in the garden fastened to the wood between two robbers, and from the height of the wood he observed both [sc. robbers] as a symbol of two nations of evildoers: on the one hand the nations in whom lie the evils of the present age, and on the other the Jews, the murderers of the prophets. These are two nations of evildoers, whose symbol was two robbers, among whom hung an innocent man. One blasphemed (God), but the other truly confessed that [sc. on the cross] an innocent man suffered injustice. But Jesus watched the blasphemer and the confessor from the watch-timber:

discussion since Harnack).

63. On these etymologies, see Burini, *Pseudo Cipriano*, 193–94.

he saved the confessor and destroyed the blasphemer. And so he did with the two nations. (De duobus montibus Sina et Sion 7.2)

This is followed by a further depiction of aspects of the passion and crucifixion of Jesus, the aim of which is to justify the condemnation of Israel. The combination of the psalm and the passage from the Song of Songs used here is, as far as we know, not otherwise documented in ancient Christian literature; however, it allows us to see into the workshop of the homilist. One starting point is the text of the psalm, which actually speaks of a place without water and not a place rich in water. The combination of "Lord," "temptation," and "watery place" forges a connection to the passion of Jesus. The mutual relationship is described in the passage as an "image" (or "mirror"). Jesus is the Lord; the "Jews," whom the text understands as Jesus's executioners, are the tempters. It is possible to identify the watery place with a garden by combining it with the Song of Songs, which at least in our homilist's *Vorlage* speaks of an orchard.[64] Our homilist takes the Song of Songs passage out of its context and now understands Christ, instead of the original speaker (i.e., the woman guardian of a vineyard), as the speaker of the passage. It is now possible to understand him as the one who looks down from the high wood like a watchman at the two thieves (and subsequently the two nations): One of them, the repentant, good thief, is understood as a model for the peoples who are shown mercy; the other as a type (*typos*) of condemned Israel.

(3) New aspects of the memory of Jesus could also be associated with specific geographical locations. In a later chapter, we will discuss in more detail pilgrimage traditions that could connect with aspects of Jesus's life, whether in the Holy Land or in Egypt (in connection with the flight of the holy family).[65] Here we emphasize that the memory of Jesus could be linked to specific places in a way that prompts the development of existing Jesus traditions and the emergence of new ones. Our example returns to the aforementioned Unknown Gospel on Papyrus

64. The critical texts speak of a vineyard.

65. On the flight of the holy family, see ch. 5 below.

Egerton 2.[66] As already indicated, the scene on fragment 2 verso, which has survived only with large lacunae, has no clear parallel in the canonical Gospels. A plausible reconstruction of the text has therefore been impossible until quite recently. From the little that has survived, it could only be concluded that it is a miracle narrative that is either set by (or otherwise connected to) the Jordan River and that it somehow involves sowing and reaping a surprising harvest. No such scene is found in the New Testament or other known apocryphal gospels. However, two ancient pilgrims mention a local tradition in Jericho and Gilgal that might be comparable: While the pilgrim Theodosius (§§ 118) offers only a brief allusion, the pilgrim of Piacenza (§13), writing in the late sixth century CE, has a more detailed text.[67] The latter writes:

The stones that the Israelites took from the Jordan are set up not far from the city of Jericho in a basilica behind the altar; they are very large. In front of the basilica is a field, the "Lord's field," which the Lord has sown with his own hand. It yields up to three bushels of seed and is harvested twice a year. It is never sown, rather it grows by itself. It is harvested in February and used for communion at Easter. As soon as the harvest has been brought in, it is plowed over and then the rest of the harvest is brought in again; it is then plowed and left as it is.[68]

This reference, as well as the idea that the prophet Elisha also performs miracles at the Jordan in Second Kings (2 Kgs 2:13; 6:7; also retold by Josephus), has helped Lorne Zelyck to reconstruct the crucial passage as follows:[69] "Then Jesus, as he walked, stood on the bank of the

66. The following passage is based on a more detailed text in Nicklas, "Zwischen Redaktion und 'Neuinszenierung,'" 324–27. The detailed discussion of the original texts and the secondary literature can be found there.

67. For an introduction to this writing from the late sixth century (around 570), see Herbert Donner, *Pilgerfahrt ins Heilige Land. Die ältesten Berichte christlicher Palästinapilger (4.–7. Jh.)*, 3rd ed. (Katholisches Bibelwerk, 2011), 226–42.

68. Translation Donner, *Pilgerfahrt ins Heilige Land*, 255–56.

69. See Lorne R. Zelyck, "Elisha Typology in Jesus' Miracle on the Jordan River (Papyrus Egerton 2, 2v.6–14)," *NTS* 62 (2016): 149–56, and Zelcyk, *Egerton Gospel*, 83, 142–62. In the following, since we do not cite a specific edition, we do not

Jordan River; and reaching out his right hand, he took salt and scattered it upon the river. Then he poured out much water upon the ground. He prayed, and it was filled before them. Then it brought forth a crop of great abundance, produced by an everlasting gift for all these people" (Papyrus Egerton 2, fragment 2 verso, lines 6–15). Although the scene described here shows motifs we find elsewhere in the Jesus tradition (such as the motif of "bearing fruit," e.g., Mark 4:7, 8, 29, in relation to the seed), it appears to have originated independently of the canonical Gospels. Of course, it remains unclear whether the Unknown Gospel took this scene from an older tradition, perhaps local to the Jordan region, or whether its author developed the tradition from Elisha's salt miracle. What's more, we can no longer know exactly what prompted the narrative. The canonical Gospels establish connections between Jesus and the prophet Elijah in different ways (see, e.g., Mark 8:28 par. Luke 7:11–17 and John 1:21); it is possible that, in places where the prophet Elisha was active, he and his deeds may also have become interesting for the depiction of Jesus's ministry.

Similarly, the canonical Gospels depict Jesus passing through more or less the whole of Israel but mention or provide anecdotes that take place in only a handful of specific locations; it is also possible that the resultant geographical gaps prompted the composition of further episodes. While the Unknown Gospel does not name the location on the Jordan where the miracle took place, the pilgrimage tradition recounted above does seem to be attached to a specific place, at which the effects of the miracle continue to be observable. At the same time, the episode provides a concrete illustration of Jesus's talk of the grain of wheat that must fall into the ground and "die" in order to bear abundant fruit (John 12:24–25; see also 1 Cor 15:37–38; Apoc. Pet. 4).[70] That Jesus's work miraculously gives life (even to the point of raising the dead) can

indicate which letters are uncertain, but we will differentiate between additions to the lacunae and the passages on the fragment.

70. See, e.g., Tobias Nicklas, "Resurrection—Judgment—Punishment: Apocalypse of Peter 4," in *Resurrection of the Dead: Biblical Traditions in Dialogue*, ed. G. Van Oyen and T. Shepherd, BETL 240 (Peeters, 2012), 472.

be seen in the field of Jericho. "The Lord" himself had sown in this place, and the field continued to bear fruit. Further, this fruit is now used for another healing, life-giving purpose: communion at the celebration of Easter, at which the very event that is figuratively alluded to in the saying about the grain of wheat is celebrated. In other words, the miracle recounted in this apocryphal episode makes a saying of Jesus tangible in a specific location while at the same time developing the symbolism of what the saying originally expressed. Again, such narratives add nothing to our knowledge of the historical Jesus. They do, however, demonstrate that remembering Jesus was not simply about recalling and repeating logia that were assigned to him; remembering Jesus could also involve the materialization of sayings and stories in connection with concrete locations.

3. Jesus Discourses and the Apocrypha

When we take one further step and consider Jesus narratives as statements in more complex theological discourses—as statements that might complement, relativize, deepen, or oppose other such statements—we begin to recognize the invaluable importance of apocryphal works and parabiblical traditions for revealing a fuller picture of the history of Christianity. Once again, we can present only a few representative examples.

(1) Most contemporary Christianities understand, though with different emphases, the following three moments in the life of Jesus as decisive: the incarnation, his suffering and death on the cross, and his resurrection from the dead. Other moments, such as Jesus's baptism, are almost completely overshadowed.[71] But, this was by no means always the case. At least in some texts composed and used by early Christ-followers,

---

71. Decisive aspects of what we present below can be found in more detail in Tobias Nicklas, "History and Theology in the Non-canonical Gospels," in *History and Theology in the Gospels*, ed. Tobias Nicklas et al., WUNT 447 (Mohr Siebeck, 2020), 250–55. There you will also find a detailed discussion of the original texts and the relevant secondary literature.

his baptism is understood as a moment in which something pivotal happens. This can already be surmised by looking at the canonical Gospels. The scene in Gospel of Mark is particularly revealing: If we read it without its canonical context—that is, without adding the infancy narratives of the Gospel of Matthew or Gospel of Luke or the prologue of the Gospel of John—the Gospel of Mark tells the story of a certain Jesus who comes from Nazareth in Galilee to the Jordan to be baptized by John, like many others. As readers of the text, we know from Mark 1:1 that Jesus is to be understood as Christ, the anointed one, and (possibly) as the Son of God.[72] The text probably also already presupposes Christ-followers as its addressees. However, the plot of the narrative indicates that something decisive happens in the baptism scene in Mark 1:9–11. In Mark 1:9, Jesus is described as a man like all the others, seemingly someone who comes from Nazareth by chance; there is no hint that John the Baptist recognizes him as the one he refers to 1:7–8. Jesus alone sees "the heavens torn apart and the Spirit descending like a dove upon him" (Mark 1:10). It is also unclear whether anyone else hears the following voice from heaven: "You are my Son, my Beloved, with you I am well pleased" (Mark 1:11). This event is followed by an apparently complete change in the life of Jesus of Nazareth: The spirit that has entered him casts him out into the desert (Mark 1:12), where he is tempted by Satan for forty days but also lives together with wild animals, while angels minister to him (Mark 1:13). Once he has been prepared in this way, he begins to proclaim his own good news in Galilee after the "handing over of John" (Mark 1:14–15).

In Mark 1:10, Jesus of Nazareth thus becomes a bearer of the Spirit of God (see Isa 61:1–2), whose actions are now completely determined by that Spirit. At the moment of baptism, he is also proclaimed to be the Son of God. Depending on which other intertexts one includes when interpreting the divine speech in Mark 1:11, associations with the binding of Isaac (see "beloved son," Gen 22:2) and the "suffering servant

72. The presence of the phrase "son of God" in Mark 1:1 is text-critically uncertain.

of God" ("well pleased," Isa 42:1), on whom God has placed his Spirit, resonate. However, the decisive point of reference seems to be Psalm 2:7, where the Lord God calls out to the anointed king of Israel: "You are my son, today I have begotten you." Does the fact that the second part of this sentence ("today I have begotten you") is absent in the Gospel of Mark indicate an author consciously distancing himself from the possibility that Jesus was only adopted by God as his son at his baptism? Or is the author perhaps not even aware of this theological issue? With their accounts of the conception and birth of Jesus (Matt 1–2; Luke 1–2) as well as the prologue (John 1:1–18), the other three canonical Gospels make it very clear that, from their perspectives, adoption at baptism is an unacceptable notion. The Gospel of John even goes so far as to identify Jesus as the divine Logos made flesh, who was already with God and was God before all creation (John 1:1–14).

The significance of Jesus's baptism thus recedes into the background, even if parts of the textual tradition of the Gospel of Luke still include the phrase "today I have begotten you" from Psalm 2:7[73] and some manuscripts of the Gospel of John assume that John the Baptist testifies to Jesus after his baptism not as the "Son of God" but as the "chosen one of God" (John 1:34; see Isa 42:1). The latter could also indicate that the baptism, at which the Spirit descends on Jesus according to all canonical Gospels, reflects a special moment of election by God. If we restrict ourselves to canonical Gospels, then the situation is fairly clear: These canonical works (at least the Gospels of Matthew, Luke, and John) reject with varying degrees of clarity the idea that christologically decisive things happened at the baptism of Jesus. Any form of adoptionism (i.e., the idea that God only made Jesus his son at his baptism) is refuted as a theological error.

The discussion of Jesus's baptism has thus become uninteresting for systematic theology. But other theological impulses emerge when one takes a broader view of the sources and considers apocryphal traditions.

73. See, for example, Codex Bezae Cantabrigiensis and parts of the Latin tradition.

One of the most interesting parallel traditions of Jesus's baptism is found in the so-called Gospel of the Ebionites, of which only a few quotations survive today in the so-called *Panarion* (Gr. "medicine chest") against heresies by Epiphanius of Salamis (ca. 315–403).[74] The Ebionites must have been a group of Jewish followers of Jesus who saw themselves as "the poor," possibly those to whom Jesus had promised the kingdom of God (see Luke 6:20). The text itself was probably written in the middle of the second century; it shows clear signs of dependence on the Synoptic Gospels. Our knowledge of the Ebionites is fragmentary and conveyed only via heresiologists, that is, early Christian authors who attempted to demonstrate that their opponents' beliefs were deficient and false. Pseudo-Hippolytus of Rome, for example, imputes to Ebionites a rather naive form of Christology and soteriology: Jesus was a man who became an anointed one because he followed the commandments of the Torah in an exemplary manner.[75] Epiphanius, on the other hand, describes the Ebionite Christology as a bit more complex: According to his account, they distinguished between the man Jesus (frag. 1, Epiphanius, *Haer.* 30.13.2) and the heavenly Christ, the ruler over the angels (frag. 6, Epiphanius, *Haer.* 30.16.4–5), who was identical with the Holy Spirit (frag. 4, Epiphanius, *Haer.* 30.14.3–4). These two were united at the baptism of Jesus in the Jordan. This is described as follows:

When the people had been baptized, there came also Jesus, and he was baptized by John. And, as he came up from the water, there opened the heavens and he saw the Holy Spirit in the form of a dove, coming down and entering into him. And a voice from heaven, saying: "You are my son, the beloved one; in you am I well pleased." And again: "Today

74. Edition: Andrew Gregory, *The Gospel According to the Hebrews and the Gospel of the Ebionites*, Oxford Early Christian Gospel Texts (Oxford University Press, 2017), 171–264. Notes on the introduction also in Frey, "Die Fragmente judenchristlicher Evangelien," and Jörg Frey, "Die Fragmente des Ebionäerevangeliums," in Markschies and Schröter, *Antike christliche Apokryphen*, 1:560–92, 607–22.

75. Sources in A. F. J. Klijn and G. J. Reinink, *Patristic Evidence for Jewish-Christian Sects* (Brill, 1973), 112–13.

I have begotten you." And immediately there shone around the place a great light. When he saw it, it says, John said to him: "Who are you, lord?" And again, a voice from heaven came to him: "This is my son, the beloved, in whom I am well pleased." And then, it says, John fell down before him and said: "I entreat you lord, you baptize me." But he prevented him, saying: "let things be, for in this way it is fitting that all things be fulfilled." (Epiphanius, *Haer.* 30.14.3–4)[76]

The baptism narrative therefore develops in several stages. First, there is talk of Jesus being baptized by John. As in the Gospel of Mark, only Jesus sees the descent of the Holy Spirit in the form of a dove,[77] which now quite obviously takes up residence inside him.[78] The heavenly voice that is apparently heard here by all those present is identical to the one we find in the Synoptic Gospels. However, an addition is deliberately emphasized: "Today I have begotten you" (see Ps 2:7). This moment, obviously the moment in which the Holy Spirit and the man Jesus unite, is accompanied by a sudden shining light, a motif that is also found in two other accounts of Jesus's baptism (see Justin Martyr, *Dial.* 88.2; Papyrus Aberdeen 3). Only now does John address Jesus as "Lord." Furthermore, it is also revealed to him that Jesus is the beloved Son of God. Only this leads to his request to be baptized by him, the Lord. In the Gospel of Matthew, which also mentions this motif, it is not without reason that it occurs in the opposite place, namely, *before* Jesus's baptism (Matt 3:14): Jesus is here, after all, already the Son of God before his baptism. The event serves only to proclaim the one who is already the Son of God; the narratives of the Gospels of Matthew, Luke, and John take pains to emphasize Jesus's superiority over John.

The situation is even more complicated in the Gospel of Philip. This text is usually assigned to the group of Valentinians often classified as

76. Translation: Gregory, *Gospel According to the Hebrews*, 226–27.

77. The canonical Gospels are ambiguous here; it is quite possible that the texts do not describe the form of the Spirit but rather the way in which it descends. The Gospel of the Ebionites, however, clearly speaks of the form or appearance of a dove.

78. The text clearly speaks of the Spirit not settling on Jesus but entering him.

"gnostic."[79] It was likely composed in the late second or early third century[80] and is extremely difficult to interpret. It has survived in a single Coptic manuscript in the Nag Hammadi library. Within this gospel, there is a baptism scene that is unfortunately only fragmentary (NHC II 3, p. 70.35–71.8):

Jesus revealed [at the Jo]rdan the [fullness of the kingdom] of heaven. He who [was begotten] before all things was begotten again. He [who was anointed] first, was anointed again. He who was redeemed, was redeemed again. Indeed it is fitting to speak of a mystery! The Father of all things joined with the Virgin who came down, and a fire illuminated him. On that day he revealed the great bridal chamber. It was because of this that his body came into being on that day.[81]

The Gospel of Philip rewrites the idea hinted at in the Gospels of Matthew and Luke, that is, that Jesus was conceived by the Virgin and the Holy Spirit, in a very creative way. The text basically speaks of two bodies of Jesus (and thus takes seriously the fact that the canonical Gospels also distinguish between the body of the risen Christ and that of the earthly man Jesus). For the Gospel of Philip, Jesus seems to have been born through Mary with an earthly body; this body, in turn, unites with the Holy Spirit at his baptism, who is referred to here as the "virgin who descended" (p. 71:5). The *baptism* of Jesus, who can also be described as the "Father of all things," thus incorporates motifs from

79. The term *gnostic* is rightly contested today in general, but especially in relation to the school of Valentinus. For a more balanced account of the Valentinian movement, see, e.g., Ismo Dunderberg, *Beyond Gnosticism: Myth, Lifestyle, and Society in the School of Valentinus* (Columbia University Press, 2008).

80. The dating of this writing is particularly controversial. For more detail on introductory questions see, e.g., Hans-Martin Schenke, "Das Philippusevangelium (NHC II,3)," in Markschies and Schröter, *Antike christliche Apokryphen*, 1:527–57.

81. Translation: Lundhaug, *Images of Rebirth*. The following thoughts largely follow Christine Jacobi, "Jesus' Body: Christology and Soteriology in the Body-Metaphors of the *Gospel of Philip*," in *Connecting Gospels: Beyond the Canonical/Non-canonical Divide*, ed. Francis Watson and Sarah Parkhouse (Oxford University Press, 2018), 77–94.

the *birth* of Jesus: A new, second body of Jesus emerges from the connection between Jesus/Father of all things on the one hand and the Holy Spirit/Virgin on the other. This baptism narrative includes, then, not only aspects of Jesus's birth but also elements that the canonical Gospels link to his resurrection from the dead. Jesus's baptism moves from the theological periphery to the center in this kind of thinking, which can hardly be described as naive adoptionism. While these ideas cannot easily be integrated into the Christologies of the various contemporary Christian denominations, they could provide an impetus to reflect on whether some dead ends in the history of theology could be reopened in creative ways.[82]

Apocryphal gospels can thus point to problems and raise questions that are essentially disregarded in contemporary Christianities. How, for example, are we to imagine the divine Son of God, the Logos of God made flesh (John 1:14a), through whose mediation the whole of creation came into being (John 1:3), as a small child in the village of Nazareth? The question may seem banal, but it takes the idea of an incarnated God to its logical conclusion. While the Gospel of John avoids it, the Infancy Gospel of Thomas (also known as the Paidika), which has been handed down in a variety of textual forms, basically follows this path.[83] Taking up the statement from the end of the nativity account in the Gospel of Luke that the young "Jesus increased in wisdom and in years and in divine and human favor" (Luke 2:52), the Infancy Gospel offers

82. For a completely different example emerging around the baptism of Jesus, see Michael E. Stone and Emanuela Timotin, *The Cheirograph of Adam in Armenian and Romanian Traditions. New Texts and Images* (Brepols, 2023), who refer to a tradition according to which, after the expulsion from paradise, Adam had to make a contract with the devil to learn farming. This contract—another aspect of humanity's fall—is destroyed during Jesus's baptism.

83. Edition of the Greek text forms: Tony Burke, ed., *De Infantia Iesu Evangelium Thomae Graece* (Brepols, 2010).

episodes that respond to questions such as[84] how a simultaneously divine and human child might deal with the fact that miraculous powers dwell within him, or to what extent such a child can and must learn, or what it might mean to educate this child as a teacher or as a parent. The Infancy Gospel, which describes an often violent, largely unsympathetic young Jesus who (perhaps) gradually changes in the sense of Luke 2:52, addresses these questions in narrative form. "How did boy Jesus behave with the neighborhood kids?" may sound like a silly or naive question, and one may or may not find the answers on offer in the Infancy Gospel satisfactory, but it is hardly the case that contemporary Christianities offer better responses. For the most part, the topic seems to be simply forgotten.

(2) The spectrum of theological ideas concerning the cross and resurrection of Jesus also changes enormously when we include apocryphal testimonies. The question of what it might mean that Jesus, the Son of God, was crucified at the end of his ministry touches the core of Christian theology. Perhaps no answer has yet been found that can fully withstand all the questions that can be posed in response to the cross of Christ existing alongside the idea of an all-powerful, just, and loving God.[85] Perhaps it is still most convincing to think that it is God himself who, in Christ on the cross, fully and compassionately dares to take an infinitely long step toward the world and humanity, which can no longer find its way to God due to their transgressions. But what does it mean to speak of a God who suffers? Is it even possible to think of such a God? At least some apocryphal texts take this question very seriously and therefore consciously differentiate between the one who is crucified and

84. For the following thoughts, see in more detail Tobias Nicklas, "Elements of a Narratival Plot About the Child Jesus in the *Infancy Gospel of Thomas* (Codex Sabaiticus 259, fols. 66r–77v [H])," in *The Infancy Gospel of Thomas*, ed. David Cielontko and Tobias Nicklas, Studies on Early Christian Apocrypha (Peeters, forthcoming, 2025).

85. Among the canonical Gospels, this ambivalence of the figure of God is particularly evident in the Gospel of Mark.

the divine Logos. This phenomenon is particularly clear in the "gospel flashback" embedded in a speech by the apostle John in the early Acts of John (87–105).[86] Sections 94–96 offer a hymn of Christ, which he sings together with his disciples before his arrest and which is described as a "dance" at the beginning of section 97. In 97–102, the mystery of the cross is revealed to John; John, in turn, flees from the sight of the crucified one to the Mount of Olives and weeps. While darkness falls, the Lord appears to him in a cave on the Mount of Olives and instructs him (97.7–12). A cross of light is revealed to him (98.1–6),[87] followed by the heavenly voice of "the Lord" delivering instructions (98.7–101.16):

It is necessary that one man should hear these things from me, O John, for I have need of someone who will hear. This cross of light is sometimes called the Word [= Logos] by me for your sakes, sometimes Mind, sometimes Jesus, sometimes Christ, sometimes Door, sometimes Way, sometimes Bread, sometimes Seed, sometimes Resurrection, sometimes Son, sometimes Father, sometimes Spirit, sometimes Life, sometimes Truth, sometimes Faith, sometimes Grace. Thus it is called for man's sake. But in truth, as known in itself and spoken to us, it is the marking off of all things and the uplifting and foundation of those things that are fixed but had been unstable, and the harmony of the wisdom and indeed the wisdom of the harmony. (98)[88]

A distinction is made between the cross of light and the wooden cross, on which someone other than the Lord himself is obviously crucified (99). John is standing at the top of the Mount of Olives and receives a revelation of the truth from the Lord, while the crowd below at the wooden cross is looking at the body on the cross. The latter, of course, refers to the woefully misled Christ-followers who follow a more

86. The passage is preserved in only a single manuscript of the Acts of John. On the edition and transmission of this text, see Junod and Kaestli, *Acta Iohannis*, vol. 1.

87. Further references to the meaning of a cross of light appear in comparable literature in Irenaeus of Lyons, *Haer.* 1.1–5; Pseudo-Hippolytus, *Haer.* 6.31.5–7; Clement of Alexandria, *Exc.* 22.4, 42.1; Tertullian, *Adversus Valentinianos*.

88. Translation: Elliott, *Apocryphal New Testament*, 320.

"orthodox" interpretation of the cross of Jesus. The cross of light appears as a manifestation of the Lord himself, who is thus seen simultaneously by several people in different guises, a phenomenon known as polymorphy.[89] "Jesus" (or a Jesus-like body) hangs on the wooden cross, but to John the Lord appears shapeless at the top of the cross of light and in the form of the cross itself (see 98). The aim of the vision is to show John the fate of humanity, in which divine sparks of light are present. The cross of light marks the boundary between the lower and upper worlds, and it is filled more and more with the light of those who belong to Christ: In this cross they are united with Christ. For the Acts of John, the actual salvation event is therefore not connected with the wooden cross on which Jesus of Nazareth hangs and suffers (101). Contrary to what the canonical Gospels emphasize, there is nothing of import to be seen there. Rather, salvation consists in the gift of knowledge and union with the divine Lord, on the basis of which redemption from this world is made possible.

The crucifixion scene in the Acts of John is just one example that in fact adds more than a few elements to the theology of the cross as laid out in the canonical Gospels. If other writings were added, quite a different picture would emerge: from the Gospel of Thomas, in which the cross is largely ignored, to the Gospel of Peter, in which the cross disappears into heaven together with the resurrected Lord, to the aforementioned homily De Duobus montibus, in which the cross becomes a tall tree from which judgment is passed on the nations, to the Coptic Apocalypse of Peter from Nag Hammadi (NHC VII 3), in which we read that the living Jesus stands next to the cross and laughs because only his fleshly body, his substitute, was crucified (p. 81). With these (and many other) additional texts and traditions in view, an astonishing spectrum of ideas emerges, to which historical and theological criticism must of course be applied, but which evinces the explosive power inherent in the idea that the Son of God is crucified and suffers.

89. Paul Foster, "Polymorphic Christology: Its Origins and Development in Early Christianity," *JTS* 58 (2007): 1–34.

4. Conclusion

In our view, the task of tracing discourses such as those briefly touched on here and of mapping the testimony of apocryphal works and parabiblical traditions is still in its infancy. And while even just the handful of works and themes discussed in this chapter have enormous potential for further study, we have barely scratched the surface of the available material: The above account, for example, has completely ignored the role that pictorial representations of Jesus and associated material culture[90] may have played in the discourses alluded to. Neither have we turned our attention to what it means to approach the life and work of Jesus in different liturgical traditions: Even where liturgical traditions are based entirely on canonical sources, this always gives rise to virtual narratives that have different emphases from the canonical Gospels and in many cases go far beyond them.

The sheer amount of material available to scholars (and all interested interpreters) for studying how Jesus has been understood—how he has been presented and re-presented—throughout the history of Christianity is daunting. But the first task is surely to cast a wide net—one that will pull in a much wider range of written sources (from world chronicles to apocalypses) but also one that can encompass a variety of media. These traditions do not exist in isolation; to the contrary, they influence each other in a constant dynamic interplay, forming ever new constellations of meaning, consolidating them, and breaking them up again.[91] However, this move from an investigation of apoc-

---

90. One example here is the tradition of the theologically highly interesting "swaddling clothes of Jesus," with the help of which it is possible to demonstrate that Jesus must have been "truly human" from the beginning. On this, see Tobias Nicklas, "From Gospel Book to Virtual Reality: A Neglected Aspect of the Gospel of Matthew's Ancient Reception History," in *The Gospel of Matthew in Its Historical and Theological Context*, ed. Mikhail Seleznev et al., WUNT 459 (Mohr Siebeck, 2021), 22.

91. That's why Stephanie Hallinger describes this phenomenon as "entangled traditions" in "Entangled Traditions About Judith: From Heroine to Camp," in

ryphal texts to closely interwoven parabiblical traditions has not yet been attempted. A large field of research lies ahead of us for at least another generation.

Characters in Mind: The Migration of Characters in Early Jewish, Early Christian and Greco-Roman Literature and Art, ed. Jan Rüggemeier and Tobias Nicklas, Diegesis in Mind 2 (Bonn University Press, forthcoming).

CHAPTER 2

Apocryphal Traditions Memorializing Apostles and Apostolic Figures

With the phrase "apocryphal traditions memorializing apostles and apostolic figures,"[1] we mean, above all, the works generally referred to as the apocryphal acts of the apostles. This new phrase—admittedly a mouthful—is intended both to broaden the category and to decouple it somewhat from the canonical Acts of the Apostles: On the one hand, we would broaden the category to include works concerning figures who were not, strictly speaking, apostles; on the other hand, we would underscore that, while many narratives about apostolic figures draw on Acts in both form and content, these works develop in distinctive ways that have little to do with the canonical narrative. Both of these shifts also allow us to recognize the continuity between apocryphal acts and lives of the saints or hagiography. Whether we are thinking in terms of form, content, authorship, compositional techniques, use, or transmission history, there is every reason to reckon many apocryphal acts and lives of the saints as closely related to each other, if not

1. Sections of this chapter are adapted from an article published in German: Janet E. Spittler, "Apokryphe Apostelerzählungen und ihrer Funktion in der Geschichte des Christentums," *Zeitschrift für Neues Testament* 51 (2023): 55–77.

representing developments of a single genre.[2] Another shift is evident in our use of the term *traditions* (as opposed to *acts*), which allows us to look beyond prose narratives to other media (e.g., apostolic lists and gospel prefaces, visual arts, etc.) that memorialize apostolic figures.[3] Finally, with the verb *memorialize* we are signaling what we view as the primary function of apostolic traditions, that is, to construct communities and landscapes of memory for Christians across a wide span of time and space.

Many readers of this book will be familiar (at least by title) with works commonly referred to as the five major apocryphal acts of the apostles: the Acts of John, Acts of Andrew, Acts of Peter, Acts of Paul (including the Acts of Paul and Thecla), and Acts of Thomas.[4] Those who have taken an interest in these works will know that we typically date them to the last half of the second century or first half of the third;

---

2. For an overview of the state of the art at the end of the twentieth century, see the still highly influential essay by Wilhelm Schneemelcher, "Apostelgeschichten des 2. und 3. Jahrhunderts: Einleitung," in *Neutestamentliche Apokryphen*, vol. 2, *Apostolisches, Apokalypsen und Verwandtes*, ed. Wilhelm Schneemelcher (Mohr Siebeck, 1997), 71–81. The distinction between Christian apocrypha and hagiographic literature was related to the closure of the NT canon around the fourth century CE; it assumes that apocryphal works were intended for inclusion in the canon but for whatever reason didn't make the cut. But this is simply not the case for many, if not most, apocryphal works. The artificial distinction, however, obscures our understanding of important developments, including the influence of some older material beyond late antiquity. That's why we prefer definitions of Christian apocrypha that do not employ arbitrary time limits (see the introduction of the present volume).

3. See, for example, the use of the term "parabiblical traditions" in Tobias Nicklas, "The 'Beyond Canon' Project: Questions, Topics, and Results," in Nicklas, *The Canon and Beyond: Collected Essays on the History and Hermeneutics of Biblical and Parabiblical Traditions*, WUNT 525 (Mohr Siebeck, 2024), 1–22.

4. For a first introduction and overview, see, e.g., Tobias Nicklas, "Second Century Apocryphal Acts," in *Second Century Christianity: A Sourcebook*, ed. Michael Bird and Scott Harrower (Baylor University Press, forthcoming), or the relevant articles in Edwards, *Early New Testament Apocrypha*.

they will also likely know that these works were negatively assessed by early church leaders (such as Eusebius, who called them "absurd and impious")[5] or that they were associated with various "heretical" groups, such as Encratites, Manichaeans, or the so-called gnostics. The very well-informed will also have read that, with the exception of the Acts of Thomas, these works are extant only in fragments—that the texts we read in modern translation in collections of apocryphal works are the reconstructions of scholars.

It is always risky to generalize, but if one were to attempt to summarize what most students and scholars of early Christianity know about the apocryphal acts, it might run something like this: The apocryphal acts are a set of early Christian narratives that, due to the unorthodox Christian thought they present, were suppressed and ultimately lost, only to be rediscovered and reconstructed by modern scholars, who have thus brought to light lost and forgotten forms of early Christianity. This statement is not entirely wrong. Much of the effort of nineteenth- and twentieth-century scholarship on apocryphal acts was dedicated to reconstructing "original" texts, and the reconstructed works do indeed offer a window into second- and third-century Christianities; the view they afford, moreover, is different—broader—than the view afforded by canonical and patristic sources alone.

That said, the notion of lost scriptures rediscovered or secret scriptures revealed (to unfairly pick on the titles of two excellent books by two very fine scholars)[6] obscures the true nature of most apocryphal acts. These works—the five acts mentioned above and many, many more—were exceedingly long-lived: They were translated into (or composed in) all the major languages of Mediterranean antiquity (from Greek to Arabic), and then, centuries later, they were translated into (or composed in) all of the European vernaculars (from Church Slavic

5. Eusebius, *Hist. eccl.* 3.25.

6. Bart D. Ehrman, *Lost Scriptures: Books That Did Not Make It into the New Testament* (Oxford University Press, 2003); Tony Burke, *Secret Scriptures Revealed: A New Introduction to New Testament Apocrypha* (SPCK; 2013).

to Icelandic); their narratives were adapted to a host of purposes and settings (both liturgical and secular), being rewritten in new literary genres and adapted to new media (above all the visual arts). The terms *lost*, *secret*, and *forgotten* hardly apply. It is true that the earliest versions of apocryphal acts (that is, the second- and third-century compositions in Greek) are generally not extant in their "original" forms, but what we *do* have is *so much more*.

In this chapter, we will present three case studies that illustrate some of the various ways in which apostolic figures were memorialized, beginning in the late second century CE and continuing through the Byzantine/medieval period and beyond. Each case involves apocryphal apostolic traditions that surely changed (in form, language, and content) over time but also evince a notable consistency and endurance. While some elements of each tradition do indeed grant us insight into ideas, beliefs, and practices that might be characterized as fringe (not to say heretical) Christianity, a broader truth is that the various permutations of these apocryphal traditions grant us insight into the ideas, beliefs, and practices of a long series of Christianities—most of them entirely orthodox—within which the traditions were adapted, read, and valued.

We'll begin with the Acts of John, a second-century Greek work describing the missionary activities and ultimately the death of John, understood as the beloved disciple and son of Zebedee.[7] The Acts of John was roundly criticized by proto-orthodox authors of the second, third, and fourth centuries and was ultimately condemned at an ecumenical council in the eighth; nevertheless, large sections of the work—either circulating independently or adapted and/or translated as new works—enjoyed continuous popularity, with some elements of the apocryphal

---

7. For an overview of basic issues regarding this text, see, e.g., Jan N. Bremmer, "The *Apocryphal Acts*: Authors, Place, Time and Relationship," in Bremmer, *Maidens, Magic and Martyrs in Early Christianity*, WUNT 379 (Mohr Siebeck, 2017), 219–34; and (solely on the Acts of John) Attridge, "Acts of John," 216–33 (including secondary literature). See also Janet E. Spittler, "John, Acts of," in *Brill Encyclopedia of Early Christianity* (Brill, 2022).

narratives finding their way into the canon itself. Next, we'll turn to the Acts of Thecla, another second-century narrative that was criticized by proto-orthodox authors, above all Tertullian. As we will see, however, the Thecla narrative—including the aspects that Tertullian found most problematic—enjoyed immense popularity and in some sense was considered highly authoritative. Finally, we'll turn to the Acts of Andrew and Matthias in the City of the Cannibals—a work that presents the apostles evangelizing at the northeastern edge of the known world and, a thousand years later, would itself have a remarkably prominent place within the literature of the northwestern edge of that world.

1. The Acts of John: The Persistent Success of a Condemned Work

An exceedingly rich body of texts and images attest to Christianity's abiding interest in John, son of Zebedee, understood from an early period to be the beloved disciple of the Gospel of John as well as that gospel's author. Multiple apocryphal narratives describe his activities in Asia Minor and/or Rome, along with his death by mostly natural causes in Ephesus. The most well-known narrative to contemporary readers is the "early" or "primitive" Acts of John, the Greek text of which was edited at the end of the nineteenth century by Maximilian Bonnet and more recently by Éric Junod and Jean-Daniel Kaestli, and has been translated widely into modern languages.[8] Generally dated to the second half of the second century, this work is not extant in its early (that is, second-century) form; rather, it has been reconstructed from two main sources: (1) a small subset of manuscripts of the Acts of John by Prochorus (a fifth-century work that will be discussed below), into which extended excerpts from the early acts were interpolated, and

8. Editions: Maximilian Bonnet, "Acta Iohannis," in *Acta Apostolorum Apocrypha*, ed. post Constantin Tischendorf by Richard Adalbert Lipsius and Maximilian Bonnet (Hermann Mendelssohn, 1858), 151–216; Junod and Kaestli, *Acta Iohannis*, vol. 1. For an overview of modern translations, see "e-Clavis Acts of John."

(2) independently circulating episodes from the early acts, above all the Metastasis (that is, the account of John's death).

The beginning of the early Acts of John is lost; the earliest of the extant episodes (that is, the one that seems to come first within the timeline of the narrative) presents John on the road from Miletus to Ephesus, already in the midst of his missionary activities. The extant material is in five large chunks: (1) a report of John's arrival in Ephesus, the raising of Cleopatra and Lycomedes, and the painting of a portrait of John (numbered as chs. 18–36 in modern editions); (2) an account of John's destruction of the Temple of Artemis of Ephesus and the conversion of a parricide (numbered as chs. 37–55 in modern editions); (3) an account of John's stay at a bedbug-infested inn while traveling, and a long episode involving the Christian Drusiana, wife of Andronicus (also a Christian), and the wicked Callimachus, who would force himself on her (numbered as chs. 58–86 in modern editions); (4) a "gospel flashback," in which John recounts for his audience his experiences with the living Jesus (numbered as chs. 87–105 in modern editions); and (5) the Metastasis, that is, the account of John's death (numbered as chs. 106–115 in modern editions). It is all but certain that each of these chunks belonged to the early Acts of John, but it is not entirely clear in what order these chunks appeared, what and how much is missing, and how close the extant texts are to their second-century form. That there has been disagreement among scholars as to how best to order the extant material is clear even to a casual reader of a modern translation, who will certainly notice that the work begins with chapter 18 (lacking chs. 1–17 entirely) and that chapters 87–105 are placed between chapters 36 and 37. Likewise, a casual reader will notice that some specific content is missing, above all a narrative about the conversion of Drusiana and Andronicus—the main characters of chapters 63–86—as well as an account of the allocation of Asia to John as missionary field and his travels there. The question of how close the extant texts come to the form of the earliest version of the work is rather more difficult to answer. There is significant scholarly debate, for example, about whether chapters 87–105 show signs of adaptation and/or interpolation—specifically, whether some sections (e.g., the hymn of Christ in chs. 94–96)—were later, "gnostic" additions.[9] Generally, we simply cannot know how close the early Acts of John's modern editors have come to approximating the text as written by its second-century author, but this is not an unusual circumstance: All editions of ancient works involve this type of (very learned) guesswork.

But the reader might ask why scholars were looking for material that might have belonged to this early work: How did scholars know there was an early Acts of John in the first place? We know that a work called the Acts of John existed in the earliest centuries of Christianity because multiple early Christian authors refer to it by name, while other early Christian authors refer to content recognizable in the reconstructed text. These references are both approving and disapproving. As one might expect, multiple "orthodox" authors (including Eusebius of Caesarea, Epiphanius of Salamis, Philaster of Brescia, Innocent I, and Turibius of Astorga) condemn the work, while approving use by "nonorthodox" Christians is evident, for example, in references to characters and episodes from the early Acts of John in the third-century Manichaean Psalm Book and in the work's apparent use by Priscillianists.[10] But the

9. On the so-called gnostic interpolation, see, e.g., Paul G. Schneider, "A Perfect Fit: The Major Interpolation in the Acts of John," in *Society of Biblical Literature 1991 Seminar Papers* (Scholars Press, 1991), 518–32; Pieter J. Lalleman, *The Acts of John: A Two Stage Initiation into Johannine Gnosticism*, Studies on Early Christian Apocrypha 4 (Peeters, 1998), 25–68; and Gerard Luttikhuizen, "A Gnostic Reading of the Acts of John," in *The Apocryphal Acts of John*, ed. Jan N. Bremmer, Studies on the Apocryphal Acts of the Apostles 1 (Kok Pharos, 1995), 119–52.

10. On attestation and use of the early Acts of John, see Éric Junod and Jean-Daniel Kaestli, *L'histoire des actes apocryphes des apôtres du IIIe au IXe siècle: le cas des Actes des Jean* (Imprimerie La Concorde, 1982); for an overview, see Knut Schäferdiek, "The Acts of John," *NTApoc*, 2:152–56. On use by "nonorthodox" Christians, see Junod and Kaestli, *L'histoire des actes apocryphes*, 50–102. On Priscillian (and his followers), see—besides the classical study by Henry Chadwick, *Priscillian of Avila: Occult and Charismatic in the Early Church* (Oxford University Press, 1976)—most recently Augusto Diego Piay, *Priscillian: The Life and Death of a Christian Dissenter in Late Antiquity* (Gorgias, 2024).

reception of the early Acts of John was not entirely so straightforward: Clement of Alexandria seems to refer to the work with no hint of critique, and while Augustine is very disparaging of apocryphal works and the Christians who use and value them, his critique of Priscillianist use of an apocryphal hymn of Jesus (from the Acts of John 95) is *not* that its content is heretical, but precisely that its meaning *is already contained* within canonical works.[11] Ultimately, however, the early Acts of John was roundly condemned—and explicitly so at the Second Council of Nicaea in 787.[12]

Thus far, we have presented a brief history of a late second-century Greek work that had in the third and fourth centuries fairly broad circulation, finding acceptance among splinter groups of early Christianity (e.g., so-called Manicheans and Priscillianists) and coming to the generally disapproving attention of "orthodox" authors. The work largely recedes from view by the end of the fifth century, reappearing again during the iconoclastic controversy of the eighth century,[13] only to be strongly condemned at the Second Council of Nicaea (787 CE). While this is an accurate account (or the best we can do with existing evidence) of a single work (the early Acts of John), it is by no means a full account of the apocryphal traditions about John, many of which had their start in the early acts. But before offering a glimpse of several key pieces of this broader extant tradition, we would remind the reader that, while

11. Augustine, *Ep.* 237. Clement, in his *Adumbrations* on 1 John 1:1, refers to "traditions" that report that when John the disciple touched Jesus's body, his hand met no resistance; while scholars have debated whether Clement had a full text of an early Acts of John before him, it is clear that he refers to a story that is narrated in Acts of John 93. The *Adumbrations*, extant only in a Latin translation by Cassiodorus, was edited by Otto Stählin and Ludwig Früchtel, *Clemens Alexandrinus*, 2nd ed., GCS 17 (Akademie, 1970); the passage in question is at 210.12–15.

12. On the role of the Acts of John in the iconoclastic controversy, see Stephen Gero, *Byzantine Iconoclasm During the Reign of Constantine V*, CSCO 384 (Secrétariat du Corpus SCO, 1977), 63.

13. For a historical overview of the iconoclastic controversy, see Leslie Brubaker and John Haldon, *Byzantium in the Iconoclast Era, c. 680–850*, 2nd ed. (Cambridge University Press, 2015).

the extant material is quite substantial, it is still just a small fraction of the materials that apparently circulated. A prime illustration of this fact is the discovery of two episodes, almost certainly part of the early Acts of John, that are extant (in very fragmentary form) in a fourth-century uncial Greek codex from Oxyrhynchus (Papyrus Oxyrhynchus VI 850) as well as (in a full version) in a fifteenth-century Irish codex (the so-called Liber Flavus).[14] Scholars have identified no trace of a transmission history of this episode; it exists only in these two codices. Nevertheless, it *was transmitted*, so we must imagine the web of copies, translations, and adaptations (and indeed the copyists, translators, and editors) that must have connected these two codices across a thousand years, from Egypt to Ireland, from the Greek language to Irish.

1.1. The Metastasis

While, as noted above, the main narrative of the early Acts of John survived antiquity only by the skin of its teeth (and incomplete, at that), the same cannot be said of the final section of the work, which describes the apostle's death. We call this section the Metastasis (Gk. μετάστασις, "departure") rather than "martyrdom" because John—exceptionally, among the apostles—was not martyred. To the contrary, this final section of the early Acts of John (typically numbered chs. 106–115) reports that he lived to a ripe old age in Ephesus. When it is time for him to die, he asks his disciples to dig a grave for him, in which—after delivering a farewell discourse—he lies down and gives up the ghost. In contrast to the main narrative of the early Acts of John, the Metastasis has a robust manuscript tradition: It is extant in more than twenty Greek manuscripts, as well as in translation into Latin, Syriac, Coptic, Armenian, Georgian, Arabic, Ethiopic, and Church Slavic.

The diverse character of this manuscript tradition means it is quite difficult to work with—but also quite rewarding. The Greek manuscripts of the Metastasis (the earliest dating from the tenth century) differ from

14. See Martin McNamara, *The Apocrypha in the Irish Church* (Dublin Institute for Advanced Studies, 1975); a translation of the Irish is available in Máire Herbert and Martin McNamara, *Irish Biblical Apocrypha* (T&T Clark, 1989), 89–94.

each other in a way that makes it impossible to choose which represents the most "original" or earliest version of the work; the best the most recent editors could do is sort the various textual witnesses into three distinct recensions.[15] However, the translations—many of which were likely made quite early—can also be compared with the Greek texts. Particularly valuable is the Syriac translation, which was likely made as early as the second half of the third century and therefore may well preserve a form of the text that is more "original" than what we find in the extant Greek manuscripts.[16] The Armenian translation, too, is quite helpful: Not only was it likely made at an early date (the fifth century), but the Armenian Metastasis was transmitted within biblical manuscripts, with the result that its text was less likely to be changed in the process of transmission. The Syriac and Armenian translations (along with the Coptic and Georgian) have allowed editors to reconstruct with a relatively high degree of certainty the form of the early Greek Metastasis.

What does this complicated manuscript tradition tell us about how and why this section of the early Acts of John was preserved? Quite a lot. First, it is clear that individual sections of a work could be separated from the whole and circulated independently. This phenomenon was particularly common with narratives of the deaths of apostles: These sections were often separated from their longer narrative contexts for inclusion—as a distinct work with its own title—in the developing hagiographic collections (menologia) that provided reading material for the celebration of a saint's feast day (normally celebrated on the day of their death).[17] Thus, to give one concrete example, we find the Acts

15. See Junod and Kaestli, *Acta Iohannis*, 1:293–343; 2:564–80.

16. On the Syriac version of the work, see Jacob A. Lollar, *The History of John the Son of Zebedee: Introduction, Texts and Translations*, Texts from Christian Late Antiquity 56 (Gorgias, 2020).

17. On the developing hagiographical collections, particularly the "premetaphrastic" collections to which our Metastasis often belonged, see Christian Høgel, *Symeon Metaphrastes: Rewriting and Canonization* (Museum Tusculanum, 2002).

of John 106–115 in an eleventh-century Greek manuscript held at the Vatican Library (Vaticani graeci 866, 32r-33v), presented as a discrete work with the title "Final Rest of John the Theologian" (Gk. Ἀνάπαυσις Ἰωάννου τοῦ θεολόγου) and placed among 117 other works recounting the lives and deaths of saints.[18]

The variability of titles in these manuscripts likely has some explanatory value for the continued copying and circulation of works (or sections of works) that were condemned even in the most explicit terms, as the early Acts of John was. The Second Council of Nicaea's discussion of the Acts of John concludes with the council agreeing: "No one is to have copies made! And we decree not only this but also that it deserves to be consigned to the flames."[19] However, while the council had before them a copy of the work we would call the Acts of John (this is absolutely clear from their long quotations of the work), their copy bears the title "Journeys of the Holy Apostles";[20] thus, even if we imagine an organized and concerted effort to discover and burn copies of this "heretical" work (itself an unlikely scenario), we could also imagine a potential book burner happily flipping past the Metastasis (or Anapausis) of John the Theologian.

As the hagiographical literature developed further (in the eighth century and beyond), episodes drawn from apocryphal narratives became deeply entrenched in the tradition. Virtually all hagiographical accounts of John's death are ultimately indebted to the Metastasis, and Symeon Metaphrastes's (d. ca. 1000 CE) highly influential *Life of*

18. A digitized version of this manuscript can be viewed on the Vatican Library's website: https://digi.vatlib.it/view/MSS_Vat.gr.866.

19. *The Acts of the Second Council of Nicaea (787)*, trans. Richard Price, Translated Texts for Historians 68 (Liverpool University Press, 2020), 402.

20. And, indeed, this text may well have been something like what Photius read in the ninth century; Photius, in his *Bibliotheca* 114, describes a work titled "Journeys of the Apostles" (τῶν ἀποστόλων περίοδοι), which comprises the "Acts" (πράξεις) of Peter, John, Andrew, Thomas, and Paul. See edition by René Henry, *Photius: Bibliothèque* (Société d'édition les Belles lettres, 1959–1977).

John includes the account of his composition of the Fourth Gospel on a mountain at the island of Patmos, with Prochorus as scribe.[21] Therefore, while it is true that the Acts of John is not extant in its original form and was in fact condemned in the most explicit terms, it is also true that its important final episode has been in continuous circulation for eighteen hundred years.

1.2. Writing, Rewriting, and Translating the Apocryphal John

The brief summary of the history of the early Acts of John given above notes that the work disappeared from view in the second half of the fifth century. We have already seen that this statement does not apply to the final section of the work, the Metastasis, but it is true that after the end of the fifth century we no longer find church authors railing against the Acts of John either by title or with references to content recognizable as coming from other sections of the work. That said, there is no dearth of works about John in the late fifth and sixth centuries; to the contrary, we can date to this period the composition of multiple new narratives about John's activities.

One of these, the Acts of John by Prochorus, clearly uses the early Acts of John as a source. This lengthy Greek work (likely composed at the end of the fifth century, perhaps in Antioch)[22] begins with all the apostles gathered in Gethsemane, where they decide to draw lots to determine their missionary fields. The narrator recounts that John draws the lot for Asia and that he himself, Prochorus (presumably identical with the Prochorus of Acts 6:5), draws the lot to accompany John (Acts John Pro. 1–5). The narrative that follows can be divided into three basic sections: (1) the account of John's activities in Ephesus,

---

21. To our knowledge, the only critical edition of Symeon Metaphrastes remains J.-P. Migne, *Commentarius in divum apostolum Joannem evangelistam ac theologum*, PG 116 (Migne, 1864), 684–705. On Symeon more generally, see Høgel, *Symeon Metaphrastes*.

22. See Junod and Kaestli, *Acta Iohannis*, 2:718–49; Spittler, "Acts of John by Prochorus," 262–361.

ending with his exile to Patmos; (2) the account of John's activities on Patmos, ending with John's composition of the Fourth Gospel on the island and his return to Ephesus; and (3) John's death in Ephesus. The middle section, taking place on Patmos, is the bulk of the narrative, some 70 percent of the whole. These episodes are quite new: No previous work recounts anything about John's activities while in island exile. The final section parallels the account of John's death from the early Acts of John, though in markedly abbreviated form; the author of the Acts of John by Prochorus had before him, then, at least the Metastasis (which, as we have seen, circulated independently). The first section, however, makes clear that the author had read more of the early work: Like the early Acts of John, the Acts of John by Prochorus reports the apostle's destruction of the Temple of Artemis of Ephesus. The episode is told in a substantially different (and expanded) way, but there are enough verbal parallels to suggest a literary relationship with the episode as it appears in the early Acts of John.[23] Again: It is impossible to determine whether the author of the Acts of John by Prochorus had the *entirety* of the early Acts of John before him: Like the Metastasis, the episode of the destruction of the temple may have circulated independently.[24] Nevertheless, we can safely say that this late fifth-century author had read and rewritten multiple sections of the early work.

Two further Greek narratives from the same period, the Acts of John in Rome and the Acts of Timothy, present—like the middle section of Prochorus—totally new material about John. As its English title suggests, the Acts of John in Rome, extant in two distinct recensions, recounts the apostle's adventures in the capital city: John is arrested (for reasons that vary depending on which of two recensions one is reading) and transported to Rome for trial before the emperor (either Domitian or Hadrian, again depending on the recension); a short exchange between

---

23. See Janet E. Spittler, "The Acts of John by Prochorus in Patmos Ms. 188: A Test-Case Illustrating the Composition and Development of Later Apocryphal Acts," in Nicklas et al., *Apostles Peter, Paul, John*, 192–214.

24. See Junod and Kaestli, *Acta Iohannis*, 2:718–36; cf. Spittler, "Acts of John by Prochorus Patmos Ms. 188," 208n27.

apostle and emperor concerning the appropriate attitude for a Christian to assume toward a human king results in the apostle drinking a poison draught—not as a death penalty per se but rather as a test of John's trustworthiness and the power of his god. In both recensions the apostle survives the poison with no ill effects, but, as an end to the narrative, he is sentenced to exile on Patmos nevertheless. The Acts of Timothy, despite its English title, is a short work that involves John as much as its titular apostle. The narrative takes place in Ephesus: The second half describes the martyrdom of Timothy, but the first half focusses on an event that took place before Timothy's arrival in the city, namely, John's composition of the Fourth Gospel there and, very interestingly, his editing of the three Synoptic Gospels.[25]

Neither of these works can be dated with precision. The emphasis on a Christian's attitude toward a human king in the Acts of John in Rome suggests a post-Constantinian date, inasmuch as this emphasis suggests a moment in which Christianity was attempting to negotiate a new relationship toward its rulers; further, the author may well have used Eusebius's *Ecclesiastical History* as a source. A *terminus ante quem* is possibly established by a probable reference to the text by Ephraim of Antioch, who wrote in the first half of the sixth century, leaving us

25. This fascinating work has received much-deserved new attention over the last decade or so. See Claudio Zamagni, "Passion (Ou Actes) de Timothée. Études des Traditions Anciennes et Édition de La Forme BHG 1487," in *Poussières de Christianisme et de Judaïsme Antiques. Études Réunies En l'honneur de Jean-Daniel Kaestli et Éric Junod*, ed. Rémi Gounelle and Albert Frey (Éditions du Zèbre, 2007), 341–75; Cavan Concannon, "In the Great City of the Ephesians: Contestations over Apostolic Memory and Ecclesial Power in the Acts of Timothy," *JECS* 24 (2016): 419–46; Meira Kensky, "Ephesus, Loca Sancta: The Acts of Timothy and Religious Travel in Late Antiquity," in *The Narrative Self in Early Christianity: Essays in Honor of Judith Perkins*, ed. Janet E. Spittler, WGRWSup 15 (SBL Press, 2019), 91–119; Jan N. Bremmer, "Timothy, John and Ephesus in the Acts of Timothy," in Nicklas et al., *Apostles Peter, Paul, John*, 215–39; Janet E. Spittler, "The *Acts of Timothy*, Luke's Prologue, and Gospel Prologues: Accounts of the Composition of Early Christian Narratives," in *Narrative Hermeneutics, History, and Rhetoric. A Festschrift for David P. Moessner*, ed. Robert Matthew Calhoun et al., NovTSup 194 (Brill, 2024), 454–83.

with a probable date of composition between the end of the fourth and first half of the sixth century. The Acts of Timothy is similarly difficult to date, but—for various reasons[26]—the decades following the Council of Chalcedon (that is, the second half of the fifth century) seem a likely moment for Timothy's martyrdom to take literary form.

At roughly the same time that the Acts of John by Prochorus, Acts of John in Rome, and Acts of Timothy were composed, a similar compositional interest in John is evident in Latin: Two extant narratives, the Passio Iohannis by Pseudo-Melito[27] and the Virtutes Iohannis, recount John's missionary activities and death. These two works are independent of each other, but both authors used the same Latin narrative (no longer extant) when composing their own narratives.[28] Both of these works (and, clearly, their common source) incorporate episodes drawn from the early Acts of John, including the lengthy account of the resurrection of Drusiana (though told in a much abbreviated way in the Passio Iohannis), the destruction of the Temple of Artemis of Ephesus, and the Metastasis. Both also have an interesting point of overlap and contrast with the Acts of John in Rome: They include an episode in which John miraculously survives a draught of poison, but instead of in Rome before the emperor, this episode takes place in Ephesus before Aristodemus, priest of Artemis. Again, it is impossible to date these works with precision, but it is clear that the Passio Iohannis and the Virtutes Iohannis were composed at some point between the mid-fifth century and the end of the sixth century. Their common Latin source, of course, must predate them; and assuming this Latin source was itself a translation of a

26. See Bremmer, "Timothy, John and Ephesus," 217–22.

27. The Passio Iohannis is available in two editions: F. M. Florentinus, *Vetustius occidentalis ecclesiae Martyrologium* (Ex Typographia Hyacinthi Pacij, 1668), 130–37 (reprinted in J. A. Fabricius, *Codex apocryphus Novi Testamenti* (B. Schiller & Joh. Christ. Kisner, 1719), 3:604–23); G. Heine, *Bibliotheca anecdotorum* (T. O. Weigel, 1848), 1:109–17 (reprinted in PG 5:1239–50).

28. On the relationship of these two works, see Junod and Kaestli, *Acta Iohannis*, 2:764–92; Jean-Daniel Kaestli, "Le rapport entre les deux Vies Latines de l'apôtre Jean," *Apocrypha* 3, no. 1 (1992): 111–23.

Greek work that compiled various existing Johannine traditions (a point argued persuasively by Junod and Kaestli), we have yet another work to place on our timeline, perhaps in the fourth century.[29]

At the very moment when the early Acts of John was "disappearing from view," then, we find not a lack of interest in traditions concerning the beloved disciple and evangelist but a flourishing of *new* narratives about him. These narratives preserve and adapt episodes from the early Acts of John (e.g., the Metastasis, the destruction of the Temple of Artemis of Ephesus, and the story of Drusiana) and other sources but also supply new episodes that fill in an increasingly busy timeline of the apostle's life. What prompted the composition of these new works in (or around) the fifth century? In the broadest terms, we must conclude that interest in the activities and deaths of apostles and apostolic figures—information generally *not* included in canonical works—was increasing rather than waning in this period. Some works, such as the Virtutes Iohannis (and perhaps even more so the lost Greek work that likely served as its basic source), evince a compilatory impulse, that is, an impulse toward collecting and assembling various traditions about John's life from diverse sources and fitting them together into a chronological narrative. Thus, we find in the Virtutes Iohannis several traditions otherwise known only from brief mention in patristic sources (e.g., Tertullian's report that John was boiled in oil at Rome and Clement's report concerning John and the robber)[30] stitched together with longer preexisting narratives (drawn from the early Acts of John and presumably other sources) to produce a cohesive whole.

---

29. See Junod and Kaestli, *Acta Iohannis*, 2:790.

30. Tertullian, *Praescr.* 36.3; Clement of Alexandria, *Quis div.* 42; cf. Eusebius, *Hist. eccl.* 3.23.5–19. See "e-Clavis John and the Robber," North American Society for the Study of Christian Apocryphal Literature, accessed February 1, 2025, https://www.nasscal.com/e-clavis-christian-apocrypha/john-and-the-robber/. For an introduction and translation to this episode, see Rick Brannan, "John and the Robber: A New Translation and Introduction," in Burke and Landau, *New Testament Apocrypha*, 1:362–70.

Other works represent a different type of compilation, aiming to collect not *everything* that was known about an individual figure but a summary of information on each of a large number of figures. Works of this sort are the "apostolic lists," which present in list form basic biographical information (including origin, alternative names, field of missionary work, and circumstances of martyrdom or death) about the twelve apostles and the seventy disciples (mentioned in Luke 10:1).[31] These apostolic lists seem to have originated at the end of the fourth century (in Greek and/or Syriac), but new versions continued to be composed for centuries and are extant in all the languages of Mediterranean Christianity. As one might expect, given the dearth of information available in the canonical New Testament, apocryphal texts and traditions were clearly drawn on in the creation of these lists. But the flow of information may have gone in the other direction as well: It is possible that authors picked up data points included within these lists and used the information as a basis for a new narrative.

This may be the case with the Acts of John by Prochorus. As noted above, this work includes an account of John's composition of the Fourth Gospel while in exile on the island Patmos. Attentive readers may have stumbled over that sentence since Patmos is (at least for most contemporary readers) famously the location where the Revelation of John—not the Gospel of John—was composed. Revelation itself claims that Patmos was the location of the vision recounted (Rev 1:9), and various early Christian authors assert Patmos also as the location of the work's composition. As for the Fourth Gospel, multiple early Christian authors assert Ephesus as the location of its composition (as does the Acts of Timothy). But the earliest apostolic lists name *Patmos* as the location where John composed his Gospel. For example, the list referred to as "Anonymous 1" has, "John (preached) in Asia; after having

31. On apostolic lists, see François Dolbeau, *Prophètes, apôtres et disciples dans les traditions chrétiennes d'Occident. Vies brèves et listes en latin,* Subsidia hagiographica 92 (Société des Bollandistes, 2012); Christophe Guignard, "Greek Lists of the Apostles: New Findings and Open Questions," *ZAC* 20, no. 3 (2016): 469–95. See, e.g., Irenaeus *Haer.* 3.1.1 (quoted in Eusebius, *Hist. eccl.* 5.8.4).

been exiled to Patmos on account of the Word of God he wrote his Gospel."[32] At least one scholar has suggested that this very brief notice is what prompted the author of the Acts of John by Prochorus to take up his stylus and compose a full narrative of John's activities on the island, culminating in the composition of the gospel. Regardless of what prompted its composition, this account of John's composition of the gospel was enormously influential, leaving a striking impression within the canonical Bible itself.

1.3. The Inclusion of Apocryphal Johannine Traditions Within Biblical Manuscripts

Another type of work that developed in late antiquity is the gospel "preface" or "prologue." Gospel prefaces offer information about the life of the evangelist, including information on where he composed his gospel. These works are often described as biblical paratexts, in that they are found alongside canonical works within biblical manuscripts.[33] Most gospel prefaces are short—not much longer than the accounts of the evangelists in the apostolic lists. Some, however, are rather lengthy, incorporating traditions—again—largely drawn from apocryphal works.

The Memorial of Saint John the Theologian, for example, clearly draws quite heavily on the Acts of John by Prochorus in its detailed account of John's composition of the Fourth Gospel. The Memorial begins with a very brief report of John's overturning of the idols in Asia

32. See Dolbeau, *Prophètes, apôtres et disciples*, 184; Christophe Guignard, "La tradition grecque de la liste d'apôtres 'anonyme I' (BHG 153c), avec un appendice sur la liste BHG 152n*," *Apocrypha* 26 (2015): 188.

33. The study of biblical paratexts is a burgeoning field; see, e.g., Patrick Andrist, "Toward a Definition of Paratexts and Paratextuality: The Case of Ancient Greek Manuscripts," in *Bible as Notepad. Tracing Annotations and Annotation Practices in Late Antique and Medieval Biblical Manuscripts*, ed. Liv Ingeborg Lied and Marilena Maniaci (de Gruyter, 2018), 130–49; Garrick V. Allen and Anthony P. Royle, "Paratexts Seeking Understanding: Manuscripts and Aesthetic Cognitivism," *Religions* 11, no. 10 (2020): 1–25; and most recently, Allen, *Words Are Not Enough*.

and "seeding of the Word" there, followed by an equally brief notice of his exile to Patmos; there follows a transcription of a letter allegedly sent by Dionysius the Areopagite[34] to John on Patmos, predicting his release and return to Asia; next is a brief report that, when Trajan became emperor, John was released, but the Patmians would have him stay on the island. Then we find the following: "Though he feels the desire to leave, the Patmians ask him not to go. And because they cannot convince him, they ask to possess his writings in his place. And he, after agreeing, first commands himself to fast, and the very same for everyone else, as well as separation from evil things. Then, after John takes Prochorus along with him, he reaches the mountain ridge, in order that the former should interpret what comes from God, and the latter, what comes from the former." There follows an account of the composition of the gospel that is clearly an adaptation of the same episode in the Acts of John by Prochorus.

In sections 1.1 and 1.2 above, we have emphasized the fact that so-called apocryphal works about John and the traditions that first appeared within them were in no sense hidden; to the contrary, while the early Acts of John was indeed condemned and the bulk of its content nearly lost to history, a wide range of apocryphal traditions about John, many of which had their origin in the early acts, were broadly circulated and widely known. But with respect to the prefaces to the Fourth Gospel, we must draw an even more surprising conclusion: Inasmuch as these prefaces precede the gospel within biblical manuscripts, the apocryphal traditions about John have literally been included within the canon (as is the case with the thirteenth-century Manuscript 727, in the University of Chicago's Goodspeed Manuscript Collection, on folios 192(b)v–192(c)v:

34. Dionysius the Areopagite is mentioned very briefly in relation to Paul's stay in Athens (see Acts 18:34); he is an example of a character who is quite marginal within the canon but develops into a key figure of Christian thought of the early medieval period, when a whole set of mainly philosophical writings were attributed to him.

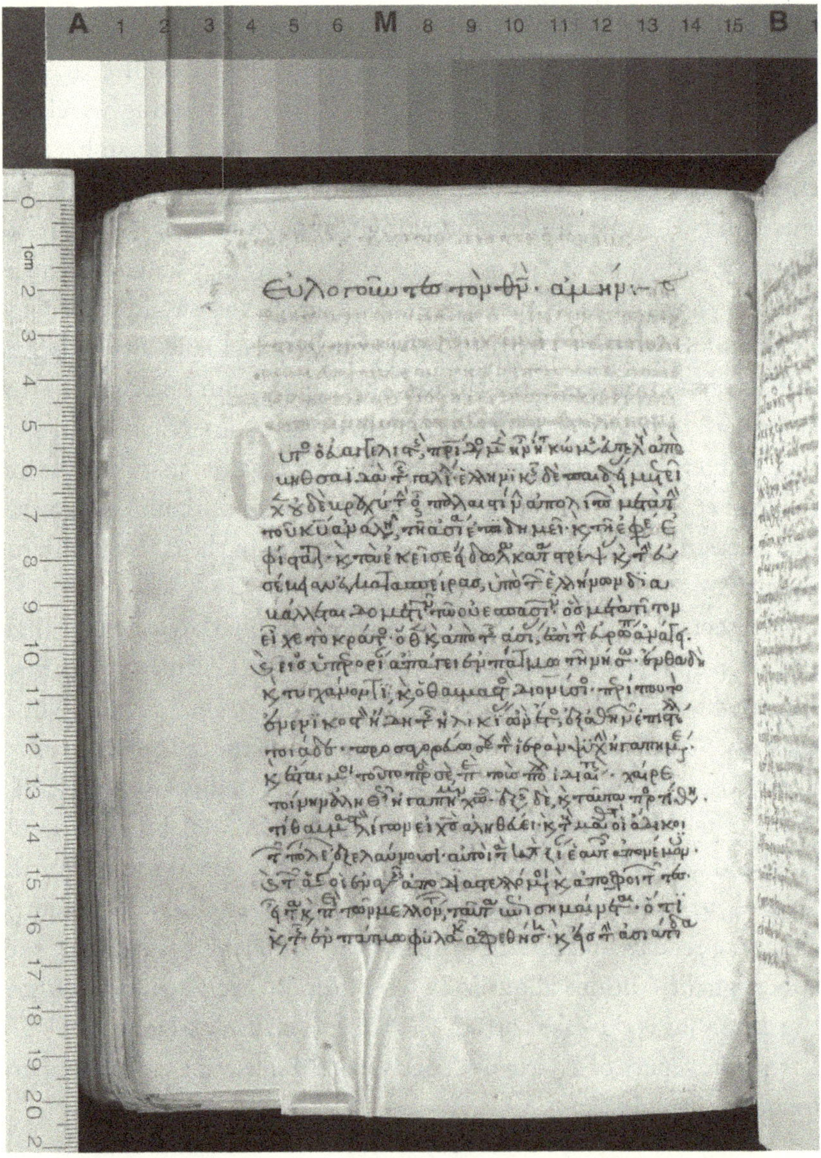

Goodspeed Manuscript Collection, Manuscript 727, New Testament Gospels (Georgius Gospels), Greg. 2266, thirteenth century, fol. 192(b)v and 192(c)r, Hanna Holborn Gray Special Collections Research Center, University of Chicago Library.

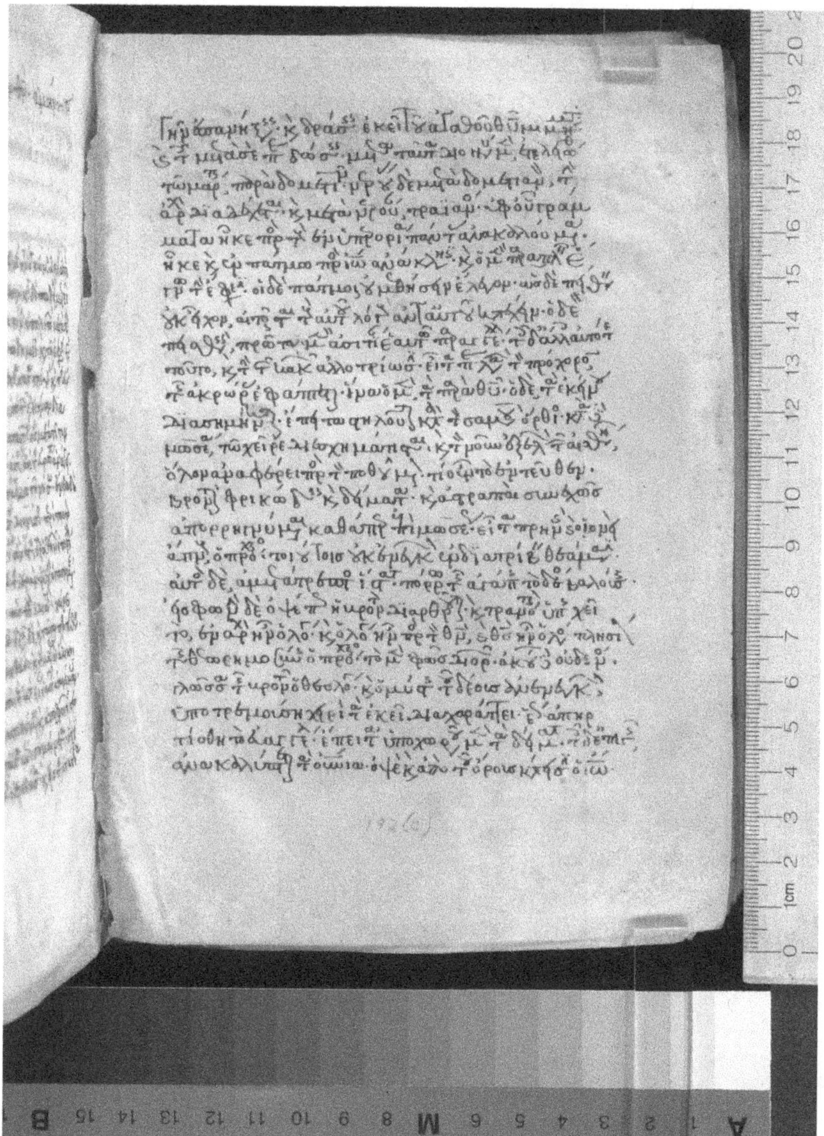

Goodspeed Manuscript Collection, Manuscript 727, New Testament Gospels (Georgius Gospels), Greg. 2266, thirteenth century, fol. 192(b)v and 192(c)r, Hanna Holborn Gray Special Collections Research Center, University of Chicago Library.

Moreover, some of the most common iconography of John depicts the evangelist composing his gospel in the way described by the Acts of John by Prochorus, that is, with the apostle standing on a rocky mountain on Patmos, often accompanied by lightning, dictating the gospel to a seated Prochorus.

Chester Beatty Collection, Manuscript W 135, Gospel Book, eleventh–twelfth century, fol. 166v. CC BY – 4.0.

This image of John is exceedingly common, even within biblical manuscripts that do not include a gospel preface; thus many biblical manuscripts that do not include a *text* of the apocryphal episode nevertheless include a decisive aspect of the *tradition*.

1.4. Drusiana in Art and Literature

As noted above, a significant portion of the early Acts of John (chs. 63–86) involves Drusiana, a wealthy woman who converted to Christianity. This material is extant as a long episode interpolated into a handful of manuscripts of the Acts of John by Prochorus; it narrates the second half of Drusiana's story.

When this episode begins, Drusiana is already a Christian, living in a chaste marriage with her husband Andronicus, also a Christian; she is plagued by the sexual advances of a certain Callimachus to the point of desperation, so grieved to be the object of Callimachus's sinful desires that she ultimately dies. But Callimachus, mad with lust, is not deterred by her death: He plots with a servant to get access to her tomb and is stopped from raping her corpse only by the miraculous appearance of an enormous snake, who frightens him to death. When John discovers what has happened, he raises both Drusiana and Callimachus, with the latter coming to belief in Christ.[35] We know that this is the second half of Drusiana's story (and not its entirety) because reference is made to Drusiana's conversion to Christianity and the conflict it provoked with her not-yet-Christian husband Andronicus—neither of which are narrated in the extant material; moreover, in another extant section of the early Acts of John, we encounter the not-yet-Christian Andronicus, referred to as a villain (in ch. 31). It is clear, then, that there was a narrative in the early Acts describing Drusiana's conversion, the conflict with Andronicus, and his eventual conversion, but it has not survived. Nevertheless, a broad outline of Drusiana's full story can be pieced together from existing materials.

In the Greek tradition, Drusiana's story largely disappears from view with the early Acts of John; she plays no role in the Metastasis, and she is not mentioned in the Greek hagiographical works (of Nicetas the

35. For a broader interpretation of the story see, e.g., Michael Theobald, "'Stirb, damit du lebst!' Die Totenauferweckungen des Kallimachos, der Drusiana und des Fortunatus) ActJoh 63–86, bes 74–84," in *Kompendium der frühchristlichen Wundererzählungen 2: Die Wunder der Apostel*, ed. Ruben Zimmermann (Gütersloher Verlagshaus, 2017), 385–99.

Paphlagonian [late ninth to tenth century CE] or Symeon Metaphrastes [d. ca. 1000 CE], for example) or in any of the gospel prefaces. In the Latin tradition, however, Drusiana comes to the fore: In the Virtutes Iohannis (the fifth- or sixth-century Latin narrative described above), the second half of Drusiana's story (that is, the narrative of the early Acts of John chs. 63–86) is presented in full in section IV. The story is situated within a new timeline of events, following immediately on John's return from exile on Patmos and before his interaction with the philosopher Craton—neither of which occurs in the extant sections of the early Acts. But the Drusiana episode itself is essentially a Latin translation that follows the Greek quite closely.[36] The differences between the Virtutes Iohannis IV and Acts of John 63–86 primarily involve the speeches, which—as one might expect—is where the bulk of the explicitly theological content of the work is conveyed. The Virtutes Iohannis, then, offers valuable insight into shifting theological ideas at the time of its composition, both through what it says and through what it changes and omits from the early Acts of John—though we are on slightly less firm ground with the latter, as we don't know precisely what the source our author/editor/translator had before them when carrying out this work.[37]

Drusiana also appears in the Passio Iohannis (described above), though her story has been significantly adapted and abbreviated. Like

36. The Latin follows the Greek so closely, in fact, that the Latin translation is useful in establishing the original form of the Greek text. See Junod and Kaestli, *Acta Iohannis*, 2:790–92.

37. Notably, the account of Drusiana's death and resurrection was even rewritten as a play by tenth-century canoness and playwright Hrotswitha of Gandersheim. Hrotswitha, who composed in a wide range of genres, wrote a series of dramas in which, according to her own preface, she attempts to glorify the chastity of Christian virgins, including a play titled *Resuscitatio Drusianae*, which hews very closely to the narrative as we have it in the early Acts of John and the Virtutes Iohannis. For an interesting study of Hrotswitha's work, see Barbara K. Gold, "Hrotswitha Writes Herself: *Clamor Validus Gandeshemensis*," in *Sex and Gender in Medieval and Renaissance Texts: The Latin Tradition*, ed. Barbara K. Gold et al. (SUNY Press, 1997), 41–70.

in the Virtutes Iohannis, the Drusiana episode is placed immediately on John's return to Ephesus after exile in Patmos, but the similarities end there: The episode is dramatically abbreviated, and the content is significantly adapted. When John returns, Drusiana has just died, and the Ephesian Christian community is in mourning. Neither Callimachus nor Andronicus appears in this now very short episode. Drusiana's death is still brought on by grief, but this is no longer associated with any sort of sexual harassment; rather, as is briefly reported, she grieves and ultimately dies because of John's absence while in exile: "Drusiana, who had always followed him and had been worn out by longing for his arrival, was carried out (on a bier)" (*Drusiana, quae semper sequuta eum fuerat, et adventus eius desiderio fuerat fatigata, efferebatur*).[38] This fact is what now grieves the community: They are carrying her body out for burial at the very moment John reappears, lamenting that she has just missed his arrival. They tell John how she used to say, "I would like to see the apostle of the Lord with my own eyes before I die" (*videam Apostolum Domini oculis meis antequam moriar*) and bemoan that "you have come, and she is not able to see you" (*tu venisti, et te videre non potuit*). John, of course, immediately resurrects her. This episode is repeated in much the same way by Jacobus de Voragine in the Legenda Aurea (= the "Golden Legend").[39]

This version of the Drusiana episode (in which she dies just before John's return to Ephesus and is resurrected as his first act upon reappearing in the city) is the version that was most prominently taken up by artists in the West. The basic scene—with John and Drusiana, rising from bier, surrounded by a crowd of Christians, often depicted against a backdrop of city walls—was particularly popular in Italy, most famously painted by Giotto (in the Peruzzi Chapel), Filippino Lippi (in the Strozzi Chapel), Donatello, Giovanni di Paolo, and others.

---

38. I quote here from the text as printed by Fabricius, *Codex Apocryphus*, 607.

39. See the chapter *De sancto Iohanne apostolo et evangelista*. Edition: *Jacobus de Voragine: Legenda Aurea. Goldene Legende*, 2nd ed., ed. Bruno W. Häuptli, Fontes Christiani (Herder, 2022), 226, 228.

Drusiana's episode was taken up and further transmitted in the medieval period by, for example, Aldhelm of Sherborne (ca. 639–709/10 CE), who seems to rely on both the Virtutes Iohannis and the Passio in his Latin prose work *De virginitate*, and Ælfric Grammaticus (955–1020 CE), who seems to rely primarily on the Passio in his Old English work on the life of John (the *Assumptio Sancti Iohannis Apostoli*).[40] Yet another adaptation of the episode is presented in the Anglo-Norman Life of John: Here we find a new development, which identifies the baptism of Drusiana as the cause of John's arrest in Ephesus.[41] Much like the episode describing John's composition of the gospel on Patmos with Prochorus taking dictation, the episode describing Drusiana's resurrection also enters the canonical, biblical tradition through imagery: Multiple thirteenth-century "picture books" of Revelation from England depict scenes from the life of John, with an emphasis on the Drusiana episode. In Bodleian Library Auctarium D.4.17 and Pierpont Morgan Library M.524, for example, Revelation is presented as a series of illustrations with captions embedded within a broader story of John's career, with Drusiana's story serving as something like bookends for the vision: Drusiana's baptism is among the first moments in John's life that is depicted, and it is presented as the immediate cause of his arrest, trial, and exile to Patmos; there follows the

40. See English translation of Aldhelm's *De virginitate* by Michael Lapidge and Michael Herren, *Aldhelm: The Prose Works* (D. S. Brewer, 1979), 59–135, at 80. The unnamed "matron" whom "the final destiny had sentenced with a double urn of death" is clearly Drusiana. In a footnote on this passage (194n11), Lapidge and Herren wonder why the urn of fate is described as "double" (*gemina*); I suspect Aldhelm here refers to Drusiana's multiple deaths and resurrections, as described in the early Acts of John and the Virtutes Iohannis. On Aldhelm's use of the Virtutes Iohannis, see Aideen M. O'Leary, "Apostolic Passiones in Early Anglo-Saxon England," in *Apocryphal Texts and Traditions in Anglo-Saxon England*, ed. Kathryn Powell and Donald Scragg (D. S. Brewer, 2003), 111. On Ælfric's use of the Passio Iohannis, see Brandon Hawk, *Preaching Apocrypha in Anglo-Saxon England* (University of Toronto Press, 2018).

41. See Ian Short, "The Translation of the Life of St John and the Apocalypse" and "The Life of St John the Evangelist from Paris, BNF fr. 19525," in *The Trinity Apocalypse (CD-ROM Accompanying)*, ed. David McKitterick (British Library, 2005), 16, 88.

illustrated version of Revelation. The manuscripts continue with further images from John's life, beginning with illustrations of John's return to Ephesus and resurrection of Drusiana. Here again, then, an apocryphal episode, first composed and circulated as the central episode of the early Acts of John, has found its way into a biblical manuscript, included alongside the canonical Revelation.

1.5. Conclusions

This account of the continuous transmission and wide popularity of apocryphal traditions concerning John could be greatly expanded, were we to look more closely at the Coptic tradition, the Armenian tradition, the Church Slavic tradition, and so on. But the point is, we think, quite clear: This apocryphal apostle narrative was neither lost, secret, nor hidden; to the contrary, it has played a central role in the history of Christian literature. The fact that works such as the early Acts of John were repeatedly adapted and dramatically changed over time may seem like a shortcoming, an obstacle to be overcome only by the painstaking reconstruction of the earliest accessible version. It is surely true that the exceedingly complicated textual traditions and trajectories make for difficult study. But we would argue that the complex lives of such texts—the multiple versions, translations, and transformations—are a feature, not a bug: The phenomenon of change is what gives us insight into the interests, concerns, and practices of each successive generation or community of Christians who valued the text enough to reproduce it. This stands in stark contrast to the early Christian literature that would be ossified by inclusion in the canon.

2. The Acts of Thecla

The Acts of Thecla (often also called the Acts of Paul and Thecla) describes the adventures of a young woman, who, sitting at the window of her home in Iconium, hears Paul preaching a message of asceticism and is immediately convinced. She leaves behind her fiancé (and a very angry mother) to join Paul as a disciple; as a consequence, she faces trial and execution twice, miraculously escaping in both instances. The earliest form of the narrative ends with Thecla leaving Paul to return to Iconium, then continuing on her own to Seleucia, where (it is very briefly reported) she eventually dies. Composed in Greek, likely toward the end of the second century CE, the Thecla narrative was enormously popular throughout late antiquity and indeed for the majority of the history of Christianity—a conclusion that, for the early period, is abundantly evident in the textual witnesses (the Acts of Thecla is better attested in papyri than several canonical texts), in the large body of artifacts related to the Thecla cult, and in the popularity of the name Thecla (which occurs for the first time in our text) in the late antique period and beyond.[42]

The early Greek narrative may well be familiar to readers of this book.[43] Among the apostle narratives, the Acts of Thecla has surely been the object of the most intensive study, in no small part because of the striking role gender plays throughout the narrative. The work depicts a female apostle who rejects marriage and family life in favor of Christianity; she baptizes herself and is charged by Paul to "go and teach" (ch. 41), a command that contradicts the opinion attributed to Paul in, for example, 1 Timothy 2:11–15, where we read, "I permit no woman to teach" and "she will be saved through childbearing." The early Christian author Tertullian (ca. 150–ca. 220 CE) certainly found contradiction; in his *De baptismo* 17, he writes:

> But if the writings which wrongly go under Paul's name, claim Thecla's example as a license for women's teaching and baptizing,

42. For images and analysis of ancient Thecla manuscripts, see Thomas A. Wayment, *The Text of the New Testament Apocrypha (100–400 CE)* (Bloomsbury, 2013) 17–35, 223–44. On the large body of artifacts related to the Thecla cult, see Stephen J. Davis, *The Cult of St Thecla: A Tradition of Women's Piety in Late Antiquity*, 2nd ed., OECS (Oxford University Press, 2009); Jeremy W. Barrier et al., eds., *Thecla: Paul's Disciple and Saint in the East and West*, Studies on Early Christian Apocrypha 12 (Peeters, 2017). On the name Thecla, see Jan N. Bremmer, "The Onomastics and Provenance of the *Acts of Paul*," in *Philologie, Herméneutique et Histoire des Textes entre Orient et Occident. Mélanges en Hommage à Sever J. Voicu*, ed. Francesca P. Barone et al. (Brepols, 2017), 527–47.

43. For an introduction and translation, see, e.g., Ehrman, *Lost Scriptures*, 151–63.

> let them know that, in Asia, the presbyter who composed that writing, as if he were augmenting Paul's fame from his own store, after being convicted, and confessing that he had done it from love of Paul, was removed from his office. For how credible would it seem, that he who has not permitted a woman even to learn with over-boldness, should give a female the power of teaching and of baptizing! "Let them be silent," he says, "and at home consult their own husbands."[44]

Tertullian's is the only reference we have to this unnamed presbyter in Asia; we have no other evidence with which to judge the accuracy of his report. As we will see below, assessments of the aspects of the work that Tertullian found objectionable (that is, the notion that women might baptize and teach—and that such a thing was sanctioned by Paul) varied across time and location, with some Christians finding these elements utterly unproblematic and others adapting the text to remove or revise them. Much of modern scholarship on the Acts of Thecla has focused on gender, and for good reason: Beyond the central figure of Thecla, almost the entire cast of characters within the narrative is defined by gender, with female beasts protecting Thecla from raging male beasts in the arena, and with human women—both en masse in crowds and individually—defending her from various assaults by human men. Whether or not the early Greek Acts of Thecla is a work by women for women, as some have suggested,[45] it is at least in part *about* gender—though the centrality of the theme also varies across time and location.

---

44. Tertullian, *De baptismo* 17, trans. S. Thelwall, *ANF* 3. Tertullian's text and its translation, however, have been a matter of debate. For a close discussion, see Anton Hilhorst, "Tertullian on the Acts of Paul," in *The Apocryphal Acts of Paul and Thecla*, ed. Jan N. Bremmer (Kok Pharos, 1996), 150–63; and Gérard Poupon, "Encore un fois: Tertullien, *De baptism* 17.5," in *Nomen Latinum. Mélanges André Schneider*, ed. Denis Knoepfler (Université de Neuchâtel, 1997), 199–205.

45. See, e.g., Stephen L. Davies, *The Revolt of the Widows: The Social World of the Apocryphal Acts* (Bardic Press, 1980), 95–96; Virginia Burrus, *Chastity as Autonomy: Women in the Stories of the Apocryphal Acts*, Studies in Women and Religion 23

Tertullian's comment in *De baptismo* notwithstanding, the Acts of Thecla never faced the formal condemnation that the early Acts of John received at the Second Council of Nicaea—nor indeed could the Acts of Thecla be described as fringe or marginal in any sense. Unsurprisingly, the work was translated into a host of languages (including Latin, Coptic, Syriac, Armenian, Arabic, and Church Slavic, among others) and rewritten in Greek.[46] Moreover, Thecla—as saint and protomartyr—has been venerated throughout the vast majority of the history of Christianity. In the following short section, we will treat just a few snapshots within the broader Thecla tradition.

2.1. Thecla and New Testament Manuscripts

We saw above that a scene from the Acts of John by Prochorus as well as other Johannine traditions originating in apocryphal works were regularly included within biblical codices. A variation on that phenomenon is evident with Thecla traditions. The activities of the apostle Paul in the Acts of Paul (of which, as noted above, the Acts of Thecla may or may not have been an original part) are difficult to place on a timeline alongside his activities as recounted in the canonical Acts or referenced in the Pastoral Epistles;[47] a harmonization of these works, in which all the events described take place sequentially, would require substantial contortions. The same is not entirely true of the Acts of Thecla. Or, more to the point: Copyists of biblical manuscripts were occasionally

(Edwin Mellen, 1987) 108; and (much more cautious) the discussion by Bremmer, "*Apocryphal Acts*: Authors, Place, Time," 225.

46. For an English translation and introduction, see Andrew S. Jacobs, *The Life of Thecla*, Early Christian Apocrypha 11 (Cascade, 2024); for text, introduction, and German translation, see Bernd Kollmann and Burghard Schröder, *Pseudo-Basilius von Seleukia: Vita et Miracula Sanctae Theclae. Leben und Wunder der Heiligen Thekla*, Fontes Christiani 93 (Herder, 2021).

47. It is not entirely clear that the author of the Acts of Paul had any interest—or even knowledge of—the canonical work. See Julia Snyder, "Relationships Between the Acts of the Apostles and Other Apostle Narratives," in *Between Canonical and Apocryphal Texts: Processes of Reception, Rewriting and Interpretation in Early Judaism and Early Christianity*, ed. Jörg Frey et al. (Mohr Siebeck, 2018), 319–41.

moved to indicate the points of connection either alongside or even *within* the biblical text.

Readers of this book who own a copy of Nestle-Aland's Greek New Testament in its twenth-fifth, twenty-sixth, or twenty-seventh edition might turn to the text of 2 Timothy 3:10–11, where "Paul"[48] briefly summarizes his suffering as follows: "Now you have observed my teaching, my conduct, my aim in life, my faith, my patience, my love, my steadfastness, my persecutions, and my sufferings, the things that happened to me in Antioch, Iconium, and Lystra. What persecutions I endured! Yet the Lord rescued me from all of them." The Greek text of verse 11a is the same in all four editions—τοῖς διωγμοῖς, τοῖς παθήμασιν, οἷά μοι ἐγένετο ἐν Ἀντιοχείᾳ, ἐν Ἰκονίῳ, ἐν Λύστροις—but the information given in the critical apparatus changes. If your Nestle-Aland Greek text is the twenty-fifth or twenty-sixth edition, you will find in the apparatus after Ἀντιοχείᾳ the phrase α δια την Θεκλαν επαθεν ("which he suffered on account of Thecla"), found in the tenth-century Manuscript 181, held at the Vatican Library. If you have instead Nestle-Aland's twenty-seventh edition before you, you will find τουτεστιν α δια Θεκλαν πεπονθεν ("this is what he suffered on account of Thecla"), found in the ninth-century Manuscript K (18), held at the State Historical Museum of Moscow. Both manuscripts include the canonical Acts, the Catholic Epistles, and the letters of Paul; Manuscript K also includes commentaries. As Thomas J. Kraus has detailed, both variants of 2 Timothy 3:11a are marginal glosses, that is, they provide supplementary information explaining the biblical text.[49] In other words, for readers who might wonder when the Paul of 2 Timothy refers to the persecutions, sufferings, and other things that happened to him in Antioch and Iconium, these scribes explain that he must mean the events described in the Thecla narrative.

An even more notable variant occurs in later in Manuscript 181's text of 2 Timothy. Second Timothy 4:19, the closing of the letter,

48. Like the vast majority of NT scholars, we regard the Pastoral Epistles to be pseudepigraphical and probably quite late.

49. See Kraus, "Thecla and the *Acts of Thecla*," 127–31.

reads as follows: "Greet Prisca and Aquila, and the household of Onesiphorus" (ἄσπασαι Πρίσκον καὶ Ἀκύλαν καὶ τὸν Ὀνησιφόρου οἶκον). In the canonical New Testament, the name Onesiphorus appears only in 2 Timothy (here and at 2 Tim 1:16). He is, however, a prominent character in the first sections of the Acts of Thecla, in which he and his wife, Lectra, and sons Simmias and Zeno host Paul at their home in Iconium. In Manuscript 181's text of 2 Timothy 4:19, we find (again, noted in NA[25], NA[26], NA[27], but dropping out in the NA[28]) precisely these additional individuals named. As opposed to 2 Timothy 3:11, however, they do not appear in a marginal gloss; their names are seamlessly included in the main text, which reads as follows: "Greet Prisca and Aquila, Lectra his wife, Simmias and Zeno his sons, and the household of Onesiphorus." The same reading occurs in Manuscript 460, a thirteenth-century trilingual manuscript held at the Biblioteca Nazionale Marciana in Venice.

We are not suggesting that any of these variants represent the original reading of 2 Timothy; that is certainly not the case. The point is that, as Kraus puts it, in these manuscripts a "phrase from a text *outside the canon* has been integrated into 2 Tim 4:19 or, in other words, has been put *inside the canon*."[50] And this circumstance is a clear indication of position the Acts of Thecla held throughout the first millennium of Christianity and beyond: Not only was the narrative so widely familiar that a brief reference such as we find in these marginalia could be understood, but the narrative had *explanatory value* for the interpretation of canonical works. We note, too, that these references to Thecla and elements of the Acts of Thecla are found within the Pastoral Epistles. While Tertullian may have regarded the content of the Acts of Thecla contradictory to what is written in 1 Timothy, in these manuscripts we find references to the Acts of Thecla existing unproblematically alongside and even within 2 Timothy.

Two further examples illustrate—quite literally—how the producers and consumers of biblical manuscripts have understood the compatibility

50. Kraus, "Thecla and the *Acts of Thecla*," 132.

of Thecla's narrative with canonical works. The first is an image found in a thirteenth-century manuscript held at the Pantocrator Monastery on Mount Athos (no. 234 = Gregory-Aland 1404). This manuscript, comprising the New Testament, a Psalter, and multiple selections from church writers such as Dionysius the Areopagite and John of Damascus, includes author portraits, including one of Paul. The manuscript is small (roughly 17 by 10 cm), fitting easily in the hand and no doubt intended for personal use. The portrait of Paul is the headpiece of the Pauline epistles; in it, the apostle is depicted as seated and writing; across from him, a woman gazes down at him from a window. The scene is almost certainly based on the beginning of the Acts of Thecla 7, in which it is reported that Thecla, "seated at the nearby window of her house, would listen night and day to the word concerning purity spoken by Paul." In any case, the woman is clearly labeled Θέκλα.[51]

Monastery of Pantokrator Manuscript 234 (Greg. 1404), New Testament with selections from the Fathers, Psalter, and other ecclesiastical writings, thirteenth century, f. 547, fol. 63r. Library of Congress Collection of Manuscripts from the Monasteries of Mt. Athos.

51. While the manuscript has not yet, to the best of our knowledge, been digitized, microfilm images are available from the Library of Congress. See "Monastery of Pantokrator 234. (Greg. 1404). New Testament with Selections from the Fathers, Psalter, and Other Ecclesiastical Writings. 13th cent. 547 f.," Library of Congress, accessed January 28, 2025, https://www.loc.gov/item/00271051633-ma/.

This image from the Mount Athos manuscript helps in the identification of an unnamed woman in the headpiece of the Pauline epistles found in Dumbarton Oaks Manuscript 3 (BZ.1962.35), a richly illustrated eleventh-century manuscript containing a Psalter and the New Testament, with portraits of the Gospel and letter writers. The portrait of Paul is found on folio 269v. The apostle is seated, writing in an open codex; he is flanked by two figures, a woman standing behind his chair and peering over his shoulder and a beardless man standing behind a desk.

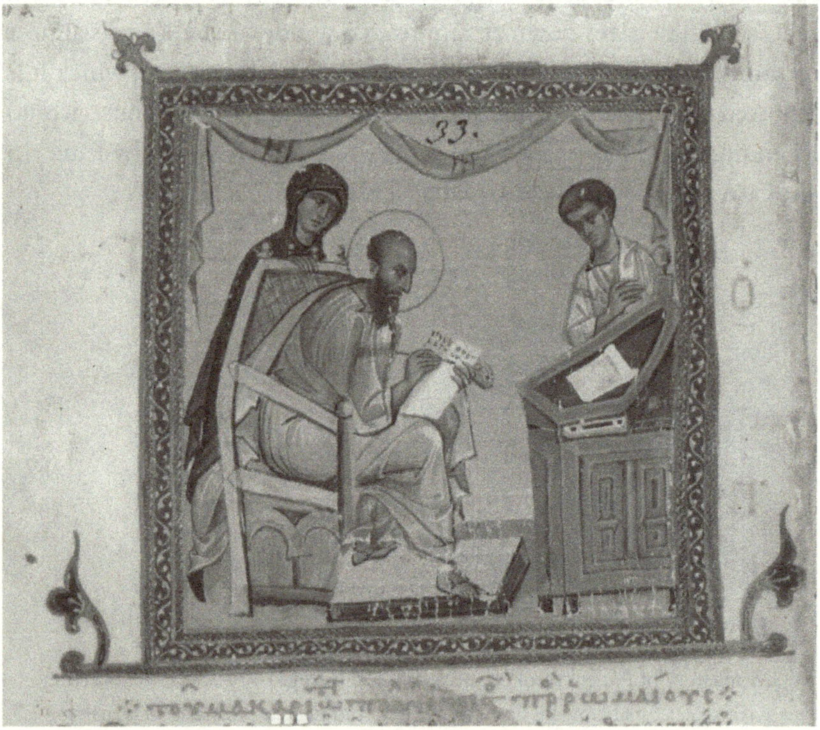

Dumbarton Oaks, Manuscript 3, Psalter and New Testament, ca. 1084, fol. 269v.

While neither figure is labeled, Sirarpie Der Nersessian identifies the woman as Thecla, both because of her costume and because she also appears in the headpiece of the Pauline Epistles in the Mount Athos manuscript.[52] Der Nersessian tentatively identifies the young man as

52. See Sirarpie Der Nersessian, "A Psalter and New Testament Manuscript at Dumbarton Oaks," *DOP* 19 (1965): 153–83.

Timothy based on the composition of the scene, which she understands as a transposition of a common iconographic type of John Chrysostom, depicting his Pauline inspiration and reflecting an episode in the life of Chrysostom (told in multiple sources). The story goes that, as John Chrysostom was composing his commentary on the Pauline Epistles, his assistant, Proclus, watching from behind the door, would see a man standing behind John, whispering into his ear. When Proclus later told John what he had seen, he pointed to an image of Paul hanging on the wall and said that that was the man he had seen whispering in John's ear. In the numerous images of this scene, John Chrysostom is depicted as seated and writing; Paul stands behind his chair to the left, and Proclus peers from behind the door on the right. Der Nersessian writes: "In this re-adaptation the inspiring figure has been transformed into that of Thekla, thus introducing an element derived from the apocryphal Acts; as for the young man who has taken the place of Proclos, John's secretary, he may be Paul's companion, Timothy."[53] This conclusion bears repeating: In Dumbarton Oaks Manuscript 3, a common iconographic type depicting John Chrysostom's inspiration by Paul has been adapted to illustrate the composition of the Pauline Epistles, with Paul taking John Chrysostom's place as author and Thecla taking Paul's place as inspiring source.

A final example moves in the opposite direction, indicating how producers and consumers of the Acts of Thecla have understood the compatibility of Thecla's narrative with canonical works. The Arabic version of the Acts of Thecla, extant in at least eight manuscripts, has until quite recently received very little scholarly attention. In two articles (from 2015 and 2017), Stephen Davis published an edition and translation of an eighteenth-century manuscript held in Los Angeles by the St. Shenouda the Archimandrite Coptic Society (ML.MS. 21). The manuscript contains a colophon that reveals its precise date of production and the name and position of its scribe: He identifies himself as Jirjis (George), a "priest and servant of the monastery of the great saint Anbā Būlus" (that is, Saint Paul the Hermit, located in the Easter

53. Der Nersessian, "Psalter and New Testament Manuscript," 179.

Desert of Egypt), completing the manuscript in 1755.[54] The Arabic Thecla narrative in this manuscript follows the plot of the early Greek version fairly closely but with the addition of framing material in a prologue and postscript. Interestingly, the prologue begins as follows: "In the name of the Father and the Son and the Holy Spirit, one God, a *Life* [*maymar*] that Saint Luke [*Lūqā*] the apostle, the physician-evangelist, related. In it he sets forth accounts of Saint Thecla the martyr apostle, her virtuous deeds and the fulfillment of her martyrdom on the twenty-fifth day of the month Abīb. Peace from the Lord, amen." Not only is the Thecla narrative still in use within a monastery in the eighteenth century, but its author is identified as Luke the Evangelist.

2.2. Thecla and Tertullian's Gender Problem

As already noted, while Tertullian strongly objected to some of the content of the Acts of Thecla—specifically the notion that Paul sanctioned a woman teaching and baptizing—the work nevertheless thrived. This is certainly the case in Tertullian's own language, Latin. Oscar von Gebhardt, who in 1902 edited the Latin witnesses, observed: "The popularity that the Thecla legend enjoyed in the Latin Church of the Middle Ages is evident from the fact that it was distributed in at least four, perhaps five, translations that each originated independently of one another, and also in several shorter versions, one of which (Epit. IV) also goes back to the original text."[55] But the Acts of Thecla was not merely translated, it was also adapted; moreover, even the most faithful

---

54. See Stephen J. Davis, "An Arabic *Acts of Paul and Thecla*: Text and Translation, with Introduction and Critical Commentary," in Barrier et al., *Thecla: Paul's Disciple*, 109.

55. Oscar von Gebhardt, *Passio S. Theclae Virginis. Die Lateinischen Übersetzungen der Acta Pauli et Theclae nebst Fragmenten, Auszügen und Beilagen,* TUGAL (Hinrichs, 1902), v. The German reads: "Welcher Beliebtheit die Thekla-Legende in der lateinischen Kirche des Mittelalters sich erfreute, erhellt aus der Thatsache dass sie in mindestens vier, vielleicht in fünf unabhängig voneinander entstandenen Übersetzungen und außerdem in mehreren kürzeren Fassungen, deren eine (Epit. IV) ebenfalls auf den Urtext zurückgeht, verbreitet gewesen ist."

translation are themselves interpretations, if not adaptions, of the original. So we might ask whether some of the elements that Tertullian objected to were toned down or simply removed in later versions; if they were, perhaps this would explain how references to the Thecla narrative coexisted with Paul's letters in the manuscripts discussed above.

We might begin with the Life and Miracles of Thecla, a fifth-century two-volume work (formerly attributed to Basil of Seleucia) that retells the Acts of Thecla in its first volume (the Life) and narrates a series of her miracles that take place at her cult site in Seleucia in the second.[56] Note that this is not a translation but the retelling of the early Acts of Thecla in a finer style of Greek and for a new generation of readers, some 250 years after the early work was in circulation. The author of the Life offers us a prologue in which he describes something of his goals, his methods, and the esteem in which he holds the earlier work. It is a rare instance in which we have rather direct access to how a late antique author is both thinking about a second-century apostle narrative and approaching his own composition of a new version, so it is worth quoting here in full:

> This text at which we have toiled is a history [ἱστορία] and an account [διήγησις] of the ancient deeds performed by the blessed Thecla, the apostle and martyr. It has been taken out of another, older history and put together following in its footsteps. Let it be known that we have embarked upon so great a task as this not as though we were saying anything more extensive or more beautiful or even more accurate than what was said before, but as a way of fulfilling our personal vow: to devote something from our meager and lowly abilities to the great martyr who, because of her goodness, takes pleasure in the smallest things. We were also eager to bring to completion the command of a pious man, of whom perhaps I shall make some mention in one way or other in my writing. Nonetheless I should see fit to note

56. Regarding introductory questions, see Kollmann and Schröder, *Pseudo-Basilius: Vita et Miracula*, 7–74.

to those who will read this text, in the present and perhaps in future, that if something additional has been said by us—for so it has been—we haven't done anything outside the purview of classical writers. For while we have followed the intent and order of what was said and done at the time of the martyrdom, just through a different (so to speak) style and vocabulary, we have adapted the task previously undertaken by others and dedicated it to the greatest martyr. By weaving speeches into it where possible, we have imparted to it (at least I think so) an old-fashioned beauty, while keeping the particular and distinct form of speech for each character. We have concerned ourselves very little with classicizing vocabulary or old-fashioned expression, instead we have paid attention to truth and clarity and to order of events, so that nothing at all of what was said or done by the apostle and martyr should be unknown, nor indeed any of the things said or done by others because of her. Herodotus of Halicarnassus and Thucydides the Athenian, and whoever after them was among those who wrote ancient or recent histories, each affirmed that they embarked upon their task of writing due to their own inclination and interest. But as for me, I embarked upon the history of the apostle and martyr Thecla after being frequently incited by a divine message and urged by the advice of the best of men—I mean Achaius, the best and wisest of all. Not out of fear that these things would become obsolete or obscure as time went on—for the actions of the saints remain forever secure, steadfast, and immortal, preserved by God both for his own eternal fame and for the benefit of the people still dwelling on earth—but so that we might adorn our own selves through this sacred task, so that we might fulfill that vow which we brought forth long ago, and so that we might make clear to future people the man who charged us to do it. This is also what the wondrous Luke has clearly done in both the divine Gospel and in the book concerning the apostles, affixing Theophilus at

> the beginning, to whom indeed he dedicated the entire task of the divine writing. Now I shall begin here the virginal history.[57]

There is clearly much to be discussed in this fascinating passage—far more than we can attempt in the present book. Hopefully, the following brief observations will suffice: (1) The author understands the early Acts of Thecla as some form of "history" (ἱστορία), clearly designating it as such in the first line but also invoking Greek historians Herodotus and Thucydides—along with Luke the evangelist—as models; (2) the author's compositional method will be to follow the plot rather closely but expand the work by "weaving speeches into it where possible"; and (3) the author was motivated to carry out this work by a human patron (the "pious man" and "best of men—I mean Achaius") but also by the desire to fulfill a "personal vow: to devote something from our meager and lowly abilities to the great martyr." This last point about motivation is particularly intriguing, inasmuch as the author notes that he is *not* attempting to expand the earlier narrative or to produce a "more accurate" (ἀκριβέστερον) account, as one might expect.

Leaving aside the prologue, how does the author actually shape the narrative? What is different in this adaptation, and do those differences involve the elements so objectionable to Tertullian? The short answer to the latter question is no. The episode in which Thecla baptizes herself is presented much as it is in the early Acts of Thecla; the final episode in which Paul explicitly commands Thecla to teach is, if anything, amplified. Compare the following passages:

> And taking her by the hand, Paul led her into the house of Hermias, and he heard everything from her, with the result that Paul marveled and all those listening were strengthened and prayed for Tryphaena. And standing up, Thecla said to Paul: "I am going to Iconium." And Paul said: "Go and teach the word

57. We quote here the translation by Jacobs, *Life of Thecla*.

> of God." And Tryphaena sent to her much clothing and gold, so that she might leave it with Paul for the ministry of the poor. (Acts of Thecla 41)
>
> [After a long speech in which Thecla details all she has come to learn through Paul, the apostle responds] "Now you have done well in all these things, virgin, and through all of them the might of the faith has accrued to you; already you have prevailed in the apostolic toils and races, such that you now lack nothing for the apostleship and succession of the divine preaching. So go and teach the word, and finish the gospel-spreading race, and share my eagerness on behalf of Christ. This is why Christ has chosen you through me: so that he might acquire you for the apostleship, and so that he might put in your hands some of those cities which have not yet been catechized. For it is necessary for you to multiply the talents of gold." When Paul had said such things, the martyr left behind for Paul the property that had been given to her from Tryphaena—there was a lot of gold and expensive clothing—for the care of the poor; responding to these things with "Commend me to Christ!" she took the road to Iconium. (Life of Thecla 26:23–25)

It would be ludicrous to suggest that the notion of Thecla teaching and preaching has been toned down in this passage; to the contrary, Thecla's status is enormously elevated. As Andrew Jacobs notes, throughout this work the author identifies Thecla specifically as both "girl" (ἡ κόρη) and as "apostle"; moreover, the latter, a masculine noun, is rather conspicuously paired with the feminine definite article (ἡ ἀπόστολος). Jacobs writes: "The author of the Life and Miracles is innovating only insofar as no one had, to that point, described someone as a 'she-apostle,' an honor that seems to remain unique to Thecla well into the Middle Ages."[58]

58. See Jacobs, *Life of Thecla*, 38.

Our author, then, in no way avoids depicting Thecla as a woman doing the things that—according to Tertullian and "Paul" as presented in 1 Timothy—women cannot do. Indeed, the point is reiterated in the last chapter of the work, where her activities are summarized as "preaching the good news," "catechizing," "baptizing" and "performing miracles." But what of the notion of using "Thecla's example as a license for women's teaching and baptizing" in general? Here, the Life of Thecla is rather less clear—and the very uniqueness of Thecla may be relevant. Again, Jacobs writes: "As an apostle, she does what other first-century apostles did: she preaches, teaches, and baptizes. Our fifth-century author does not portray this behavior as problematic even though he lived in a time when Christian women may have taught, rarely preached, and probably never baptized."[59] Does our author intend for Thecla to be a model for contemporary, fifth-century women? The few scholars who have dealt with the Life of Thecla tend to think not; they read the depiction of Thecla in the Life of Thecla as exceptional and anomalous, rather than exemplary.[60] Jacobs notes multiple places where the Life of Thecla actually reinscribes gender norms, as for example when, during her first attempted martyrdom, Thecla remains silent. In the Acts of Thecla, she silently gazes upon Paul (or, rather, Christ disguised as Paul) in the crowd; in the Life of Thecla, her silence is explained as feminine modesty: "For nothing is so proper for a woman, nothing so fitting, as silence and keeping quiet."[61] With this narratorial statement, we are nearly back at 1 Timothy 2:11. In other words, the tension of referencing Thecla's story either alongside or within the Pastoral Epistles in manuscripts here exists within the Life of Thecla itself.

Elsewhere, however, Thecla clearly did serve an exemplary function—if primarily for exceptional women. As Klazina Staat argues, multiple

59. Jacobs, *Life of Thecla*, 38.

60. See further discussion in Jacobs, *Life of Thecla*, 27–28; see also Elizabeth Castelli, *Martyrdom and Memory: Early Christian Culture Making* (Columbia University Press, 2004), 150–53.

61. See Jacobs, *Life of Thecla*, 43.

late-antique biographical and hagiographical accounts of women explicitly invoke Thecla as a model. In his *Life of Macrina* (a biography of his own sister), Gregory of Nyssa (ca. 335/40–after 394 CE) recounts how their mother, Emmelia, while pregnant with Macrina, had a vision in which a man addressed her unborn child as Thecla. Gregory interprets that vision as follows: "Thecla, therefore, was Macrina's secret name. The visionary being seemed to me to proclaim this name not so much to guide the mother in the choice of the name as to foretell what the life of the virgin would be and to show, through the identical character of the name, that she would choose the same way of life as Thecla did."[62] As Staat notes, Gregory does not explain the specific ways in which Macrina follows Thecla's example, though she chooses celibacy and asceticism after the untimely death of her fiancé. Instead, Gregory assumes that his audience will be quite familiar with Thecla's story, able to recognize the similarities on their own.

The situation is similar with the anonymous Greek Life of Olympias (Bibliotheca Hagiographica Graeca 1374); this hagiographical account of Olympias (a noble woman born sometime around 360 or 370 CE who chose chastity after a brief and childless marriage) offers a short resume of the Thecla narrative before affirming, "Olympias walked in the footsteps of this saint, Thecla, in every virtue of her divinely-inspired conduct."[63] In the narrative, Olympias is presented as an ardent follower of John Chrysostom, much as Thecla was of Paul. Other hagiographical narratives about women adopt and adapt plot elements from the Acts of Thecla without mentioning her by

62. Quoted from Klazina Staat, "'Useful' Models: The Reception of the Apocryphal *Acts of Paul and Thecla* in Late-Antique Hagiographical Narratives About Female Virgins," in Nicklas et al., *Apostles Peter, Paul, John*, 155.

63. Translation slightly adapted from Staat, "'Useful' Models," 157. For a broader discussion of Thecla as a role model for Olympias, see also Tobias Nicklas, "An 'Apocryphal' Role Model Allowing for a Different Lifestyle: Olympias as a Late Antique Thecla," *ETL* 96 (2020): 503–19.

name; still others both name Thecla as model *and* adopt plot elements from her narrative.[64]

A particularly interesting example is the Latin Passion of Eugenia, in which a text of the Thecla narrative is explicitly mentioned and plays a role in the plot. The work begins when "a letter of the blessed apostle Paul and the story of the virgin Thecla came into her hands" (*pervenit ad manus eius beati Pauli Apostoli epistola et virginis Teclae historia*); "reading it secretly every day, she wept; and although she was the child of pagan parents, she began to become Christian in her heart."[65] As Staat writes, "The story itself can be read as the imitation and mirror of Thecla's story."[66]

2.3. Thecla from Armenia to Tarragona

The early Acts of Thecla was translated into Armenian (from Syriac) at the very beginning of Armenian literature. The Armenian alphabet was created by Maštoc' at the turn of the fifth century, and the Acts of Thecla was translated at some point within the next fifty years.[67] This Armenian Thecla tradition has come quite clearly into view just in the last decade, thanks to the outstanding efforts of Valentina Calzolari, who has completed a critical edition of the Armenian texts and produced numerous interpretive essays revealing the significance of Thecla within the Armenian tradition as well as the connections between the Armenian tradition and both the Byzantine and Latin Christianities from late antiquity through the Middle Ages. The resulting picture is absolutely fascinating. At moments, there are clear commonalities with

64. See, e.g., the Life of Helia and the Life of Syncletica, both discussed by Staat.

65. English translation adapted from Staat, "'Useful' Models," 168.

66. Staat, "'Useful' Models," 169.

67. Valentina Calzolari, "The Legend of St. Thecla in the Armenian Tradition: From Asia Minor to Tarragona Through Armenia," in Calzolari, *The Apocryphal Acts of the Apostles in Armenian*, Studies on Early Christian Apocrypha 18 (Peeters, 2022), 84–85.

the Thecla trajectories of the Greek tradition—with Thecla serving as *exemplum* for the depiction of women ascetics and martyrs.[68] At other times, Thecla is put to use in ways more specific to the Armenian context, as in her appearance in the *History of Armenia* by the late fourth- or fifth-century historian Faustus of Byzantium as a patroness of Nicaean orthodoxy (and Armenian cultural construction more broadly).[69]

Most surprising and remarkable, however, is the very direct connection between the Armenian and the Catalonian Thecla tradition in the fourteenth century—the year 1321, to be precise. In a truly fascinating chapter (and in more detail within her critical edition of the Armenian texts), Calzolari describes what happened.[70] As noted very briefly above, the primary cult site of Thecla is Seleucia (modern Silifke in Turkey); in the fourteenth century, the site was within the Armenian Kingdom of Cilicia (which existed as a principality from 1080 and as a kingdom from 1198 to 1375). During this time—and with direct access to the Mediterranean—Armenia developed close connections with kingdoms in the Occident, including James II's Crown of Aragon. These connections were above all political and economic, but ecclesiastical and religious matters also, of course, played a role—with Ošin, king of the Armenian Kingdom of Cilicia, favoring a union with the Roman Church. A series of James II's letters, held in Barcelona in the General Archives of the Crown of Aragon, involve the transfer of Thecla relics from Armenia to Tarragona. In a letter of 1319, addressed to Ošin, James II announces the completion of a cathedral in Tarragona, dedicated to Thecla; he notes that Thecla's body is located in the now Armenian city of Seleucia and requests that Ošin send her relics to Tarragona to be installed for veneration in the new cathedral.

68. See Calzolari, "Legend of St. Thecla," 86–87.

69. See Valentina Calzolari, "St. Thecla as a Patroness of Nicean Orthodoxy in the *History of Armenia* by Faustus of Byzantium (*Buzandaran Patmut'iwnk'*)," in Calzolari, *Apocryphal Acts of the Apostles in Armenian*, 125–47.

70. This section draws heavily from Calzolari's chapter "Legend of St. Thecla."

Here we must pause for a moment to discuss the various traditions surrounding Thecla's death. Although she is often dubbed "protomartyr" (the first female martyr, often paired with Stephen, the first male martyr [see Acts 7:54–60]), in the narrative she is not martyred at all—at least not successfully. In the Acts of Thecla she faces the death penalty twice: First she is to be burned at the stake, and later she faces the beasts in the arena; in both instances, she is miraculously rescued. The oldest version of the Acts of Thecla ends with a very brief notice of her death, presumably at Seleucia. A later adaptation of the Acts of Thecla[71] provides an expanded account of the end of Thecla's life, in which she takes up residence in a cave just outside Seleucia, where she collects a group of ascetic women, performs healing miracles, and ultimately runs afoul of local physicians. These physicians, attributing Thecla's power to heal with her sexual purity, plot to rape the saint, thereby, they imagine, destroying her ability to heal. When the attempt is made, Thecla prays to God, who allows her to escape by opening the rock wall for her to slip inside and sealing the rock behind her. The Life of Thecla has a similar version of the moment of her departure, though without the narrative concerning the wicked physicians: There we are told that "she by no means died but sank down while still living and went down into the earth, as it was pleasing to God to separate and split open for her that ground in the place." The author continues to describe how that location "is a place of healing for all people," closing the work with a veritable invitation to pilgrims.

Notably, none of these narratives offers up the possibility of relics. Multiple scholars have suggested that this amounts to an apology of sorts for the absence of relics at Thecla's main cult site.[72] Nevertheless, a relic of Thecla's body was indeed transferred from the Armenian Kingdom of Cilicia to Tarragona in 1321. How was this circumstance explained

71. This version is extant in two manuscripts; see Richard Adelbert Lipsius, *Acta Apostolorum Apocrypha* (repr., Wissenschaftliche Buchgesellschaft, 1959), 2.2:271–72.

72. See, e.g., Davis, *Cult of Thecla*, 45.

and understood? Ten folios of a fourteenth-century manuscript held at the cathedral of Barcelona (MS 105, fols. 282–292) contain a very interesting answer, in the form of a Latin Acts of Thecla (BHL 8022b–c) with an expanded ending. The manuscript's colophon indicates that the work was translated from Armenian to Latin by Nicolas de Rays (a known historical figure in the chancellery of the Kingdom of Cilicia) at the request of King Ošin. While, generally speaking, translations from Armenian into Latin are very rare, Calzolari has confirmed that the text is indeed a translation of the Armenian Acts of Paul and Thecla followed by a translation of the Armenian Prodigies of Thecla, the latter ending with a version of the attempted rape and Thecla's miraculous escape into the opening of the rock wall.

The material that follows is an account of the more recent, divinely assisted search for Thecla's body. After much prayer, an angel appears to the patriarch of Seleucia, indicating to him the location of Thecla's rock. A large procession of Christians hold a vigil at the site for three days, after which the following happens: "The place holding the virgin's limbs started to separate and the stone split in the middle, and the mount opened and, visibly in the presence of all who observed and assisted, as a very perfumed odor of consolation filled the whole region, the right hand of Thecla and her arm to the elbow emerging from the rock offered itself to those who desired it with devotion." The account continues with details of the chain of custody, so to speak, closing with the request by James II and King Ošin's donation of the relic to the new cathedral at Tarragona. There are no Armenian versions of this final section, so it cannot be conclusively demonstrated that it, like the first two sections, is a translation from Armenian to Latin; perhaps it was instead composed in Latin by the Catalans. That said, as Calzolari argues, it is entirely plausible that the text was composed by the Armenians "to offer a kind of certified guarantee of the relic itself."[73]

In either case, in the Latin Acts of Thecla from the Barcelona manuscript we see a fascinating development of the Thecla tradition—and

73. Calzolari, "Legend of St. Thecla," 101.

a new *political* use to which apocryphal narratives are put. As briefly noted above, King Ošin was a proponent of union between the Armenian Church and the Roman Church; this attitude is quite understandable in the fourteenth century, when the tiny Kingdom of Cilicia and Cyprus were quite isolated within a Muslim region. Calzolari writes:

> The text concludes with the wish that Thecla would continue to consider both Kingdoms of Aragon and Armenia worthy of her protection, she who had lived and died in the land of the Armenians, while sustaining their "passion" [*nostra passionem sustinuit*], she who had thereafter been transferred to the Kingdom of Aragon. By the invocation of a double protection bestowed on both kingdoms, Thecla endorsed the role as patroness of the alliance that united them. It is interesting to note how the stakes of diplomacy and international Armenian politics contributed to a new aspect of Thecla's legend.[74]

An intersection of politics and religion is surely nothing shocking, and there are certainly many more examples to be found of apocryphal narratives leveraged for quite specific political purposes.[75] But it is an area that has thus far received relatively little attention from scholars.

2.4. Thecla in Church Slavic

The final example in our case study of Thecla narratives is chronologically the most recent: Here we take up the Church Slavic "Life and Suffering of Saint Thecla, Protomartyr and the Equal to the Apostles," produced by Dymytrii Tuptalo at the end of the seventeenth century.[76]

74. Calzolari, "Legend of St. Thecla," 102.

75. For a broader overview see, e.g., Tobias Nicklas, "Clashing Claims to Apostolicity in Late Antique Apostle Narratives: East and West," in *Apostolicity and Mission in the Early Church*, ed. Tobias Nicklas et al., WUNT (Mohr Siebeck, forthcoming).

76. In this section, we rely on the work of Dariya Syroyid, particularly her essay "The Church Slavonic Redaction of the *Acts of Paul and Thecla* by Dymytrii Tuptalo," in

Tuptalo (1651–1709), who studied at the Kyiv Mohyla Academy in the 1660s, took it as his life's work to produce a collection of the Lives of the Saints (*Chetii Minei*) in Church Slavic—a menaion for daily reading. The work was published by the Kyiv Cave Monastery press in four volumes between 1689 and 1705 and has since been reissued many times. A leading figure within the Ruthenian Orthodox Church, Tuptalo lived in a difficult period in which the Kyiv metropolis was annexed to the Moscow patriarchate—thus his work bears in a different way the mark of the intersection of politics and religion. Dariya Syroyid writes: "Unexpectedly for Tuptalo (and for other people involved in this publishing project), the work was required to pass censorship in Moscow before printing. The censors made several remarks about the use of 'heretical' sources and demanded that corrections be made."[77] Interestingly, Tuptalo kept a diary—still extant—during his work on the project, in which he comments on his labors; he records how some of the saints "appeared to him in dream visions and 'took part' in the narration of their holy lives."[78]

At the beginning of each *Life*, he briefly notes the author or authors used as the primary sources of his own composition. For some *Lives*, this is an individual author; for others, a long list of sources might be given. In the margins, Tuptalo provides further information on the sources of individual sections of the text. Syroyid has demonstrated that Tuptalo's basic source for the plot of his Thecla narrative was a preexisting Church Slavic version of the Acts of Thecla, but at the beginning of the text, he writes only that "many Holy Fathers attest to it."[79] In the margins he refers to Basil of Seleucia, John Chrysostom, Gregory of Nyssa, Epiphanius of Salamis, John of Damascus, Cyprian, and Jerome; the majority of marginal citations, however, point to canonical sources,

Nicklas et al., *Apostles Peter, Paul, John*, 175–91.

77. Syroyid, "Church Slavonic Redaction," 178.

78. Syroyid, "Church Slavonic Redaction," 177–78.

79. Syroyid, "Church Slavonic Redaction," 179.

including Acts, the letters of Paul, the Gospels, and Psalms. Syroyid further argues that Tuptalo's aim was to eliminate any details that might prove problematic for the early modern church, particularly the censors in Moscow. As a result, "his basic approach was to attempt to correlate the apocryphal [Acts of Thecla] with the canonical Acts: that is, to bring what was 'beyond canon' within the fold."[80]

This approach is evident, as Syroyid shows, in the very first sentence of the work: "When the holy apostles Paul and Barnabas, bringing the Good News to the world, went to Iconium, they stayed in the house of Onesiphorus, who is mentioned by Paul in the epistle to Timothy, saying: 'May the Lord show mercy to the household of Onesiphorus because he often refreshed me and was not ashamed of my chains.'"[81] Here we see the same connection drawn in the Greek manuscripts surveyed above: The Thecla narrative is essentially grafted onto Paul's career as referred to in the Pastoral Epistles. But Tuptalo does not stop there: His description of Paul's (and, now, Barnabas's) activities in Iconium closes with a citation of Acts 14:1: "At Iconium, Paul and Barnabas went as usual into the Jewish synagogue. There they spoke so effectively that a great number of Jews and Greeks believed."[82] What's more, Tuptalo relates Thecla's behavior toward Paul to the behavior of Mary, sister of Martha and Lazarus, in the Gospel of Luke: "She was sitting and listening to Paul's talking three days and three nights as if forgetting herself, not thinking of food and drink, nor of bodily rest, like Mary who was sitting by Jesus' feet immersing the whole mind in God."[83]

As one might expect, gender plays a significant role Tuptalo's version of the Thecla narrative. Here, her roles as preacher, teacher, and baptizer are greatly diminished—a shift that Syroyid takes to reflect his effort to produce an acceptable "orthodox" text. Tuptalo's simplified ending

80. Syroyid, "Church Slavonic Redaction," 181.

81. Syroyid, "Church Slavonic Redaction," 182.

82. Syroyid, "Church Slavonic Redaction," 183.

83. Syroyid, "Church Slavonic Redaction," 184.

is particularly striking in this respect: Thecla asks Paul for permission to follow him, but Paul declines; thus she departs—with no mandate to teach—to Seleucia, where she fasts and prays, performing miracles and healings. Intriguingly, Tuptalo explains Paul's rejection with an otherwise unknown saying of Jerome to the effect that no one goes to war with his bride.

2.5. Conclusions

As noted above, Thecla narratives—above all the early Greek Acts of Thecla—have received far more scholarly attention than other apocryphal apostle narratives. That said, the full scope of the Thecla tradition has only recently come into view. In the preceding pages, we have offered snapshots from Greek, Arabic, Armenian, and Slavic sources; we did not touch on the robust Syriac, Coptic and Ethiopian sources, nor the full Latin tradition.[84] We have seen that the Thecla narrative offers readers and writers multiple opportunities to draw connections with canonical sources—and that readers and writers take advantage of these opportunities in multiple creative ways. Further, we have seen that gender—both Thecla's enactment of her own gender and what that might mean for readers—is a topic of continued interest in the various iterations of the Thecla narrative and in other narratives that refer to it. Above all we have seen that, like the apocryphal narratives about John, the Thecla narrative *traveled*: through translation, adaptation, and—at least once—by boat from Cilicia to Catalonia.

3. Andrew and Matthias in the City of the Cannibals

As a final example we turn, much too briefly, to a work that is exactly as exciting as its title suggests: the Acts of Andrew and Matthias in the

84. For more information see, e.g., the contributions in Ghazzal Dabiri and Flavia Ruani, eds., *Thecla and Medieval Sainthood: The Acts of Paul and Thecla in Eastern and Western Hagiography* (Cambridge University Press, 2022).

City of the Cannibals.[85] This Greek work was likely composed at the end of the fourth century CE; like so many of the apostle narratives, it is extant also in a host of other languages (Latin, Coptic, Arabic, Ethiopic, Syriac, Armenian, Georgian, Church Slavic, etc.). But this work has *not* received the sort of attention from scholars that the Acts of Thecla has; it is not generally included in sourcebooks of Christian apocrypha and is rarely the topic of articles and essays, let alone monographs. It is possible that readers of this book have never even heard of such a work; if that describes you, you may be surprised to learn that this was an *enormously popular* work throughout antiquity and the Middle Ages.

The Greek narrative begins (ch. 1) with the apostles casting lots to divide up the world for their missionary activities. The apostle Matthias—who, if we attach this narrative to the story world of the canonical Acts, has just drawn the lot to replace Judas as the twelfth apostle (see Acts 1:15–26)—now has the unbelievably bad luck of being allotted to the "region of the cannibals" (εἰς τὴν χώραν τῶν ἀνθρωποφάγων). And lest the reader imagine that the city can't be as bad as it sounds—the narrator describes it as follows: "The people of that city neither ate bread nor drank wine, but were eating the flesh of humans and drinking their blood. Therefore, every person who enters their city—they seize them, pluck out their eyes, and after taking away their eyes they force them to drink a potion prepared with sorcery and magic, and when they drink the potion their heart is changed and their mind is deranged [ἠλλοιοῦτο αὐτοῦ ἡ καρδία καὶ ὁ νοῦς αὐτοῦ μετηλλάσσετο]." Matthias dutifully travels to the city and, as soon as he arrives at the gates, is captured and treated exactly as the narrator has warned: His eyes are plucked out and he is given the potion to drink, but by divine intervention it has no effect (ch. 2). Matthias prays to Jesus, who hears

85. See "e-Clavis Acts of Andrew and Matthias," North American Society for the Study of Christian Apocryphal Literature, accessed February 1, 2025, https://www.nasscal.com/e-clavis-christian-apocrypha/acts-of-andrew-and-matthias/. An easily available edition of the Greek (plus English translation) is offered by Dennis R. MacDonald, *The Acts of Andrew and the Acts of Andrew and Matthias in the City of the Cannibals*, SBLTT 33 (Scholars Press, 1990), 63–169.

his prayer, restores his sight and tells him that he is sending Andrew to rescue him, but he must wait twenty-seven days (ch. 3). After twenty-seven days, Jesus appears to Andrew in Achaea, telling him to rescue Matthias; Andrew and his disciples thus go down to the sea and board a boat, not knowing that the captain is Jesus in disguise and the shipmates two angels. When his disciples become seasick, Andrew prays that they will fall asleep; they do, leaving the disguised Jesus and Andrew alone to talk (chs. 4–9). The disguised Jesus then asks Andrew questions about Jesus—specifically why the Jews did not believe in Jesus, suggesting that they perhaps had not witnessed the miracles he performed; Andrew counters the notion, quickly rehearsing the many miracles (familiar from the canonical Gospels) that Jesus performed before them; the disguised Jesus then suggests that, while the people witnessed these public miracles, the high priests may not have (ch. 10).

At this point, Andrew describes at length a "secret" (ἐν τῷ κρυπτῷ) miracle (chs. 11–16) that Jesus performed before the high priest. The miracle—presented essentially as a flashback to Andrew's experiences of the living Jesus—takes place inside a temple of the gentiles, which is decorated with two statues of sphinxes. Jesus commands one sphinx to step down from its pedestal and speak in refutation of the chief priests, who do not believe in him. The sphinx immediately obliges, delivering a speech that identifies Jesus as the God who created the world, the one who spoke with Abraham. The chief priests are not convinced: They attribute the statue's speech to magic; more specifically, they doubt that the notion that Jesus could have spoken with Abraham, who died long before he was born.[86] In response, Jesus sends the sphinx to the tomb of the patriarchs to call out Abraham and two others (presumably Isaac and Jacob); these three return with the sphinx to refute the chief priests. Jesus then dismisses the patriarchs to their tomb and the sphinx to his pedestal. The chief priests, of course, still refuse to believe, and the flashback ends. This section of the narrative closes with Andrew

86. The motif is possibly influenced by John 8:48–59.

falling asleep, and Jesus commanding his angels to carry Andrew and his disciples to the gates of the city of the cannibals.

When Andrew awakens and finds himself and his disciples at the gates of the city, he realizes that the captain was Jesus in disguise; he proceeds into the city, quickly dispatches the prison guards, and frees Matthias and the other prisoners; all but Andrew are then miraculously transported by cloud to a mountain where Peter is teaching (chs. 17–21). Meanwhile, the cannibals discover the empty prison, eventually finding and capturing Andrew; they punish him for destroying their food supply by dragging him naked around the city for three days; Andrew calls out for Jesus in desperation, and Jesus comforts him (chs. 22–28). Finally, Jesus heals Andrew, and Andrew handles the cannibals: He causes an alabaster statue to spew forth poisonous water, also praying to Jesus and the archangel Michael to surround the city with a wall of fire; the cannibals finally beg for mercy and express belief in Jesus; Andrew resurrects all but the most wicked cannibals, baptizes them, and builds a church; at Jesus's insistence, Andrew stays an additional seven days in the city to preach; finally, he takes his leave as the (former) cannibals pray to Jesus (chs. 29–33).

This is clearly an exciting narrative—one might even call it epic. In fact, Dennis R. MacDonald—one of very few contemporary scholars who have dedicated sustained attention to the work—has argued that it represents part of an extended imitation and transformation of Homeric themes.[87] While MacDonald's thesis in its strongest form is not entirely convincing, potions that derange and bodies dragged around cities are certainly plot elements that ring Homeric bells. In any case, we will have occasion to return to the topic of epic poems below.

3.1. Quoting from the Canon in the City of the Cannibals

Like the Johannine and Thecla traditions discussed above, the Acts of Andrew and Matthias in the City of the Cannibals has many points of

87. Dennis R. MacDonald, *Christianizing Homer: The Odyssey, Plato and the Acts of Andrews* (Oxford University Press, 1994).

contact with the canonical New Testament. Here we will highlight a phenomenon that is rather different from what we have observed thus far. The episode in which Andrew is dragged around the city of the cannibals is notable for a number of reasons (beyond the potential point of comparison with the treatment of Hector's body in the *Iliad*); in this scene of near-martyrdom, the depiction of the apostle's experience and expression differs substantially from typical depictions of early Christian suffering. In typical martyr accounts, the martyr's pain and suffering is *not* the focus; to the contrary, they are often described as miraculously insensate.[88] This is not the case in the Acts of Andrew and Matthias; as Andrew is dragged by the neck around the city for the third day in a row, with chunks of his flesh and hair sticking to the ground, he cries out in pain and weeps, begging Jesus to end his suffering: "Lord Jesus Christ, these tortures are enough; for I am exhausted [ἐξητόνησα γάρ]."[89]

Even more interesting, however, is how Andrew attempts to persuade Jesus to help him. First, Andrew compares his own suffering to Jesus's suffering on the cross, asking Jesus to "recall" (μνήσθητι) that he had spent just three hours on the cross when he "grew faint" (or "discouraged," ὠλιγοψυχήσας) and called out "My God, my God, why have you forsaken me" (Andrew quoting here from Jesus's last words in the Gospel of Mark and Gospel of Matthew). Further, the apostle accuses Jesus of not keeping his word: "Where are your words, Lord, which you spoke to us to strengthen us when we walked with you, saying to us: 'You will not lose one hair from your heads.' Well, look, Lord, and see that my flesh and the hairs of my head are stuck to the ground!" Here Andrew quotes a saying of Jesus from Luke 21:18, tossing it back in moment of despair. Jesus responds (in the form of a voice from heaven), quoting yet another synoptic saying: "Our Andrew, heaven and earth will pass away, but my words will never pass away" (Mark 13:21 and par.). The voice then directs Andrew to look again to see what has happened to his fallen

88. See L. Stephanie Cobb, *Divine Deliverance: Pain and Painlessness in Early Christian Martyr Texts* (University of California Press, 2016), passim.

89. MacDonald, *Acts of Andrew*, 28.

flesh and hair; Andrew sees that it has sprouted large fruit-bearing trees. Andrew then confirms (in an inversion of his quotation of Jesus's words from the cross): "I know then, Lord, that you have not forsaken me."

The result of the episode, then, is an affirmation of the veracity of a statement ("not a hair of your head will perish") made in a canonical text (at Luke 21:18), even though the plot of the narrative (and, for that matter, many other early Christian narratives in which believers suffer) might be understood to contradict it. Moreover, with Andrew's last statement in this scene, the Acts of Andrew and Matthias offers a sense of closure to an otherwise rather difficult element of the canonical crucifixion scenes, that is, Jesus's wretched query: "Why have you forsaken me?" This work clearly states the answer that is, at best, implicit in the canonical works: "You have not forsaken me."

This episode is just one example; references to the canonical Gospels occur throughout the work. This is particularly notable because Acts of Andrew and Matthias does not have obvious ties to the canonical Gospels in the way that the Johannine material does (inasmuch as John is understood to be the beloved disciple, both a character within and the author of the Gospel of John) or the Thecla narrative does (inasmuch as the presence of Paul ties the work both to the canonical Acts and the letters attributed to Paul, as does the setting of the narrative in cities well traversed in canonical sources). Andrew and Matthias are at best minor characters in the canonical Gospels and Acts; neither does the setting of the narrative in the city of the cannibals offer much opportunity for canonical tie-ins. Nevertheless, the author of this work was clearly deeply invested in interweaving his narrative with canonical works, particularly the Gospels. He carries out the task primarily through direct discourse, having his hero, Andrew, refer to things that Jesus says and does in the canonical Gospels. Conspicuously, the work's greatest addition to the canonical accounts—his recounting of the miracles involving the sphinx performed in secret before the high priests—is paired with a highly canonical list of the miracles Jesus publicly performed, and, perhaps as an additional assurance of reliability, the secret miracle is reported in direct discourse by Andrew to Jesus himself.

3.2. Andrew and Matthias, from One End of the Earth to the Other

While the location of the "city of the cannibals" is not explicitly identified in the Acts of Andrew and Matthias, there is little doubt that what is imagined is the northeastern edge of the known world, the region inhabited by Scythians. While there is variation in the details, there is broad agreement in our Greek and Roman sources about what—and who—was at the edges of the known landmasses: At the western edge was the Iberian Peninsula, terminating at the Pillars of Hercules; at the eastern edge was India; at the southern edge was Ethiopia; and at the northern edge, Britain and Ireland to the West, Scythia to the East.[90] This commonplace knowledge is repeated in multiple ancient works. The following passage from first-century geographer Strabo is a good illustrative example:

> Within the area of small countries it involves no very great discrepancy if a given place be situated more towards the north, or more towards the south; but when the area is that of the whole round of the inhabited world [τῆς οἰκουμένης] the north extends to the remote confines of Scythia and Celtica, and the south to the remote confines of Ethiopia, and the difference between these two extremes is very great. The same thing holds true also as regards a man's living in India or Iberia; the one country is in the far east, the other in the far west; indeed, they are, in a sense, the antipodes of each other, as we know. (Strabo, *Geogr.* 1.1.13; trans. Jones, LCL)

The inhabitants of the northern edge of the *oikoumenē* in particular were regularly identified as either the very worst or very best of humanity.

90. See Janet E. Spittler, "Christianity at the Edges: Representations of the Ends of the Earth in the Apocryphal Acts of the Apostles," in *The Rise and Expansion of Christianity in the First Three Centuries CE*, ed. Clare Rothschild and Jens Schröter, WUNT 301 (Mohr Siebeck, 2013), 353–77.

Strabo, here quoting the historian Ephorus, refers to these widely varying accounts concerning the Scythians in the far northeast: "Previous writers, Ephorus says, only tell about the savagery of the Scythians . . . but he, for his part, says that one must do the opposite of this, and depict exemplary models of humanity. Thus he resolves to write about those Scythians, who are fed on the milk of horses, and who surpass all men in justice."[91] Strabo himself adopts this notion of the "noble savage" in his descriptions of the Scythians and their society, with which his own Greco-Roman society suffers by comparison.

For those taking the negative view, Scythians were quite simply bloodthirsty cannibals. This view is repeated again and again. Pliny writes: "We have pointed out that some Scythian tribes, and in fact a good many, feed on human bodies."[92] Aulus Gellius, the second-century Roman author, likewise writes: "The most remote of the Scythians, who pass their life in the far north, eat human flesh and subsist on the nourishment of that food, and are called ἀνθρωποφάγοι, or cannibals."[93] Other reports are more graphic: "The so-called man-eaters of the Scythians drink from human skulls and fashion the skin of their enemies' heads into hand towels. Having flayed the rest of the body with their fingernails, they put [the skin] on their horses."[94] Similar reports circulated about the inhabitants of what was understood as the northwest edge of the inhabited earth. Strabo writes:

> Besides some small islands round about Britain, there is also a large island, Ierne (Ireland), which stretches parallel to Britain on the north, its breadth being greater than its length. Concerning this island I have nothing certain to tell, except that

91. Strabo, *Geogr.* 7.3.9; quoted from James S. Romm, *The Edges of the Earth in Ancient Thought* (Princeton University Press, 1992), 46.

92. Pliny, *Nat.* 7.9 (trans. Rackham, LCL).

93. Aulus Gellius, *Noct. att.* 9.4.6 (trans. Rolfe, LCL).

94. Paradoxographus Vaticanus, 47.

> its inhabitants are more savage than the Britons, since they are man-eaters as well as heavy eaters, and since, further, they count it an honourable thing, when their fathers die, to devour them, and openly to have intercourse, not only with the other women, but also with their mothers and sisters; but I am saying this only with the understanding that I have no trustworthy witnesses for it; and yet, as for the matter of man-eating, that is said to be a custom of the Scythians also.[95]

Here it is important to note both the similarities and differences between the fabulous reports of the inhabitants of the far north in early Greek sources such as Herodotus and Ctesias and the reports of first-century Greco-Roman authors such as Strabo and Pliny. To be sure, all these authors delighted their readers with descriptions of the amazing, sometimes shocking, characteristics and behaviors of the people who lived in these regions. But when we lump Herodotus's reports of the happy Hyperboreans and Ctesias's one-eyed griffin-fighters with later accounts of the shocking behavior of the inhabitants of Scythia and the British Isles as described by Strabo, we risk suggesting that the Scythians and the Irish were understood by readers in the first centuries CE as quasi-mythical populations. This was not at all the case. To the contrary, as is clear particularly in the last quotation of Strabo above, these were very real people who may (or may not, as Strabo emphasizes with respect to the Irish) have practiced cannibalism. Anyone traveling to the northern edge of the inhabited world might expect to encounter such behavior, and so it is really no surprise that in imaging the adventures of the apostles sent out in this direction, one early Christian author composed a narrative set in the city of the cannibals.

The Acts of Andrew and Matthias, then, represents in narrative form the fulfillment of what the risen Jesus tells his disciples when they are gathered in Jerusalem: that they will be his witnesses (μάρτυρες) not

95. Strabo, *Geogr.* 4.5.4 (trans. Jones, LCL).

just in Jerusalem and all of Judea and Samaria but even to the "end of the earth" (ἕως ἐσχάτου τῆς γῆς, Acts 1:8). Andrew and Matthias reach this goal, find it exactly as horrifying as the worst reports suggest, but convert the entire population to Christianity nonetheless. In a fascinating coincidence, the narrative itself would reach and conquer, so to speak, the northwestern end of the earth, that is, Britain.

In addition to Syriac, Armenian, Georgian, Coptic, Arabic, Ethiopic, and Church Slavic, the Acts of Andrew and Matthias was translated, via Latin, into Old English—notably in the form of an epic poem, generally referred to as Andreas. It is difficult to overstate the importance of Andreas in the history of English literature, but some numbers might help put it in perspective: Extant poetry in Old English amounts to some thirty thousand lines of verse; *Beowulf*, at 3,182 lines, accounts for a full 10 percent of the total; Andreas, in turn, has 1,722 lines. In other words, our "obscure" narrative—of Matthias with his eyes gouged out, Andrew dragged around the city, and a population of cannibals ultimately brought to Christian belief—accounts for upward of 5 percent of the *entirety* of extant Old English poetry. It is no wonder, then, that the vast majority of scholarship touching on the Greek Acts of Andrew and Matthias has been published by medievalists working in English departments.

From this scholarship, we learn that Andreas, extant in the famous Vercelli Book, was likely composed in the late ninth century for the court of Alfred in Winchester. Its most recent editors, Richard North and Michael D. J. Bintley, argue for a more specific scenario: "Other theories may do better, but ours is that priest adventurer Æthelstan, some time after returning from the shrines of St Bartholomew in Macedonia and St Thomas in Asia Minor, and very approximately in 890, composed *Andreas* for the court in Winchester, and that he left a copy in Ramsbury when he died there as bishop of Wiltshire in 927."[96] Regardless of whether this scenario is accurate (and we are not well

96. Richard North and Michael D. J. Bintley, *Andreas: An Edition* (Liverpool University Press, 2016), 115.

equipped to judge), its plausibility adds to our developing image of how apocryphal apostle narratives traveled from one location (and language) to another.

The shift in genre from prose to epic poem is a particularly interesting development. Whereas, as noted above, MacDonald's theory of Homeric imitation in the Greek narrative has been met with substantial skepticism, medievalists are broadly agreed that Andreas imitates *Beowulf*, whether in a ham-fisted way (as earlier generations of scholars suggested) or in a sophisticated play, in which *Beowulf*'s apologetic attitude toward heroes and heathens is mocked (as North and Bintley suggest).[97] In either case, it is clear that the basic plot of Andrew and Matthias's story held real appeal to a poet familiar with monsters who eat people.

We'll close this section by quoting a section of the poem (in modern English translation by North and Bintley) to give readers a flavor for its style; here, then, is the Old English version of Andrew's lament to Jesus, as he is dragged around the city:

> Then in dejection did he call upon God,
> hard man from shackles, with holy voice;
> wept on exhausted and uttered these words:
> "Never did I undergo at Lord's will
> under heaven's vault any harder condition
> anywhere I had to preach the Gospel!
> My limbs are dislocated, body sorely broken,
> bone-house blood-stained; the wounds well up,
> gory sinew-gashes. See, O Keeper of Victory,
> Healing Lord, how dejected You were
> with the Jews in the space of one day,
> when You, from the gallows, as Living God,
> Lord of Old Labours, called to the Father,

97. North and Bintley, *Andreas: An Edition*, 66.

the Glory of Kings, and spoke thus:
'Father of Angels, I will ask You this,
why forsake me, Author of light and the Life?'
And now it is three days I have had to endure
torments grim as death! God of Hosts,
I beg You for leave to give up my spirit
into Your Own hand, Feast-Giver of Souls.
You promised this by Your sacred word
when You started to strengthen us twelve,
that no warfare of maniacs would harm us,
nor any body-part be suddenly torn away,
nor sinew or bone have to lie on the path,
nor any lock from the head be lost,
if we would just follow Your teaching.
Now sinews are torn, my blood has dripped out,
lying over land my locks have been scattered,
my hair on the ground. Parting from life for me
is preferable by far to this care of living!"[98]

Conclusions

What we have discussed here is just a narrow slice of the world of apocryphal apostle narratives. But even this brief encounter with a handful of works is revealing. When we broaden our perspective to take in works beyond the oldest forms of these traditions, when we open the boundaries between apocryphal acts and hagiography, and when we attend to media beyond the written word, we discover that many of these narratives, which are often perceived as marginal today, were in fact central in the history of Christianity. Their influence can hardly be overestimated, as successive generations of authors and editors turned to these

98. *Andreas*, lines 1398–1428 (trans. North and Bintley, *Andreas: An Edition*, 193–94).

stories to develop and explain theological ideas, to work through social issues, to understand their own place in the world, and to tell and enjoy an entertaining story. Fascinating scholarship, which takes up the long lives of these stories across multiple geographies, languages, and cultures, is currently underway—but the sheer bulk of the material means that scholars (and graduate students) will have plenty to work with for generations to come.

CHAPTER 3

This World and Other Worlds

Is this world chaos or cosmos? If it is cosmos—that is, if it is ordered—to what extent is the underlying order recognizable and navigable?[1] How is it possible to lead a good, even happy, life within it? And how does the part of the world we live in relate to parts we do not know? What strange peoples, dangerous monsters, paradisiacal places, and unimaginable treasures are hidden in the unknown parts of the world, and how can we explore them? Apocryphal and parabiblical traditions engage in discourses about the world we live in, its limits, and what might be found beyond. In some cases, the result is entertaining; indeed, as we shall see, some works have traces of subversive humor. Often, however, these traditions raise extremely serious questions. In efforts to confront various versions of the problem of theodicy—whether this world is confronted with a just God or perhaps

1. This is one of the fundamental questions behind biblical wisdom literature. In the course of this chapter, as in biblical literature, we will present a juxtaposition of texts in which fundamental principles of order are given and texts in which they are called into question again. The more difficult it is to recognize consistent principles of order in the given world that guarantee a successful life, the more necessary it becomes to expand the existing world with other worlds. The other alternative is to give up the idea that this world (and therefore the God who created it) is ultimately good and just.

a malevolent or even ignorant demiurge—some narratives leave this world and tell of journeys to spheres beyond, which can be reached through raptures, through the opening of gates to other worlds,[2] or through dreams and new levels of consciousness. In many cases, what is described in the afterlife has a direct impact on this world, which can be mirrored, distorted, or deconstructed in its logic. The strange, other spaces described can be dystopias, utopias, and heterotopias; as such, they offer new ways of perceiving this world with its challenges and dangers, new ways of redefining the present.[3] In some cases, they provide reason for confidence in times perceived as precarious or crisis-ridden; in other cases, they simply offer space for one's own fantasy

---

2. A typical example of this can be found in the Apocalypse of John, where, according to Rev 4:1, the seer enters the heavenly throne room through an open door.

3. Here we discuss spaces as places that are given multidimensionality through elements of communication. In this way, a place can become a space through narratives, rituals, memories, and the interaction of things that are interpreted in relation to it. What constitutes the Temple Mount in Jerusalem cannot be understood if we simply define it geometrically in terms of its dimensions as a place like others. Only the interpretations associated with it, some of which are in conflict with each other and generated by the most diverse dimensions of communication, make it the highly effective space that it is. In the background of the use of the term *heterotopia* is, broadly speaking, the definition by Michel Foucault, "Andere Räume" [1967], in *Aisthesis. Wahrnehmung heute oder Perspektiven einer anderen Ästhetik. Essais*, ed. Karlheinz Barck (Suhrkamp, 1993), 39. What is meant are "real places, effective places that are drawn into the institution of a society, counter-placements or abutments, so to speak, actually realized utopias, in which the real places within culture are simultaneously represented, contested, and turned, places outside of all places, so to speak, even though they can actually be located." Unlike Foucault, however, we consider the underlying distinction between real places or places that can actually be located and nonreal places to be artificial. Some of the following examples prove this. Today, "India" would surely be understood as a real, locatable place, but the "India" of Prester John is anything but such a place, instead functioning excellently as a heterotopia. We have sought to show the extent to which apocalyptic writings can have the function of providing a "redefinition of the present" by means of the interpretation of 2 Thessalonians. On this, see Tobias Nicklas, *Der zweite Thessalonicherbrief*, KEK 10/2 (Vandenhoeck & Ruprecht, 2019), 63–66.

and imagination.[4] The following chapter traces two types of narrative: In the first, the protagonists remain in this world; in the second, they enter otherworldly realms such as heaven and hell. As we will see, however, the difference between the two types of narration is less than the contemporary reader might imagine.

1. The Ends of the Earth as Utopia and Dystopia

One of the most important self-designations of the followers of Christ in the canonical Acts of the Apostles is as "the way" (or also the "new way"; see Acts 9:2; 19:9, 23; 22:4; cf. 18:25).[5] It is fair to say that Acts paints a picture of a movement carried by the Spirit of God, whose work extends to the ends of the earth (see Acts 1:8). Although something like a center of the then known world, Rome,[6] is reached at the end of Acts, the book's rather open conclusion indicates that the ultimate goals have not yet been reached, and that the dynamics of this journey have by no means come to an end. As we have seen in the previous chapter on apocryphal apostle narratives,[7] many of these works inscribe themselves into these dynamics, narrating how the apostles, their disciples, and other figures continue to win new parts of the world for Christ. The key point for the present chapter is that truly liminal spaces are also traversed. From these borders and ends of the earth, impulses emanate that change the (self-)understanding of the places understood as at the center.[8]

4. The various options are by no means mutually exclusive.

5. See also the comparable self-designation as the "way of righteousness," as we find it in 2 Peter and the Apocalypse of Peter.

6. Of course, this is written from a very Mediterranean-centered point of view.

7. See ch. 2.

8. If the texts discussed below were largely written in Europe or the Mediterranean region, this is because research into apocrypha has been limited primarily to these places; overcoming this is a task for the coming generation of research into apocrypha or (even better) parabiblical traditions. Fundamental information on the problem of the extent to which nineteenth-century Europe-centrism represents an anachronism

The Greek Passion of Bartholomew (CANT 259),[9] which can probably be dated to the sixth century at the earliest, presents India as a locale with very little geographical or cultural specificity that might differentiate it from places more familiar to the Greek audience; this work, like many other narratives, is primarily concerned with portraying the apostle (as the representative of Christ) as the victor over demonic powers that rule the land. The work also raises the question of how it is possible that healings may also have taken place in the pagan cults.[10] The absence of geographical knowledge regarding India is indicated by a tradition, associated with the work, that the body of the apostle was washed from India to Lipari, off the north shore of Sicily, where his relics were actually venerated from the year 580, before being transferred to Benevento in 838.[11]

Similarly, the narrated "India" of the Acts of Thomas is not fundamentally different from the locations described in other apocryphal apostle narratives; however, the liminal character of Thomas's journey is hinted at in his encounters with "exotic" animals, including the Indian

---

for the understanding of earlier epochs can be found in Dorothea Weltecke, *Die drei Ringe: Warum die Religionen erst im Mittelalter entstanden sind* (Beck, 2024), 21–41.

9. To our knowledge, the text is not yet available in a modern critical edition; an introduction and translation of it, which will appear in Tobias Nicklas, *Zwischen apokryph und hagiographisch: Spätantike Apostelerzählungen in ihrer Zeit*, Tria Corda Lectures (Mohr Siebeck, forthcoming), is therefore based on the edition by Maximilian Bonnet, "Passio Sancti Bartholomaei apostoli," in *Acta apostolorum apocrypha*, ed. Richard Lipsius and Maximilian Bonnet (repr., Olms, 1959), 2.1:128–50.

10. The text's answer is quite original: powerful beings do indeed live in the images of the gods of the pagan cults; however, they are not deities but demons. On behalf of their ruler, the devil, they are initially able to make people ill. When they then withdraw from them as a result of sacrifices at a temple of the gods, this has the effect of a cure, but the result is fatal. Those healed begin to worship the demonic powers like gods and, possibly physically healed, fall even more under their spell mentally.

11. The complex legendary narrative of the invasion of Lipari and the relocation of the relics to Benevento is also recorded in Jacobus de Voragine's *Legenda Aurea* 123. See de Voragine, *Legenda Aurea*, 1614–17.

wild ass and a serpent of enormous size.[12] The presence of the latter perhaps points toward the influence of Satan in this far-flung edge of the world (e.g., §§30–38). The connection between Thomas and India seems to have remained in the cultural memory[13] of Latin Europe well into the Middle Ages. From the twelfth century onward, due to the introduction of a new legend involving India, it gained significance that should not be underestimated, especially during the Crusades.[14]

Narratives about Prester John, a legendary ruler from India, are not usually found within modern collections of Christian apocrypha. The anonymous writing De adventu patriarchae Indorum ad urbem sub Calisto Papa IIo probably dates back to the first half of the twelfth century.[15] This work reports that in the fourth year of the reign of Pope Calixtus II (1119–1124), that is, in 1122 or 1123, there arrived in Rome a "patriarch of the Indians," specifically from the part of India known as the most distant edge of the earth (§5). His coming (as the first representative of his country in living memory) is already understood as a miracle (§5). This person is referred to as "Patriarch John" (5, 11), who, after his election as patriarch of India, first traveled to Byzantium to receive confirmation of his election and the corresponding insignia (§8). There he learned from Roman legates at the court of Constantinople that Rome was the real head of the world (§12).[16] Upon hearing this information, he set off for Rome. We are then told how he presents his country to Pope Calixtus and a select circle of listeners (§18 and following). His

12. On animals in the Acts of Thomas, see Janet E. Spittler, *Animals in the Apocryphal Acts of the Apostles: The Wild Kingdom of Early Christian Literature*, WUNT 2/247 (Mohr Siebeck, 2008), 190–223. On representations of the ends of the earth in ancient literature, see Spittler, "Christianity at the Edges."

13. We use this term according to the use of Assmann, *Das kulturelle Gedächtnis*.

14. The sources referred to below are summarized in Keagan Brewer, *Prester John: The Legend and Its Sources*, Crusade Texts in Translation 27 (Routledge, 2015). The dating of the sources mentioned below is based on this volume.

15. Latin text according to Brewer, *Prester John*, 30–33, first edited by Friedrich Zarncke, *Der Priester Johannes: Zwei Teile in einem Band* (repr., Olms, 1980), 837–43.

16. Of course, this is written from a clearly Western perspective.

description of the capital, Hulna, which may remind today's readers of a mixture of the heavenly Jerusalem, paradise, and Eldorado, shows that Prester John actually comes from a different, fantastic world: It takes four days to cross the city from one side to the other, and its walls are so wide that two carriages can fit side by side on them (§§20–21). One of the rivers of paradise, the Physon (or "Pison"; Gen 2:10–12), runs through the center of the city, carrying gold and jewels and thus helping the land to achieve indescribable wealth (§23). The city can be inhabited only by believing Christians—anyone else who tries to do so will die within a short time (§§24–25).

The real miracle, however, is to be found near the city on a high mountain, surrounded by a deep lake, on the summit of which is the mother church of St. Thomas the apostle (§§26–28). According to the text, this church was inaccessible all year round; only once a year did the patriarch celebrate the Eucharist there. Eight days before and eight days after the feast of St. Thomas the apostle, the water of the lake miraculously disappears. During this period, people come from great distances to be miraculously healed by the apostle of their various illnesses (§29). The narrative describes a kind of holy of holies in the innermost part of the church:

> In fact, within the holy of holies of this aforesaid church is a *ciborium* of wonderful workmanship, interwoven with gold and silver and decorated with various most precious stones of the sort which the river of paradise named the Physon deposits there. Within this *ciborium* is a most precious silver shell hanging from silver chains, as that history of the apostle tells; but although it is placed in valuable metal, the greater treasure is within it. Inside it, the holy body of the apostle is preserved to this day whole and unharmed as though on the day of its burial. The body is seen standing erect above the shell as though living, and a golden lamp full of balsam hangs by ropes of silver in front of it. (§§30–33)[17]

17. Translation by Brewer, *Prester John*, 36.

Whoever is anointed with the balm of the golden lamp receives immediate and perfect healing. But that is not all. During the celebration of the Eucharist, the apostle's body is placed on the apostle's throne. The patriarch presents the apostle with the Eucharist on a golden pan; Thomas then reaches out like a living person, holds it in his right hand, and offers it to the faithful. Sinners, however, are denied it: They must decide to repent immediately or die.

This narrative, to which the pope and other audiences react with great astonishment and praise of God (§51), is only vaguely connected to the early Acts of Thomas (though a version of that work is undoubtedly what is meant by "the history of the apostle").[18] It clearly presupposes the veneration of the miracle-working relics of Thomas and his connection with India. In its ideas about the miraculous powers of the apostle's relics, this narrative goes to the outermost limits of what is believable—appropriate for its setting at the outermost limits of the inhabited world.[19] The space described by Prester John is a utopia located at an almost unimaginable distance from Rome, in which decisive aspects of what human and ecclesiastical hopes are directed toward have already been realized: immeasurable prosperity, direct access to the sacred, and the concomitant healing of body and spirit. Added to this is the possibility of keeping sinners and dissenters in check, an aspect that is expressed on several levels. This world is a perfect world (at least from the perspective of those who formulate it) because in it the problem of "sin," injustice, and religious dissent resolves itself, both for those who want to inhabit the city and for those who receive the Eucharist through the apostle. Reliable punitive miracles make this world just in a verifiable way. At the same time, however, there is no definition as to who should be considered a sinner.

18. See Brewer, *Prester John*, 35n2.

19. On the one hand, the credibility of certain forms of miracles is culturally and contextually determined; however, this text also shows that the place in which they are located may play an additional role. For fundamental observations of this kind, see the contributions in Tobias Nicklas and Janet E. Spittler, eds., *Credible, Incredible. The Miraculous in the Ancient Mediterranean*, WUNT 321 (Mohr Siebeck, 2013).

What is interesting about this text, however, is not only the imaginative description of the wonders of India but also the depiction of events in Rome, where this narrative—incredible on so many levels—is apparently adopted without any sign of doubt: "When the patriarch of the Indians had finished reporting such things in the Lateran court, Pope Calixtus II and the rest of the Roman assembly calmly glorified Christ, with their hands raised to heaven, because so excellent and great a miracle did not cease to be performed through his holiness the apostle every year, with the father and the holy spirit living forever and ever. Amen" (§51). Two other sources from around the same time shift this perspective in two different directions. The first is the *Letter to Count Thomas*, also from the first half/mid-twelfth century, in which Odo of Saint-Remi (Rheims) claims to have been[20] a witness to the Indian patriarch's visit to Rome and mentions, much more succinctly than the *Adventus*, his reports of miracles associated with the relics of Thomas. According to Odo's letter, however, these reports were initially rejected by the pope, and he threatened the "archbishop of India" (i.e., Prester John, who is not named) with excommunication if he lied (§21). Only when the archbishop swears an oath on the gospel does the pope believe him (§22–23). Odo's letter thus plays with the element of doubt in his narrative,[21] describing both its presence and how it is ultimately overcome.

The second—and certainly most influential—Prester John source is a (pseudepigraphical) letter from Prester John to the Roman *gubernator* Manuel (i.e., the Byzantine emperor Manuel), which appears around a generation later.[22] In this incredibly successful letter, which has survived in various forms, the connection between India and Thomas

20. Edition: Zarncke, *Priester Johannes 1*, 845–46; Latin text and English translation also in Brewer, *Prester John*, 39–42.

21. The account in Otto von Freising, *De Duabus Civitatibus* 7.33, from 1157, is once again much more sober—without mentioning the apostle's miracles (edition: MGH. SS.RGUS 45, 363–67; Latin original and English translation in Brewer, *Prester John*, 43–45).

22. We assume the Latin text given in Brewer, *Prester John*, 46–66; there it is also indicated which passage is to be assigned to which interpolation.

largely recedes,[23] but the descriptions of the country and its animals—from fantasy creatures such as the *methagallinarii* and *cametheternis*, to tigers, jackals, and hyenas, to well-known mythical creatures such as the phoenix, centaurs, fauns, and dog-headed humans—exceed all boundaries. It is not possible to present this text, which has little to do with biblical motifs, in more detail here, but it is likely the reason why the legend of Prester John and his land of virtually unlimited possibilities became a *lieux de mémoire* (that is, a crystallization point of social memory),[24] which was able to unfold its power once again during the time of the Fifth Crusade (1217–1221). Keagan Brewer goes so far as to link the failure of the Fifth Crusade to the crusaders' belief in support from Prester John:

> Belief in Prester John here had an important impact on world history, being partly responsible for the failure of the crusade as a whole. Whilst the Fifth Crusaders were in northern Egypt after having made a few conquests there, news reached them of the first conquests of Chingis Khan in Asia, which called to mind Prester John. Around the same time, the leaders of the Fifth Crusade discovered a book of prophecies in Egypt that said that a king from the west and a king from the east would meet in Jerusalem and destroy Islam forever. This they took to mean that Prester John was coming from the east to help them win the crusade. . . . The leaders of the crusade waited some six months for Prester John to arrive, and wrote letters to the

23. A brief note that the body of St. Thomas the apostle rests in outer India can be found in §12. For detailed information on the state of transmission, see Brewer, *Prester John*, 299–320. This extremely successful text has survived (in various forms) in more than 200 manuscripts in Latin; in addition, there is evidence of medieval translations into at least eighteen languages.

24. This term also goes back to Pierre Nora; Etienne François, "Pierre Nora und die 'lieux de mémoire,'" in *Erinnerungsorte Frankreichs*, ed. Pierre Nora (Beck, 2005), 7–14, provides a good, brief introduction. On this text, see Istvan Bejczy, *La Lettre du Prêtre Jean: Une Utopie Médiévale* (Imago, 2001).

> major political figures of the time in Europe, including Pope Honorius III, informing them that Prester John was on his way. But when nothing eventuated, the crusaders made their offensive southwards toward Cairo in July 1221, and were thoroughly repulsed by the Muslims. The delay in waiting for Prester John was pivotal.[25]

In other words, the parabiblical tradition around Prester John, at least in part due to its relationship to biblical writings and to the apostle Thomas in the Acts of Thomas, indicates how strongly our ideas of the world are influenced by our fantasies about its edges; the Prester John legend and its reception in the thirteenth century lays plain the tremendous attraction utopias can have. Margins become central because we project our wishes and hopes onto them. They become particularly powerful (and perhaps even dangerous) when we no longer perceive projections as such and are no longer able to differentiate between wishes and reality.

However, dystopian elements can also be present at the edges of the earth. This can already be seen to some extent in the lists of the animal species of India contained in the letter of Prester John, but certainly also in the number of texts that connect the human inhabitants of the edges of the earth with danger, interpreting them as ciphers for demonic powers.[26] One such passage, which seems to play with sadomasochistic fantasies, can be found in the Latin Acts of Peter (the Actus Vercellenses), the original composition of which likely dates to the end of the second century. In this narrative, the senator Marcellus, one of the protagonists, tells Peter about a dream before his confrontation with his opponent Simon Magus, in which the basic structure of the plot is expressed.[27] Marcellus narrates: "As I . . . fell asleep for a moment, I saw you [sc. Peter] sitting before a large crowd, and a very ugly woman, in

25. Brewer, *Prester John*, 97 (for sources see 98–139).

26. See John Block Friedman, *The Monstrous Races in Medieval Art and Thought* (Harvard University Press, 2000).

27. For more on the thinking behind this writing, see Tobias Nicklas, "Inszenierung 'petrinischer' Theologie in den *Acta Petri* (*Actus Vercellenses*)," in *Peter in the Early*

appearance an Ethiopian and not an Egyptian, but completely black with dirt, clothed in rags, but with an iron yoke on her neck and a chain on her hands and feet, and she was dancing" (§22). This woman is understood as an image of Simon's evil powers and therefore of Satan himself. Cutting off her head also means defeating Simon and thereby one of the devil's representatives.

The scene is not isolated. A parallel can be found in the Passio Perpetuae 10.6, where—also in a dream—the martyr Perpetua encounters the devil in the form of an Egyptian who wants to fight with her;[28] similarly in the aforementioned Greek Passion of Bartholomew, the apostle frees an Indian temple from its demon and forces it to show its true form: "(He was) like an Ethiopian black as coal dust; his face pointed like a dog's, with a thin beard, hair down to his feet, with fiery eyes. Sparks came out of his mouth, and from his nostrils smoke as of brimstone; he had wings with spines like a porcupine, his hands were bound with fiery chains, and he was held fast with power" (§8).[29] Such motifs cannot be explained solely by the fact that the color black can stand for the devil (Barn. 4:10 and Athanasius, *Vit. Ant.* 6.1) or the place where sinners are tormented (Greek Apoc. Pet. 21; Visio Pauli 39).[30] The references to Egypt—and even more so Ethiopia—seem, rather, to reflect the understanding of these locales as situated at the southern edge of the earth, here perceived as completely "other" and to be feared.[31]

Church: Apostle—Missionary—Church Leader, ed. Judith M. Lieu, BETL (Peeters, 2021), 243–82.

28. Edition: SC 417:136.12–15.

29. Translation by Tobias Nicklas.

30. The examples cited here are taken from Marietheres Döhler, ed., *Acta Petri: Text, Überstezung und Kommentar zu den Actus Vercellenses*, TU 171 (de Gruyter, 2018), 230–31, 271.

31. However, the canonical Acts of the Apostles (see Acts 8:26–40) describes a completely different picture of an Ethiopian who is to be counted among the first baptized of the "new way." See also David Brakke, "Ethiopian Demons: Male Sexuality, the Black-Skinned Other, and the Monastic Self," in *Journal of the History of Sexuality* (2001): 501–35.

With respect to the ends of the earth, the Acts of Andrew and Matthias in the City of the Cannibals is particularly worthy of consideration.[32] Much of this narrative is set in the city of the cannibals (in Latin manuscripts dubbed "Myrmidonia")—a setting that is not further localized but was later identified with Sinope on the Black Sea.[33] As discussed at length in the previous chapter, the presence of cannibals is a clear indication that the northeast edge of the known world—the region inhabited by Scythians—was the understood location. But whether readers believe in the existence of such a city is here of secondary importance.[34] The narrative is, of course, intended to entertain, perhaps by giving readers a taste of the disgusting. Beyond that, however, the text, in its play with miracle and magic, also attempts to inscribe itself into the great basic narrative that connects many apocryphal apostle stories: Christ's message, the gospel, and his reign really do reach the limits of the earth—and thus also the limits of the human, transforming bloodthirsty brutes into sane people. Perhaps this text even plays on prejudices against Christianity, including the well-known accusations that cast the celebration of the Eucharist as the cannibalistic consumption of flesh and blood. The story then shows the opposite: Christians are not cannibals; rather, their gospel and the power of Christ transform the world and the worst it has to offer. This is true even for cannibals, who are transformed into civilized people through their encounter with Christ and his representatives, the apostles. From the borders and through the description of other places, such works say something important about identity formation in the Christian movement—if in a thoroughly entertaining manner.

32. We follow the edition by MacDonald, *Acts of Andrew*.

33. See the report by Archdeacon Theodosius (sixth century) on his pilgrimage to the Holy Land (*Theodosii de situ terrae sanctae* 13).

34. What is told here also lies on the borderline between the credible and the no longer credible.

2. Other Worlds: Visions and Dreams of the Afterlife, Journeys into the Hereafter

Not all of the texts mentioned above address crossing borders in the same way. Some texts simply report of an individual's arrival at a distant place or—as in the traditions surrounding Prester John—repeatedly emphasize the length of the journey. In the Vision of Zosimos, also known as the History of the Rechabites, the hermit Zosimos can reach the paradise-like place where the lost tribe of the Rechabites, together with angels, lead a life similar to that of Adam and Eve before the fall (see Vision of Zosimos 12:3) only with God's help.[35] After forty years of fasting in solitude, his request to visit the blessed who were raptured from this world in the days of Jeremiah is granted (see Jer 35; Vision of Zosimos 1). After a forty-day journey with an angel, he collapses, whereupon an unspecified animal takes him for many days to the shore of the "great ocean," in the middle of which the land of the Rechabites is located, seemingly completely unreachable and shrouded by a cloud (§2). Crossing the ocean is achievable only with a miracle:

> And suddenly two luxuriant and very stately trees, larger than any I had ever seen, appeared on the shore of the sea. And then one of the trees bent itself down and I securely grasped its branches. And it stretched out toward the height (of heaven) and lifted me up and carried me in its summit until the cloud was beneath (me). And also that other tree bent itself down toward it; and the one from here curved its summit and held me out to the one which was from the other side. And descending,

35. Ronit Nikolsky, "The Adam and Eve Traditions in the Journey of Zosimos," in *Things Revealed: Festschrift Michael E. Stone*, ed. Esther Chazon, JSJSup 89 (Brill, 2004), 345–56. For a summary of the text and important information on the introduction and secondary literature, see Folker Siegert, *Einleitung in die hellenistisch-jüdische Literatur. Apocrypha, Pseudepigrapha und Fragmente verlorener Autorenwerke* (de Gruyter, 2016).

> it dropped me in the midst of it. And thus by God's guidance I passed over the great ocean and the cloud.[36]

The land of the Rechabites is thus described as being technically in this world, but so far removed from any human civilization ("taken away from worldly life" [Vision of Zosimos 1][37]) and so inaccessible to any normal person that it is difficult to decide whether this text should be classified as an earthly or otherworldly journey. The boundaries between descriptions of journeys to distant lands (or the appearance of people from these other worlds) and journeys to the afterlife (which in some cases may also be described as visions of the afterlife or dreams about the afterlife) can thus be blurred.[38] Even when concentrating on late antiquity, it is impossible to offer a complete overview of such writings.[39] In the following, we offer four examples to illustrate a central theme: Glimpses into the afterlife express something about the (imagined) order of the world. While the narratives of our first examples attempt in various ways to restore faith in the justice of God within a sinful and unjust world, the last text does the exact opposite: A radical gaze into dystopia calls everything into question.

2.1. The Greek Apocalypse of Peter

The so-called Greek-Ethiopic Apocalypse of Peter (not to be confused with the Coptic Apocalypse of Peter from Nag Hammadi [NHC VII 3]) was probably written in Alexandria in the first half of the second

---

36. English translation by James H. Charlesworth, "History of the Rechabites," *OTP*, 2:451; the edition of the Greek text also goes back to Charlesworth. See Charlesworth, *The History of the Rechabites*, vol. 1, *The Greek Recension*, SBLTT 17 (Scholars Press, 1982).

37. Translation by Charlesworth, "History of the Rechabites," 450.

38. Of course, this does not mean that they will disappear in every case.

39. Good overviews are offered (with clearly different emphases) by Bart D. Ehrman, *Journeys to Heaven and Hell: Tours to the Afterlife* (Yale University Press, 2022), and Meghan R. Henning, *Hell Hath No Fury: Gender, Disability, and the Invention of Damned Bodies in Early Christian Literature*, ABRL (Yale University Press, 2021).

century.[40] This text was recognized as authoritative by at least some early Christian authors, especially in the East. From the fifth century onward, however,[41] it was increasingly superseded by the Apocalypse of Paul, which, in its Latin version as Visio Pauli, achieved great influence. The Apocalypse of Peter is particularly interesting because it is the first Christian text to venture a detailed look into hell. This is not simply for the sheer pleasure of describing grotesque punishments; rather, the work addresses the fundamental problem of understanding the relationship between God's justice and his mercy.[42] Today the text has been transmitted in different versions, which makes it largely impossible to draw conclusions about its original form. Furthermore, the various extant versions offer different answers to the problem of God's justice. Here we concentrate on the extensive Greek fragment that, together with the text we usually refer to as the Gospel of Peter and an extensive section of 1 Enoch, has come down to us in the so-called Akhmîm Codex from the sixth or seventh century.[43] In the

40. This is only a brief summary of the now extensive discussion on the origin of the text. For the following discussion, it is also not necessary to decide whether the original text may have originated in Alexandria (Nicklas's thesis) or elsewhere. (Jan N. Bremmer, "The Apocalypse of Peter: Place, Date and Punishments, in his *Maidens, Magic and Martyrs in Early Christianity*, WUNT 379 [Mohr Siebeck, 2017], 281–94, at 293.) This discussion is put into perspective once again if we concentrate in our interpretation on text forms that have survived in specific manuscripts. Note that aspects of the following material are also treated in Tobias Nicklas, "Weltwahrnehmung in christlichen Apokalypsen: Johannesapokalypse und Offenbarung des Petrus" (lecture at the conference of the Wissenschaftliche Gesellschaft für Theologie, Heidelberg, September 2024).

41. For examples of their early reception see, e.g., Kraus and Nicklas, *Das Petrusevangelium und die Petrusapokalypse*, 87–100.

42. On this, see also Eric J. Beck, *Justice and Mercy in the Apocalypse of Peter*, WUNT 427 (Mohr Siebeck, 2019), 169–79, who, however, concentrates on a text that he has reconstructed with the help of the Ethiopian tradition.

43. Edition: Kraus and Nicklas, *Das Petrusevangelium und die Petrusapokalypse*, 101–17.

following, we will refer to its text as the Apocalypse of Peter for the sake of simplicity.

Any analysis of the content of the Apocalypse of Peter is, of course, subject to the proviso that it is an (extensive) fragment. The situation to which the text responds is similar to that of other apocalyptic writings. As the opening verses 1–3 suggest, the Christ-followers addressed find themselves in a situation of distress (v. 3), in which they nevertheless seem to prove themselves. The key motif of the text, from which the plot develops with a total of three successive visions, can also be understood against this background: The twelve disciples ask Jesus, the "Lord," to show them what the righteous who have died look like (v. 5). Seeing their likeness should not only give the disciples courage in times of distress but also encourage others in the same situation. That the righteous are mentioned here is no coincidence: At no point does the text refer to its addressees as Christians. Comparable to 2 Peter, the Christian group that made use of this text seems to have understood itself as the "way of righteousness." The members of the way of righteousness, however, seem to be confronted with a world that they experience as unjust; indeed, some seem to have already left the way. In response to this problem, however, the text does not question God's justice but broadens the view. The decisive question is, "What comes after death?"—and this question is answered with a look at the righteous who have died and at two worlds "outside this world."[44]

This view, in turn, is intended to change the understanding of one's own experience of the world in the present. This happens on three levels:

44. Aspects of the following—with slightly different questions—also appear in Tobias Nicklas, "'And I Saw Another Place . . .' (ApcPet 21): The Greek Apocalypse of Peter and Its Otherworldly Landscape of Memories," in *Social Memory Theory and Conceptions of Afterlife in Jewish and Christian Antiquity*, ed. Thomas R. Hatina and Jiří Lukeš, Studies in Cultural Contexts of the Bible 8 (Brill and Schöningh, 2023), 251–66.

(1) In response to the disciples' prayer, two men "suddenly" appear with all the signs of belonging to another, heavenly world or sphere.[45] The basic message of this first vision is the simple thought that the righteous will not only be indescribably beautiful after their death, but that they, from whom light shines forth and who are clothed in splendor or glory (see v. 7), also participate in a kind of supernatural existence in close relationship with God—a relationship that is barely comprehensible to human judgment. This means that earthly righteousness will be transformed into heavenly splendor and supernatural beauty. The few verses in which the righteous are described could hardly be more densely packed with terms from the realm of beauty, light, and splendor (vv. 6–11). Added to this is the image of their hair woven into a wreath of flowers and the comparison with a rainbow that seems to emanate from them (v. 10). In other words, the flawlessness of a character, that is, its righteousness, will be revealed after death in transfigured, flawless beauty.

(2) In a second vision, the text turns from the figure of the righteous who have died to the place they have gone: The "aeon in which they are" (v. 14) again matches their description in crucial respects. It is "a great land outside this world," the characteristics of which are again described as light and brightness and the rays of the sun, as well as beautiful and fragrant flowers, herbs, and fruits. The place is paradisiacal, although nowhere is it explicitly called a paradise. Once again, the narrative describes the appearance of the inhabitants: They wear shining robes and are like angels (v. 17); they are all glorious in the same way. But another observation is important. This "land outside this world" (v. 15) is "*their* place," that is, the place of the righteous (v. 20). If we take the formulation seriously, then this also applies, at least to some extent, to

45. More extensively in Tobias Nicklas, "'Our Righteous Brethren': Reflections on the Description of the Righteous Ones According to the Greek *Revelation of Peter* (Akhm. 2)," in *Empsychoi Logoi: Religious Innovations in Antiquity: Studies in Honor of Peter Willem van der Horst*, ed. Alberdina Houtman et al., AJEC 73 (Brill, 2008), 329–46.

the members of the way of righteousness who do not yet inhabit this place (v. 17). The expansion of this world by a large country that lies "outside" (v. 15) creates a space for those who feel oppressed as the righteous in this world. Their affliction in this world corresponds to the glory "in that place" (vv. 17, 19), which is also "their place" (v. 20).

(3) Without another question as prompt, the perspective now shifts to "another place" directly opposite. This is basically the opposite of the paradisiacal garden that has just been described. Darkness takes the place of light, and the angels there wear dark robes instead of shining ones. Instead of communion with angels, we read of angels of punishment; instead of the scent of flowers, we find burning dung or the mud of hell. There is no community among those who inhabit that place; rather, we find individual compartments, isolated spaces within the one "other place," in which different sinners are punished. This is truly hell, although the term is not encountered here, and we should not be too quick to assume that this hell must be understood as eternal.[46] It is not necessary here to examine each individual compartment.[47] The key point is that this hell, in contrast to the paradisiacal garden just described, is the place *where other people are*.[48] Or, to put it more provocatively, in this hell are *the others*. In some cases, it is occupied by those who prepare hellish things for the righteous in this world. In other cases, it is filled with those who have detached themselves from the community. We find those who have "turned away from righteousness" (v. 23), those who have "persecuted the righteous and delivered them up" (v. 27), those who have "blasphemed the way of righteousness and spoken evil of it" (v. 28), those who have become "witnesses of lies" (v. 29), and finally those who have "forsaken the way of God" (v. 34). Although the other offenses represented in this hell can largely be derived from the Torah, it is a selection

46. On the development of this idea, which seems self-evident today, see, e.g., Ehrman, *Journeys to Heaven and Hell*, 203–10.

47. Beck, *Justice and Mercy*, 125–68, who, however, concentrates on a text that he has reconstructed by comparing the Ethiopic and Greek versions.

48. Here, of course, we are playing with the well-known line from Jean-Paul Sartre's play *No Exit*: "Hell is other people." ("L'enfer, c'est les autres.")

that could hope for a fairly broad social consensus among its first audiences.[49] We read about adulteresses (v. 24), murderers and their accomplices (v. 25), women who have aborted their children (v. 26), usurers (v. 31), and people in homoerotic relationships (v. 32). More typical of a Jewish background are the people mentioned who "did not have mercy on widows and orphans" (v. 30) and the makers of images of gods (v. 33). If we take this combination seriously, a second conclusion emerges: In this hell there are many who would be described as "the others" *by most people*, that is, also by those who do not feel that they specifically belong to the way of righteousness. It is true that this is the place where those who now harm the path of righteousness experience God's justice. At the same time, however, it is also the place that can convince those who do not (yet) seem to belong to the way of righteousness that they are not far removed from its ethics. Above all, however, it is not a distant future place but one in which God is already providing justice (see v. 25).

The combination of this world with two other worlds—such that all three are related to one another—thus aims to educate us to a different view of *this* world. What is mixed up in *this* world—the inseparability of the righteous and the unrighteous, the persecutors and the persecuted, the oppressed and the afflicted—is only one part of a larger order. What meets without separation in this world remains in direct opposition even after death (v. 21), but the difference reveals itself in complete separation—although at least in one case (that of the murderers and their victims) a certain proximity leveraged as punishment remains (v. 25). The differences that those who see themselves as righteous already perceive in their affliction in relation to their opponents are embedded in a world order where, after death, the differences become the basis of an

49. See the important studies by Wolfgang Grünstäudl, "Enthüllung im Fragment: Notizen zu Überlieferungsgestalt und Figureninventar der Offenbarung des Petrus," in Verheyden et al., *Shadowy Characters and Fragmentary Evidence*, 109–23, esp. 119–22; and Michael Sommer, "The Ethics of Hell: Righteousness in the Apocalypse of Peter and Early Christian Discourses About Ethics," in *The Apocalypse of Peter in Context*, ed. Daniel C. Maier et al., Studies on Early Christian Apocrypha 21 (Peeters, 2024), 93–111.

assignment to different places, even separate worlds.[50] The circumstances are simply reversed after death. The end-time judgment of God or Christ can fade into the background because a postmortem judgment is already active now—and for all times. But it occurs in other places, in parallel worlds. Whether *this* world will continue to exist is therefore at best a secondary question for works such as the Apocalypse of Peter. Although a new creation or a completion of creation is not necessary (unlike, for example, in Revelation), according to the Apocalypse of Peter, this world remains provisional for those who inhabit it. After all, two other worlds already exist that seek to permanently compensate for the injustice of these worlds; the ideal, light-filled world belongs to the righteous. It is "their place."

2.2. The Long Form of the Latin Visio Pauli

This perspective changes in the Visio Pauli.[51] This text also offers a juxtaposition of places of otherworldly human fulfillment and damnation. With origins in an elite monasticism,[52] this text develops a highly pessimistic view of humanity and its fate. Only very few will be saved, and

50. A close parallel to this can be found in Luke 16:19–31, where the rich man and Lazarus, who never really meet in this world (even if it were possible for the rich man), are forever separated in the Otherworld.

51. On current introductory questions, see Bremmer, "Apocalypse of Paul," 427–45; on the transmission of the text and its meaning in the Latin Middle Ages, see Lenka Jiroušková, *Die Visio Pauli: Wege und Wandlungen einer orientalischen Apokryphe im lateinischen Mittelalter unter Einschluß der alttschechischen und deutschsprachigen Textzeugen* (Brill, 2006). Edition of the Latin texts: Theodore Silverstein and Anthony Hilhorst, *Apocalypse of Paul: A New Critical Edition of Three Long Latin Versions*, Cahiers d'Orientalisme 21 (Patrick Cramer, 1997).

52. An original form of the text probably goes back to Pachomian monks in Egypt. See, e.g., Kirsti Copeland, "Mapping the Apocalypse of Paul: Geography, Genre and History" (PhD diss., Princeton University, 2001), 177–78. Also important is Emiliano Fiori, "Death and Judgment in the *Apocalypse of Paul*: Old Imagery and Monastic Reinvention," *ZAC* 20 (2016): 92–108. Lautaro Roig Lanzillotta and Jacques van der Vliet, *The Apocalypse of Paul (Visio Pauli) in Sahidic Coptic*, Supplements to Vigiliae Christianae 178 (Brill, 2023).

even their salvation is not fulfilled in an open space of hope, such as the heavenly Jerusalem of Revelation: Paul is initially led to a paradisiacal place that in many respects comes close to chiliastic ideas of the millennial reign of Christ (§22).[53] Part of human fulfillment here consists in the possibility of satisfying hunger and thirst in a garden full of trees with countless fruits—a garden through which a river of milk and honey flows. But this place is by no means the pinnacle of what is to be hoped for. Within this garden is the city of Christ, which is clearly different from the description of Revelation's heavenly Jerusalem.[54] According to the long form of the text, only men who have preserved their chastity may enter this city. In the city itself, there is a strict hierarchy: The decisive criteria for how close one can come to the innermost part of the city are the renunciation of any kind of pride (§24), complete submission to God's will (§25), chastity and purity (§26), hospitality (§27), and the singing of psalms to God without pride (§28). The highest level of godliness, however, seems to be achieved through a kind of holy simplicity described in section 29. When Paul asks who sits on the golden thrones in the innermost part of the city, the angel replies: "These thrones belong to those who had goodness and understanding of heart, but made fools of themselves for the Lord God's sake, not knowing the Scriptures nor many psalms, but observing one chapter of the commandments of God and hearing what it contained, they acted with great zeal and had a true zeal before the Lord God" (§29, text from the Codex Parisinus).

All of this can be interpreted as the rhetoric of a rather dangerous discourse on power: The ideal image of fulfilled humanity thus

---

53. The greatest similarity in early Christian literature is probably the description of the millennium by Papias of Hierapolis (quoted by Irenaeus of Lyons, *Haer.* 5.33.3–4). Important aspects of what is described below go back to the much more detailed contribution by Tobias Nicklas, "The Latin *Apocalypse of Paul*: Ideas and Images of Humanity," in *Images of the Human Being*, ed. Karl-Wilhelm Niebuhr et al., WUNT 521 (Mohr Siebeck, 2024), 41–62.

54. On the relationship of the city of Christ to the heavenly Jerusalem of Revelation, see Tobias Nicklas, "From the Heavenly Jerusalem to the City of Christ: Revelation and the Visio Pauli," in *Revelation's New Jerusalem in Late Antiquity*, ed. Nathan Betz et al., History of Biblical Exegesis 6 (Mohr Siebeck, 2023), 123–36.

corresponds to a man without sexual relations, who controls his desires and focuses only on what is explained to him as "God's will," that is, a man who functions well in a monastic community. This text is not interested in the prospect of salvation for women. This fact goes hand in hand with a certain hostility toward any kind of freedom of thought, or, more to the point, a lack of interest in any kind of critical human mind. A person's critical mind seems to be an obstacle rather than a good guide to the city of Christ. In the order of this world, the ascetic monastic groups and communities living on the margins of civilization move to the center of the end-time city of Christ. Inside it, they will do what they are already doing: singing psalms and praising God.

The salvation of such an elite is possible only because those individuals largely withdraw from the actions of other people. This is evident not only in the opening chapters of this work, in which the elements of creation turn to God to complain about the sinful actions of humanity (§§3–7), but also in the detailed descriptions of hellish places. As in the Apocalypse of Peter, hell consists of a multitude of compartments in which sinners are tortured in unimaginably sadistic ways, depending on their transgression; aspects of the corporeality of the punished are repeatedly emphasized. Unlike in the Apocalypse of Peter, these punishments clearly also affect Christians, including members of the church hierarchy and administration. In this hell, we find a presbyter, a bishop, a lector, and even a deacon (§§34–36). Sin, and therefore punishment, does not stop at the gates of the church. Also unlike the Greek fragment of the Apocalypse of Peter discussed above, the Visio Pauli mentions the reaction of the traveler to the afterlife. When Paul sees the fate of the damned, he weeps and laments over the human race (§§33, 40, 42). The concern in the Visio Pauli is therefore somewhat different from the Apocalypse of Peter: It too is interested in a complex form of God's justice, which manifests itself in a hierarchy of rewards, on the one hand, but also in a precise allocation of punishments for specific transgressions on the other. The apostle's view of the punishments of the damned, however, leads to a somewhat different question than in the Apocalypse of Peter: How far does the mercy of the righteous God go, when so few people achieve the perfection necessary for salvation? This is underscored in a cry that is apparently joined by all the damned, as well as Paul and even the archangel Michael: "O Lord God! Have mercy on your creation, have mercy on the children of men, have mercy on your image!" (§43).[55]

Although it is actually too late for God's mercy, the call is heard and the "Son of God" descends from heaven, crowned with a diadem (in the version of the Paris and St. Gall codices). However, even his response does not initially open the door to further mercy. In view of his own passion, he emphasizes that those now being punished have been given the opportunity to repent: "And you did not want to repent" (§44).[56] The suffering of the Son of God on the cross, which neither found mercy nor led to human repentance, leaves no room for mercy for the condemned. Nevertheless, a final form of mercy is still granted to the damned. Although redemption is no longer attainable for them, on one day of the week they receive a respite from their torment through the intercession of Paul and the archangel Michael (§44).[57] Of course, this day is Sunday, in remembrance of Christ's resurrection. It may be debated whether this remission of punishment is really to be understood as a sign of mercy (rather than a particularly perfidious form of sadism). But this is hardly the perspective of the text. From the point of view of people who see themselves as a special elite—who have already left this world as far as possible during their lifetime—it is emphasized that only the very best of them will receive the full reward in the innermost part of the city of Christ. And what happens there will not be very different from what they are already striving for now: an existence of constant praise to God.

The extremely pessimistic—perhaps even arrogant—views of this group toward the rest of humanity (including other Christians who do not follow the same ideals) is already evident in the first chapters of the Visio Pauli: The lamentations of creation formulated there probably

55. This is the version of the Paris Codex.

56. Version of the Paris Codex (with slight deviations in the St. Gall Codex and without parallel in the codices of the Escorial and Arnheim).

57. This corresponds to the version of the Paris Codex.

correspond to the opinions of the sponsoring group on the rest of humanity. If, in view of this, heaven and hell are to be understood here, as in the Apocalypse of Peter, as additional places of divine justice that balance out the disorder of this world, hell must be overwhelmingly large and full. Paul's view of the mass of the damned can thus ultimately be identified with that of the group of bearers: Here too, hell is filled with *other people*. The dividing line, however, does not run between Christians and their persecutors but also through the mass of believers, only a few of whom follow higher ideals.[58] Intercession for the damned, which may also reflect the practices of the elite, does not break one's own worldview but actually confirms it.[59] According to this logic, successful intercession is possible only for the few who (like Paul) are on the right side. The result of intercession in turn confirms one's own way of thinking. The punishment of the damned is and remains in accordance with God's justice. Christ himself introduces into this hellish world an aspect of order, which, because of his resurrection, also gives this world its temporal order: Sunday rest.

3. The Medieval Vision of Tnugdal

The Vision of Tnugdal, which is little known today, takes us to yet another time and place. This journey to the afterlife, which was probably written in Latin in the thirteenth century by an otherwise unknown monk Marcus, in the Scottish monastery in Regensburg, Germany, was extremely successful in its day.[60] Compared to the texts mentioned so

58. This is also fitting at a time when more and more people were converting to Christianity because they hoped it would bring them benefits.

59. Detailed information on the topic of "intercession for the dead" in ancient Christian literature can be found in Thomas J. Kraus, "Fürbitte für die Toten im frühen Christentum. 'I Will Grant . . . the One They Ask for Out of Punishment,'" in *Das Gebet im Neuen Testament*, ed. Hans Klein et al., WUNT 249 (Mohr Siebeck, 2009), 355–96.

60. The otherwise unknown author introduces himself in the prologue as *frater Marcus*. His knowledge of and interest in Ireland makes it likely that he originally came from there. For more detailed information with references to the discussion

far, it differs in a number of details, including the fact that it differentiates an apparently *eternal* part of hell from *temporary* punishments for transgressions. Another aspect, however, is particularly interesting: We do not read here about a vision of the afterlife by an apostle (as in the Apocalypse of Peter) or an apostle's journey to hell (as in the Visio Pauli). In this work, an Irish knight named Tnugdal—anything but a saint—is sent to hell, where he not only observes the torments of the damned but suffers some of them himself. This means that the motif of compassion for the damned falls away, replaced by the protagonist's fear of suffering a similar fate himself. Intercession for the damned is replaced by a plea for mercy for one's own fate (and repentance after returning to this world). This journey to the afterlife can be read in different ways. Our primary observation is that the text plays with the genre of the journey to hell precisely through this shift in perspective, and that, at least in some places, the monk Marcus's *Schadenfreude* at the fate of the knight, who must change his life entirely after his traumatic experiences in the afterlife, is recognizable.[61] This form of humor, which creates distance and superiority over the knight who normally asserts himself by force, is yet another way of creating order already in *this* world.

The story begins in Cashel in Ireland (present-day County Tipperary), whose king Cormac MacCarthaigh (d. 1138) was probably connected with Regensburg's monastery of the *Scoti* (that is, monks from Scotland and Ireland).[62] According to the text, "a certain man

in the older secondary literature, see Hans-Christian Lehner and Maximilian Nix, *Marcus von Regensburg, Visio Tnugdali. Vision des Tnugdal*, Fontes Christiani 76 (Herder, 2018), 15–17 (including a discussion of the question of whether Marcus was active in the Scottish monastery). The edition by Lehner and Nix (19) speaks of 150 manuscripts (as well as numerous prints). It is interesting to note that the text must therefore have been much more widely distributed than the Song of the Nibelungs (19n48).

61. We developed this thesis in dialogue with Dr. Stephanie Hallinger, University of Regensburg.

62. This also explains the prominent depiction of the end-time fate of the king, who, according to §18, lives in a kind of heavenly house modeled on Solomon's palace but

named Tnugdalus" (1.7) came from there.[63] Tnugdal is described as a handsome knight, bursting with strength, yet cruel and without a care about his own salvation (1.7–11). He wants to collect the debt of three horses from one of his friends. When the friend is unable to make good on the debt, Tnugdal is ready to set off in anger. Only with difficulty can he be persuaded to have a meal before leaving (1.17–21). What it means that Tnugdal is "full of rage" is revealed in passing: Before he sits down to eat, he must first put aside the war ax he is holding (1.22).[64] This is the moment, however, when he collapses, seemingly lifeless. For several days—from Wednesday to Saturday (1.29)—he shows no sign of life. Only a slight residual warmth in his body prevents him from being buried (1.30). On Saturday, however, he comes back to life before a multitude of witnesses,[65] vows to repent completely, and begins to tell others about what has happened to him (1.31–36).

Here we focus only on a few elements of the narrative in which one might feel *Schadenfreude*—particularly as a reader who may have had bad experiences with the brutality of knights in the monastery. The *Schadenfreude* certainly begins with the fact that Tnugdal, who once took such care of his body (1.8–9), finds himself in the afterlife as a trembling "soul" (*anima*, §2) that has left the body (2.1).[66] The knight, whose most important problem just a few lines ago was putting down his battle-ax before eating, is completely unsettled in his new surroundings:

must suffer punishment there for three hours a day for adultery and the murder of a follower (18.19–21).

63. The text is not uniformly transmitted here. Most manuscripts do not mention the name here.

64. Lehner and Dix, *Marcus von Regensburg, Visio Tnugdali*, 76n33, write: "It is striking how often the axe is mentioned in the following scenery. The constant carrying of the war axe seems to have been an Irish custom that was probably not known outside Ireland." Whether this may have been the case remains to be seen. The function of the motif, however, is clearly to characterize Tnugdal.

65. This also sets Tnugdal's revival apart from the Easter narratives of the NT.

66. However, it is not understood to be completely incorporeal, because it can suffer punishments and sometimes walk difficult paths within the afterlife.

"Indeed she [Tnugdal's soul] was afraid, but what she was afraid of she did not know. . . . And when she had been behaving like this for quite a long time, weeping and trembling and howling, not knowing what to do, she finally saw so many unclean spirits coming to her that they not only filled the whole house and courtyard where the corpse was staying, but also over all the streets and squares of the city there was no place that was not full of them" (2.2–5).[67] The spirits of the dead, who suddenly appear everywhere, intimidate Tnugdal's soul (2.6–8), but God sends him his personal (protective) angel,[68] whom Tnugdal's soul meets with tears in his eyes (3.3). Tnugdal, who once emphasized all the attributes of aggressive masculinity, behaves like a small child. Tnugdal's language also changes in the course of the journey. His speech begins to resemble that of the angel, containing more and more biblical quotations (see esp. 6.8; 7.37–40; etc.). After a few stops in hell, the former knight sounds like a contrite, pious man.

The journey beyond that follows is rich with opportunities for future investigation. We briefly present a few stations here, which illustrate our main points. The two travelers to the afterlife, Tnugdal and his angel, first pass through a valley filled with glowing coals where the souls of murderers are tortured;[69] Tnugdal is told that he himself also deserves this punishment (4.10). Tnugdal, however, gets away once more, and they witness the punishment of the deceitful and dishonest (§5). Some of the places in hell, then, can hardly be distinguished from what we also find in other texts: An important source of

67. Translations are based on Lehner and Dix, *Marcus von Regensburg, Visio Tnugdali.*

68. The abovementioned Visio Pauli already speaks of personal angels for each individual.

69. Obviously, this is an eternal part of hell. Lehner and Dix, *Marcus von Regensburg, Visio Tnugdali*, 34, write: "Thus, unlike others, the first punishment room of the murderers (ch. 4) is not a transit room, i.e., not a room that must be crossed in the punishment, as, for example, the bridges must be crossed by the sinners as part of the punishment. . . . The spatial fixedness of the place suggests a perpetuating character of the punishment, since the room cannot simply be crossed, which would end the punishment."

the *vision* is certainly the *Elucidarium* of Honorius Augustodunensis (PL 172.1109–76).[70] The key scene, which clearly shows that the Vision of Tnugdal can also be read differently from the usual journey to the afterlife, is found in section 8, which describes the hell for thieves and robbers. In the valley of the arrogant (§6), Tnugdal's soul already had to cross a bridge a thousand paces long but only one foot wide, full of fear.[71] Only with the help of the angel, who keeps a cheerful face even in the midst of the stinking sulfur smoke and the howling of the damned from the depths, does he succeed (6.2–9), although another punishment is already prophesied for him here. This comes to him a little later: In the hell for thieves and robbers there is also a "very wide and stormy lake," with terrible beasts in great numbers that seek to devour the souls that must cross the lake (8.4–5). The path across the lake, however, is even more dangerous than in the valley of the arrogant. There is also a bridge across it, but it is now two miles long and only a hand's breadth wide (8.6–8). Even worse, it is studded with sharp nails that would "pierce the feet of all who crossed it, so that no foot, once it touched them, could escape unharmed" (8.9). Tnugdal sees another soul, laden with large bundles of grain, being forced to cross the bridge and at the same time threatened with being devoured by the huge beasts from the abyss (8.13–15).

Now the angel no longer comes to the aid of Tnugdal's soul; Tnugdal must cross without him. But that is not all. Tnugdal must

70. For sources of the text, see Lehner and Dix, *Marcus von Regensburg, Visio Tnugdali*, 25–28. Like Marcus, Honorius probably came from Ireland and stayed in Regensburg at the end of his life (mid-twelfth century). For more details on his work and its transmission, see Dagmar Gottschall, *Das "Elucidarium" des Honorius Augustodonensis: Untersuchungen zu seiner Überlieferungs-und Rezeptionsgeschichte im deutschsprachigen Raum mit Ausgabe der niederdeutschen Übersetzung*, Texte und Textgeschichte 33 (de Gruyter, 1993).

71. Peter Dinzelbacher, *Die Jenseitsbrücke im Mittelalter*, Dissertationen der Universität Wien 104 (Verband der wissenschaftlichen Gesellschaften Österreichs, 1973), is still the most important study on this motif and its (still not fully clarified) background.

take an untamed cow, which he once stole from his neighbor, to the other side and hand it over to the angel unharmed (8.24–27). Readers can sense the joy the author of the text feels when he describes how Tnugdal and the cow cross the bridge: "When [Tnugdal's] soul had begun to continue on its way, the cow did not want to go with it. Why do we hesitate any longer? When the soul stood, the cow fell, and when the cow stood, the soul fell, and in this way, they stood and fell alternately until they came to the middle of the bridge" (8:34–36). The scene is already comically absurd. But what happens in the middle of the bridge? Oncoming traffic! The soul that had just been sent across the bridge with huge bundles of grain on its back has now also arrived from the other side. The narrator's comment is telling: "I mean [those with the bundle of grain], not those about whom it is said, 'But those who are coming will come with rejoicing, carrying their bundles' [Psalm 125:6], but those who are threatened elsewhere in Scripture: 'Woe to you who laugh now, because you will weep and mourn' [Luke 6:25]" (8.38). While the two souls in the middle of the bridge do weep and mourn (8.39), this comment, with its quotation of Luke 6:25, is completely superfluous to the development of the plot. It makes sense only if the intention is to warn—with a wink—against laughing *too* loudly in response to this scene.

The next hellish place is the inn of a certain Phristinus,[72] where the two (perhaps alluding to a habit of Tnugdal's during his lifetime?) "cannot pass by in any way" (8.48). Although the innkeeper now asks to receive new guests all the time, he does not treat them hospitably at all (8.49). The following chapter shows that Tnugdal must again suffer at least some of the torments that he inflicted on the guests of this place in life.

The Vision of Tnugdal, then, can be read as an edifying text that guides us to a better way of life and offers instructions for personal piety. This is also the aim stated in the text itself (in the heading for §1:

72. According to Lehner and Nix, *Marcus von Regensburg, Visio Tnugdali*, 115n78, this name is possibly derived from the Latin *pistrinum* ("bakehouse").

"composed for the edification of many") and would probably have been the case in most instances.[73] Additionally, the text serves something like a political function. Certainly the Irish local color becomes very clear (with visions of the otherworldly fate of Irish saints including Saint Patrick [§§24–25], but also regional Irish kings [§§17–18]). However, some of the motifs mentioned would not be necessary if the text had been written *only* for such purposes. Although it is certainly not composed as a thoroughgoing parody of a journey to the afterlife, at least in some places it makes space for the gleeful smiles (or even snorts of laughter) of the monks of central Ireland (and Regensburg) as they contemplated Tnugdal's fate in the hereafter. After all, these monks—and probably also the monks of the Regensburg Scottish monastery—likely had experience with the mercilessness of knights.

Excursus: Historical Individuals and Their Afterlives

At the transition from late antiquity to the Middle Ages at the latest, we find passages in visions of the afterlife in which the punishments of historically identifiable individuals are described alongside the usual inventory of punishments in hell, in which the specific offense or sin is of particular interest. These are not necessarily the typical arch-sinners, such as Judas Iscariot or Herod. Instead, contemporary figures come into focus. Such depictions naturally provide a perspective on historical events and historical personalities. Two examples illustrate this phenomenon. The likely Byzantine Apocalypse of Anastasia tells of the journey to the afterlife of a nun named Anastasia, who lives an exemplary ascetic life (placed in the time of Emperor Theodosius, without clarity as to which of the historical emperors of that name is intended).[74] Anastasia

73. I repeat here the functions of visions as discussed in Lehner and Nix, *Marcus von Regensburg, Visio Tnugdali*, 11–13.

74. On this writing, which is not normally dealt with in the usual collections of Christian apocrypha, see Jane Baun, *Tales from Another Byzantium: Celestial Journey and Local Community in the Medieval Greek Apocrypha* (Cambridge University Press, 2007). There (401–24) you will also find translations of two main versions of this apocalypse.

falls into a deathlike state, from which she awakens only after three days. She then reports her experiences in the afterlife to the spiritual father of the monastery. She saw the heavenly throne and the gate of heaven, the place of the punishment of sins, paradise, a kind of administration room where angels' reports on people's behavior are kept, and more. Especially exciting is a report about an area in which high-ranking sinners—such as priests, bishops, and even former emperors—suffer hellish punishments. Section 42 is particularly specific (here in the version of the Apocalypse of Anastasia from the Paris and Milan manuscripts):[75]

> And I saw there the throne of an emperor, and he did not have imperial state, and behind him there was a somber man. And the angel said to me, "This is John, the one also <called> Tzimiskes, and he killed Nikephoros the Emperor, he neither has respite, nor was he worthy of a throne." And when I stared at him, I also saw Nikephoros the Emperor, standing and cross-examining him: "Kyr John—why did you do this unjust murder to me? Why did you not pity your own soul? Do you not understand that we put our hands <together> in the Hagia Sophia, and made peace with one another, so that there would not be treachery between us? But you did not keep these things, and not for the kind of deed you did, you have received what was your due." But that one, lamenting, said nothing, save only "Ah me" and "woe is me, ah me, ah me."

The scene, from which the dating of the text at the turn of the tenth to the eleventh century can also be derived, recalls the brutal seizure of power in December 969 CE by the former successful general of Armenian origin John Tzimiskes by instigating the murder of his predecessor, Nikephoros II Phokas (963–969 CE). John Tzimiskes, who had only just returned to court from four years of house arrest in Asia Minor and was (probably wrongly) accused of plotting with Empress

75. The translation follows Baun, *Tales from Another Byzantium*, 410–11; a parallel version can be found on 422.

Theophanu (941–976), was in fact able to assert himself as Byzantine emperor from 969 to 976. The ecclesiastical punishment imposed on him by the then patriarch Polyeuktos (956–970) seems to have demanded financial penance and the punishment of two people involved in the murder. In fact, he proved to be a ruler who was not only militarily capable but who was viewed very differently by posterity.[76] While the history of Leon the Deacon, written in 995, describes both emperors (Nikephoros and John) in a positive way, this text clearly represents a different perspective: John's legitimacy is still fundamentally rejected because of the way in which he came to power; he is condemned as a peacebreaker and murderer, who from now on is constantly confronted with the interrogation by his victim Nikephoros.[77]

The situation in the Vision of Tnugdal is slightly different. In the heavenly and hellish places Tnugdal passes through on his journey to the afterlife, he also encounters the otherworldly sojourns of some Irish kings of his time. He describes in particular detail the fate of Cormac MacCarthaigh (d. 1138), who as king of Desmond was probably connected to the Scottish monastery of St. James in Regensburg, where Marcus, author of the work, lived (Visio Tnugdali 18). Tnugdal and the angel accompanying him arrive at a marvelous palace on the other side, in which there is a richly decorated throne; they see

> a marvelously adorned house, whose walls and entire structure were of gold and silver and of all kinds of precious stones; but there were no windows or doors there, and yet all who wished to enter entered. The house was as brilliant inside as if, I don't want to say a single sun, but as if many suns were shining there. The

76. For detailed information on the government of Johannes Tzimiskes, see Anthony Kaldellis, *Streams of Gold, Rivers of Blood: The Rise and Fall of Byzantium, 955 A.D. to the First Crusade* (Oxford University Press, 2017), 65–80 (on the judgments of posterity, see esp. 79).

77. It is not entirely certain whether the punishment is intended to be eternal. Our modern ideas of an eternal hell do not always work when applied to ancient and medieval writings.

> house itself was very spacious and round and not supported by any pillars, and the whole courtyard was covered with gold and precious stones. But when [Tnugdal's] soul was pleased in such buildings, she saw, as she looked around, a golden seat adorned with precious stones and silk and all kinds of ornaments, and saw the lord king Cormac sitting on that very throne, clothed in such garments as neither he himself nor any of the kings of the earth could ever be clothed in. (18.1–4)

The former patron of the monastery, Cormac, whose brother Donnchadh MacCarthaigh held the throne of Desmond until 1144, is portrayed in this scene (and in the following) as a kind of otherworldly King Solomon in a palace of indescribable splendor.[78] In Tnugdal's world, this now virtually unknown ruler of an Irish empire occupies a central place, through which his historical kingship also appears in a splendor that can be explained a few years after his death only from the perspective of a person who was either directly or indirectly dependent on this kingship. And yet the Vision of Tnugdal is brave enough to break this splendor and to relativize the glory, inasmuch as Cormac also has sins to atone for: The same king who has just been depicted enthroned in his heavenly palace is shown shortly afterward "in flames up to his navel and clothed from the navel upwards with a garment of atonement" (18.17). Although the deceased king is allowed to rest in the splendor of his heavenly palace for twenty-one hours a day, he must suffer for three hours a day "because he has defiled the legal sacrament of marriage. And from the navel upwards, he wears the penitential garment because he has commanded the death of followers close (to the church of) St. Patrick" (18.21). Today it is no longer possible to ascertain the specific background of Cormac's

78. For more detail, see Herrad Spilling, *Die Visio Tnugdali: Eigenart und Stellung in der mittelalterlichen Visionsliteratur bis zum Ende des 12. Jahrhunderts*, Münchener Beiträge zur Mediävistik und Renaissance-Forschung 21 (Arbeo-Gesellschaft, 1975), 126–29.

transgressions described here.[79] However, this passage clearly shows a thoroughly differentiated view of historical personality: The connection to Desmond and the temporal proximity to Cormac's reign compel Marcus to grant him a prominent position in the afterlife as well. The description of otherworldly splendor, transcending all that is humanly possible, is, however, delivered from a critical distance: Even a largely just king such as Cormac is subject to God's justice.

4. Ka-Tzetnik 135633, *Shivitti*

As we have seen, talking about hell can be entertaining.[80] But entertainment should not have the last word at a time when people in many parts of the world have experienced and continue to experience hell. That is why the last example in this chapter is intended to remind us that the inner distance with which we tend to read many ancient and medieval journeys to hell today should collapse in the moment that we recognize those who suffer the horrors of hell as no longer distant *others* but people who could be ourselves. Perhaps even more extreme, but to be taken extremely seriously, is the question of how it is possible that regular people—people like us, people like you—can also actively create or be a hell for other people.[81] The last text to be addressed in this

79. See von Regensburg, *Visio Tnugdali*, 165nn136–137 (with additional literature on the discussion of the problem).

80. The following explanations are based on the edition titled *Shivitti*, which was published in 2005 in the series Der Grüne Zweig 250 by Werner Pieper and the Grüne Kraft. However, it probably goes back to the 1998 edition published by Gateway Verlag (with an additional foreword by Claudio Naranjo in 1998). The German first edition was published in 1991 by Antje Kunstmann Verlag. The English version, titled *Shivitti: A Vision*, was published by HarperCollins in 1989 and republished in 1998 in the Gateway Conscious Classics series. The original was published in Hebrew with the title *The Code: E.D.M.A.* and was published in Tel Aviv in 1987.

81. Very valuable and helpful reflections along similar lines can be found, for example, in historian Timothy Snyder, *Bloodlands: Europe Between Hitler and Stalin*, 7th ed. (Beck, 2022), 381–410, under the title "Humanity."

chapter stands out from all the others but should be included because it addresses these questions in the most radical way possible.

As much as all the journeys to hell described so far depict hell as a space that at least rhetorically and in our imagination extends into this world, hell has remained a space beyond in all these works. The last work we would like to present breaks through the generic constraints once again. The location of this hell can be found on earth. It is a place beyond that which we would like to conceive of as the world in which we live, but it can still be entered today: Auschwitz. It may seem highly disconcerting to relate a twentieth-century novel, written by a survivor of Auschwitz, to research on apocrypha. Of course, the attribute *Christian* is excluded from the outset. But the extraordinary, gripping, and deeply moving novel *Shivitti* by Jewish survivor of Auschwitz Yehiel de Nur, born Yehiel Feiner (1909–2001), who wrote under the pseudonym Ka-Tzetnik 135633 (in memory of the number branded on him), plays so much with the genre of the journey to the afterlife and is so full of biblical quotations and allusions that one can dare to bring it into dialogue with parabiblical literature. It does not directly recount the years that the author spent in Auschwitz; instead, the autobiographical novel is set in 1976 and tells of trauma therapy sessions using LSD that the author underwent with the Dutch therapist Jan C. Bastiaans.[82] Accompanied by Bastiaans, these sessions lead Ka-Tzetnik 135633 back to the places of horror in a controlled manner. As we understand it, however, the text is not simply a record of what he experienced during his therapy sessions but is an act of digesting them, which led to a process of healing.[83] What we present below does not approach an adequate overall interpretation of this novel. Instead, we have selected just a few passages to show how the novel deals with biblical texts, motifs, and images and how, unlike all the other texts we have looked at, it has something decisive to say about

82. Bastiaans himself has his say at the end of the text edition on which this is based.

83. At least this is how the author's final chapter, titled "Foreword and Afterword," can be interpreted.

the underlying thesis of this chapter: Exploration of other worlds leads to a redefinition of our understanding of the world in which we live.

The transition provoked by LSD from one world to the other—that is, from the patient's room in Amsterdam back to the hell of Auschwitz—is introduced in the same way in every chapter: the word PLÖTZLICH ("SUDDENLY"), written in capital letters. The two worlds remain connected, clearly seen by the fact that the visions are interspersed with calls from the attending physician—also written in capital letters—which are necessary to prevent the patient from being lost within the vision. What is described in the visions is always based on the author's concrete experiences in Auschwitz, for example, the moment when he is to be driven to the crematorium together with other people condemned to death and is able to save himself by hiding in the coal box of the truck.[84] The author's memories, however, are repeatedly combined with visions. In the sky above Auschwitz, he sees the *Shivitti*, the prayer formula with which Psalm 16:8 is introduced: "I have the Lord constantly before my eyes":

> I raise my eyes to the sky of Auschwitz. And there, hovering as a vision above the horizon, is the *Shivitti*; just as it always hung framed before the eyes of the prayer leader in the synagogue. But the *Shivitti* of our synagogue looks quite different here, against the sky of Auschwitz. Here it blazes like a torch, in the glowing colors of the rainbow. But—and this is the unusual thing about it—its light only shines inwards and upwards. It is as if Auschwitz and the sky above it had never existed, while the *Shivitti* fills the entire horizon, from the earth to the sky. Awe grips me. I stand on the truck, a skeleton in the mass of many; stand and stare at the letters YHWH shining out of the *Shivitti*; an unearthly light.[85]

84. Ka-Tzetnik 135633, *Shivitti*, 23–24.

85. Ka-Tzetnik 135633, *Shivitti*, 26.

His cry is directed into this situation: "God! God! Who has determined it? Who has determined it? God! God! Auschwitz—whose work is it?"[86] When he tries to see the face of God in the initials of God's name, however, he sees the "face of the SS man standing under the tailboard of the truck," who yawns as he carries out his daily murderous routine. The renewed cry, "God, who created Auschwitz?" is followed by a new, terrifying realization that leads to a series of terrible questions and consequences.

> And I'm standing on the rolling truck, a naked skeleton in the middle of a mass of naked skeletons, carted to the crematorium under the watchful eye of a yawning German. I stare at him, and his yawn, and suddenly ask myself: does he hate me? He doesn't even know me. He doesn't even know my name. I still stare at him and ask myself: Do I hate him? I don't even know his name, just as I don't know the names of all the others who are now being taken to the crematorium. I know nothing more about this German than that on such a cold morning he would surely have preferred to stretch out under his warm comforter rather than get up so early because a load has to be shipped to the crematorium. Suddenly I am seized by an additional horror, one that I have never known before: for if it were so, he could be standing here in my place, while I could be standing there in his, on a cold morning like this, doing my duty and sending him and millions like him to the crematorium—and like him I would yawn, for like him I would certainly prefer to stretch out under my warm comforter on such a cold morning. . . . O God, gracious and merciful God, is it I who created Auschwitz? . . . O God, Lord of heaven over Auschwitz, enlighten my ignorance of Your works so that I may recognize who this being in me is who is now being transported to the crematorium—and why? And who is the being in him who is transporting me to the crematorium—and why? For You know that both of us, the

86. Ka-Tzetnik 135633, *Shivitti*, 27.

> murderer and the murdered, are at this moment equally sons of man, both created by You, in Your image.[87]

Even reading such a short excerpt makes clear the dramatic density with which the text addresses not only the topics mentioned at the beginning, which are inescapable. It also shows how radically the question of God and being human removes all naivety here. The author experiences four additional visions called "gates," some of which are separated by longer periods of time, before he ends the therapy and, after some time, is able to write down what he has experienced in the present form.[88] The breathtaking texts present the experiences with almost unbearable immediacy; at the same time, they are imbued with motifs from the Bible and traditional Jewish literature, with a focus on ideas from the Kabbalah.[89] The shoemaker Vevke, who carries a shoemaker's bench on the procession from the ghetto to the camp, turns into the Messiah, son of Joseph, for a moment. His bench is a cross to which his hands are nailed; it melts like one of Salvador Dali's clocks and becomes "Jacob's ladder to heaven, on which the angels ascend and descend."[90] The place to which Vevke is fastened in Auschwitz like a crucified man and then beaten to death is the "Akeda site."[91] When he is cremated, none other "than Ashmodai, king of the underworld, emerges from the crematorium in the smoke. On his right hovers Shamash, on his left Asael, as I know them from the Book of Enoch the Black."[92]

---

87. Ka-Tzetnik 135633, *Shivitti*, 27–28.

88. This is discussed in the supplementary chapter "Preface and Afterword" (117–23).

89. Isaac Herschkowitz, "Asmodeus and Nucleus on Planet Auschwitz. Kazentnik's Theological and Demonological Kabbalah" (unpublished paper), https://www.academia.edu/3316135/Asmodeus_and_Nucleus_on_Planet_Auschwitz_Katzetnik_s_Theological_and_Demonological_Kabbalah. It is interesting to note that even very basic motifs such as the cross are taken from the NT.

90. Ka-Tzetnik 135633, *Shivitti*, 50–51.

91. Ka-Tzetnik 135633, *Shivitti*, 52.

92. Ka-Tzetnik 135633, *Shivitti*, 55.

We deliberately stop at this point. Readers of this volume may decide for themselves how far they want to go on this deeply disturbing journey, to what extent they wish to expose themselves to the questions posed by this text, and how far they wish to explore the answers already hinted at. What is decisive for the topic of this volume is that the examination of the genre of otherworldly journeys is by no means a topic of the past only—or a topic of marginal importance. The last example in particular shows that the texts are concerned with nothing less than the question of what it means to be human in a world whose order—for whatever reason—is fragile and questionable. In different ways, many journeys to the afterlife address the injustice experienced, the imbalance in this world and its horrors. They try to save the idea of an orderly cosmos by adding other worlds that balance out what is perceived as chaotic in this world. *Shivitti* reverses this: As much as the LSD trip to Auschwitz seems to lead to another world, it says something fundamental about *this* world, about God, and about humanity. No sense of a good creation can be saved here. In one of the last visions, the author sees his own family, murdered in Auschwitz, before the throne of God:

> I've already caught up with mom, she's standing before God's throne. Her screams cut the air. "Look at this, God! Look at it!" She drags seventeen-year-old Daniella forward and tears the cloth from the brand between her daughter's breasts: "Look at this, God! Look at her, your *field whore!*"[93] And he looks. God sees. Now mom pulls eleven-year-old Moni forward. "Look at that, God! Look at him, your *peep* from Auschwitz!"[94] And Mum's screams cut through the air: "Don't run away from me, God! Look at me, God! They have delivered me to you naked, without hair on my head, and my children are sobbing: Mama!

---

93. The fate of Daniella is at the center of the novel *House of Dolls* (Simon & Schuster, 1955).

94. Moni's fate is at the center of the novel *Piepel: The Most Terrible Story Ever Told* (Anthony Blond, 1961).

> Mommy! Did you hear the crying of my child, the *Peep*? Did you hear my child, the *Field Whore*, sobbing? I am the mother of these sobbing children. And you, God, tell me, who are you? And he looks. God sees—me. He sees me sitting on my throne under the flaming mushroom, while I see myself standing next to Block 14, the skeleton of a Muselmann in Auschwitz, and knows that I see my family rising in the smoke from the opening of the chimney, while my eyes watch me: Nucleus! I am Nucleus![95] Oh my God![96]

95. This is the name of a demon who plays a key role in the novel alongside the better-known Asmodeus.

96. Ka-Tzetnik 135633, *Shivitti*, 113.

CHAPTER 4

Apocryphal Chronologies

Perspectives on Time, History, and the End of the World

What is the future of humanity? How many more generations will continue to find a home on this earth? What will the world we live in look like in ten, twenty, or a hundred years? Will our cities and towns continue to be habitable? These are burning questions in the twenty-first century—in the truest sense of the word. Just a few years ago we experienced a global pandemic that, despite the best efforts of the wealthiest and most technologically advanced countries, could not easily be brought under control; almost daily we see new images of the effects of a climate catastrophe that can be stopped only if the whole of humanity dramatically rethinks and changes its actions. At the same time, the power blocs that defined the world in the twentieth century are breaking apart, and the international situation is increasingly unstable: Democratic states are losing their balance, dangerous ideologies are taking on a new face, and the power of unscrupulous autocrats and dictators is growing in many places. Social media is not helping.

It is surely true that the most urgent problems of our day—above all the climate catastrophe—are unprecedented in human history; nevertheless, our view of the future has interesting parallels to what we know of certain perspectives from late antiquity.[1] Sulpicius Severus

1. The following example (as well as additional examples) are presented in much greater detail in Tobias Nicklas, "From Historical Apocalypses to Apocalyptic

(363–425 CE), for example, who is known today primarily as the first biographer of Martin of Tours (316–397 CE) and the author of a significant *Chronology of the World*, was extremely pessimistic about the future of the world.[2] Severus lived at a time of dramatic upheavals in the Western Roman Empire, in which the influence of the central power was barely perceptible, and signs of decline were increasingly clear. Given a worldview within which the Roman Empire and its representative, the emperor, could be linked with the *katechon* of 2 Thessalonians (that is, the figure and/or principle that held back the appearance of the antichrist), one can imagine that the end seemed to have come.[3] Competing calculations as to which year since the beginning of creation humanity was now living in—which point on the timeline humanity currently occupied—took on more urgent significance. It was expected that the world would reach an age of six thousand years (six so-called world weeks) by the time it ended. While an author such as Jerome (347–420 CE) calculated the end of the world at around the year 800 CE in his

History: Late Antique Historians and Apocalyptic Writings," in *Dreams, Visions, Imaginations: Jewish, Christian and Gnostic Views of the World to come*, ed. Jens Schröter et al., BZNW 247 (de Gruyter, 2021), 433–60.

2. On the understanding of time in this text, see Veronika Wieser, "Die Weltchronik des Sulpicius Severus. Fragmente einer Sprache der Endzeit im ausgehenden vierten Jahrhundert," in *Abendländische Apokalyptik: Kompendium zu einer Genealogie der Endzeit*, ed. Veronika Wieser et al., Kulturgeschichte der Apokalypse 1 (Akademie, 2013), 661–92. On the success and significance of *Life of Martin*, see Peter Brown, *The Rise of Western Christendom. Triumph and Diversity, A.D. 200–1000*, 3rd ed. (Wiley Blackwell, 2013), 83: "The *Life of Martin* soon became a classic of Latin hagiography. He was a saint for a new, less quiet times: a prophet raised up by God in the West, to warn a generation of tepid Christians of the swift approach of the Last Days."

3. On the catechism (*Katechon*) in the history of interpretation and contemporary interpretation, see Paul Metzger, *Katechon: II Thess 2,1–12 im Horizont apokalyptischen Denkens*, BZNW 135 (de Gruyter, 2005); Fritz W. Röcker, *Belial und Katechon: Eine Untersuchung zu 1 Thess 2,1–12 und 1 Thess 4,13–5,11*, WUNT 2/262 (Mohr Siebeck, 2009), as well as (more concise and based on both) Nicklas, *Der zweite Thessalonicherbrief*, 142–50.

translation of the *Chronicle* by Eusebius of Caesarea,[4] Severus, following Martin of Tours, assumed that he was living in one of the last generations before the end. One passage in his *Dialogues*, in which he also refers to Martin's last words, underscores his perspective:[5]

> But when we questioned [Martin] concerning the end of the world, he said to us that Nero and Antichrist have first to come; that Nero will rule in the Western portion of the world, after having subdued ten kings; and that a persecution will be carried out by him, with the view of compelling men to worship the idols of the Gentiles. He also said that Antichrist, on the other hand, would first seize upon the empire of the East, having his seat and capital in Jerusalem, while both the city and the temple would be restored by him. He added that his persecution would have for its object to compel men to deny Christ as God, while he maintained rather that he himself was Christ, and he ordered all men to be circumcised according to the law. He further said that Nero was to be destroyed by Antichrist, and that the whole world, and all nations, were to be reduced under the power of Antichrist and that the impious one should be overthrown by the coming of Christ. He told us, too, that there was no doubt but that Antichrist, having been conceived by an evil spirit, as already born, and had, by this time, reached the years of boyhood, while he would assume power as soon as he reached the proper age. Now, this is the eighth year since we heard these words from his lips: you may conjecture, then how nearly about to happen are those things which are feared in the future. (*Dial.* 2.14.4)

4. More extensive in James T. Palmer, "The Ordering of Time," in Wieser et al., *Abendländische Apokalyptik*, 607–8; it is clear that this naturally led to intense speculation about the approaching end around 800 CE, i.e., in the West in connection with the reign of Charlemagne (768–814 CE). See, e.g., James T. Palmer, *The Apocalypse in the Early Middle Ages* (Cambridge University Press, 2014), 130–58.

5. Edition Jacques Fontaine, SC 510; translation: *The Works of Sulpicius Severus. On the Life of St. Martin, Letters, Dialogues, Sacred History* (2012), 124.

No specific date for the end time is named, but the time remaining is reduced to just a few years, a generation at most. The narrative presentation of the chronology builds a dire sense of urgency for the reader: When Martin spoke, the antichrist had already been born and reached boyhood, but that was eight years before the composition of the text; how much more time passed between composition and the reader's encounter with the text? The basic scenario is certainly rooted in interpretations of texts from the canonical Revelation, 2 Thessalonians, and—with the specific mention of the antichrist—perhaps the Johannine Epistles (1 John 2:18, 22; 4:2; 2 John 7).[6] And yet it is not simply biblical, as it creatively combines various end-time scenarios from different texts that stand side by side in the New Testament but are not easily compatible with one another—a phenomenon that can be observed in many other works.[7] In this chapter, we hope to reveal the central role played by apocryphal texts and traditions whenever Christians (of different times and places) have attempted to determine their position in time and history, particularly with respect to the end time. The amount of extant material is enormous, so we make no attempt at a comprehensive survey. Instead, we treat a small selection of the most pronounced features of such material, taking a few lesser-known works as examples.

1. Example 1: Where Do We Stand in Time? The Long Form of the Apocalypse of Thomas

The Latin Apocalypse of Thomas is one writing of late antique Christianity that has hardly been studied to date.[8] This lack of atten-

6. The fact that the history of the figure of the antichrist was able to detach itself very quickly from these biblical origins is shown by the fascinating study by Bernard McGinn, *Antichrist: Two Thousand Years of the Human Fascination with the Evil* (Columbia University Press, 2000).

7. Using the example of the disputes in the so-called Donatist controversy (with a focus on the figure of Tyconius), see, e.g., Karol P. Kulpa, *The Relevance of the Reception of 2 Thess 2:3–12 for Tyconius: A Theological Reading of Tyconius' Insights*, History of Biblical Exegesis 4 (Mohr Siebeck, 2022).

8. An easily accessible recent English translation with an introduction based on the latest research is offered in Matthias Geigenfeind, "The Apocalypse of Thomas," in

tion is accounted for in part by a continued skepticism toward apocalyptic literature in research but may also be attributed to the work's difficult textual tradition. An attempt at a critical edition was made at the beginning of the twentieth century by Ernst von Dobschütz (1870–1934) but then shelved for decades. Until a new edition is made available, it is therefore still best to use the texts of specific manuscripts of the Apocalypse of Thomas as a basis.[9] The pluriformity of the work is interesting for the present purposes, inasmuch as the long version develops a concept of time and history that is clearly different from that of the short version.[10]

The following discussion focuses on the long version of the text, which is preserved (partly fragmentarily, partly combined with other writings) in a total of five manuscripts, the oldest of which (dated to the sixth or seventh century) is found in the Biblioteca Capitolare in Verona. While the short version of the writing concentrates on the description of the last days of creation and the world's gradual dissolution, the long version precedes all this with a detailed outline of the events that

---

New Testament Apocrypha: More Noncanonical Scriptures, ed. Tony Burke (Eerdmans, 2020), 2:580–604. Parts of the following material are taken from Tobias Nicklas et al., "Die Deutung der Weltgeschichte in der Langform der Apokalypse des Thomas (Codex Palatinus: §§2–10)," *ETL* 94 (2018): 257–74. However, while this older contribution still concentrates quite clearly on the reconstruction of possible historical events behind the presentation of the text, here a meta level will be aimed at more clearly, on the basis of which the technique of the text in dealing with historical events and the perspective on these will take center stage.

9. On the specific history of the text, in which, in addition to a short and a long text, there is also an abbreviated form (compared to the long one), see the current overview in Geigenfeind, "Apocalypse of Thomas," 581–82; on the fluidity of the text, see Charles D. Wright, "Rewriting (and Re-editing) the *Apocalypse of Thomas*," in *Écritures et réécritures: la reprise interpretative des traditions fondatrices par la littérature biblique et extra-biblique*, ed. Claire Clivaz et al. (Peeters, 2012), 441–54. As we understand it, Wright is working on a new edition to be published in Corpus Christianorum Series Apocryphorum.

10. On this, see in more detail Tobias Nicklas, "Signs for the End of the *Saeculum*: Time in the *Apocalypse of Thomas* (Short Version, Codex N)," in *Apocalyptic Time*, ed. Emanuela Grypeou and Stephanie Rabe (forthcoming).

will take place before the last days. An interesting technique is used here. Paragraph 2 of this text (in Codex Palatinus [Vatican; Biblioteca Apostolica Vaticana, Pal. Lat. 220, fols. 48v–53r., ninth century]) presents a chaotic situation:[11] "There will be famine and war and earthquakes in various places and sword and great drought, and many dissensions among the people, blasphemy, iniquity, zeal, indolence, hatred, pride and intemperance, so that everyone will speak that which pleases them." Such a description cannot, of course, be placed at a specific historical moment; rather, it combines various catastrophic scenarios, including natural disasters and war but also general human misconduct. What these events and behaviors have in common is not just their threatening, frightening nature; it is important that they also would seem to destroy a sense of order—the sense that everyone has their place in the world and should know what that place is. The disorder is further demonstrated by the fact that people do not know what they are allowed to say to God and to other people and instead blaspheme God and say whatever they please. In turn, sections 3–4 contain statements that concentrate on a crisis in the worship of God:

> My priests will not have peace among themselves; they will sacrifice to me with deceitful mind. Therefore, I will not look upon them. Then the priests will behold the people departing from the house of God. They will turn back to the world and they will set up a boundary in the house of God. They will judge for themselves many places that were lost. And they will be subject to Caesar as they were before, paying the poll-taxes of their city, gold and silver. And the leaders of the towns will be condemned. They will fill the treasuries of the kings with (their) payment. For there will be a great disturbance throughout all the people: the house of God will perish in the wilderness, and their altars

11. The translation follows Geigenfeind, "Apocalypse of Thomas," 591–94. This is of course a simplification, since it is hardly possible to reconstruct an original text of the Apocalypse of Thomas—and the texts of the long form differ from one another in details. The deviations (also carefully noted by Geigenfeind) are kept in view where necessary.

> will be abhorred, so that a spider will weave (its web) within it. The place of holiness will be corrupted, the priesthood will be polluted. Zeal will be broken, virtue will be diminished, joy will perish, and gladness will depart. In those days, evil will abound, there will be favoritism, truth will be no more, covetousness will abound, <and> an upright priesthood will not be found.

While this passage includes more specific, concrete elements—especially with regard to developments in the church—it is still not possible to clearly link what is described here to specific historical moments.[12] Depending on which (inner-Christian) perspective one adopts, almost any situation within a church that is perceived as problematic and for which a priesthood is important could be described in this way. Whether the motif of apostasy from God before the end of time (also described in 2 Thess 2:3) is dealt with here in a free form cannot be clearly established. Nor is it clear whether concrete heresies and political events are alluded to in this passage; again, what is described can certainly be applied to many situations. In other words, Apocalypse of Thomas 2–4 in its long form reflects a deeply pessimistic view of a world that seems to have come apart at the seams and whose order is no longer recognizable without the prophetic gaze of the text. This text, however, does not yet offer any historical orientation. Do the events described lie in an as yet undetermined and indeterminable future? Or are we already in a time in which what is presented is valid?

Answers to such questions first begin to appear in section 5: "Suddenly, near the last time, a king will arise, a lover of the law. He will not rule for long. He will leave two sons. The first is named after the first letter, the second after the eighth. And the first will die before the second." What at first glance appears to be a highly mysterious

12. The motif of the boundary within the house of God could possibly be associated with architectural innovations, which are also accompanied by a cultic innovation (see, e.g., the testimony of Eusebius of Caesarea, *Hist. eccl.* 10.4.44, about the consecration of a church in Tyre). See also Nicklas et al., "Die Deutung der Weltgeschichte," 264.

prophecy of the end of times proves on closer inspection to be a *vaticinium ex eventu* that can be deciphered quite clearly. The king portrayed so positively here, who will "arise near the end of time," is none other than Theodosius I.[13] He was installed as Augustus of the East in January 379 by the Western emperor Gratian and ruled until his death on January 17, 395 CE. However, he became the sole ruler of the Roman Empire, also recognized in the West, only after he had defeated his rival Eugenius (who claimed the title of Western Roman Augustus from 392) in the famous Battle of Frigidus on September 6, 394. Thus, he really only ruled as sole emperor for a few months.[14] It was not only the Apocalypse of Thomas that saw this emperor as a special figure. Theodosius's victory over Eugenius, allegedly made possible by miraculous events, was increasingly understood in the course of tradition as a sign of his divine election.[15] Theodosius's two sons are clearly referred to in our text: His elder son Arcadius is "named after the first letter" (A) and his second son, Honorius, "after the eighth" (H). After Theodosius's death, the two were appointed as his successors: Arcadius in the East (395–408 CE) and Honorius in the West (395–423 CE).

This collection of details—the short reign of Theodosius, the allusions to the names of his two sons, and the information that the first would die earlier than the second—makes the identification of these rulers unambiguous. Moreover, the interrelation of the statements provides clues as to the dating of the passage. It must, of course, have been written after the death of Arcadius—and may look back to the death of Honorius as well. At the same time, this cannot have happened too

13. As Édmund Hauler, "Zu den lateinischen Bruchstücken der Thomasapokalypse und eines apostolischen Sendschreibens im Codex Vind. Nr. 16," *Wiener Studien* 30 (1908): 332, mentions, the identification goes back to Ernst von Dobschütz.

14. A very good account of the reign of Theodosius I is provided by Hartmut Leppin, *Theodosius der Große: Auf dem Weg zu einem christlichen Imperium*, Gestalten der Antike (Wissenschaftliche Buchgesellschaft, 2003).

15. H. A. Drake, *A Century of Miracles: Christians, Pagans, Jews, and the Supernatural, 312–410* (Oxford University Press, 2017), 27–48, offers an interesting depiction.

many decades later because it is already said of Theodosius I that he rose "near the end." The data point that the latter reigned only briefly is best understood from a Western rather than Eastern perspective, a conclusion that is also supported by the fact that our text is transmitted (and was probably composed) in Latin. Given that Theodosius is also described as a "lover of the law," the text may also have been written from the perspective of a Nicene-Constantinopolitan orthodoxy, which opposed multiple groups that were polemically, if imprecisely, described at the time as Arians. Whatever the case, we are obviously dealing here with an author who, like Sulpicius Severus (though likely somewhat later), looks to the approaching end of times in the fifth century of our era. The situation, however, grows more complex, as further details follow in the next few paragraphs:

> Thereafter the two will arise as principes[16] to oppress the nations, under whose days there will be a great famine in the south. Nation will arise against nation and the people will be driven out from their own borders. Again, another king, a cunning man, will arise. And he will command a golden image of Caesar to be made, so that one is bidden to worship it in the house of God. And martyrdom will abound. Then faith will return to the servants of God, and holiness will be multiplied and zeal increased. The mountains will be comforted and will drip sweetness of fire from the face, so that the number of the saints will be accomplished. After a little time there will arise a king out of the east, a lover of the law. The house of God will abound in all necessary things. He will show mercy to the widows and to the needy and he will grant a royal house to the priests. In his time there will be abundance of all things. After that, again a king will arise in the southern part of the world and he will hold rule for a little time. In his days the treasury will fail because of the

16. We depart here from Geigenfeind's translation, which offers the following suggestion: "Thereafter two princes will arise. . . ." Both translations are grammatically possible; Geigenfeind's, however, creates problems in terms of content.

> wages of the Roman soldiers, so that all the acquaintances of the powerful might be commanded to be shared with the same king. Thereafter, there will be abundance of grain and wine and oil, but great inflation, so that gold and silver will be given for grain. There will be very great scarcity at that time.

This passage is perplexing. Just a moment ago, readers thought they had solid ground under their feet, a clear historical reference point. Now, however, that clarity eludes us, with the introduction of figures and events that are much more difficult to associate with specific times and places. This impression may partly be attributed to corruption in transmission—a perennial possibility with literature preserved in manuscripts. We, however, would prefer to attribute this effect to the intentional blending of typical apocalyptic motifs (some with a recognizable biblical background) with more concrete details that feel at least potentially comprehensible as historical reminiscences (as the references to Theodosius and his sons in §5 clearly are). However, the extent to which the two (that is, the general motifs of biblical-apocalyptic literature and possible historical reminiscences) are intertwined here is evident throughout.

Biblical allusions are offered, for example, by section 6, with the motif that "one people will rise above another" (see Mark 13:8) or section 7, with the idea that "the mountains will give comfort and trickle down sweetness" (Amos 9:13; Joel 4:18) and the "number of the saints must be filled" (Rev 6:11; see also 4 Ezra 4:36). Other motifs are less specifically related to individual texts: Discussion of mercy toward widows and the needy (§8) takes up a motif from central prophetic texts, which makes demands with respect to social welfare and was widely used as a Christian proprium in early Christian discourses.[17] Mention of a king rising from the south of the earth (§9) is of course reminiscent of Daniel 11:5, and in the case of the dearth of grain one might think of

17. See further Michael Sommer, *Witwen, Recht und Gerechtigkeit: Diskurse über Witwen im frühen Christentum als Rezeptionsorte prophetischer und weisheitlicher Kultkritik gelesen*, WUNT (Mohr Siebeck, forthcoming).

the opening of the third seal in Revelation (Rev 6:5–6), though parallels are not so close as to suggest a quotation or even a specific allusion. The speeches about famines, martyrdoms, great distress, and so on are also motifs that commonly appear in apocalyptic works, without being linked to specific events. However, the fact that section 5 contains a specific reference to Theodosius I and his sons Arcadius and Honorius prompts the reader to search for such references in other passages as well.

The possibilities are, of course, manifold. Already in section 6—depending on the translation of the words *duo principes*—the reader might continue thinking of Arcadius and Honorius or of others. But what does it mean specifically that they "oppress the nations"? And who is the "other king" from section 7, referred to in at least one manuscript? One could think of the North African usurper Gildo (d. July 398), whose reputation among "orthodox Christians" was extremely poor.[18] But how does our text imagine this event in relation to the later events reported in sections 5–6? And to what extent can Gildo be said to have ordered a "golden image of Caesar to be made" and worshipped "in the house of God"? Perhaps what we have here is simply an apocalyptic motif that developed from the synoptic end-time discourse (Mark 13:14 par Matt 24:15).[19] There is a somewhat greater chance of identifying an historical referent in section 8: The renewed "lover of the law" rising up in the East could very well be Theodosius II, who reigned 408–450 CE and who played an important role in the implementation of

18. Thus already Hauler, "Zu den lateinischen Bruchstücken," 333. See, however, a somewhat more reserved view in Nicklas et al., "Die Deutung der Weltgeschichte", 268–69. That Gildo is described by Claudian as a "barbarian" from a typical Roman perspective—a trait that would also have suggested itself for the Apocalypse of Thomas but is absent here—speaks against the identification with Gildo. For more on this, see Guy Halsall, *Barbarian Migrations and the Roman West 376–568*, 2nd ed. (Cambridge University Press, 2014), 137.

19. The background of this motif, which may originally have alluded to Caligula's plans to erect his statue in the temple in Jerusalem, can probably be found in Dan 9:27; 11:31; 12:11.

Nicene-Constantinopolitan orthodoxy.[20] But what is said about this king is so cryptic that we are left in the dark. The mystery surrounding the king from the south is even greater. Is it about the Western Roman emperor John (423–435 CE)?[21]

Or have we already fallen into the text's trap with all these questions? Perhaps our author has intentionally combined clearly identifiable elements with broader prophetic and apocalyptic scenarios precisely to provoke the reader to make identifications even where the text evades them. We find similar strategies in Revelation; consider, for example, Revelation 13:18, where the number 666 is described as the number of a human name that can (or even should) be calculated.[22] Even more ambiguous is the description of the seven kings in Revelation 17:9–11, who are followed by an eighth, who is one of the seven. The history of interpretation of the text is full of suggested decipherments with widely varying degrees of plausibility. It is the ultimate ambiguity of the text, combined here with hints at the understanding and knowledge necessary to decipher it, that continually provokes readers to attempt decoding.[23]

That such texts occasionally allow a glimpse of their historical location but never do so consistently (and almost never unambiguously) also enables readers of later generations—in times when the original *vaticinia ex eventu* have lost their function—to continue to make use of the works' logic: An apocalypse is not simply a description of historical events but

20. See further, e.g., at Timothy E. Gregory, *A History of Byzantium*, 2nd ed., Blackwell History of the Ancient World (Wiley-Blackwell, 2016), 103–14.

21. Thus again the interpretation of Hauler, "Zu den lateinischen Bruchstücken," 334.

22. The interpretation of Emperor Nero, which many authors take for granted today, dates back only to the nineteenth century. We are indebted to Regis Burnet for this reference.

23. On the reception history of both passages, see, e.g., Judith Kovacs and Christopher Rowland, *Revelation*, Blackwell Bible Commentaries (Blackwell, 2004), 157–58, 177–89.

an *interpretation of experienced time*. What is described and alluded to is, as in any historical account, the result of selection, and the criteria of selection used by the apocalyptic author are often different from those of the (contemporary) historian. Both, however, must choose and thus both adopt a perspective. This perhaps becomes even clearer if we consider which events the Apocalypse of Thomas apparently does not mention: We read nothing about the catastrophic defeat of Emperor Valens (Eastern Roman emperor 364–378 CE) at Adrianople (on August 9, 378)—an event that was interpreted by other authors as the beginning of an unstoppable decline of the Roman Empire.[24] Despite the author's apparently Western perspective, we also read nothing about the fall of Rome in August 410 CE at the hands of Visigothic warriors led by Alaric (ca. 370–410 CE).[25] And despite the obvious interest in an orthodox Christian point of view and despite a multitude of allusions to the status of the church, there is no reference to the great councils of the fifth century. The apocalyptic view of the world thus shows us in the extreme how much each of our perspectives on time and history is based on our own criteria for selection. In each case, images of what has happened and what is still to be expected are created, which at best reflect parts of the whole. What may interest us as historians of the twenty-first century differs significantly from what the author of the Apocalypse of Thomas considered decisive. And yet he seems to have been successful, inasmuch as his text continued to be copied centuries after it was written.

One could attribute this peculiar, seemingly distorted view of time and history to the generic features of apocalypse. Something similar,

24. Noel Lenski, *Failure of Empire: Valens and the Roman State in the Fourth Century* (University of California Press, 2002), 320–67, offers a detailed account of this event, which was traumatic for later Roman history because the emperor fell on the battlefield.

25. For more on Alaric and his campaigns, see Mischa Meier, *Geschichte der Völkerwanderung: Europa, Asien und Afrika vom 3. bis zum 8. Jahrhundert n.Chr.*, 2nd ed. (Beck, 2020), 191–223.

however, can also be found in historiographical literature.[26] The world chronicle of Hydatius of Aquae Flaviae (ca. 395/400–ca. 469 CE), written in roughly the same era, offers a particularly fine example of this.[27] Hydatius, who was probably influenced in his interpretation of history by a series of prophetic and apocalyptic texts such as Daniel, Ezekiel, Joel, 2 Thessalonians, Revelation, and perhaps also a version of the Apocalypse of Thomas that is no longer extant,[28] wrote his work shortly before his death, being of the opinion that the end of the world was imminent. He repeatedly describes historical events in the light of prophetic writings: This is particularly evident in the short section on the marriage of the Visigothic king Athaulf (374–415 CE) to the Roman princess Galla Placidia (392–450 CE) in 414 (*Chron.* 57):[29] "Athaulf married Placidia at Narbona. By this event it is thought that a prophecy of Daniel was fulfilled who says that the daughter of the King of the South was to be united with the King of the North, but no offspring of his by her would survive" (see Dan 11:8).[30] Like the author of the Apocalypse of Thomas, Hydatius seeks to understand the signs of the times sent by God. Perceiving these and interpreting them in an appropriate way is at least as important as a description of the "great events"

---

26. On the following example, see in detail Nicklas, *Historical Apocalypses*, 443–50.

27. Edition (with introduction and German translation): Jan-Markus Kötter and Carlo Scardino, eds., *Chronik des Hydatius. Fortführung der Epitome*, Kleine und fragmentarische Historiker der Spätantike G 9–10 (Schöningh, 2019).

28. On the possible dependence of Hydatius on the Apocalypse of Thomas for the first time, see Richard W. Burgess, *The Chronicle of Hydatius and the consularia Constantinopolitana. Two Contemporary Accounts of the Final Years of the Roman Empire*, OCM (Clarendon, 1993), 31–32, as well as additional arguments in Nicklas, *Historical Apocalypses*, 446–49.

29. For a more precise historical classification, see Hagith Sivan, *Galla Placidia. The Last Roman Empress*, Women in Antiquity (Oxford University Press, 2011), 9–36.

30. The following translations are aligned with the text by Kötter and Scardino, but adapted from Burgess, *Chronicle*.

of world history. This is the only way to explain the mysterious words with which Hydatius's history of the world ends:

> And even a number of signs and prodigies were recognized in areas of Gallaecia. In the river Minius at around the fifth milestone from the town of Lais, four fish of unique appearance and type were caught, as the Christians and pious men who had caught them related. They were inscribed with Hebrew and Greek letters, but with the numbers of Spanish *aeras* in Latin, which thus embrace the cycle of the three hundred-and sixty-fifth year.... And there were many other portents which would take too long to recount. (*Chron.* 253)

These closing words of a world chronicle, which places itself shortly before the end of the world, are not concerned with the description of a great battle or the fall of a dynasty or a world empire. Instead, the focus is a small tale from a fishing trip that took place at the edge of the known world—though perhaps at the center of Hydatius's world. What clearer indication could there be that we have reached the end of history—that there is nothing more to tell?

Texts such as these may seem crude and marginal in their narrow perspectives and their seemingly strange selection of events worth telling. But are the perspectives of today's newspaper reports in Europe and the United States, which regularly ignore events in huge swaths of the globe (e.g., in sub-Saharan Africa, large parts of Asia, or Latin America) while taking an interest in the private lives of athletes or actors, any less narrow and strange?

2. Example 2: A Reinterpretation of Biblical End-Time Scenarios—The Tiburtine Sibyl

The second example is closely related to the first, though it goes one important step further. The undertaking of placing one's own position on a timeline of human history can also (directly or indirectly) have a political dimension. We already know this from the writings of the New

Testament. As much as we can discuss the extent to which Revelation should be seen as an anti-imperial writing,[31] it is clear in any case that this text calls on us to take a stand, to bear witness to the God of Israel and his end-time messenger, the Lamb, in this world, to submit to him almost as if enslaved, and to serve him in every way possible.[32] Where this form of total devotion encounters other, contradictory claims, these must be rejected in the strongest possible terms. This opposing side can be represented by various motifs: the devilish dragon and the beasts associated with it in chapters 12–13, the "kings of the earth" subjected to them, or Babylon condemned to destruction, which also stands for Rome without being completely absorbed by it (Rev 17–18).

At least in its reception, something similar can be said about the second chapter of 2 Thessalonians. Very early on, the mysterious *katechon* mentioned in 2 Thessalonians 2:6–7 was identified with the Roman Empire and its representative, the emperor.[33] The Roman Empire and its order, represented by the emperor, therefore prevented the appearance of the antichrist and thus the expected events of the end times: the parousia of Christ and his final victory over the forces of evil. Initially, this could be seen as something negative: Rome (as *katechon*) was delaying the much longed-for return of Christ. Over time, however, this perspective began to shift. The continued existence of the Roman Empire guaranteed that the chaos expected at the end times could *still* be held back. This is certainly one of the impulses that led to the motif that a "last emperor"

31. In this regard, see Warren Carter, "Revelation and Roman Rule in First-Century Asia Minor," in *The Oxford Handbook of the Book of Revelation*, ed. Craig R. Koester (Oxford University Press, 2020), 133–52 (with detailed bibliography).

32. See further Tobias Nicklas, "Gott und Identität: Das Gottesbild der Johannesoffenbarung und ihre Identitätskonstruktion," in *Die Johannesapokalypse: Geschichte – Theologie – Rezeption*, ed. M. Sommer et al., WUNT 508 (Mohr Siebeck, 2023), 135–52.

33. This interpretation can already be found in Tertullian (*Apol.* 32) and in the *Commentary on Daniel* by Hippolytus of Rome. Additional examples can be found in Nicklas, *Der zweite Thessalonicherbrief*, 144–45.

would appear at the end of time, who would ultimately place his power in the hands of Christ or God.[34] The latter is, of course, a variation of what we read in 1 Corinthians 15:24–28. In this model, however, it is not Christ who destroys the enemies of God and ultimately hands over all power to him but the emperor of the (or rather, *a*) Roman Empire representing Christ on earth.

One of the most fascinating texts to illustrate this model is the so-called Tiburtine Sibyl.[35] This apocalyptic writing, which was probably originally written in Greek, is extant in a large number of Latin manuscripts. An extant Greek version probably represents a later text form than the core of the Latin writings. There are also witnesses in Ethiopic and Garshuni, but we leave these aside at present. In the course of its transmission, the text was repeatedly subjected to new additions, through which later emperors from the medieval Carolingian and even Salian dynasties were able to inscribe themselves in the text. These later interpolations are, at least in most cases, quite easily identified. The plot of the text is more important: it takes place at the beginning of Rome's history, specifically—and quite anachronistically—under an emperor of Trojan origin (Tiburtine Sibyl 2.1).[36] One hundred senators dream

34. Foundationally in Gerhard Podskalsky, *Byzantinische Reichsideologie: Die Periodisierung der Weltgecshichte in den vier Großreichen (Daniel 2 und 7) und dem tausendjährigen Friedensreiche (Apok. 20), Eine motivgeschichtliche Untersuchung* (Fink, 1972); Paul J. Alexander, *The Byzantine Apocalyptic Tradition* (University of California Press, 1985); and especially in Hannes Möhling, *Der Weltkaiser der Endzeit: Entstehung, Wandel und Wirkung einer tausendjährigen Weissagung*, Mittelalter-Forschungen 3 (Thorbeke, 2000).

35. On the decisive questions concerning textual transmission and introduction discussed below, see Stephen J. Shoemaker, "The Tiburtine Sibyl," in Burke and Landau, *New Testament Apocrypha*, 1:510–25. The following translations also come from this article (or are adapted from it). Translation of the Greek in Rieuwerd Buitenwerf, "The Tiburtine Sibyl (Greek)," in Bauckham et al., *Old Testament Pseudepigrapha*, 1:176–88. Latin edition in Ernst Sackur, *Sibyllinische Texte und Forschungen. Pseudomethodius, Adso und die tiburtinische Sibylle* (Niemeyer, 1898).

36. This of course includes the mythical Trojan origin of the Roman people.

the same dream on the same night, in which nine suns appear to them. The sibyl, who is in Rome at the time, interprets this dream for them as a prefiguration of the history of Rome in nine ages. The depiction of the ninth "generation" in chapter 3 of the text is very reminiscent of what we also discovered in the long form of the Apocalypse of Thomas in its technique of creating identifiable parallels to historical events:

> The ninth sun is the ninth generation, and the leaders of Rome will rise up in the ruin of many. . . . And after that two kings will arise from Egypt and four kings will conquer and kill them and all their army, and they will reign for three years and six months. After them will rise another king, with the name of C, mighty in battle, who will reign for thirty years and will build a temple to God and will fulfill the law and establish justice on earth for God's sake. And there will be a great city, and many will dwell in it, namely the seventy-two languages [!]. Do not rejoice with joy: they will not rule from Byzantium within sixty years. Then other kings will arise, and one of them will be burned with fire. (3.14–16)

While some of the statements in this passage remain obscure—in part due to the ambiguous Latin[37]—it is nevertheless possible to make clear identifications with figures from Roman history at the beginning of the fourth century of our era. It is very likely that the "four kings" refer to the Roman tetrarchy, which was introduced under the Augusti Diocletian and Maximian and the Caesares Galerius and Constantius I Chlorus from 293 CE. However, the fact that our text speaks here of a reign of only three and a half years, while the aforementioned shared power until 305 CE, suggests that it is not the first but the fourth and last tetrarchy with the Augusti Galerius and Licinius as well as the Caesares Maximinus Daia and Constantine (who shared power from 308–311)

37. For example, note Shoemaker, "Tiburtine Sibyl," 521.

that is meant here.[38] If we now identify C with Constantine I and start counting from his years as Caesar of a tetrarchy, we arrive at around thirty years of rule before his death in 337 CE. Given that the text was probably written three generations after Constantine's reign, we need not expect too much precision here. The characterization of Constantine as a church builder and promoter of justice naturally corresponds to his reputation for asserting "orthodoxy." And of course, it is obvious that the great city mentioned here refers to his city, Constantinople, which is referred to by its old name, Byzantium, in the following sentence.[39] The final sentence of Tiburtine Sibyl 3.16 is the last historical allusion that is recognizable in the noninterpolated text: It can refer only to the Battle of Adrianople on August 9, 378, in which the reigning emperor Valens (Eastern Roman emperor 364–378 CE) lost his life—one of the deepest traumas of late Roman history. If this event represents the transition between *vaticinium ex eventu* and prophecy of the future, then it is highly probable that the original text of the Tiburtine Sibyl could have been written no more than a generation after it took place.[40]

Unlike the Apocalypse of Thomas, in which the historical prologue then leads into a depiction of the last seven days of a creation that is gradually disintegrating, the Tiburtine Sibyl develops a highly complex scenario of the things that must happen first. If the clearly medieval additions (with allusions to Carolingian rulers, for example), especially in chapters 4 and 6, are removed from the text, the following scenario emerges: Chapter 5 describes the dissolution of all order in the world in apocalyptic images, including wars, plagues of locusts, and sexual

38. For a more detailed account of the historical events, see, e.g., David S. Potter, *The Roman Empire at Bay. AD 180–395*, 2nd ed., Routledge History of the Ancient World (Routledge, 2014), 275–84 (on the emergence of the first tetrarchy) as well as 326–56 (on the fall of this system and the rise of Constantine).

39. For additional information on the founding of Constantinople, see Albrecht Berger, *Konstantinopel. Geschichte – Topographie – Religion*, Standorte in Antike und Christentum (Anton Hiersemann, 2011), 1–20.

40. Similar arguments can be found in Shoemaker, "Tiburtine Sibyl," 512–15.

transgressions. Chapter 7 then arrives at the conclusion that, at that time, no one was in a position to stop the continuing destruction. Only with Tiburtine Sibyl 7.4 does this picture change:

> Then will arise a king of the Greeks, whose name is Constans, and he will be king of the Romans and the Greeks. He will be tall in stature, handsome in appearance, shining in countenance, and well-built in all of his bodily features. And his reign will end after 112 years. Therefore, in those days there will be great riches, and the earth will bring fruit abundantly, so that a measure of wheat will be sold for one denarius, a measure of wine for one denarius, and a measure of oil for one denarius. And the king will have before his eyes a Scripture that says: "The king of the Romans will claim the entire kingdom of the Christians for himself." Therefore, he will devastate all the islands and cities of the pagans and destroy all their temples of idols. He will call all the pagans to baptism, and the cross of Jesus Christ will be erected in all the temples. . . . Whoever will not worship the cross of Jesus Christ will be punished by the sword. And when 120 years have been completed, the Jews will be converted to the Lord, and his sepulcher will be glorified by all. In these days Judah will be saved and Israel will encamp in confidence.

The name Constans is unlikely to refer to Constantine's son, Constans I, who reigned from 337–350 CE; rather, it is clear from the description of this king that he is a kind of superhuman figure, almost a superhero in contemporary terms. In his end-time reign there is once again a great flourishing, as carefree conditions prevail and messianic prophecies relating to the end times (such as the conversion of all Jews to Christianity)[41] are fulfilled. Some formulations are somewhat pecu-

41. The text supports this with a citation of Jer 23:6a and a possible allusion to Isa 11:10. It is also conceivable, however, that there is an influence from Rom 11:25–26—the prophecy of the salvation of all Israel.

liar, including but not limited to the discrepancy between 120 years and 112 years as the length of the ruler's reign. Ideas such as the punishment with the sword of those who do not venerate the cross of Christ or the idea that "his sepulcher will be glorified by all" (perhaps a cipher for an end-time pilgrimage to Jerusalem) may have been added after the fourth century.

The origin of the peculiar "scriptural passage" quoted here ("the king of the Romans will claim the entire kingdom of the Christians for himself") is of course unclear. It is possible, however, for any ruler who sees himself as Roman or as a successor to Rome to use the title "king of Rome" to legitimize a claim to world dominion. The concluding eighth chapter shows that this claim, as well as the forcible conversion of unbelievers, can be legitimized as the will of God or the end-time plan of salvation. Apparently at the time when the last emperor reigns, the antichrist also appears, and the nations of Gog and Magog, once enclosed by Alexander the Great, rise up. The nations Gog and Magog are, of course, already known from canonical Revelation; the text of the Tiburtine Sibyl clearly alludes to Revelation 20:8.[42] There, too, they represent the last enemies of God to be defeated before the final judgment. However, while in Revelation they surround "the camp of the saints and God's beloved city" (probably Jerusalem?) and are destroyed by heavenly fire (Rev 20:9), the focus here shifts to Rome: The Roman emperor gathers his army and destroys it in an end-time battle. Only then is his task complete:

> Then he [the emperor] will come to Jerusalem, and there having laid down the diadem of his head and all his royal garb, he will hand over the kingdom of the Christians to God the Father and Jesus Christ his Son. And when the Roman Empire will have come to an end, then the Antichrist will be

42. The background to the idea can probably already be found in Ezek 38–39. The connection between Alexander the Great and the peoples of Gog and Magog also reappears in Islam.

> openly revealed, and he will sit in the House of the Lord in Jerusalem. Nevertheless, while he is reigning, two most distinguished men, Elijah and Enoch, will go forth to announce the coming of the Lord and the Antichrist will kill them. After three days they will be resurrected by the Lord. Then there will be a great persecution, such as there was not before nor as will follow thereafter. Nevertheless, the Lord will shorten those days for the sake of the elect, and the Antichrist will be slain by the power of the Lord by the Archangel Michael on the Mount of Olives.

This is followed by the final judgment by the Lord, who will reign from now on in a new heaven and a new earth (cf. Rev 21:1) among his "saints." All of this is exciting in many respects: While we still perceive the canonical Revelation as a text that—in whatever concrete form—calls for a form of total devotion to Christ from a perspective that sees itself as marginalized, and while Revelation may be understood as directed against the Roman Empire and its claims, here we find the opposite: It is the last Roman emperor himself who takes on Christ's tasks in a world order that is now understood in a completely different way. From the perspective of this text, the last part of the history of the world *is Roman history*. With the procession of the last emperor to Jerusalem, the "kingdom of the Christians"—now understood as *identical to the Roman Empire*—comes to an end. It passes over into the kingdom of God (or the kingdom of Christ), which is identical with the new world in which Christ reigns over the saints. This happens through a gesture of the Roman emperor, who, by handing over his power into the hands of God and Christ, basically accomplishes what 1 Corinthians 15:24 expects of Christ in relation to his Father.

What comes next can be understood as a reception of important aspects of 2 Thessalonians 2 without explicitly quoting this text: Only when the restraining principle and its representative (that is, the *katechon*, understood as the Roman Empire and the Roman emperor) no longer play a role will the antichrist (here described as the "man of lawlessness") be revealed (2 Thess 2:6–8). The idea that he will sit in the house of God in Jerusalem also goes back to 2 Thessalonians, albeit with the variation that the Jewish temple is replaced here with a church (perhaps the Church of the Holy Sepulcher in Jerusalem). The appearance of Elijah and Enoch, which functions here to delay the parousia, is probably derived from Revelation 11:1–3; the motif of the last time of persecution, in which the Lord will shorten the time for the elect, in turn probably goes back to the Matthean end-time discourse (Matt 24:21–22). The victory of Michael over the antichrist on the Mount of Olives is not biblical, but it is reminiscent of Michael's victory over Satan and the subsequent fall of Satan described in Revelation 12:7–12. The fusion of various motifs developed from the canon, but ultimately anchored in a Christian cultural memory[43] (or a "Bible in the mind"), results in an impression of continuity with early traditions—despite the fact that this work reinterprets that tradition in a radical way. It will be the Roman ruler alone who, following God's will for history, can bring earthly history to its final phase before the parousia. An eschatology that, in the first century, deconstructed worldly power has become a view of the world, time, and history that affirms precisely that power.[44]

3. Example 3: Escape from the World and from Time—The Long Form of the Latin Visio Pauli

The Visio Pauli (that is, the longer, Latin version of the Apocalypse of Paul discussed in ch. 3) addresses a completely different level of the question of the relationship between humanity, time, and the world.[45] Although this text is known today for its depiction of otherworldly

43. On this concept, see especially Assmann, *Das kulturelle Gedächtnis*.

44. Of course, it should not be underestimated that the Apocalypse of John consciously inscribes itself into power discourses with the greatest self-confidence and in a highly aggressive manner.

45. An English translation, which of course cannot capture the diversity of the various textual witnesses of this work, is in Elliott, *Apocryphal New Testament*, 616–44. The following translations have been adapted from this translation; they are oriented

places (above all a detailed description of hell) its perspective on time and history is also fascinating. Unlike the examples presented so far, however, the text does not present material that can be linked to specific historical figures or events (apart from the legend about its alleged discovery "under the consulship of Theodosius Augustus the Younger and Cynegius" in 388 CE).[46] Instead, the work is presented as an account of what Paul only hints at in 2 Corinthians 12:2–4, that is, the apostle's rapture to the third heaven and paradise, though it does not elaborate on what he saw and heard. In the brief discussion that follows, we focus on the work's temporality vis-à-vis humanity.[47]

Before the text offers its well-known detailed descriptions of heaven and hell, it lays out fundamental statements on the situation of humanity in the world. As opposed to describing specific moments of human history or referring to identifiable events or personalities, the Visio Pauli provides a general view of the role of human action in time and history. The basic idea of the first part of the work can be summarized in a single sentence. *Because of its disobedience to God, humanity is worse than any other part of creation*. This is illustrated as the various parts of creation speak to God and complain about the actions of humanity. The voice of the earth goes furthest:

> Lord God Almighty, I above every other of your creatures am harmed, supporting the fornications, adulteries, homicides, thefts, perjuries, magic and ill-doings of human beings and all the evil they do, so that the father rises against the son, and the son upon the father, the alien against the alien and each one defiles his neighbor's wife. The father mounts the bed of his own son, and the son likewise ascends the couch of his own father;

on the critical edition by Silverstein and Hilhorst, *Apocalypse of Paul*, but nevertheless are by Tobias Nicklas.

46. See also Hugo Duensing and Aurelio de Santos Otero, "Apokalypse des Paulus," in Schneemelcher, *Neutestamentliche Apokryphen*, 2:648n5.

47. The following section partly uses material that is presented in more detail (and partly from a different perspective) in Nicklas, "Latin *Apocalypse of Paul*."

> and in all these evils they who offer sacrifice to your name have defiled your holy place. (§6)[48]

From this perspective, there is no such thing as a history or a development of humanity. Although humanity has a special destiny from creation (§3), namely, to rule over the creatures of the earth, it violates this destiny from the very beginning. In contrast to the apocalypses we have looked at so far, the focus is *not* on specific historical catastrophes or the particular injustice of individual people; rather, humanity *as such*, beyond all geographical and historical localization and also beyond all affiliation to a specific group (whether to a chosen people, to the Christian church, or a part of it), falls short. From the perspective of this apocalypse, however, being human means (at least implicitly) being a man. Thus, the focus within this catalog of vices is also on sexual transgressions, which are formulated from the perspective of men and with men in mind. And among these men, the focus is particularly on priests who dishonor the sanctuary of God through their way of sacrificing. In fact, the original Apocalypse of Paul seems to have been formulated in an ascetic context, perhaps Pachomian monastic communities in Egypt.[49]

Such a context may explain why, instead of looking at the events of history, the focus is on another aspect: time itself. In section 7, the focus turns from concrete human sins to an appropriate practice of prayer. The decisive passage reads: "Bless God, the Lord, unceasingly, every hour and every day, but more especially when the sun sets."[50] This rather odd statement is explained by the idea that every human being has a personal angel at their side. These are not simply guardian angels but angels who regularly give an account to God at sunset of the deeds of the person assigned to them. These angels would gladly belong to those "who have renounced this world for the sake of your holy name, who wander as

48. The translation follows MS P.

49. On this, see the foundational work by Copeland, "Mapping the Apocalypse of Paul," 177–78, as well as the recent work Fiori, "Death and Judgment," 92–108.

50. Translation according to P (Codex Paris).

pilgrims in the caves of the rocks, weeping every hour they are on earth and hungering and thirsting for the sake of your name, who have girded their loins, who hold the incense of their hearts in their hands and pray and bless every hour" (§9). But even if human beings behave appropriately, they—and the angels assigned to them—suffer under the conditions of the world. According to the Visio Pauli, perfection is possible only if one escapes from a world full of devilish temptations—a world in which neither baptism nor faith in Christ alone is sufficient for salvation. This is evident in the lamentations of the angels assigned to people whose lives do not correspond to the highest ideals: "We have come from those who have called on your name, and the obstacles of the world have made them miserable, thinking up many occasions every hour and not even making a single pure prayer, not even with all their heart, in all the days of their lives" (§10). That these are not unbelievers or pagans is underscored in the text of a manuscript in Arnhem the Netherlands, which adds that the angels speak of people "over whom your name has been called." The task that the work sets for its readers—who were probably exclusively men—is not to find their appropriate place on a timeline that leads inevitably to no good end, but to drop out of the world and time altogether. This is what each man must do to be found righteous at the approach of his own death—a point made quite explicitly in the detailed descriptions of the fate of the soul of a righteous man and the fate of the soul of an unrighteous man within the work.

4. Example 4: 5 Ezra—A Turning Point or a New Perspective on the History of Israel?

Christian questions about time and history, however, are concerned not only with the problem of positioning oneself on a historical timeline that leads to the end time or the problem of how a connection to heavenly worlds beyond time can be established *now*. The Pauline writings already show that the followers of Jesus of Nazareth assumed from the earliest times that they were living in a new quality of time—indeed, that with the death and resurrection of Jesus, decisive events of the end time had already begun. This is why it was possible for the old walls of separation between Israel and the nations to break down, why a new hope for the resurrection from the dead "in Christ" arose, and much more. The range of consequences resulting from this new understanding of time is vast—and it is impossible to grasp without also considering apocryphal writings. One of several surviving statements of how this new quality of time could be understood can be found in 5 Ezra, an early Christian prophetic writing that has repeatedly been associated with the notion of a turning point in time after which Israel lost its election as God's people. Here we want to show that such an anti-Jewish interpretation of the text is probably wrong.

Fifth Ezra, which is preserved today only in combination with 4 Ezra and 6 Ezra (and was perhaps composed on the basis of 4 Ezra), is extant only in Latin in two recensions.[51] It is difficult to date the work with certainty; it presupposes Revelation, and there is no evidence of a clear reception of it until the fifth century. Theodore Bergren suggests a very broad period "before 300 CE" as its date of composition,[52] but the middle of the second century seems the most likely. The work may react to the events of the Bar Kokhba War of 132–135 CE, but it is not possible to be certain about this. In any case, 5 Ezra can be placed within a stream of texts in which the biblical figure of Ezra is received and interpreted as a prophet or apocalyptic seer.[53] The work places itself chronologically in the "days of King Nebuchadnezzar." During this time, the word of the Lord is given to "Ezra the son of Chusi" (5 Ezra 1:1); a large part of the work consists of reproaches from the Lord against his once chosen

51. For a discussion of introductory questions (and an edition), see Theodore A. Bergren, *Fifth Ezra: The Text, Origin and Early History*, SCS 25 (Scholars Press, 1990). More concise and updated (with the English translation, which is also used as a basis in the following) is Bergren, "Fifth Ezra," 467–82; on the concrete tradition in more detail, see Lilia Milbach-Schirr, "Die Rezeption jüdisch-apokalyptischer Traditionen in christlichen Schriften, untersucht anhand des Verhältnisses von 5. und 6. Esra zu 4. Esra" (PhD diss., Humboldt Universität at Berlin, 2020).

52. Bergren, "Fifth Ezra," 473.

53. See the contributions in Jan N. Bremmer et al., eds., *Figures of Ezra*, Studies on Early Christian Apocrypha 13 (Peeters, 2018).

people. The text first recalls the great deeds of God during the exodus and the taking of the land. Despite all this, Israel had never stopped sinning and had never been obedient to its Lord (5 Ezra 1:7–24). That is why God will give the destroyed house to another people: "Thus says the Lord Almighty: Your house is desolate! I will drive you out as the wind drives straw. And your children will not have offspring, because they have neglected my commandment and have done evil in my presence. I will hand over your house to a people coming from far away, and those who have not known me will believe me, and those to whom I have not shown signs will do what I have said" (5 Ezra 1:33–35).

In older secondary literature, this new people is often simply identified with "the Christians" or even "the Christian church";[54] in this case, we would be dealing with an early example of the supersessionist idea of replacing the old people of God, Israel, with a new people, "the Christians." This simplistic reading, however, would not do justice to the text on several levels. First of all, we should not be too quick to presuppose "Jews" and "Christians" as clear categories where they are not explicitly used.[55] Although we can already find individual supersessionist writings in the first half of the second century, we cannot assume that they represent a majority opinion or even a generally valid use of the categories. Even texts such as the letters of Ignatius of Antioch, in which a very clear distinction is made between "Judaism" and "Christianity" (e.g., Ign. *Magn.* 8–10; Ign. *Phld.* 6), should be interpreted as only one (accidently preserved) voice among many;

54. So also Bergren, *Fifth Ezra*, right down to the headings of his translation (formulated by him and interpreting the text).

55. A good example that shows how problematic this is, is the Ascension of Isaiah, a text discussed in more detail in the following chapter: Analyzing the categories used there for self-definition shows very clearly that the usual question of whether this text must be understood in Jewish or Christian terms is anachronistic. Further arguments can be found in Henning and Nicklas, "Questions of Self-Designation," 175–98. On the problematic nature of the "parting(s) of the ways" model, see also (among others) the contributions in the volume by Jens Schröter et al., eds., *Jews and Christians—Parting Ways in the first Two Centuries CE? Reflections on the Gains and Losses of a Model*, BZNW 253 (de Gruyter, 2021).

moreover, these early efforts at differentiating "Jews" and "Christians" may indicate not a status quo but the need for such categories to be established in the first place.[56]

Instead of clear and unambiguously defined boundaries between "Jews" and "Christians," many recent investigations have shown that there were spaces in which adherence to Christ *and* Judaism was not necessarily mutually exclusive. This was not only the case in the earliest times; it was also possible in later periods, in different regions, and in different groups in different ways. For its part, 5 Ezra never uses the word *Christians*, nor does it speak of *a* or *the* "Christian church." Its concept of future generations is also by no means clearly defined, instead remaining open in many respects;[57] it clearly includes important figures from the history of Israel, as is made explicit in 5 Ezra 1:38–40: "Now, father, look with glory and see the people coming from the east. I will lead them, (I) together with Abraham, Isaac, and Jacob, Elijah and Enoch, Zechariah and Hosea, Amos, Joel, Micah, Obadiah, Zephaniah, Nahum, Jonah, Malachi, Habakkuk, and twelve angels with flowers." Here the great figures in Israel's history are still to be understood as part of God's people (or standing for its future); likewise, the enigmatic motif of the *twelve* angels with flowers may suggest a certain form of continuity. At the same time, the reader is struck by who is included on and who is missing from this list: On the one hand, the text mentions the patriarchs (Abraham, Isaac, and Jacob), who initially stand for the beginnings of Israel. Simultaneously, however, Abraham can be understood as the "father of many nations"

56. For a discussion of this passage against this background, see, e.g., Nicklas, *Jews and Christians?*, 1–10. The early dating of the letters still advocated there, however, can probably not be maintained; see now the convincing argument by Jan N. Bremmer, "The Place, Date and Author of the *Ignatian Letters.* An Onomastic Approach," in *Die Datierung neutestamentlicher Pseudepigraphen: Herausforderungen und neuere Lösungsansätze*, ed. Wolfgang Grünstäudl and Karl Matthias Schmidt, WUNT 470 (Mohr Siebeck, 2021), 405–33, who places the texts in the middle of the second century.

57. Analyzed in more detail in Hirschberger, *Ringen um Israel*, 271–75.

according to Genesis 17:5. This is followed by figures who can all be categorized as prophets in different ways: Elijah and Enoch are figures who, as those once raptured, have a special role to play in the events of the end time; the others are all authors of prophetic books (of the Dodecapropheton). Later, in 5 Ezra 2:17, further names are added: Jeremiah, Isaiah, and Daniel. In comparison to Ignatius of Antioch, who says of the prophets of Israel that they "lived after Christ Jesus" (Ign. *Magn.* 8:2), there is no suggestion here that those named should be attributed to Christ in any way (or that they should be interpreted as already living in a "Christian" way).

Interestingly, Moses is missing from this list. This may be insignificant, but it could also be explained by two further observations.[58] First, it is noticeable that the final vision of an enormous Son of God together with the end-time individuals who are crowned does not characterize these individuals as a people composed of twelve tribes,[59] a clear difference from Revelation 7:14. The vision is introduced in the following way: "Mount Zion receive your number. Bring to completion your people clothed in white, who serve you with obedience, because they have fulfilled the law of the Lord. Since formerly you wished your children to come, complete their number. Ask the authority of the Lord that the people may be sanctified, because they were called from the beginning" (5 Ezra 2:40–42). Here there is still a connection between the people of God and Mount Zion. But how is it conceivable that it is now understood as "called from the beginning"? With these words alone, it is completely impossible to interpret 5 Ezra as an example of a work that stands

58. Interestingly, Moses is also missing in the NT genealogies of Jesus (Matt 1:1–17; Luke 3:23–38).

59. On the reception of the Revelation of John in 5 Ezra, see Tobias Nicklas, "Rezeption und Nicht-Rezeption der Offenbarung des Johannes durch antike christliche Apokalypsen," in *Christian Apocrypha: Receptions of the New Testament in Ancient Christian Apocrypha*, ed. Jean-Michel Roessli and Tobias Nicklas, Novum Testamentum Patristicum 26 (Vandenhoeck & Ruprecht, 2014), 336–40, as well as (in greater detail) Hirschberger, *Ringen um Israel*, 174–241.

for the substitution of Christianity for the nations for Israel. Unless we assume that the text is completely inconsistent, a second observation is necessary: The people who are to be brought to perfection are characterized by the fact that they have fulfilled "the law of the Lord."[60] Once again, it is interesting that the text does not speak of the law of Moses. But this is perhaps best explained by another short passage in the text spoken by God himself: "When you offer sacrifices to me, I will turn my eyes from you, for I did not command you (to observe) feast days, new moons, sabbaths, and circumcisions" (5 Ezra 1:31). This completes the picture: 5 Ezra hardly stands for a theology in which—even because of the Christ event of the cross and resurrection—a new phase of history has dawned wherein Christians have replaced Israel as God's chosen people. To the contrary, 5 Ezra goes much further.

By stating that God himself had never wanted important aspects of the Torah—from sacrificial cults to Sabbath observance and circumcision—this text actually develops a new perspective on history, but in this case first and foremost the history of Israel. Important events in this history remain: The liberating actions of God in the exodus are still remembered. And yet this cannot simply be understood in terms of the Torah of Moses. The Torah of the Lord takes its place. The focus of *this* Torah, however, is solely on socially relevant aspects. Fifth Ezra is aware that it does not break with the tradition of Israel but rather ties in with prophetic traditions that lie precisely along these lines. This is shown, on the one hand, by the fact that it places the prophets alongside the people of God, and, on the other hand, by the fact that, within the world of intertexts that it alludes to, passages of prophetic cult criticism such as Isaiah 1 and 58, Jeremiah 6–7, and Zechariah 7–8 probably play the most decisive role. The new people of God therefore does not simply follow diachronically from the old; nor does it break from and stand in opposition to Israel. Instead, it is defined by an aspect of Israel's

60. The following thoughts are based on the chapter on 5 Ezra in Sommer, *Witwen Recht und Gerechtigkeit*. The outstanding significance of Jer 7 for the understanding of 5 Ezra is also emphasized by Hirschberger, *Ringen um Israel*, 91–124.

tradition. Vocation, however, does not refer to commandments such as those rejected in 5 Ezra 1:31. Instead it relates—from the beginning—to the will of God, which is directed toward social justice. According to 5 Ezra, this is obscured in aspects of the Torah of Moses but already shines forth in the tradition of Israel through the corresponding prophetic texts. Now it is open to all peoples.

CHAPTER 5

Christian Apocrypha and "Landscapes of Memory"

Memories of Christian origins were liturgically staged from the very beginning, perhaps by the historical Jesus himself. With different emphases, the various accounts of the institution of the Last Supper (in the NT at 1 Cor 11:23–25; Mark 14:22–24; Matt 26:26–28; Luke 22:19–20) emphasize the *anamnesis* of Jesus;[1] the communal celebration of the Eucharist creates a chain of remembrances of Jesus—remembrances that are expanded with interpretive words about the meaning of his death. And the chain continued: A few generations after Jesus's death, after decades of oral tradition incorporating the words and stories of Jesus, a new stage of memory and memorialization began with the writing of the first Gospels and, later, the Acts of the Apostles. The individual memory of those who had once been companions of the earthly Jesus was naturally superseded by the social memory of the various groups of followers of Jesus that formed in different places in the first decades.

"Social memory" or "group memory" refers to a notion of memory that is accessible even for members of a group who did *not* participate in

1. Predrag Bukovec, *Die frühchristliche Eucharistie*; WUNT 499 (Mohr Siebeck, 2023), offers an excellent history of the development of the early Christian Eucharist, taking full account of apocryphal traditions.

the remembered events of the past—typically a memory that is of decisive importance for the identity construction of that group. The idea goes back in its basic features to French sociologist and philosopher Maurice Halbwachs, who died in the Buchenwald concentration camp in March 1945.[2] Studies of this phenomenon suggest that some four generations after the remembered event, the form of stabilization and transmission of the group's social memory changes significantly once again: Egyptologist and religious studies scholar Jan Assmann (1938–2024) speaks of "cultural memory"[3] from this point on. The theories that have become most prominent and differentiated in cultural studies over the last few decades have now also found their way into the historical study of religion and theology.[4] Within biblical exegesis, in turn, various fruitful branches of memory studies or memory theory have emerged, some of which are quite different from each other. Particular emphasis has, of course, been placed on memories of the historical Jesus.[5] This is not, however, the only way in which such approaches can be used to understand Christianity, in both its origins and history.

2. Especially important is Maurice Halbwachs, *Das Gedächtnis und seine sozialen Bedingungen*, 6th ed., Suhrkamp Wissenschaft 538 (Suhrkamp, 2019). For more on Halbwachs's life and thought, see 11–18. The standard English translation is *On Collective Memory* (University of Chicago Press, 1992).

3. Assmann, *Das kulturelle Gedächtnis*; as well as Jan Assmann, *Religion und kulturelles Gedächtnis*, 3rd ed. (Beck, 2008).

4. Huebenthal, *Gedächtnistheorie und Neues Testament*, offers an excellent introduction to the significance of memory theories for NT exegesis (and thus for the study of early Christianity).

5. See Jens Schröter, *Erinnerung an Jesu Worte: Studien zur Rezeption der Logienüberlieferung in Markus, Q und Thomas*, WMANT 76 (Neukirchener, 1997). Especially important now is Chris Keith et al., eds., *The Reception of Jesus in the First Three Centuries*, 3 vols. (T&T Clark, 2020). For an initial overview of some very diverse approaches, see the contributions in the volume by Butticaz and Norelli, *Memory and Memories in Early Christianity*.

This chapter takes up the related concept of *lieux de mémoire*, that is, "places of memory," developed by French scholar Pierre Nora.[6] We will underscore the significance of extracanonical, apocryphal traditions for the development of these types of social memories within Christian communities. Where more complex structures arise from the mutual relationship between different locales, we will also speak of not just individual places but full "landscapes of memory."[7] Before taking a concrete look at the relevant texts and associated traditions, however, a few preliminary remarks are in order. It is not easy to identify a concise definition of the phrase "places of memory" in Nora's extensive oeuvre; rather, the idea seems to evolve across multiple publications. It is therefore perhaps easiest to refer to the later work *Deutsche Erinnerungsorte* ("German Places of Memory"), edited by Hagen Schulze and Etienne François, which takes Nora's notion as its basis. Here we find the following workable definition: "[Places of memory] are long-lasting crystallization points of collective memory and identity that transcend generations and are integrated into social, cultural, and political practices; [these crystallization points] change to the extent that the way they are perceived, appropriated, and transmitted changes."[8] In his introduction to the German edition of Nora's volume *Erinnerungsorte Frankreichs*, François adds the following elements: A place of memory can be material, but also immaterial, and is "characterized by an excess of symbolic and emotional dimensions."[9] Several conclusions can be drawn from this: Places of memory do not

6. Fundamental are the volumes by Pierre Nora, ed., *Les lieux de mémoire*, 3 vols. (Gallimard, 1984–1992); English version: Pierre Nora, ed., *Realms of Memory: Rethinking the French Past*, 3 vols. (University of Chicago Press, 1998).

7. See already Tobias Nicklas, "New Testament Canon and Ancient Christian 'Landscapes of Memory,'" *EC* 7 (2016): 5–23, as well as Nicklas, "Neutestamentlicher Kanon, christliche Apokryphen," 588–609.

8. Etienne François and Hagen Schulze, "Einleitung," in *Deutsche Erinnerungsorte*, ed. Etienne Francois and Hagen Schulze (Beck, 2009), 1:18.

9. François, "Pierre Nora und die 'Lieux de mémoire,'" 9.

have to be *real* places in a physical sense, that is, places that can be entered or visited. In many cases, even more important are figurative places that become the "crystallization points of collective memory." The volume *Erinnerungsorte des Christentums*, published in 2010 by Christoph Markschies and Hubert Wolf, discusses the Bible, the cross, Mary, and others among such "transferred places."[10]

The basic notion of the long-lasting or enduring quality of places of memory—across generations—quite naturally indicates that testimonies from the New Testament canon alone will hardly be sufficient to describe such places. To the contrary, the aim must be to trace developments that, due to their inherent durability, immediately exceed the limits of the canonical works. However, this point already speaks to another aspect of the definition: Places of memory (and associated landscapes of memory) are by no means stable. They change in their composition but also in how they are perceived and how they function. Describing the "surplus of symbolic and emotional dimension" recognizable in places of memory—particularly as they develop over time—enables a special form of historiography that "encompasses many voices and corresponds better than 'classical' history to the scientific and social needs of our time."[11] This type of historiography—one that takes the central importance of the symbolic seriously, while remaining historical in a critical way—is particularly appropriate to the task of working on the history of religion, and particularly the history of Christianity.

This concept of places of memory, in both its concreteness and its flexibility, can be used to develop exciting new questions and avenues of inquiry. An obvious first step is to trace the development of an individual place of memory across all extant and accessible sources that describe or determine how it is perceived. Such a study makes it possible to chart the changing functions of a place of memory across time. There is, however,

---

10. See Christoph Markschies and Hubert Wolf, eds., *Erinnerungsorte des Christentums* (Beck, 2010).

11. François, "Pierre Nora und die 'Lieux de mémoire,'" 9.

also the possibility—which in many of the cases discussed by Nora tends to recede into the background—of recognizing that one and the same place of memory can be perceived in very different ways at the *same* time, and that one place of memory might have a tense or even contentious relationship to other places of memory. This is obvious in the context of the history of Christianity because there is not and has never been a single, uniform version of the religion.[12] Instead, we can assume (in antiquity as in the present) a diversity of groups with geographical, social, and theological differentiations, leading to different perspectives. At least in some cases, we can see quite clearly that this has also led to different, even competing, perspectives on individual places of memory.[13] Of course, we always come up against limits: Our sources from antiquity are simultaneously fragmentary and extraordinarily numerous. We are by no means in a position—and never will be—to fathom and describe all the functions of places of memory. The following examples are intended to illustrate the possible insights that this type of investigation might yield, always emphasizing that apocryphal and parabiblical traditions are indispensable for any understanding of the history of Christian symbols and practice.

12. Very helpful models for describing the diversity of the development of early Christianity up to the time of Constantine the Great are presented by David Brakke, *The Gnostics. Myth, Ritual, and Diversity in Early Christianity* (Harvard University Press, 2010), 5–18. In addition to and against this background, see also Tobias Nicklas, "Parting of the Ways? Probleme eines Konzepts," in Alkier and Leppin, *Juden – Heiden – Christen?*, 37–38 (using a picture by Andreas Merkt).

13. The most famous example of this is certainly the Temple Mount in Jerusalem. In the Holy Land, however, we can think of a multitude of places that are of (sometimes differing) importance to Jews, Christians, and Muslims. We do not, however, have to remain in Israel. We can also find exciting examples in connection with the Caucasus in the volume by Igor Dorfmann-Lazarev, ed., *Sharing Myths, Texts and Sanctuaries in the South Caucasus: Apocryphal Themes in Literatures, Arts and Cults from Late Antiquity to the Middle Ages*, Studies on Early Christian Apocrypha 19 (Peeters, 2022).

1. Example 1: The Holy Family's Flight to Egypt

The first example alone indicates that the concept of the place of memory can be understood in many different ways and on several levels.[14] Even the story of the flight of the holy family to Egypt can be interpreted as a *lieux de mémoire* in the figurative sense: It continues to produce new texts, new narratives, and new traditions in different contexts to this day. One example of how far this can go to this day is Otfried Preußler's novel *Die Flucht nach Ägypten*, which takes the holy family through the Bohemia of the declining Austro-Hungarian monarchy.[15]

When analyzing the place of memory "flight to Egypt," it is irrelevant whether such a flight is historically plausible or whether it actually took place (in whatever form). Even if there is no historical kernel within the story, the question of the origin and significance of this place of memory, as well as its connection with real places that become a walkable and visitable landscape of memory, is historically extremely interesting. The oldest accessible starting point of the tradition is found in the Gospel of Matthew. The evangelist narrates how, after the departure of the magi (Matt 2:1–12), an angel tells Joseph in a dream to flee to Egypt with his family because Herod wants to kill the child, whom he sees as a rival to the throne. Joseph sets off with his wife and child that very night, remaining in Egypt until Herod's death. The short scene leads to a fulfillment quotation that refers back to the prophet Hosea: "Out of Egypt I have called my son" (Matt 2:15; see Hos 11:1). The fate

---

14. The following section largely relies on material from Tobias Nicklas, "New Testament Canon," 9–18. Such material is compiled in even greater detail by Gavdat Gabra, ed., *Be Thou There: The Holy Family's Journey in Egypt* (American University in Cairo Press, 2001), as well as François Bovon, "L'enfant Jésus durant la fuite en Égypte: Les récits apocryphes de l'enfance comme légendes profitables à l'âme," in *The Apocryphal Gospels Within the Context of Early Christian Theology*, ed. Jens Schröter, BETL 260 (Peeters, 2013), 249–70; interesting beyond that is Gavdat Gabra and Gertrud J. M. van Loon, *The Churches of Egypt: From the Journey of the Holy Family to the Present Day* (American University in Cairo Press, 2007).

15. Otfried Preußler, *Die Flucht nach Ägypten: Königlich böhmischer Teil* (dtv, 1996).

of Jesus, the Immanuel (Matt 1:21–24), is thus narratively closely linked to the fate of Israel.[16]

Apocryphal infancy gospels have reenacted this short narrative in various ways and added further elements. The highly successful Protevangelium of James (probably written toward the end of the second century) offers an alternative tradition: Mary saves the child by hiding him in a manger (Prot. Jas. 22:2).[17] Elizabeth in turn flees to the mountains, where the rock face splits to receive and hide her and her son John, who will later become the Baptist. On the whole, however, the basic elements of the flight to Egypt as narrated in the canonical Gospel of Matthew are widely accepted: The motif of the angel of the Lord appearing to Joseph in a dream (Matt 2:13) is taken up with slight variations in the Arabic Infancy Gospel and in the early medieval Gospel of Pseudo-Matthew.[18] The so-called History of Joseph the

16. Matthias Konradt, *Das Evangelium nach Matthäus*, NTD 1 (Vandenhoeck & Ruprecht, 2015), 44, writes, "In Hos 11:1, 'my son' refers collectively to Israel. By transferring the phrase to Jesus, Matthew reinforces the connection between the story of Jesus and God's history with Israel, which could already be observed in 1:1–17. The story of Jesus is colored with biblical strokes: in a sense, Israel's basic experience is repeated in his journey under God's guidance. But unlike Israel, Jesus will prove his sonship to God in the desert." (Translation of the German original: Jacob Cerone.)

17. The Irish Leabhar Breac 121–125 also offers a detailed expansion of this tradition. Text in relation to Prot. Jas. 22:2 in J. Keith Elliott, *A Synopsis of the Apocryphal Nativity and Infancy Narratives*, NTTSD 34 (Brill, 2006), 108–9, whose synopsis I will continue to follow.

18. For a helpful overview of the Arabic Infancy Gospel, see "e-clavis Arabic Infancy Gospel," North American Society for the Study of Christian Apocryphal Literature, accessed February 1, 2025, https://www.nasscal.com/e-clavis-christian-apocrypha/arabic-infancy-gospel/. An English translation of the Arabic Infancy Gospel (in individual passages) can be found in Elliott, *Synopsis*; an excellent introduction to this writing, which essentially dates back to pre-Islamic times and whose place of origin can only be vaguely classified as the ecclesiastical East, is provided (including a German translation) in Gerhard Schneider, *Apokryphe Kindheitsevangelien*, Fontes Christiani 18 (Herder, 1995), 173–95, as well as in Maria Josua and Friedmann Eißler, "Das arabische Kindheitsevangelium," in Markschies and Schröter, *Antike*

Carpenter 8 adds to the motif of the holy family being accompanied by Salome.[19] In addition to these and other minor variations, however, it is particularly interesting how much certain texts expand on and flesh out the events that take place on the way to Egypt or in Egypt itself. Latin texts of the Paidika, also known as the Infancy Gospel of Thomas, the Gospel of Pseudo-Matthew, the Arabic Infancy Gospel, and the Irish Leabhar Breac[20] offer accounts of various miracles performed

---

christliche Apokryphen, 1:963–82. A French translation of the lesser-known long form offered in Biblioteca Laurenziana codex orientalis 32 can be found in Charles Genequand, "Vie de Jésus en arabe," in *Écrits apocryphes chrétiens*, ed. François Bovon and Pierre Geoltrain, Bibliotèque de la Pléiade (Gallimard, 1997), 1:211–38. For an English translation of the Gospel of Pseudo-Matthew, with extensive introduction and notes, see Brandon W. Hawk, *The Gospel of Pseudo-Matthew and the Nativity of Mary*, Early Christian Apocrypha 9 (Cascade, 2019). See also Elliott, *Apocryphal New Testament*, 84–99; good introductions can also be found in Schneider, *Apokryphe Kindheitsevangelien*, 213–56, and Oliver Ehlen, "Das Pseudo-Matthäusevangelium," in Markschies and Schröter, *Antike christliche Apokryphen*, 1:983–1002.

19. The History of Joseph the Carpenter has been preserved in (fragmentary) Sahidic, Bohairic, and Arabic versions; an original Greek version is possible but cannot be reconstructed. Parallels to the Egyptian cult of the dead suggest an origin in Egypt. The dating of the text is disputed; one can think of the turn of the sixth to the seventh century. An English translation is provided by Elliott, *Apocryphal New Testament*, 114–17. For a more detailed introduction (with German translation), see Schneider, *Apokryphe Kindheitsevangelien*, 69–73, 271–83, as well as U. Ulrike Kaiser, "Die Geschichte von Joseph dem Zimmermann," in Markschies and Schröter, *Antike christliche Apokryphen*, 1:308–42.

20. For an English translation of the Paidika (or the Infancy Gospel according to Thomas), see Elliott, *Apocryphal New Testament*, 68–83, as well as the corresponding passages in Elliott, *Synopsis*. In all translations, however, it must be borne in mind that this text has been handed down in a highly fluid form and often simply reproduces the text of a manuscript. A good introduction (with German translations of several traditions) is provided by U. Ulrike Kaiser (with the collaboration of Josef Tropper), "Die Kindheitserzählung des Thomas," in Markschies and Schröter, *Antike christliche Apokryphen*, 1:930–59; fundamental is the monograph by Reidar Aasgaard, *The Childhood of Jesus: Decoding the Apocryphal Infancy Gospel of Thomas* (Wipf & Stock, 2009). The decisive new edition of the Greek text is Burke, *De infantia Iesu Evangelium Thomae graece*, as well as (for the Syriac text) Tony Burke,

by the infant Jesus on the way to Egypt and while there. In narrative interpretations of Psalm 148:7 and Isaiah 65:25, there are reports of encounters with dragons, lions, and panthers, all of whom worship the child; we also find sheep who follow the holy family together with wolves. A palm tree bows down and offers its fruit to Mary and Jesus (Ps.-Mt. 19–20). The extent to which the flight had already become part of the cultural memory of Christian groups in Egypt in the second century is shown by the fact that the Alexandrian philosopher Celsus was able to use the tradition to critique Christianity in his polemic *Alethes Logos*: In Celsus's estimation, Jesus's sojourn in Egypt shows that he was neither a miracle worker nor god but a charlatan who had learned practices of sorcery and magic during his years in Egypt (Origen, *Cels.* 1.28).[21]

Especially interesting, however, are developments that show that the figurative place of memory "flight to Egypt" was increasingly able to connect with real places in Egypt, with new locations and traditions being added up until the very recent past.[22] These individual places developed into a complex landscape of memory with multiple itineraries, through which Christians have connected in different ways with the flight of the holy family.

The Syriac Tradition of the Infancy Gospel of Thomas: A Critical Edition and Syriac Translation, Gorgias Eastern Christian Studies 48 (Gorgias, 2017). Leabhar Breac is an Irish manuscript from the fifteenth century, which contains an older form of an infancy gospel. A brief introduction is provided by Elliott, *Synopsis*, xviii; this volume also contains English translations of some sections.

21. However, Celsus does not speak of the royal Son of God fleeing to Egypt. Instead, Jesus moved there out of poverty and hired himself out as a day laborer. On this occasion, he learned magical practices. For a more detailed interpretation of the scene, see Horacio E. Lona, *Die "wahre Lehre" des Kelsos*, Kommentar zu frühchristlichen Apologeten – Erg. 1 (Herder, 2005), 98–100.

22. An example of this can be found in the Church of the Holy Family in Matariya, Cairo, which was built only in the early twentieth century. The Marian visions on the site of today's Church of the Virgin of Zayton (in Cairo) date back to 1968. See Gabra and van Loon, *Churches of Egypt*, 156, 160.

Here we will discuss in more detail just two aspects of these itineraries, in the development of which the interpretation of canonical and apocryphal traditions are interwoven:

(1) In his *Demonstratio evangelica* 6.20 and 9.2, Eusebius of Caesarea (ca. 264/65–ca. 339/40), who probably encountered local traditions during his own flight to Egypt at the time of the Diocletian persecution, offers a highly interesting interpretation of Isaiah 19:1. The verse from Isaiah reads as follows (here translating the LXX's Greek translation): "A vision of Egypt. Look, the Lord [κύριος] sits on a light cloud and will come to Egypt; the hand-crafted idols of the Egyptians will tremble before him, and their hearts will crumble within them." What the Septuagint still understands as the epiphany of God (κύριος, the Lord), Eusebius interprets as a prophecy of Jesus's flight to Egypt and thus his saving appearance among the Egyptians, the people who were most in need of salvation:

And surely this part of the prophecy was literally fulfilled, when the angel of the Lord appeared in a dream to Joseph and said: "Arise, and take the young child and his mother, and flee into Egypt, and stay there until I tell thee." For then, the Lord God the Word, uniting with the child's growth, and present in the Flesh that had been furnished him of the Holy Virgin, visited the land of the Egyptians. . . . But the cause of his journey there is as follows. When it is remembered that the first origin of idolatrous error was in Egypt, and the Egyptians seemed to be the most superstitious of men, and bitter enemies of the people of God, and as far removed from the prophets as possible, we can see why the power of God came to them first of all. And therefore the word of Gospel teaching has waxed stronger among the Egyptians than among any other men. Hence this prophecy foretells that the Lord will sojourn among them. But it does not say that the Egyptians will come to the land of the Jews, nor worship him at Jerusalem, nor become Jewish proselytes there according to the enactments of Moses, nor sacrifice at the altar in Jerusalem. It says nothing of this, but that the Lord will himself visit the Egyptians, and will think these men worthy of his presence, and will be the occasion of great blessings to them. (*Dem. ev.* 6.20)[23]

Parallels to these ideas can also be found in several apocryphal narratives; however, they link this to specific places in Egypt. This is particularly well illustrated in the Gospel of Pseudo-Matthew and (in more detail, although less specifically linked to a place) in section 10 of the Arabic Infancy Gospel (see also the Syriac Cave of Treasures 47.4[24]). The narrative of the Gospel of Pseudo-Mathew reads as follows:

Both rejoicing and exulting, they arrived at Hermopolis and went into one of the cities, which was called Sohennen. And because they knew no one in that place who would put them up as guests, they went into the temple, which is called the Capitoline of this same city of Egypt. In this temple were placed 365 idols, to whom divine honors were offered, each on its own day, by the sacrilegious. Now, it came to pass that when Mary entered the temple with the little child, all together the images fell, and all of the idols of their own accord, cast down on their faces, revealed themselves quite clearly to be nothing. Then was fulfilled what the prophet said: "Behold, the Lord will come upon a

23. Translation slightly adapted from William John Ferrar, *The Proof of the Gospel. Being the Demonstratio Evangelica* (Wipf & Stock, 2001), 296–97. Athanasius of Alexandria, *Inc.* 2.33.5; 2.36.4 (SC 199) and Cyril of Jerusalem, *Catechetical Lectures* 10.10 (PG 33:673) offer something comparable.

24. The Syrian Cave of Treasures is a kind of history of the world that inscribes itself into biblical history. Large parts of the text are based on the stories of the OT, beginning with a narrative that goes back to the creation but does not stop there. The text, which can be classified in the (not unproblematic genre) *rewritten Bible*, also extends into NT history. It is thought to have been written in the late sixth or early seventh century of our era. For further reading (with an up-to-date English translation and helpful bibliography), see Toepel, "Cave of Treasures," 531–84. The passage alluded to here reads: "Know that, when Christ entered Egypt, all the idols within were cast down, fell upon the ground, and broke, so that there might be fulfilled what is written: *Behold, the Lord rides upon the swift clouds and enters Egypt, while Egypt's idols tremble before him*" (577).

swift cloud and all of the graven images of Egypt will be shaken by his presence." (Ps.-Mt. 22–23)[25]

It is highly unlikely that any knowledge of specific geographical locations in Egypt lies behind the narrative as it is presented in the Latin Gospel of Pseudo-Matthew. This is surely the case for the vast majority of its medieval readers and listeners. For many people living within the Jewish and Christian tradition, Egypt could already be described as a symbolic place of memory because of the exodus event.

That said, what we read in the Gospel of Pseudo-Matthew is unlikely to have arisen in isolation from traditions that were indeed linked with real places in the real Egypt, gaining a symbolic charge through interpretation with the help of Isaiah 19:1. The Historia Monachorum in Aegypto, probably written in the fifth century, offers a rare glimpse of the symbolically charged perception of a real place in connection with the tradition just described, in which we learn of a pilgrimage that must have taken place around the years 394/395.[26] The travelers also reach Hermopolis Magna, located between Middle and Upper Egypt.[27] There

25. Translation (very slightly adapted) from Hawk, *Gospel of Pseudo-Matthew.*

26. Andrew Cain, *The Greek Historia Monachorum in Aegypto: Monastic Hagiography in the Late Fourth Century*, OECS (Oxford University Press, 2016), offers a fundamental discussion of this text.

27. Sozomenos, *Hist. eccl.* 5.21.8–11 (see Stephen Davis, *Coptic Christology in Practice: Incarnation and Divine Participation in Late Antique and Medieval Egypt* [Oxford University Press, 2008], 132–33), offers a tradition about a sacred tree that shows Jesus was worshipped in this place: "In Hermopolis, in the Thebaïs, there is a tree called Persis, of which it is said that the branches, the leaves, and the smallest part of the bark cure diseases when touched by the sick; for it is reported by the Egyptians that Joseph fled to Hermopolis with Christ and Mary, the holy Mother of God, from the wrath of Herod. When they entered through the gate, this greatest of trees, as if it could not bear the coming of Christ, bowed to the ground and worshipped him. I am recounting exactly what I have heard from many sources about this tree. I think that this event was a sign of the presence of God in the city; or perhaps, as seems most probable, the tree, which had been worshipped by the inhabitants according to pagan custom, was shaken because of the demon that had been the object of worship went out of it [= at the sight of him who had appeared to purify it from such powers]. He was moved of his own accord; for in the presence of Christ the idols of Egypt were

the pilgrims meet a certain Apollos, who leads them through the ruins of a dilapidated temple. The text reads: "But we saw also another holy man, named Apollos, in the territory of Hermopolis in the Thebaid, where the Savior attained with Mary and Joseph in fulfilment of the prophecy of Isaiah which says, 'Behold, the Lord rides upon a swift cloud and he will come into Egypt. And the idols of Egypt will be shaken at his presence and will fall on the ground.' And indeed we saw there the temple where all the idols fell on the ground at the entry of the Savior into the city" (Historia Monachorum 8.1).[28] The connection of the figurative place of memory "flight into Egypt" with a tradition of interpretation[29] of Isaiah 19:1, which apparently developed during the period of dramatic upheavals for Christianity after the time of Constantine the Great, enables a reinterpretation of the real place of Hermopolis Magna: The ruins of the pagan sanctuary can now be interpreted as a sign of a "victory" of the Christian god over the old gods—regardless of whether this perception of the significance of the site was shared by all sides (and surely it was not).

(2) Considering its meager function for the plot of the text, the very short section 25 of the Arabic Infancy Gospel is easily passed over without notice. The text reads: "Therefore they turned aside to that sycamore that is now called Matarea, and here the Lord Jesus brought forth a fountain, in which the Lady Mary washed his shirt, and balsam was produced in the region from the sweat of the Lord Jesus that Mary

---

shaken, as the prophet Isaiah had foretold. When the demon was driven out, the tree was allowed to remain as a memorial of what had happened and was endowed with the power to heal the faithful" (translation by Tobias Nicklas).

28. Also cited in Nicklas, "New Testament Canon," 12. Greek text: André-Jean Festugière, *Historia Monachorum in Aegypto. Édition critique du texte grec et traduction annotée*, Subsidia Hagiographica 53 (Société des Bollandistes, 1971), 46. English translation adapted from Norman Russell, *The Lives of the Desert Fathers: The Historia monachorum in Aegypto* (Mowbray, 1980), 70.

29. Of course, it cannot be ruled out that this tradition could be older; however, it could only have really blossomed in contexts where the (alleged) results of the Lord's epiphany in Egypt could be made visible.

sprinkled there."[30] The function of this short episode—and the reason for its inclusion in the work—can be understood only if we consider that it refers to a real place of memory. In fact, this place can still be visited today: It stands at the site of Mataryia, located just a few kilometers northeast of the center of Cairo, where a sycamore grows that supposedly replaces the tree under which the holy family purportedly rested. The tree and the spring next to it are associated with a tradition that can be found in its most concise written form in the passage just quoted from the Arabic Infancy Gospel. The connection of the episode and this site also served another purpose: The balsam produced in the area could be linked to the sweat of the Christ child. For those who believed this tradition, such a product was no doubt valuable. This shows that the construction of places of memory could also serve economic interests.[31]

The real places that make up the landscape of memory associated with the flight of the holy family to Egypt are just as difficult to grasp in detail as the texts and traditions associated with them. The place where the holy family supposedly sailed to Upper Egypt is marked by the Church of the Holy Virgin in Maadi, about ten miles south of Cairo. In Minya, there is a stone imprint of Jesus's hand; in Sakha, the imprint of one of his feet. The monastery al Muharraq near the mountains of Qusqam in Upper Egypt (36 km south of Hermopolis) marks the house where the holy family lived in Egypt. After his resurrection, Christ himself celebrated the Eucharist there with his apostles.[32]

Each of these apocryphal and parabiblical traditions,[33] in which different media have both interconnected roles and specific functions,

---

30. Translation from Elliott, *Synopsis*, 122.

31. Additional brief information can also be found in Gabra and van Look, *Churches of Egypt*, 164. Interestingly, this is an interreligiously significant place of remembrance, also venerated by Muslims.

32. The examples are presented (and partly illustrated) in Gabra and van Loon, *Churches of Egypt*. References to this can already be found in Nicklas, "New Testament Canon."

33. For a definition of parabiblical traditions, see ch. 1 of this volume.

leaves much to be examined in detail. Overall, however, they are connected to a larger whole. First and foremost, they inscribe the origin narratives of Christianity onto the land of Egypt—and thus reinterpret Egypt as a place of memory for Christianity; the land whose pharaoh had enslaved Israel and which, in the view of the early church, had been under the rule of demonic powers, becomes the place where Christ as the Lord had already revealed himself as a child. In these narratives of the flight, the point is not the foundation of the church of Egypt in connection with later apostolic traditions (primarily associated with the evangelist Mark);[34] rather, Christ, the Lord himself, comes to Egypt—and the region thus becomes the first place where the Christian gospel is revealed. With the idea that the common Eucharist of the risen Christ with the apostles finds its starting point in Egypt, Egypt itself becomes a core point of Christian memory culture. With these developments, Egypt is placed alongside Israel itself.

In this context, it may be interesting to look at another group of apocryphal texts closely linked to Egypt, the so-called apostolic memoirs.[35] These writings, which were composed in Coptic but have also survived in later translations, resemble apocryphal gospels at first glance and are certainly closely related to them. Some of them, for example, the so-called Unknown Berlin Gospel, are still also found under the rubric "apocryphal gospels" in the usual apocryphal collections; however, it makes sense to assign them more precisely to this distinct category of literature typical of Egypt. They are basically origin narratives that attempt to lend legitimacy to the developing identity of a post-Chalcedonian miaphysite church of Egypt from the middle of the fifth century. Some of these writings are strikingly anti-Jewish.[36]

34. See Stephen J. Davis, *The Early Coptic Papacy 1* (American University in Cairo Press, 2005), for such traditions.

35. An excellent introduction to this literary genre, which has only been recognized as such in recent years, is provided by Suciu, *Berlin-Strasbourg Apocryphon*, 70–140.

36. See also the observations of Dylan M. Burns, "A Homily on the Passion and Resurrection," in Burke, *New Testament Apocrypha*, 2:48–50.

We know very little about actual Jewish life in Egypt after the diaspora revolt at the time of Trajan (115–117 CE);[37] it is therefore highly unlikely that these texts reflect confrontations with "real" Jewish people of flesh and blood at the time these writings were composed (from around the sixth century onward). But perhaps the surprisingly anti-Jewish content can be explained if we relate it to what we have just observed: With the emergence of landscapes of memory that link parts of Jesus's life to places in Egypt, a tension with Israel arises. If we look at just one text from the group of apostolic memoirs, namely, the work On the Life and the Passion of Christ, there is perhaps a chance to see more clearly.[38] A large part of this apocryphal writing focuses on the events surrounding the passion of Jesus of Nazareth. Compared to the canonical Gospels, the figure of Judas Iscariot is greatly expanded here. Judas is married in this work, and it is his wife who continuously incites him not just to embezzle money but also to betray Jesus (and his companions). The role of Judas's wife is not simply banal. The actions of Judas and his wife are presented as a type of second fall from grace.[39] With Judas, however, the Jews—who are portrayed in the most negative

37. Eldon J. Epp, "The Jews and the Jewish Community in Oxyrhynchus: Socio-religious Context for the New Testament Papyri," in *New Testament Manuscripts, Their Texts and Their World*, ed. Thomas J. Kraus and Tobias Nicklas, TENTS 2 (Brill, 2006), 13–52, offers a very helpful article on the local situation in Oxyrhynchus.

38. The edition On the Life and the Passion of Christ and all English translations follow Roelof van den Broek, *Pseudo-Cyril: On the Life and the Passion of Christ. A Coptic Apocryphon*, VCSup 118 (Brill, 2013). Like some other apostolic memoirs, this text is embedded in an alleged homily by an important church father. Of course, all such attributions are pseudepigraphal. Parts of the material used below is also published in Tobias Nicklas, "Die Judasfigur in spätantiken Apokryphen. Pseudo-Cyrill von Jerusalems *Leben und Passion Christi*," in *Bibel und Patristik. Studien zur Exegese und Rezeption von Septuaginta und Neuem Testament*, ed. Siegfried Kreuzer et al., BZSup 3 (Brill Deutschland, 2022), 337–49.

39. This is the decisive thesis of Nicklas, "Die Judasfigur in spätantiken Apokryphen."

light, filled with hatred from the outset—also renounce Jesus.[40] The basic fact that Jesus and his companions were also Jews is not reflected in this text.

Pilate, however, is developed into an unwaveringly positive figure. He would rather see his own son die than Jesus. The following is finally revealed to Pilate in a dream:[41]

> There was, as it were, a great darkness outside, spread upon the face of the entire earth. And the whole world was gathered together, blind and not seeing. And, behold, an eagle came from heaven, with a cistern of light around it and a wreath on its head, and the light shone for a short time. The eagle cried out: "The light of Charran and the light of Canaan have been given to the Land of Egypt." The people of the Hebrews at that time remained blind and they did not see. And they cried out: "Where is the eagle that has taken away our light so that we may kill him?" And the eagle came to the people of the Hebrews. They seized him, brought him upon a fruitless tress and killed him. The Egyptians gathered to the eagle, they were amazed that he immediately died. And the eagle lived (again), he flew away and while they were looking at him he went up to heaven as he had come.

Jesus in turn interprets the dream in the following way:

---

40. For example, we read sentences such as: "For what reason did the Jews hate our Savior so much that they sought to kill him from the beginning?" (31).

41. Parts of the material that follows can also be found—in a broader horizon—in Tobias Nicklas, "The Covenant in Christian Apocrypha: Fragmentary Evidence of a Spectrum of Voices," in *Covenant: Concepts of Berit, Diatheke and Testamentum: Proceedings of the Conference at Lanier Theological Library in Houston, Texas, November 2019*, ed. Christian A. Eberhart and Wolfgang Kraus, WUNT 506 (Mohr Siebeck, 2023), 578–80.

> And as to the cry uttered by the eagle, I too shall cry out: "My Father, I give my spirit into your hands." And there will be no longer a covenant made with the Hebrews but it will be made with the Egyptians. There will not arise another prophet from the race of the Hebrews forever. But the people I did not know have served me and the Egyptians you saw gathering to me as I took the likeness of an eagle will build churches to worship me therein and to continue to commemorate my resurrection and to marvel at my death.

This text brings us to a crucial point: The idea that the "Jews" seek to kill Jesus from the beginning is linked to the idea that God had once granted them a covenant, but that they had broken it from the beginning, again and again. With the death of Jesus attributed to a kind of second fall, the covenant has been taken away from Israel for all time. Israel is now replaced by Egypt—a country that, as we read in sections 56–57, had already granted Jesus life-saving asylum in his childhood. A link to the place of memory "flight to Egypt" is thus established even in this writing about Jesus's passion. According to this text, God's covenant with Israel is now replaced by a covenant with Egypt, which the miaphysite church of late antiquity traces back to the origins of Christianity with a late antique text like the one just mentioned—and thus interprets itself as the true people of God in covenant with God.

2. Example 2: Figures Between Canon and Apocrypha—The Roman Peter

If we take the definition of *lieux de mémoire* given at the beginning of this chapter seriously, figures of central import to a particular group can also become places of memory.[42] For Christianity (or various Christianities), the figure of Jesus of Nazareth is of course such a place

42. Important parts of the material used in the following are published (much more extensively and in greater detail) in Tobias Nicklas, "Antike Petruserzählungen und der erinnerte Petrus in Rom," in *Petrusliteratur und Petrusarchäologie: Römische*

of memory. Likewise, the figure of Mary, her significance, and the interpretation of her life and character demonstrate the different roles that this place of memory still plays for the various denominations today.[43] In recent years, the remembered Peter has been discussed time and again, mostly with a focus on writings from the first and second centuries.[44] In this section, we will not attempt to trace the developments of the *lieux de mémoire* of Peter in all their diversity and complexity. Instead, we will concentrate on the figure of the "Roman Peter." From a purely historical perspective, there is some evidence to suggest that Peter actually did meet his end in Rome during the reign of Nero—even if the evidence is rather thin and ultimately inconclusive.[45] This does not, however, detract from the significance of the figure of Peter as a place of memory that is strongly associated with Rome. There is no clear indication in the New Testament that Peter was in Rome and suffered martyrdom there—perhaps with the exception of 1 Peter 5:13, where Peter sends greetings from his "fellow elect in Babylon," possibly a cipher for Rome.[46] Of course, 1 Peter hardly goes back to Peter himself; thus this letter is already a testimony of the remembered Peter. The Gospel of

---

Begegnungen," ed. Jörg Frey and Martin Wallraff, Rom und Protestantismus 4 (Mohr Siebeck, 2020), 159–88.

43. See, e.g., Klaus Schreiner, "Maria," in Markschies and Wolf, *Erinnerungsorte des Christentums*, 592–613.

44. Especially important is Markus Bockmuehl, *The Remembered Peter in Ancient Reception and Modern Debate*, WUNT 262 (Mohr Siebeck, 2010), as well as Bockmuehl, *Simon Peter in Scripture and Memory: The New Testament Apostle in the Early Church* (Eerdmans, 2012). Additionally, there are at least some of the contributions in the important volume by Helen K. Bond and Larry W. Hurtado, eds., *Peter in Early Christianity* (Eerdmans, 2015).

45. Just how heated the debate continues to be can be seen in the article by Timothy D. Barnes, "'Another Shall Gird Thee': Probative Evidence for the Death of Peter," in Bond and Hurtado, *Peter in Early Christianity*, 76–95.

46. A detailed interpretation of the passage can be found, for example, in Reiner Feldmeier, *Der erste Brief des Petrus*, THKNT 15/I (Evangelische Verlagsanstalt, 2005), 170–71.

John (at 21:18), on the other hand, offers—as *vaticinium ex eventu*—a prophecy of Peter's death. Second Peter, as a literary testament, also presupposes Peter's death not only historically but also literarily (2 Pet 1:14).[47] Neither text, however, explicitly links this death to Rome. It is only apocryphal and parabiblical traditions that develop the connection between Peter, his ministry, and above all his martyrdom with the city of Rome. As with the flight to Egypt, this development includes both figurative places of memory and concrete locations within the physical landscape of the city.

The oldest extracanonical traces that refer to Peter's martyrdom in Rome (or seem to presuppose it) are found in the apocryphal Apocalypse of Peter (discussed also in ch. 4), which—written possibly in Alexandria but certainly in the East—offers a prophecy that Peter would "drink the cup promised to him by Christ" in the "city that rules over the West" (Apoc. Pet. 14:4; Papyrus Vindobonensis Graecus 39756).[48] The Ascension of

47. Overall, however, this also gives rise to an exciting additional line that has hardly been pursued to date: How far and to what extent are and were these two passages consciously or unconsciously read from apocryphal texts in their reception history?

48. On this passage in detail, see Tobias Nicklas, "'Drink the Cup Which I Promised You!' (*Apocalypse of Peter* 14.4): Peter's Death and the End of Times," in *The Open Mind: Essays in Honour of Christopher Rowland*, ed. Jonathan Knight and Kevin Sullivan, LNTS 522 (Bloomsbury, 2015), 184–93. The Apocalypse of Peter is a text reported from Peter's perspective. The center of the text is a version of Jesus's end-time speech, the description of the last judgment (including a world conflagration), and the description of otherworldly places, especially a kind of hell (without a corresponding term being used). The text has survived in its entirety only in an Ethiopic translation, though fragments of the original Greek also exist. The place of origin and date of the text are disputed: For the first half, perhaps the middle of the second century seems plausible. Alexandria, Palestine, and Syria are discussed as places of origin. A reference to the Bar Kokhba revolt (132–135 CE) is disputed. Since the usual introductions to Christian apocrypha do not reflect the latest state of the debate, reference can be made here to the fundamental work by Beck, *Justice and Mercy*. Also important now are the contributions in the volume by Maier et al., *Apocalypse of Peter in Context*. In addition, see Tobias Nicklas, "'Insider' und 'Outsider': Überlegungen zum historischen Kontext der Darstellung 'jenseitiger' Orte in der Offenbarung des Petrus," in *Topographie des Jenseits: Studien zur Geschichte des Todes in Kaiserzeit*

Isaiah,[49] in addition, refers to the persecution of the "planting by the twelve apostles" by the "unjust king" and "murderer of his mother," that is, Nero (Ascen. Isa. 4:2). In this persecution, one of the twelve was killed by Nero (Ascen. Isa. 4:3).[50] Other possible references (e.g., in 1 Clem. 5:4, Ign. *Rom.* 4:1–3, and Dionysius of Corinth [in Eusebius of Caesarea, *Hist. eccl.* 2.25.8]) also remain vague. The oldest reference to a tomb of Peter in Rome is found in Eusebius of Caesarea, *Historia ecclesiastica* 2.25, where he not only speaks of the beheading of Paul and the crucifixion of Peter in Rome at the time of Emperor Nero but also refers to the testimony of a certain Gaius, which goes back to the time of Bishop Zephyrinus of Rome (198/199–217 CE). This Gaius speaks of the "trophies" of the apostles, which Eusebius interprets as the places where the apostles are buried: "But I can point out the trophies of the Apostles. For, if you are willing to go to the Vatican or to the Ostian Way, you will find the trophies of those who founded this Church" (*Hist. eccl.* 2.25.3–5).[51]

The development becomes more exciting when we look at the apocryphal apostle narratives. The best-known form of the Acts of Peter, which is regularly presented in the usual collections of texts of the Christian apocrypha, is the Latin (also referred to as the Actus

---

und Spätantike, ed. Walter Ameling, Altertumswissenschaftliches Kolloquium 21 (Steiner, 2011), 35–48; Nicklas, "Petrus-Diskurse in Alexandria: Eine Fortführung der Gedanken von Jörg Frey," in Frey et al., *2 Peter and the Apocalypse of Peter*, 99–127.

49. The Ascension of Isaiah is a Christian apocalypse originally written in Greek. Earlier ideas that it was a Christian reworking of an originally Jewish Martyrdom of Isaiah are no longer held today. The text is probably made up of two originally independent parts, the origin of which can probably be dated to the early second century. The intensive reception of the text well into the Middle Ages by groups marginalized by the mainstream church, such as the Cathars or the Bogomils, is remarkable. An easily accessible English translation (albeit with a largely outdated introduction) is available in Michael A. Knibb, "Martyrdom and Ascension of Isaiah," *OTP*, 2:143–76. For an in-depth insight into the current discussion, see Bremmer et al., *Ascension of Isaiah*.

50. On this passage in detail, see Nicklas, "Drink the Cup," 193–99.

51. Translation from Eusebius of Caesarea, *Ecclesiastical History, Books 1–5*, ed. and trans. R. J. Deferrari, FC 19 (Catholic University of America Press, 1953), 133.

Vercellenses).[52] This work is a translation, likely originating in North Africa at the end of the fourth century, of an older Greek text, dating back to the end of the second century (probably from Asia Minor). The narrative is largely set in Rome, where Peter arrives after Paul has left for Spain and the majority of the congregation has been seduced into apostasy by Simon Magus, who is in league with Satan. The majority of these Acts of Peter revolve around Peter's ultimately successful battle (as the representative of Christ and the Christian God) against Simon.[53] This is followed by an account of Peter's martyrdom, which is only partially preserved in the Actus Vercellenses, and the story of his burial. Put simply, the Acts of Peter in this form thus offer three complexes of Peter's memory: (1) Peter's victorious battle against the representative of evil, Simon Magus; (2) his crucifixion, head down, at the time of the emperor Nero; and (3) a tradition surrounding his burial. While the battle against Simon Magus recedes in many later traditions about the Roman Peter as his martyrdom becomes more and more prominent, later texts will add two further memory complexes. First, the connection between Peter and Paul, who are increasingly understood on an equal footing as the apostles of Rome and whose martyrdoms are brought into ever closer

52. Text edition (with detailed information and German translation) is found in Döhler, *Acta Petri*; for the martyrdom of Peter, see also Otto Zwierlein, *Petrus in Rom: Die literarischen Zeugnisse*, 2nd ed., Untersuchungen zur antiken Literatur und Geschichte 96 (de Gruyter, 2010), 404–25. For an accessible English translation, see Elliott, *Apocryphal New Testament*, 390–426; for an overview of later Martyrdoms of Peter (and Paul) with short, helpful introductions, see David L. Eastman, *The Ancient Martyrdom Accounts of Peter and Paul*, WGRW 39 (SBL Press, 2015). The Latin Actus Vercellenses, on the other hand, is a version of the Acts of Peter probably written in North Africa in the second half of the fourth century and was originally native to Asia Minor. It probably dates back to the last third of the second century. In addition to the literature already mentioned, see also Jan N. Bremmer, "Aspects of the *Acts of Peter*: Women, Magic, Place and Date," in Bremmer, *Maidens, Magic and Martyrs*, 133–46.

53. On the content and theology of the text, see also Nicklas, "Inszenierung 'petrinischer Theologie,'" 243–81.

connection, will be strengthened.[54] Finally, Peter's imprisonment is associated with a motif that was initially transmitted in iconographic, rather than written, form: the idea that Peter converted the soldiers appointed to guard him in prison to Christianity, and that they were baptized by him. In order to make baptism possible in the dungeon, however, Peter, like Moses, strikes water from a rock, in a scene that is represented in numerous images. This last example clearly shows how different media (e.g., visual and literary) can work together to create a place of memory. Texts are by no means always the starting point, though they are often the easiest for us to grasp and interpret today.

In order to understand an important aspect of the development, it is important to take another look at both the Actus Vercellenses and its parallel, the oldest version of the Martyrdom of Peter. These works are indeed interested in the burial of Peter, but in a way that does not yet link Peter's place of memory with a real location in Rome where Peter was buried. One of the protagonists in these Peter narratives is the senator Marcellus. This man had become a Christian before the appearance of Peter but had then fallen away from the church under the influence of Simon Magus. Convinced by Peter, however, he not only turned back to Christianity but also gained steadfastness and firmness. After Peter's death, he—perhaps like Nicodemus and Joseph of Arimathea in the Gospel of John—arranged for Peter's royal burial. The oldest version of section 11 of the Greek largely corresponds to section 40 of the Actus Vercellenses:

> The apostle Peter gave up his spirit. But Marcellus, who had not received this idea from anyone—and this was not allowed—saw that the blessed Peter had died, and after taking the body off the cross with his own hands, he washed it with milk and wine. After he cut up fifty minas of mastic and myrrh and aloe, and another fifty minas of silphium, he embalmed his remains.

54. See the helpful and thorough treatment in David L. Eastman, *The Many Deaths of Peter and Paul*, OECS (Oxford University Press, 2019).

> And after filling a great stone coffin with a large amount of expensive Attic honey, he placed Peter in it. But the apostle Peter visited Marcellus by night and said, "Marcellus, did you not hear the Lord say, 'Leave the dead to bury their own dead'?" Then Marcellus said, "Yes." Peter said to him, "Therefore those things that you offered for the dead, you have lost, for you who are alive took care of the dead as if you were dead." But Marcellus awoke and recounted this appearance to the brothers and sisters who had been strengthened in their faith in Christ by Peter. And he himself was strengthened even more until the arrival of Paul in Rome.[55]

This scene, which revolves around the free quotation of the logion of Jesus from the Gospel of Matthew (Matt 8:22 par. Luke 9:60), offers a plethora of starting points for interpretation.[56] But with respect to the memory that is supposed to surround the figure of Peter, the statement seems clear: The point is not about the preservation of Peter's body "in the flesh." To back this up, the text subtly differentiates between, on the one hand, the Peter on the cross who appears to Marcellus in a dream, and, on the other hand, his corpse or mortal remains. What Marcellus seeks to preserve is not Peter but only his corpse. The thrust of the text is perhaps best understood in this way: Narrated memories of Peter are valuable, but to tie these memories to his bodily remains or his elaborately created grave is not. Peter remains a *mental* or *figurative* place of memory, from which the congregation's consolidation in faith is derived.

Tradition (incorrectly) attributes another version of Peter's death, the Martyrdom of the Blessed Apostle Peter, to Linus of Rome, Peter's

55. Translation in Eastman, *Ancient Martyrdom Accounts*, 23–25.

56. See further (with considerably more detail), on the material briefly presented below, Tobias Nicklas, "'Let the Dead Bury Their Own Dead' (Matt 8:22 par. Luke 9:60): A Commandment Without Impact for Christian Ethos?," in *Biblical Ethics and Application: Purview, Validity, and Relevance of Biblical Texts in Ethical Discourse*, ed. Ruben Zimmermann and Stephen Joubert, WUNT 384 (Mohr Siebeck, 2017), 75–90.

alleged successor as bishop of Rome. This work was likely composed at the turn of the fifth century.[57] It is the first time that a written version of the miracle of Peter striking water from the rock, already represented earlier particularly in funerary art, appears.[58] The passage is quite brief—containing a reference to rather than narration of the miracle—indicating that knowledge of the miracle is presupposed. Here Peter's prison guards are given the names Processus and Martinianus (§5); they report: "After we believers in this region of the Mamertine prison were baptized in the name of the Holy Trinity in a spring brought forth from stone by prayers and the glorious sign of the cross, you [Peter] went around as freely as you pleased."[59] The passage also demonstrates that the memory of Peter is now tied to concrete, real places: Peter is imprisoned in the Mamertine prison (§5), which is in itself a place of memory of the Roman Empire, as some of its most threatening enemies were imprisoned here (namely, Jugurtha, Vercingetorix, and Catiline). The apostle narrative thus augments an existing place of memory:[60] on the one hand, Peter is placed on the same level of fame and significance as the other well-known prisoners; on the other hand, for the author of the Martyrdom of the Blessed Apostle Peter, he is of course *not* the enemy of the state that his enemies consider him to be.

In the same work, Peter's cross is also localized at a specific place called Naumachia *iuxta obeliscum Neronis in montem* (§10: Naumachia,

57. Text and introduction as well as an English translation in Eastman, *Ancient Martyrdom Accounts*, 27–66.

58. On this motif in written tradition, its interpretation in the early church, and its iconographic representation on sarcophagi and in catacombs, see Dresken-Weiland, *Bild, Grab und Wort*, 119–35.

59. Translation according to Eastman, *Ancient Martyrdom Accounts*, 41.

60. The wording is based on thoughts by Andreas Merkt, "The Hetero-topography of the Forum Romanum. How Late Antique Peter Traditions Generated an Augmented Reality of Public Space," in Nicklas et al., *Apostles Peter, Paul, John*, 21–55, esp. 32–35.

next to the obelisk of Nero on the mountain[61]). Even if we can no longer identify this location with certainty today, the function of the passage seems to be to do exactly that for the work's readers.[62] At the same time, the connection between Peter's death on the cross and Nero is also reinforced. A shift in connection with Peter's burial is evident in this work: Marcellus is no longer rebuked for having buried Peter's (here) "holy corpse" (!) at great expense (§16). Instead, he is to overcome his grief, which makes him feel dead, and return to life and proclaim the kingdom of God. Peter speaks to him in a dream (§16) as follows: "Do not seem to bury and weep for the dead as if you were dead, but rather as one who is alive, delight in living and rejoicing, and leave the dead to bury their own dead. But, as for you, as you learned from me, go and proclaim the kingdom of God."[63]

A complete reinterpretation of this scene is found in the Passion of Peter.[64] This Latin text, probably from the sixth century, is dependent on the earlier writings in its description of the burial of Peter, but it supplies Peter's burial with a completely new meaning: "Marcellus, one of his disciples, did not wait for anyone's permission but took down his body from the cross with his own hands. After embalming it with the

61. Eastman, *Ancient Martyrdom Accounts*, 49.

62. On this, David Eastman writes, "The term *naumachia* refers to a mock sea battle or to the place where mock sea battles were staged. Nero was apparently the first emperor to put on such an event in an amphitheater . . . in 57 CE. He constructed this building on (or at least very near) the Field of Mars, opposite the Vatican hill (Suetonius, *Nero* 12.2–6; Cassius Dio, *Hist.* 61.9.5). Cassius Dio (*Hist.* 62.15.1) records that Nero staged a battle there in 64 CE, preceded by animal hunts and gladiatorial shows. Its exact location is unknown, but it is possible that the amphitheater and the place at which it was located could have taken on the name of the spectacles staged there" (*Ancient Martyrdom Accounts*, 49).

63. Eastman, *Ancient Martyrdom Accounts*, 63.

64. Introduction, text, and English translation in Eastman, *Ancient Martyrdom Accounts*, 67–102. On the work's mistaken attribution to Abdias, see Els Rose, "Virtutes Apostolorum: Editorial Problems and Principles," *Apocrypha* 23 (2012): 11–45; Rose, "Abdias Scriptor Vitarum Sanctorum Apostolorum? The 'Collection of Pseudo-Abdias,'" *Revue d'histoire des textes* (2013): 227–68.

most precious spices, he placed it in his own sarcophagus in a place that is called the Vatican, next to the triumphal way, where it is honored in peace by the veneration of the entire city" (§20).[65] Here Marcellus becomes a type of Roman Joseph of Arimathea, who uses his own sarcophagus (instead of his own tomb; cf. Matt 27:60) to give Peter a dignified burial. There is no more critique of Marcellus's attitude toward Peter's physical remains. Moreover, the narrative and the specific location of those physical remains in the real world are now combined: The work places them "in the Vatican next to the triumphal way." A clear parallel is found in Jerome, *De viris illustribus* 1, where we read the following information of Peter's body: It is "buried in Rome in the Vatican, next to the triumphal way, where it is honored by the whole world."[66]

Space does not allow us to follow this trail much further, but the development of apocryphal writings dealing with the death of Peter in Rome surely does not end here. To the contrary, we can observe more and more—for example, in the Latin Passion of the Holy Apostles Peter and Paul by Pseudo-Marcellus and the Greek Acts of the Holy Apostles Peter and Paul—how the martyrdom of Peter and the martyrdom of Paul are interwoven, and how commemorative days (such as June 29 for the martyrdoms of Peter and Paul, and July 2 for martyrdoms of Processus and Martinianus) are connected with them. Beyond what we have sketched here, there is a complex system of Christian symbolic history, which revolves around the Roman Peter and reappears in parts in the medieval *Legenda Aurea* of Jacobus de Voragine.[67]

The development of the place of memory "Peter in Rome" does not, however, stand on its own; in some cases, a highly tense relationship with other developments is observable. Starting with memories of Martin of Tours (316–397 CE), who is increasingly understood as the apostle of Gaul, a new landscape of real places of memory developed. Besides Martin, this landscape included saints and their miracles in

65. Eastman, *Ancient Martyrdom Accounts*, 99–101.

66. See Eastman, *Ancient Martyrdom Accounts*, 101n61.

67. On Peter in the Legenda Aurea, see de Voragine, *Legenda Aurea*, 1130–61.

areas of Gaul that were breaking away from the Roman Empire. With this landscape of memories the emerging empire of the Merovingians, quite largely detached from Roman claims, sought to form their own identity.[68] Gaul did not need a grave of Peter, nor of Paul; it had its own apostle(s), Martin and other saints. A similar phenomenon is recognizable elsewhere: Against the idea that Peter and Paul were the founders of the Church of Rome, the *Barnabas Encomium* (composed by the monk Alexander in Cyprus in the middle of the sixth century) was able to develop a perspective on early Christianity in which neither Peter nor Paul was a founder of the Church of Rome but Barnabas, the later apostle of Cyprus.[69]

Constantinople also developed its own apostolic landscape of memory.[70] As the church of the capital of the East, which was only newly founded in the fourth century, the city could not, at least initially, claim apostolic foundation. Two other techniques were used instead: (1) Various places in Constantinople were associated with the memory of Mary, who had been venerated as the mother of God since the Council

68. For important information on this, see Raymond Van *Leadership and Community in Late Antique Gaul* (University of California Press, 1985).

69. The *Barnabas Encomium* by the monk Alexander offers a significantly expanded new version of the story of the mission of Cyprus and the martyrdom of Barnabas, which is also contained in the Acts of Barnabas. Extensive traditions deal with Barnabas's alleged early missionary journeys, his relationship with Paul, and the miraculous recovery of his relics. The text can be found in Peter van Deun, "Sancti Barnabae Laudatio auctore Alexandro Monacho," in *Hagiographica Cypria*, CCSG 26 (Brepols, 1993), 5–122; Michael R. Cosby, *Creation of History: The Transformation of Barnabas from Peacemaker to Warrior Saint* (Wipf & Stock, 2017) offers an English translation of the text that is not always entirely reliable. On the political significance of the text (also in its continuation and deepening of the claims of Cyprus in comparison to the Acts of Barnabas), see Tobias Nicklas, "Barnabas Remembered," 178–87. On the dating, see van Deun, "Sancti Barnabae Laudatio," 16–21.

70. See in detail at Martina Hartl, *Leichen, Asche und Gebeine: Der frühchristliche Umgang mit dem toten Körper und die Anfänge des Reliquienkults*, Handbuch zur Geschichte des Todes im frühen Christentum und seiner Umwelt 3 (Schnell & Steiner, 2018), 159–70.

of Ephesus (431 CE) and who could be venerated as the patron saint of the city and the orthodox emperors.[71] (2) Apostolic presence was made possible through the transfer of relics. In the first stage, the memories of apostles seem to have played a less decisive role than the memory of Constantine, as Constantine the Great had ordered to be buried in his mausoleum together with the relics of Andrew and Luke. It was only a generation later, under Constantine II (ruler of the East 337–361 CE), that the memory of Constantine and the tombs of the apostles, to which the relics of Timothy were added, were separated. The fact that the Church of Constantinople also began to see itself as having an apostolic foundation can probably be traced to much later developments;[72] it is certainly no coincidence that the focus here was on Andrew, who, at least according to the testimony of the Gospel of John (John 1:35–41), was one of the first two disciples called, preceding Peter. The apocryphal traditions that report the founding of the Church of Byzantium (i.e., the predecessor of Constantinople) by Andrew (and his companion Stachys) are significantly later than the aforementioned Roman apocrypha about Peter (and Paul). Only in the Martyrdom of St. Andrew the Apostle, dating to the eighth century of our era (and not to be confused with the martyrdom of the apostle in the usual editions of the Acts of Andrew) do we read:

> [Andrew], after having sailed down through the same Pontus Euxinos [i.e., the Black Sea], which flows towards Byzantium, landed on the right bank, and after arriving at a place called Argyropolis, and having constructed here a church, he ordained one of the seventy disciples called Stachys whom also Paul the Apostle, the mouth-piece of Christ, the vessel of election,

71. On this, see Leslie Brubaker and Mary B. Cunningham, eds., *The Cult of the Mother of God in Byzantium: Texts and Images*, 2nd ed., Birmingham Byzantine and Ottoman Studies (Routledge, 2016).

72. Francis Dvornik, *The Idea of Apostolicity in Byzantium and the Legend of the Apostle Andrew* (Harvard University Press, 1958), provides a detailed account of the development.

> mentions in the Epistle to the Romans as beloved, Bishop of Byzantium, and left him to preach the word of salvation.[73]

While this work forges Constantinople's connection with one of the great apostles rather cautiously, it is notable that this type of creative narration was a viable strategy in the eighth century and beyond.

3. Example 3: Memory Beyond Texts—Objects and Rites

Up to this point, we have mainly worked in a text-oriented manner, though in some places it has already become apparent that the development of places of memory is not restricted to written sources. To the contrary, in many cases other media, particularly art and architecture, initiate, support, and further develop memory. One of the most important landscapes of memory in Christianity—also of the utmost importance for the self-definition of other religions such as Judaism and Islam—is Israel. With the word *Israel* we do not, of course, simply refer to the geographically describable stretch of land east of the Mediterranean or the modern state of Israel per se; rather, we refer to what Christians have called the Holy Land since late antiquity.[74] The phrase "Holy Land," in turn, relates to a particular perception of the space it designates as well as the complex structure of the many highly symbolic places and objects within it. All of this can be seen particularly dramatically in the city of Jerusalem: The Temple Mount, for example—a place the size of a soccer pitch—is a location that different religions understand as holy in different ways based on completely different narratives and interpretations.

---

73. Text in Maximilian Bonnet, "Martyrium Sancti Apostoli Andreae," *AnBoll* 13 (1894): 353–72. A translation of the passage is in Dvornik, *Idea of Apostolicity*, 172; a complete translation of this writing does not of yet exist.

74. The volume by Harald Buchinger et al., eds., *Extracanonical Traditions and the Holy Land: Texts, Ritual, and Material Culture in Late Antique Palestine*, Studien und Texte zu Antike und Christentum (Mohr Siebeck, forthcoming), offers a variety of traditions in relation to the Holy Land.

The following example shows the extent to which both canonical and apocryphal traditions, without a sharp dividing line being drawn between them, contribute to the development of Jerusalem as the primary place of memory within the Holy Land.[75] Among the great number of human beings who have undertaken travel to the Holy Land since the fourth century, an unknown pilgrim from Bordeaux (ca. 333–334 CE) has left us a revealing itinerary. The following passage reports on Jerusalem—or, rather, it reveals how the pilgrim perceived Jerusalem:

> There are in Jerusalem two large pools at the side of the temple, that is, one upon the right hand, and one upon the left, which Solomon made; and further in the city are twin pools which have five porticoes, which are called Bethsaida. There the ones who were sick for many years were healed; these pools have water, which is red when stirred up. Here is also a crypt, wherein Solomon tortured demons. Here is the corner of an exceedingly high tower, where the Lord ascended and the one who tempted him spoke to him and the Lord said to him: "You will not tempt the Lord your God, but only serve him." There is a big cornerstone, of which it is said, "The stone which the builders refused was made the head of the corner." . . . And in the building itself, where the Temple was, which Solomon built, they say that the blood of Zacharias that was shed upon the stone floor before the altar is there until today. . . . On this side, one ascends Sion and sees where the priest Caiphas' house was. And there is still a column where they flagellated Christ with rods. . . . From there, when you go out of the wall of Sion and walk to the Neapolis gate, at the right hand, below in the valley

75. On the role of apocryphal traditions in late antique and early medieval pilgrimage reports on the Holy Land, see Tobias Nicklas, "Beyond 'Canon': Christian Apocrypha and Pilgrimage," in *The Other Side: Apocryphal Perspectives on Ancient Christian "Orthodoxies,"* ed. Tobias Nicklas et al., NTOA 117 (Vandenhoeck & Ruprecht, 2017), 23–38. The following material is also discussed in Nicklas, "From Gospel Book to Virtual Reality," 24–28.

> are walls where Pontius Pilate's house or praetorium was. Here the Lord was questioned before the passion. On the left, however, is the small Golgotha hill where the Lord was crucified. About a stone's throw from there is a crypt where his body was laid and rose on the third day. (Itinerarium Burdigalense 2.8)[76]

The Jerusalem of the pilgrim is clearly not just a city like any other. Its houses and streets tell *the* gospel (or parts of the gospel). This gospel, however, does not simply correspond to one of the four canonical Gospels but is made up of a variety of narratives that can be linked to the story of Jesus. It is therefore a kind of "virtual narrative," or "Bible in the mind."[77] If one takes a closer look, one may discover reminiscences of the Gospel of John in the pilgrim's account—albeit in a textual form that speaks of the pools of Bethsaida, not those of Bethesda (see John 5:12).[78] There are also recognizable references to Jesus's temptation by the devil in the Synoptic Gospels (Matt 4:1–11 par. Luke 4:1–13). The reference to Solomon torturing the demons, on the other hand, calls to mind the apocryphal Testament of Solomon, though it is not clear that our pilgrim had direct knowledge of this text.[79] Analyzing the account detail by detail, one would conclude that our pilgrim recognizes in Jerusalem the representation of a virtual gospel that can only loosely be assigned to the concrete written texts of the canon. Some details, such as the mention of the pillar to which Jesus was tied during his scourging,

---

76. A Latin text is available in Kai Brodersen, ed., *Aetheria/Egeria. Reise ins Heilige Land* (de Gruyter, 2016), 54–56. Translation by Tobias Nicklas.

77. On this concept, see also the introductory chapter of the present volume.

78. The transmission history of John 5:2 is notoriously ambiguous.

79. The late antique, probably Christian Testament of Solomon compiles traditions about Solomon as the conqueror of demons. The text with an introduction and German translation can be found in Peter Busch, *Das Testament Salomos: Die älteste christliche Dämonologie, kommentiert und in deutscher Erstübersetzung*, TU 153 (de Gruyter, 2006).

are not found in any canonical text; instead, they must derive from readers' imaginations of gospel scenes.

One motif in our passage, however, is particularly intriguing: The pilgrim apparently visits the Temple Mount but offers hardly any description of it or the remaining ruins of the temple; instead, he mentions only a single specific site, the place where "the blood of Zacharias which was shed upon the stone floor before the altar is until today." At first glance, the contemporary reader might assume this refers to the Gospel of Matthew (at 23:35), where the blood of Zechariah, the son of Barachiah, who was murdered in the courtyard between the temple building and the altar, is mentioned.[80] However, the fact that the pilgrim mentions that this blood can still be seen today points to a different background. The apocryphal Protevangelium of James deals with the obvious question—not answered in the canonical Gospels—of how the young John the Baptist was able to survive the slaughter of infants conducted by Herod. As already mentioned above, according to Protevangelium of James 22 this happens through a miracle: The rock face of a mountain opens, taking in Elizabeth and the child and saving them from the persecutors. But, of course, this puts the child's father, the priest Zechariah known from the Gospel of Luke, in danger. When he does not reveal his son's whereabouts to Herod, he is murdered in the antechamber of the temple (Prot. Jas. 23). As his blood stains the altar of the Lord, an (apparently) heavenly voice is heard: "Zacharias has been slain, and his blood shall not be wiped away until the avenger comes" (Prot. Jas. 24:2). Apparently, our pilgrim is shown a stone that has itself become a place of memory: a place that represents the Christian memory that, with the murder of Zechariah, his blood desecrated the altar of the temple. This place of memory is a physical object, in this case an object linked to a narrative that finds its background (or at least one instantiation) in the Protevangelium of James. Later testimonies indicate that the place with which this memory was associated moved from the Temple Mount to the Church of the Holy

80. See also, less concretely, Luke 11:51.

Sepulcher in Jerusalem. In Breviarius de Hierosolyma, a kind of ancient pilgrim's guide to Jerusalem (probably sixth century), the following description of the Holy Sepulcher can be found: "In front of the grave is the altar where the holy Zacharias was killed and where his blood dried up" (§3, version A).

The question of whether and to what extent *objects speak in and of themselves* is controversial in modern cultural studies. Although there are indications that the world of things can exhibit analogies to the world of texts, caution is generally advisable.[81] In many cases, things require an interpretive narrative in order to be able to speak. The extent to which this also applies in the present case is shown by a somewhat later example: Abbot Adomnan of Iona,[82] who is also otherwise associated with apocryphal and hagiographic literature, handed down the account of a certain Arculf about the holy places of Jerusalem around 680 CE. Arculf also describes the stones of the Holy Sepulcher but simply depicts them as red and white. The story of Zechariah's murder and his staining blood is either unknown or does not occur to Arculf: Without the apocryphal account, the stones are simply red, with no particular significance.

However, it is not written narratives alone that are able to create and maintain a "crystallization point of collective memory and identity" that lasts for generations. In many cases, it is rituals—often tied to fixed times—that present memory in the truest sense of the word, that is, literally make it present in time and space. The task of describing this phenomenon more precisely falls within the field of liturgical studies, which in recent years has made decisive contributions to a reorientation

81. On the limits of the parallels between language and things, see the convincing thoughts of Hans Peter Hahn, *Materielle Kultur. Eine Einführung*, 2nd ed. (Dietrich Reimer, 2014), 136–44.

82. One example of this is the so-called Vision of Adomnan, an early medieval journey to the afterlife.

of research into apocryphal and parabiblical traditions.[83] Here we highlight just one aspect of this area of research: Many late apocryphal apostle narratives, situated on the borderline of apocryphal and hagiographic literature, can be interpreted as etiologies of liturgical practices, for example, in connection with the feasts of the apostles.[84] In many cases, the protagonist of such writings, usually an apostle or disciple of an apostle, can themselves be understood as a place of memory in a figurative sense. Such a narrative is then often linked to a physically accessible, real place.

In the Acts of Titus, for example, toward the end (§11), reference is made to the apostle's "revered burial place," which is describe as follows: It is "an altar on which there are manacles with which those who are under the influence of unclean spirits are bound." There also all who are worthy to embrace the place of the saint's final resting place receive "healing."[85] Before they were transferred to St. Mark's in Venice in the ninth century, this form of veneration of the relics of Titus was possible at the Basilica of Titus in Gortys in Crete—the city to which the long title of the Acts of Titus also refers: the Acts of the Holy

83. A foundational essay (with detailed further reading) can be found in Harald Buchinger, "Liturgy and Early Christian Apocrypha," in Gregory and Tuckett, *Oxford Handbook of Early Christian Apocrypha*, 361–77.

84. A more detailed presentation of the material presented below can also be found in in Tobias Nicklas, "Spätantike Apostelerzählungen als liturgiegeschichtliche Quellen," in *Ünneplő ember a közösségben. Baráti köszöntő kötet Nóda Mózes tiszteletére*, ed. Korinna Zamfir (Verbum, 2019), 97–106. Another point relevant to liturgical studies, which I would like to ignore in what follows, is that some of these texts have survived in manuscripts produced for liturgical purposes. Researching this would provide material for a large-scale project.

85. The late antique Acts of Titus tells of the first mission to Crete by the Pauline disciple Titus. Richard I. Pervo, "The Acts of Titus," in Burke and Landau, *New Testament Apocrypha*, 1:406–15, offers an English translation. See also the extensive discussion of the little-known text (with German translation) in Tobias Nicklas, "Die Akten des Titus; Rezeption 'apostolischer' Schriften und Entwicklung antik-christlicher 'Erinnerungslandschaften,'" *EC* 8 (2017): 458–80.

Apostle Titus, the Bishop of Crete, the City of Gortys, the Disciple of the Holy Apostle Paul. Something similar can also be seen in the aforementioned *Barnabas Encomium* by the monk Alexander, which points out that the tomb of Barnabas the apostle that is so important for the identity of the Church of Cyprus can still be venerated today in the monastery of Barnabas near the city of Salamis. For other texts, feasts at which the apostle is to be commemorated liturgically take place alongside the real places of memory. The Greek Martyrdom of Mark is one of the fundamental texts surrounding the figurative place of memory of Mark, who is understood as an evangelist, apostle, and missionary of Alexandria (as well as large parts of North Africa).[86] The text, which essentially dates to the second half of the fourth century, focuses on the first mission of Alexandria and the overcoming of the gods of Egypt; the decisive antagonist is the god of the city of Alexandria, Serapis. The climax of the text is, of course, the martyrdom of Mark. However, this is not the end of the text. Paragraphs 11 and 12 of the manuscript Biblioteca Apostolica Vaticana (Vaticani graeci 866, fols. 276r–277v) conclude with the following words:

> And performing prayers, they buried him according to the custom of the city. They preserved him in a place that had been hewn out with glory honoring his memories with fasting and prayers, as the first relic acquired in Alexandria, and they laid him in the eastern part (of the church). This way the blessed evangelist Mark, the first martyr for the name of the Lord Jesus Christ in Alexandria at Egypt, passed away in the month

86. An English translation of this text (or of this textual witness with variants of other versions) is offered by Tobias Nicklas, "Martyrdom of Mark," in *New Testament Apocrypha: More Noncanonical Scriptures*, ed. Tony Burke (Eerdmans, 2023), 3:375–92; see also (unfortunately already outdated with regard to the transmission history) Tobias Nicklas, "The Martyrdom of Mark in Late Antique Alexandria," in *Alexandria: Hub of the Hellenistic World*, ed. Benjamin Schliesser et al., WUNT 460 (Mohr Siebeck, 2021), 519–42.

> Parmoute, according to Romans on the 25th of April, under the reign of Caesar Gaius Tiberius, but according to us Christians, the ruling of our Lord Jesus Christ. To him be the glory and the power together with the Father and the Holy Spirit, forever and ever. Amen.[87]

This concluding passage describes neither the place where Mark's tomb can be venerated nor a precise liturgical rite. And yet—together with other places in Alexandria mentioned in the Martyrdom—a real place of worship for Mark is obviously assumed; the date of his martyrdom is given almost as a matter of protocol. We do not know whether the liturgical commemoration of Mark originated from this text or whether the work reflects an existing ritual practice. What is clear, however, is that it is the combination of the (apocryphal) text, the real place, and the practice of remembering that constitutes the place of memory of Mark in Alexandria—which, as noted above, was significant for the construction of an identity for the Church of Alexandria.[88]

---

87. Translation in Nicklas, "Martyrdom of Mark" (2023).

88. The Martyrdom of Mark certainly does not represent the intellectuals who played an important role in Alexandrian Christianity early on but rather appeals to simple circles. See in greater detail Alfons Fürst, *Christentum als Intellektuellen-Religion. Die Anfänge des Christentums in Alexandria*, SBS 213 (Katholisches Bibelwerk, 2007).

CHAPTER 6

An Epilogue

Reading Apocrypha Straight from Heaven

At some point in the early 1920s, a salesman knocked on the door of 5706 Woodlawn Avenue, Chicago, home of Edgar J. Goodspeed, professor of New Testament at the University of Chicago.[1] The salesman was selling a tract with the title "Copy of a Letter, Written by Our Blessed Lord and Saviour, Jesus Christ." Of this salesman Goodspeed would later write, "I am sure he was never so welcomed in his life as he was at my door, for I had been looking for a complete text of this curious work for years."[2] Goodspeed had already encountered this apocryphal epistle twice: He was first made aware of it by a friend, who had transcribed a copy from "a framed text . . . found hanging on the wall of a house" of an acquaintance; later, Goodspeed would be surprised to find a nearly identical edition of the letter printed in the *Chicago Evening Post* of May 16, 1917; the third and most fortuitous encounter with the work, in the form of "a tract printed in Chicago, November 17, 1917,"

1. This chapter is an adapted and abbreviated version of an essay that appeared in a festschrift for Margaret M. Mitchell: Janet E. Spittler, "Apocryphal Epistles: The Curious Case of the *Letter of Jesus Christ That Fell from Heaven*," in *Paul, Christian Textuality, and the Hermeneutics of Late Antiquity*, ed. Robert Matthew Calhoun et al. (Brill, 2023), 302–47.

2. Edgar J. Goodspeed, *Modern Apocrypha* (Beacon, 1956), 70.

that was being "peddled door to door" on the south side of Chicago,[3] seems to have solidified Goodspeed's determination to learn more.

The headline as printed in *The Post* reads: "'Letter from Christ' Warns of 'Holy Day'—Anonymous Communication to The Post Demands Sabbath Be Consecrated." The following two selections offer a flavor of the letter's contents:

> Whosoever works on the Sabbath day shall be cursed. I command you to go to church and keep holy the Lord's Day, without any manner of work. You shall not idle or misspend your time bedecking yourself in vain dressing, for I have ordered it a day of rest. I will have that day kept holy that your sins may be forgiven you. . . . And he that hath a copy of this letter written by My own hand and spoken by My own mouth and keepeth it without publishing it to others shall not prosper, but he who publisheth it to others shall be blessed by Me and if their sins be as many as the stars by night, and if they truly believe, they shall be pardoned, and they that believe not this writing and my commandments will have My plague upon you.

This last section is what has earned the Letter its reputation as the world's first chain letter, that is, a letter that demands that its readers send it on to new recipients (in German, a *Kettenbrief*). It might also be the most widely independently circulated work of Christian apocrypha—because, as Goodspeed would eventually come to know, what he had before him was not a recent composition; it was, in fact, a modern English version of a late antique apocryphal letter,[4] which purports to be a composition of Jesus himself and treats primarily the importance of keeping the Lord's Day holy, alongside vivid descriptions of the punishments in store for those who fail to do so. This work, generally referred to in modern scholarship as the Letter of Jesus Christ (but also as the Letter That Fell from Heaven, the Skyletter, or, most commonly in anglophone scholarship on the Anglo-Saxon and

3. Edgar J. Goodspeed, *Strange New Gospels* (University of Chicago Press, 1931), 101.

4. *CANT* 311, Bibliotheca Hagiographica Graeca 812i–812r.

English traditions, the Sunday Letter) is extraordinarily widespread: It is extant in Latin, Greek, Armenian, Syriac, Arabic, Ethiopic, Georgian, Church Slavic, Italian, English, Welsh, German, Icelandic, Irish, Czech, Romanian, Ukrainian, Russian, Hungarian, Polish, Bulgarian, Serbian, Norwegian, and surely other languages, and has been in continuous circulation for some fourteen hundred years. In this last chapter, we take up the Letter of Jesus Christ as a single example of the enormous breadth of transmission that an apocryphal work can achieve.

Our earliest evidence of the existence of a letter written by Jesus Christ that fell from heaven comes from the end of the sixth century CE. In or around the year 584, Licinianus, bishop of Cartagena, writes a letter to Vincentius, bishop of Ebusa (modern Ibiza). In it, Licinianus denounces a text that Vincentius has sent to him—a text purporting to be a letter written by Jesus Christ himself, which Vincentius has held to be authentic and has read out to his congregation. Licinianus's letter is extraordinarily interesting (and not broadly available in English translation), so we quote it in its entirety here. Licinianus writes:

> In the midst of various straits of tribulations—such as they are—it does not trouble us, as the charity of Christ demands, to send words to Your Holiness, acknowledging that we have received your letter and are pleased by the good news of your well-being. But we are in no small part saddened by the fact that you have, as your letter indicates, accepted a certain letter, which you have sent to us, and that you have allowed it to be proclaimed from the tribunal of the people. I, indeed, as soon as I received your dispatch, reading the preface of that letter in the presence of the messenger himself (and neither bearing it patiently nor thinking it worthwhile to read to the end of such nonsense), immediately tore it up and threw it to the ground, marvelling that you were so credulous, and that—even after the prophecies of the prophets, and the Gospels of Christ, the letters of his apostles—you believe a letter of some human being, fashioned under the name of Christ, to (really) be his, where no fine word or sound teaching is to be found!

At the beginning of that letter we read that Sunday should be honored. Honestly, which Christian does not hold it as most revered—not because of the day itself, but because of the resurrection of our Lord Jesus Christ, that on that very day he rose from the dead? But, as far as I can tell, this new preacher says this in order to compel us to Judaize—so that no one prepare for themselves on that day the necessary foods, or walk on the road! But let Your Holiness consider if this is the worst possible thing. Would that Christian people, if they do not attend church on that day, *would* do some sort of work—and not dance! It would be better for a man to tend the garden, to make a journey; for a woman to take up the spindle, and not, as was said, to dance, to leap, and to wickedly twist with dancing the limbs (that were properly assembled by God) and to call out to jesters for songs to excite lust.

God forbid, then, that Your Holiness believe that the letter was sent to us by Christ in the present time. Indeed, let what is said in the prophets themselves and through his apostles suffice! For even to these he did not send a letter from heaven; rather, he filled their hearts with the Holy Spirit. To be sure, with the exception of the Ten Commandments (which were miraculously given on stone tablets), to none of the prophets or apostles were epistles sent from heaven. Well then, you should not trust what was read—things that never happened, things that, even if they had happened, are no longer necessary after the preaching of the Gospel. If, perhaps, that novel title seduced you—that the epistle, as the trickster wrote, descended from heaven above the altar of Christ that is a memorial of the holy apostle Peter—know that it is a figment of the devil, and that all divine scriptures—epistle or epistles—are heavenly, sent to us from heaven.

Therefore, correct what Your Holiness rashly believed, and, in the presence of the people, tear up that letter, if it is in your possession: indeed, let this be your penance, because you allowed

> it to be proclaimed from the tribunal, following the teaching of the blessed apostle, which he wrote, among others, to the Galatians: "If anyone evangelizes you contrary to what you have received, let that one be cursed!" But indeed, that is what the Gospel, every law, and the prophets—all the way up to John—prophesied. From now on, if new or extraordinary things are spread among the people, Your Holiness will recognize them as utterly to be cast aside and renounced. Pray for us, holy Lord and dearest brother in Christ.

What do we learn from Licinianus's response to Vincentius? What is in this Letter of Jesus Christ, and what is it precisely that is so unacceptable to Licinianus? He seems to have two primary objections. The first involves the specific teaching concerning Sunday, which Licinianus understands as misguided "Judaizing"—misguided both in its imitation of Jewish practices per se and in the particular practices mandated (Licinianus would rather Christians work on Sunday than dance). The second objection involves the basic notion of a letter written by the risen Jesus and delivered in the present day. For Licinianus, God simply does not communicate (and has never communicated) with human beings via missive directly from heaven—though, as Licinianus acknowledges, the Ten Commandments are perhaps an exception to this rule. Moreover, Licinianus continues, the canonical Scriptures are sufficient: There is no need for new material, and a letter that claims to have fallen directly from heaven is in no sense superior to existing Scriptures. Note also that Licinianus is not impressed by the writing style: "No fine word" is to be found, so obviously Jesus didn't write it.

Licinianus's strong reaction to the Letter is mirrored in modern scholars' reaction to the work, many of whom refer to it with terms such as *artless*, *tedious*, *fraudulent*, or (as one of our favorite scholars, M. R. James, puts it) "long, very dull." It is important to imagine, then, how Vincentius's reception of the Letter might have differed from Licinianus's: In Vincentius we have a reader who must have found the opposite qualities in the same text. Which type of reader has been more numerous over the history of the reception of the Letter: the Liciniani or the Vincentii?

This chapter is not the place to explore the Letter's circulation within Western Christianity, though it is truly a fascinating journey. Key figures in the story of the Letter's reception in the West include Boniface, Pope Zacharias, the "heretic" and wonderworker Aldebert, Charlemagne, Eustace the Abbot of Flay, the chronicler Roger of Hoveden, Ecgred the bishop of Lindisfarne, and an assortment of flagellants. Here we would simply emphasize that there are *at least* as many Vincentii as Liciniani to be found among those who encountered the Letter of Jesus Christ.

One of the fundamental questions in modern scholarship on the Letter involves its language of composition: Was it written in Latin, originating somewhere in the West? Or was it perhaps a Greek composition, originating somewhere in the East? The Letter is in fact extant in quite a few Greek witnesses, from which stem, ultimately, the Armenian, Syriac, Garshuni, Arabic, Ethiopic, Georgian, and all of the various Slavic translations.[5] The first edition of a Greek witness was made in 1743 by Fabricius in the third part of his *Codex Apocryphus Novi Testamenti*.[6] In 1893, Vassiliev edited two recensions, working from six manuscripts all dated to the fifteenth, sixteenth, or seventeenth centuries; in his introduction, Vassiliev also prints two recensions of a version of the letter in contemporary (that is, late nineteenth and early twentieth century) circulation among Greek tourists and pilgrims in Jerusalem.[7] In 1906, Maximilian Bittner published a monumental work, in which he edited twelve Greek witnesses (as well as thirteen

---

5. One could add here Middle Bulgarian, Polish, Hungarian, Ukrainian, Czech, Romanian, and Serbian. On these, see Dennis Deletant, "The Sunday Legend," *Revue des études sud-est européennes* 15 (1977): 431–51.

6. Fabricius, *Codex Apocryphus*, 3:510–13. Note that Fabricius printed Latin sources for the Letter (including Licinianus's letter as well as the quotation of Letter in from the records of the synod involving Aldebert and Boniface) in *Codex Apocryphus Novi Testamenti edition secunda* (Schiller & Kisner, 1719), 308–13.

7. A. Vassiliev, *Anecdota Graeco-Byzantina, pars prior* (Universitatus Caesarea, 1893), xii–xx, 23–32.

Armenian witnesses, eight Syriac, five Garshuni, seven Arabic, and three Ethiopic). Among the twelve Greek witnesses (including the six already edited by Vassiliev), Bittner identifies ten distinct recensions, presenting editions of seven of them. Following Vassiliev, he divides these into three basic categories (*alpha*, *beta*, and *gamma*), the last of these representing the early twentieth-century pamphlets circulated in Jerusalem.[8] The online resource Pinakes lists seven additional Greek witnesses not used by Bittner.[9]

A sense of the differences and similarities between the Latin and Greek recensions can be gained by a quick look at the beginning of the work in four different versions. The Latin version that was read into the record of the Lateran Synod of 745 (this is where Boniface accused Aldebert of heresy, and the Letter was used as evidence) is as follows:

> In the name of God, here begins the letter of our Lord Jesus Christ, Son of God, which fell in Hierosolyma and was found by the archangel Michael at the gate of Ephraim; and that very letter was read and copied by the hand of a priest named Icore; and he sent it to another priest, named Talasius, in the city of Hieremia; and that Talasius sent the same letter to the city Arabia to another priest, Leobanius; and that Leobanius sent

8. The contemporary pamphlet in Greek is in fact the only Greek version of the work that Goodspeed was aware of. He refers (*Strange New Gospels*, 105–6) to a "much longer tract now current in modern Greek and published by Michael Saliveros in Athens." He continues: "This Greek form of the letter is much more violent and denunciatory than the English forms given above. It is also much more extended. The common elements of the two forms are enough, however, to make it pretty certain that the one is a development from the other, and if that be true, the Greek represents the elaborated form and the English the more primitive. Probably the patriarch, finding the shorter, milder form, developed it into the savage tirade which we find in the Greek."

9. These are Vatican City, Bibl. Vat. gr. 2235, fols. 222–29; Rome, Biblioteca Nazionale Centrale Vittorio Emanuele II, S. A. Valle 102, fols. 168–70; Paris, BnF cod. gr. 1313, fols. 1–5; Tübingen, Universitätsbibliothek, fonds principal Mb 33, fols. 133–37; and Sinai, Monastery of St. Catherine gr. 1670, fols. 130–36.

> that letter to the city Wetfavia; which letter the priest of God Macherius received and sent to Mont St. Michel. And that letter, by the hand of the angel of the Lord, arrived at the city of Rome, to the location of the tomb of Saint Peter, where the keys of the kingdom of heaven are set up; and twelve papal dignitaries, who are in the city of Rome, held a three-day vigil, continuing in fasting and prayer day and night.[10]

The version that Roger of Hoveden records begins like this:

> The holy commandment as to the Lord's day, which came from heaven to Jerusalem, and was found upon the altar of Saint Simeon, in Golgotha, where Christ was crucified for the sins of the world. The Lord sent down this Epistle, which was found upon the altar of Saint Simeon, and after looking upon which, three days and three nights, some men fell upon the earth, imploring mercy of God. And after the third hour, the Patriarch arose, and Acharias, the archbishop, and they opened the scroll, and received the holy Epistle from God. And when they had taken the same they found this writing therein.[11]

The Greek *alpha* recension begins rather differently, like this:

> Epistle of our Lord, God, and Savior Jesus Christ, sent to ancient Rome to the basilica of the holy apostle and first leader Peter, to whom Christ said, "You are Peter, and on this rock I will build my church, and the gates of Hades will not prevail against it. I will give you the keys of the kingdom of heaven, and whatever you bind on earth will be bound in heaven, and whatever you

10. Boniface, *Ep.* 67 (ed. Würdtwein, *Epistolae S. Bonifacii*, 173); we have retained the placenames as printed by Würdtwein.

11. William Stubbs, ed., *Chronica magistri Rogeri de Houedene* (London: Her Majesty's Stationary Office, 1871), 4:167; translation by Janet E. Spittler.

> loose on earth will be loosed in heaven." The epistle remained suspended in the middle of the basilica in the sanctuary. Peter, the great apostle, appeared to the bishop of Rome in a dream saying, "Get up, bishop, and see the undefiled epistle of our Lord Jesus Christ."
>
> The high priest got up trembling and went to the altar. Looking at the undefiled epistle in the middle of the basilica in the sanctuary, he cried out with tears, "You are great, Lord, and your works are wonderful, because you have made known to us the epistle for all the world." Then he summoned all the people of the great church: the clerics, priests, monks, rulers, men, women, and children. For three days and three nights they said with tears, "Show us, Lord, the richness of your mercy, to the humble and unworthy people who pray for you." Then, at around nine o'clock in the morning, the undefiled epistle came down into the hands of the high priest and he welcomed and revered it with fear and trembling. Opening it, he found these things written. And it says . . .[12]

The Greek *beta*[1] recension, where the letter falls in Bethlehem either in or on a stone, which can only be turned over by the patriarch of Jerusalem, begins like this:

> A letter of our Lord Jesus Christ. This letter fell from the sky on the fourth of September.
>
> Preface and narrative of the awesome and shocking wonder that took place among the people of Jerusalem: A small stone fell in the city of Bethlehem—well, the stone was small, but its weight was awesome. For no one was strong enough to roll it, except the patriarch of Jerusalem, having held a gathering with the high priests and priests and scribes for three days and three

12. See introduction and translation in Calogero A. Miceli, "The Epistle of Christ from Heaven," in Burke and Landau, *New Testament Apocrypha*, 1:455–563.

> nights. And then, a voice came out of heaven, saying: "Patriarch, take the stone with your hands and roll it." And when the patriarch had taken and rolled the stone, immediately the stone opened; and they found the following things written . . .[13]

As one can immediately glean, there's a lot of variation but also some moments of clear overlap across these texts—and it's not obvious what the earliest version might be. The earliest Greek witnesses are substantially later than the Latin—most date to the fifteenth century. That in itself might point to Latin as the earlier version, but not definitively.

Again, this chapter is not the place to decide this debate, though we tend to think a Western/Latin origin is most likely. The most persuasive evidence leading to this conclusion is the basic fact that the Latin Letter fits quite well in sixth-century Spain and Gaul, where treatises on the proper observance of Sunday and narrations of punitive miracles (or miraculous punishments, German *Strafwunder*) are easy to find (among, for example, the writings of Caesarius of Arles (d. 542), Martin of Braga (d. 580), the First Council of Narbonne (589), Gregory of Tours (538–594), and so on. The Letter clearly fits within that milieu of Christian thought, practice, and literature. But, as we will see, a consistent feature of the Letter—across an enormous range of temporal, geographical, and linguistic contexts—is precisely its ability to fit, its seemingly infinite recyclability.

And indeed, others have argued for the priority of the Greek. For Aurelio de Santos Otero, for example, the Greek origin of the work is obvious: "The Byzantine-Greek origin of this letter is easily recognized, not just from the comparative study of the various recensions and versions, but also from the peculiarity of the content itself. Again and again features and nuances emerge that are unique to Byzantine liturgy and piety."[14] For de Santos Otero, these elements include the supplication of

13. Translation by Spittler, "Apocryphal Epistles," 340–44.

14. Aurelio de Santos Otero, "Der apokryphe sogenannte Sonntagsbrief," *StPatr* 3, no. 1 (1961): 292.

Mary and John the Baptist on behalf of sinners and specific references to the Liturgy of John Chrysostom. There are many arguments for an Eastern/Greek origin for the text, but, again, we would single out points of contact between the Letter and the Dormition of Mary by the Apostle John. This Dormition, which is dated to the late fifth or early sixth century, is an early Greek witness to the developing traditions concerning Mary's death and assumption.[15] What it shares with the Greek Letter is an express interest in placing key events from Christian salvation history on Sundays. Thus, in Dormition 37 we read:

> You know that on Sunday the Virgin Mary was given the good news by the archangel Gabriel, and on Sunday the savior was born in Bethlehem, and on Sunday the children of Jerusalem went out with palms to meet him, saying "Hosanna in the highest, blessed is the one who comes in the name of the Lord," and on Sunday he was raised from the dead, and on Sunday he will come to judge the living and the dead, and on Sunday he will come from heaven for the glory and honor of the departure of the holy, glorious virgin who gave birth to him.

Most of these events (the annunciation, Jesus's birth, Jesus's resurrection, and judgment day) are included in the various Greek recensions of the Letter in lists of key events taking place on Sunday. Compare, for example, the list in the *beta*[1] recension:

> Do you not know, foolish and witless at heart, that it was on the holy Sunday that I announced "greetings, favored one" to my most-holy mother with the archangel Gabriel in the city of Nazareth? Do you not know, evil-doing human beings, that it was on the holy Sunday that I received baptism in the

15. There is a rich bibliography on Dormition traditions; see particularly, Stephen Shoemaker, *The Ancient Traditions of the Virgin Mary's Dormition and Assumption* (Oxford University Press, 2002), and Shoemaker, *The Dormition and Assumption Apocrypha*, Studies on Early Christian Apocrypha 15 (Peeters, 2018).

> streams of the Jordan by the hand of John the Baptist? Do you not know, foolish and witless at heart . . . that it was on the holy Sunday that I made my resurrection, so that I might raise Adam and those who came from Adam? Do you not know, foolish and witless at heart, that it was on the holy Sunday that I sojourned with Abraham at the Oak of Mamre? Do you not know, transgressors of my commandments and confounders of my divine scriptures, that on my holy Sunday I will judge the living and the dead?

There is substantial variation among the multiple Greek recensions of the Letter in the specific events included in the list; nevertheless, the basic similarity to the passage from the Dormition is quite clear and suggests a relationship of literary dependence.

There are also clear points of contact between the Greek Letter and the Apocalypse of Anastasia (discussed above in ch. 3). Jane Baun notes that both Anastasia and the Greek Letter are characterized by an urgent emphasis on the proper observance of Sunday, by the promotion of fasting on Wednesdays and Fridays, and by the depiction of an "angry Christ, whose wrath is appeased only by the prayers of his Mother."[16] She identifies multiple examples of close thematic and verbal parallels; for the sake of time we'll quote only one here, their curse formulae for those who do not copy the text:

> But if anyone should be found a fool or an enemy of the Spirit and talk nonsense and say that it was produced by a human hand, that one will inherit the curse and will be numbered along with those crying out "Away with him! Away with him! Crucify him!" And their house will be destroyed like Sodom and Gomora, and their spirit will be given to wicked angels on the day of judgment. (Letter *beta*[1])

16. Baun, *Tales from Another Byzantium*, 104.

> But whosoever does not believe these things, and blasphemes, shall have the curse of the 318 God-bearing Fathers,[17] and his portion shall be with Judas, and with those who cry out, "Away with him! Away with him! Crucify him!" And upon the earth I will not bless him, since these words have gone out from me.[18] (Anastasia)

As either a sidenote or yet another indication of the recyclability of this work, we point out that Goodspeed, who, in addition to being a New Testament scholar was also a mediocre novelist, borrowed the "curse of the 318 Fathers" in his 1935 novel, *The Curse in the Colophon.* But the literary relationship between or Letter and the Apocalypse of Anastasia is also particularly interesting because, as Baun shows, it is not possible to identify a single Greek recension that served as its source; rather, Anastasia has thematic and verbal parallels with *all* the Greek recensions edited by Bittner. Moreover, while some recensions of Anastasia seem to tone down borrowings from the Letter, other recensions retain or even augment these borrowings.

Baun concludes that "one of the earliest compilers of Anastasia, and also some of its later redactors, received the [Letter] as authoritative, and derived inspiration—and sometimes whole passages—from one or possibly several versions of the letter."[19] In other words, the literary relationship between Anastasia and the Letter is not simply a matter of an individual author using a specific text of the Letter as a source. While one or more recensions of the Greek Letter clearly served as a source in the composition of Anastasia, the two works continued to circulate and develop in the same milieu for an extended period, such that later editors of Anastasia could continue to incorporate material from multiple recensions of the Letter.

17. See Edgar J. Goodspeed, *The Curse in the Colophon* (Willett, Clark, 1933), 5.

18. Translation adapted from Baun, *Tales from Another Byzantium*, 107.

19. Baun, *Tales from Another Byzantium*, 108.

Ultimately, we can conclude that the Letter in its multiple Greek recensions was a significant strand within the complicated tapestry of Byzantine Marian literature, including both Dormition traditions and apocalypses. The most likely scenario—keeping in mind the lack of sure footing when it comes to dating and locating the earliest Dormition works—is that the Greek Letter used the Greek Dormition of Mary by the Apostle John as a source and then was itself used as source in the composition of the Apocalypse of Anastasia. That is, the Letter entered the Greek literary scene sometime after the early sixth century and was well established within it sometime before the tenth century.

What does this tell us about the origins of the Letter—East or West, Greek or Latin? On the one hand, very little: None of the information above necessarily indicates that the letter was composed in Greek; it is entirely possible that the Letter originated in the West as a Latin composition and that the elements familiar from the Dormition were incorporated at the moment of its translation into Greek (or soon after). On the other hand, the thoroughness with which the Letter was absorbed into the Byzantine tradition—such that de Santos Otero can speak with utter certainty of the obvious "Greek origin of the letter"—underscores what seems to be a fundamental characteristic of the Letter in many of its translations and adaptations: its flexibility and adaptability.

We now leap ahead to the modern printed German and English versions of the Letter, both of which circulated quite widely in the United States, the latter ultimately catching the attention of Goodspeed. As one might suspect, the German versions were particularly popular among Pennsylvania Dutch (that is, Deutsch) communities, where the German language continued to be spoken.

The Letter's flexibility and adaptability are particularly evident in its modern German tradition,[20] wherein it is typically said to have fallen to earth at some point in the eighteenth century, either in a village in Holstein, or at Magdeburg, or in various other locations, mostly within Germany. The most popular German version of the Letter on the Western side of the Atlantic was the "Magdeburg" Letter. This is

20. Karl Bartsch prints multiple versions of the Himmelsbrief in *Sagen, Märchen und Gebräuche aus Mecklenburg* (Braumüller, 1880), 2:341–47.

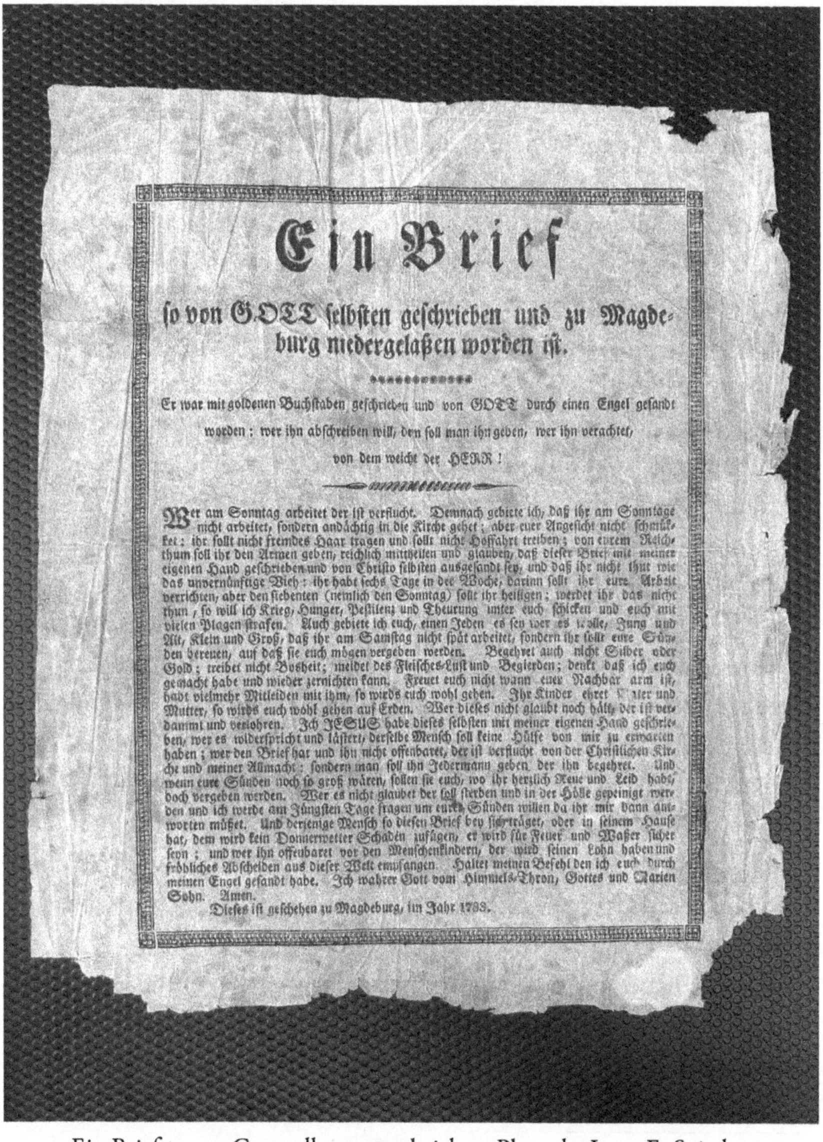

Ein Brief

so von GOTT selbsten geschrieben und zu Magdeburg niedergelaßen worden ist.

Er war mit goldenen Buchstaben geschrieben und von GOTT durch einen Engel gesandt worden; wer ihn abschreiben will, dem soll man ihn geben, wer ihn verachtet, von dem weicht der HERR!

Wer am Sonntag arbeitet der ist verflucht. Demnach gebiete ich, daß ihr am Sonntage nicht arbeitet, sondern andächtig in die Kirche gehet; aber euer Angesicht nicht schmükket: ihr sollt nicht fremdes Haar tragen und sollt nicht Hoffahrt treiben; von eurem Reichthum soll ihr den Armen geben, reichlich mittheilen und glauben, daß dieser Brief mit meiner eigenen Hand geschrieben und von Christo selbsten ausgesandt sey, und daß ihr nicht thut wie das unvernünftige Vieh: ihr habt sechs Tage in der Woche, darinn sollt ihr eure Arbeit verrichten, aber den siebenten (nemlich den Sonntag) sollt ihr heiligen; werdet ihr das nicht thun, so will ich Krieg, Hunger, Pestilenz und Theurung unter euch schicken und euch mit vielen Plagen strafen. Auch gebiete ich euch, einen Jeden es sey wer es wolle, Jung und Alt, Klein und Groß, daß ihr am Samstag nicht spät arbeitet, sondern ihr sollt eure Sünden bereuen, auf daß sie euch mögen vergeben werden. Begehret auch nicht Silber oder Gold; treibet nicht Bosheit; meidet des Fleisches-Lust und Begierden; denkt daß ich euch gemacht habe und wieder zernichten kann. Freuet euch nicht wann euer Nachbar arm ist, habt vielmehr Mitleiden mit ihm, so wirds euch wohl gehen. Ihr Kinder ehret Vater und Mutter, so wirds euch wohl gehen auf Erden. Wer dieses nicht glaubt noch hält, der ist verdammt und verlohren. Ich JESUS habe dieses selbsten mit meiner eigenen Hand geschrieben, wer es widerspricht und lästert, derselbe Mensch soll keine Hülfe von mir zu erwarten haben; wer den Brief hat und ihn nicht offenbaret, der ist verflucht von der Christlichen Kirche und meiner Allmacht: sondern man soll ihn Jedermann geben der ihn begehret. Und wenn eure Sünden noch so groß wären, sollen sie euch, wo ihr herzlich Reue und Leid habt, doch vergeben werden. Wer es nicht glaubet der soll sterben und in der Hölle gepeinigt werden und ich werde am Jüngsten Tage fragen um eurer Sünden willen da ihr mir dann antworten müßet. Und derjenige Mensch so diesen Brief bey sich träget, oder in seinem Hause hat, dem wird kein Donnerwetter Schaden zufügen, er wird für Feuer und Waßer sicher seyn; und wer ihn offenbaret vor den Menschenkindern, der wird seinen Lohn haben und fröhliches Abscheiden aus dieser Welt empfangen. Haltet meinen Befehl den ich euch durch meinen Engel gesandt habe. Ich wahrer Gott vom Himmels-Thron, Gottes und Marien Sohn. Amen.

Dieses ist geschehen zu Magdeburg, im Jahr 1783.

Ein Brief so von Gott selbsten geschrieben. Photo by Janet E. Spittler.

the version of the Letter commonly produced by Pennsylvania Dutch printers in illuminated form on broadsides;[21] this version was also trans-

21. These broadsides are widespread in the US and can still be found in antiquarian bookstores. A selection is held at the Library of Congress; see Paul Connor and Jill Roberts for the American Folklife Center, *Pennsylvania German Fraktur and Printed*

lated into English. Its introduction reads: "A letter written by God himself, and fallen down at Magdeburg. It was written with golden letters, and was sent by God through an angel. It should be given to whoever wants to make a copy; whoever despises it, the Lord departs from him." From there follows a form of the Letter, which includes proper observance of Sunday but with an increased focus on the apotropaic powers of the letter itself—both to ward off fire and pestilence when displayed in a house and to protect an individual from harm when carried on their person.

Albrecht Dieterich, who had a strong interest in the German versions of the Letter, wrote: "In the country they are worn on the body to protect against all sorts of evil, put under the roof to protect against fire, but above all they protect against shot and blow, and are taken by the soldiers to war. Many of these magic letters were found on the battlefields of 1866 and 1870—on those whom they had not helped."[22] At precisely the same time, American soldiers were doing the exact same thing on American battlefields—with both German-language and English-language versions of the letter. American folklorist Don Yoder writes: "There is plenty of evidence from Pennsylvania that the heaven-letter was carried by soldiers in all of the American wars." A friend of Janet Spittler, with whom she was associated at the Pennsylvania Dutch Folk Festival at Kutztown for many years, once presented her with a framed heaven letter in German that his father had carried with him folded up in his uniform through the Civil War.

This brings us back, finally, to the English version of the Letter with which we started and to Goodspeed. As a good New Testament scholar, Goodspeed did exactly what we might expect he would do with the three

---

Broadsides: A Guide to the Collections in the Library of Congress (Library of Congress, 1988), 42, nos. 141–49. Images of particularly fine illuminated examples can be viewed at "A Letter from God (Ein Brief von Gott)," Free Library of Philadelphia, accessed February 1, 2025, https://libwww.freelibrary.org/digital/item/6347, and at Pennsylvania German Broadside Collection, Franklin & Marshall College Library Digital Collections, accessed February 1, 2025, https://digital.fandm.edu/collections/pennsylvania-german-broadside-collection.

22. Albrecht Dieterich, "Himmelsbriefe," in his *Kleine Schriften* (Teubner, 1911), 240.

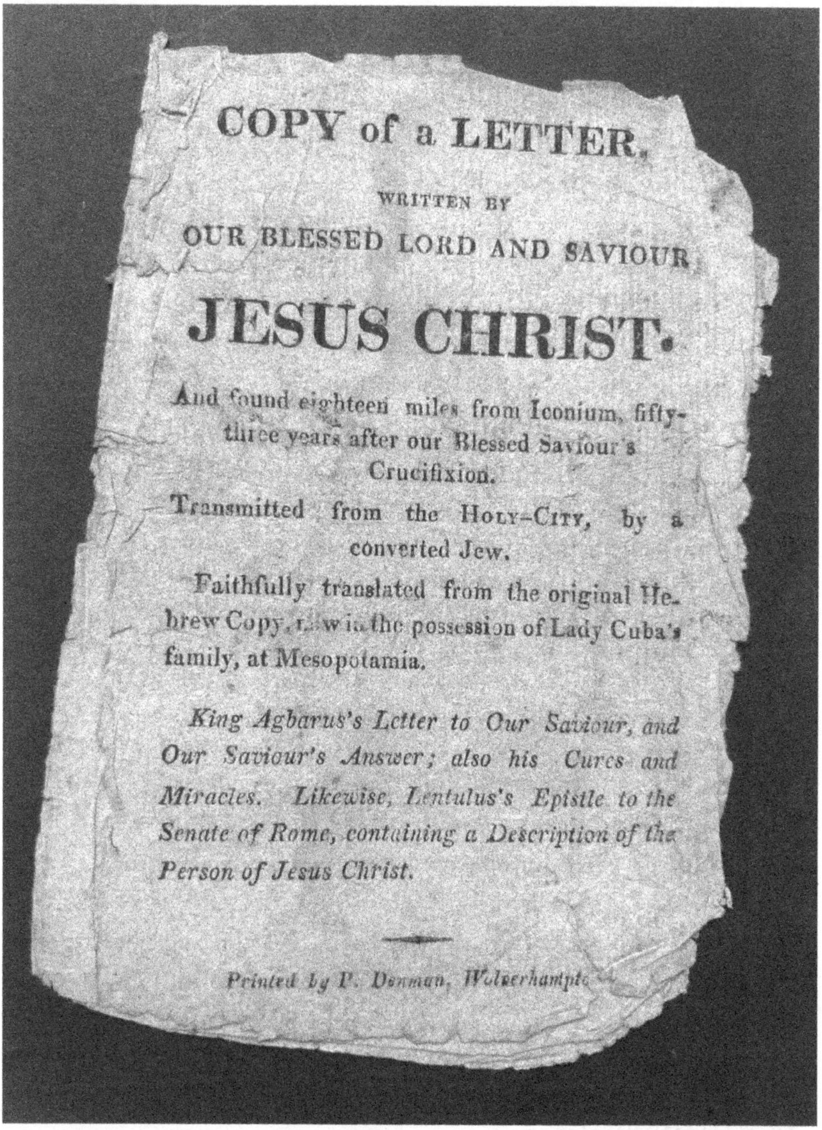

COPY of a LETTER,

WRITTEN BY

OUR BLESSED LORD AND SAVIOUR

JESUS CHRIST.

And found eighteen miles from Iconium, fifty-three years after our Blessed Saviour's Crucifixion.

Transmitted from the HOLY-CITY, by a converted Jew.

Faithfully translated from the original Hebrew Copy, now in the possession of Lady Cuba's family, at Mesopotamia.

King Agbarus's Letter to Our Saviour, and Our Saviour's Answer; also his Cures and Miracles. Likewise, Lentulus's Epistle to the Senate of Rome, containing a Description of the Person of Jesus Christ.

Printed by P. Denman, Wolverhampt...

Copy of a Letter Written by Our Blessed Lord and Savior. Photo by Janet E. Spittler.

versions he had come across: He published a synopsis, then created his own critical edition (which he published in his 1931 book *Strange New Gospels*).

Here's the full text of the introduction to the Letter:

A copy of a letter written by our blessed Lord and Saviour Jesus Christ, and found eighteen miles from Iconium sixty five

> years after his crucifixion; transmitted from the Holy City by a converted Jew; faithfully translated from the original Hebrew copy, now in the possession of the Lady Cubasse's family in Mesopotamia. This letter was written by Jesus Christ, and found under a stone large and round, at the foot of the cross. Upon the stone was engraven, "Blessed be he that shall turn me over." All people that saw it prayed to God earnestly and desired that he would make this writing known to them, that they might not attempt in vain to turn it over. In the meantime there came out a little child about six or seven years of age, and turned it over without assistance, to the admiration of every person who was standing by. Under this stone was found the following, written by Jesus Christ. It was carried to the city of Iconium, and there published by a person belonging to the Lady Cubasse. On the letter was written: "The Commandments of Jesus Christ; Signed by the Angel Gabriel ninety-nine years after our Saviour's birth."[23]

The printed English Letter was, like the German, extraordinarily widespread, though scholarly reactions to it tend to be, like Goodspeed's, isolated and prompted by serendipitous encounters.[24] We will not attempt to trace the development of the printed English Letter from its Anglo-Saxon, Old, and Middle English antecedents or other possible sources, though we note that its opening is characterized by both striking new developments[25] and puzzling coherence with much earlier versions. Like many earlier versions of the Letter, the discovery is a

23. Edgar J. Goodspeed, "The Letter of Jesus Christ and the Western Text," *AThR* 1, no. 5/2 (1933): 105–14.

24. See, e.g., Wayland D. Hand, "A North Carolina Himmelsbrief," in *Middle Ages – Reformation – Volkskunde: Festschrift for John G. Kunstmann*, ed. Frederic E. Coenen (University of North Carolina Press, 1959), 201–7.

25. That is, elements that we have not seen in the versions of the Letter reviewed above. I simply do not know when these elements enter the English tradition, or from where.

multipart story: The document first appears in one place but is transported to another. Here the initial appearance is, as in the *beta* recensions of the Greek Letter, Jerusalem, but it is then transported "by a converted Jew" to Iconium—two specific elements we have not seen before. The letter is said to be translated from Hebrew, though we are not told by whom or into which language: That the letter was somehow encased in stone is also familiar from the *beta* recension of the Greek Letter, as is the notion that no one was able to roll it over; whereas, in the *beta* recension of the Greek Letter it is only the patriarch of Jerusalem who can move the stone, in the English version, it is a child. The inscription on the stone ("blessed is he who can turn me over")[26] seems to be a new element—and it calls to mind the Sword and the Stone, the Arthurian novel. In the Greek, no such prompting is necessary: The fact that the stone has fallen from the sky is reason enough to attempt to pick it up. In Goodspeed's modern English Letter, it is in fact not clear that the stone fell from anywhere: It seems, rather, to appear at the foot of the cross.

In comparison with the German versions of the Letter, the emphasis on the time and place of the letter's composition is striking. The modern English Letter implies (or, in some versions, states clearly) that the letter was composed by Christ soon after his crucifixion.[27] The importance of this early date and holy location is underscored by the report of the letter's translation from Hebrew (presumably the language in which Christ wrote it) and the account of the chain of custody (carried by the converted Jew to Iconium, where it seems the "Mesopotamian" family of this "Lady Cubasse" took possession of it). It seems clear that the very foreignness, perhaps "orientalizing" flavor, of these reports has an authenticating function for the modern English version of the

26. As Per Beskow notes, this element calls to mind the *Sword and the Stone*; see *Strange Tales About Jesus: A Survey of Unfamiliar Gospels* (Fortress, 1983), 27.

27. The version of the letter printed in the May 16, 1917, *Chicago Evening Post*, for example, reads, "A letter written by Christ just after his crucifixion, signed by the Angel Gabriel ninety-three years after the Savior's birth and presumably deposited by him under a stone at the foot of the cross."

Letter. Just the opposite seems to be the case with the Magdeburg version, where a document written by God in German falls directly into Germany. The increased emphasis on the apotropaic qualities of the Letter that we observed in the German versions *is* evident in the English, if not quite to the same extent.

A final exceedingly interesting characteristic of the printed English Letter is that it, like some versions of the German Letter, accrued to itself other works.[28] In both pamphlets and broadsides, the modern English Letter was often printed alongside the Correspondence of Jesus and Abgar, a list of Jesus's "cures and miracles," and the Letter of Lentulus (that is, the thirteenth-century Latin work that describes Jesus's physical appearance, in this broadside misspelled as "Sentulus"). The third text alongside which the Letter was printed (the list of Jesus's "cures and miracles") comprises just a few lines, in which the miracles performed by Jesus in the canonical Gospels are recounted with extreme brevity.

Before concluding, we must call attention to the fact that the *Chicago Evening Post* was not the only newspaper (or even the only Chicago newspaper) to print the Letter: The *Chicago Tribune* had in fact already printed the full text on September 20, 1896, in an article titled, "This Letter Said to Have Been Written by Christ."[29] Alongside the

---

28. Deletant, "Sunday Legend," 440–41, has indicated an analogous phenomenon in the Polish, Hungarian, Ukrainian, and Romanian versions of the Letter, which "are inevitably copied, or printed, together with another legend, entitled 'The Dream of the Virgin Mary.'"

29. The entirety of the article is a quotation of the Letter itself (and the Correspondence of Jesus and Abgar); the only commentary to be found is in the titles and subtitles. Notably, the first subtitle reads "Georgia Negroes Are in a Ferment of Excitement Over It, Believing It to Be a Genuine Writing of the Savior, and Some Are Healed of Illness by Virtue of Possessing a Copy." This association of the Letter with Black Americans here is clearly a topic worthy of further research. Goodspeed notes that the man selling the Letter door to door in Hyde Park was Black, and it is possible that Black Christian communities, like German-American Christian communities, were particularly receptive of the Letter. That said, the tone of the subtitle (and perhaps Goodspeed's tone in describing the salesman) suggests an effort to distance the author and audience from acceptance of the Letter, placing belief in its authenticity

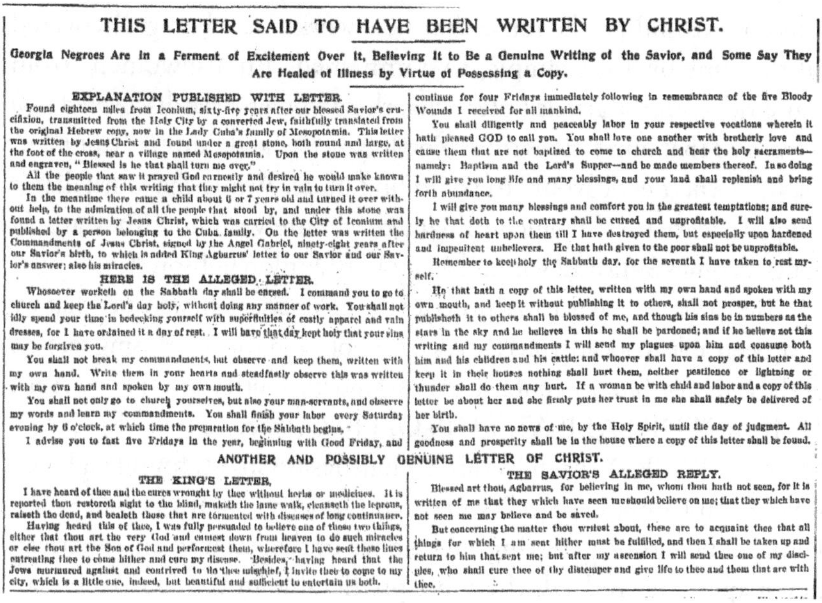

THIS LETTER SAID TO HAVE BEEN WRITTEN BY CHRIST.

Georgia Negroes Are in a Ferment of Excitement Over It, Believing It to Be a Genuine Writing of the Savior, and Some Say They Are Healed of Illness by Virtue of Possessing a Copy.

EXPLANATION PUBLISHED WITH LETTER.

Found eighteen miles from Iconium, sixty-five years after our blessed Savior's crucifixion, transmitted from the Holy City by a converted Jew, faithfully translated from the original Hebrew copy, now in the Lady Cuba's family of Mesopotamia. This letter was written by Jesus Christ and found under a great stone, both round and large, at the foot of the cross, near a village named Mesopotamia. Upon the stone was written and engraven, "Blessed is he that shall turn me over."

All the people that saw it prayed God earnestly and desired he would make known to them the meaning of this writing that they might not try in vain to turn it over.

In the meantime there came a child about 6 or 7 years old and turned it over without help, to the admiration of all the people that stood by, and under this stone was found a letter written by Jesus Christ, which was carried to the City of Iconium and published by a person belonging to the Cuba family. On the letter was written the Commandments of Jesus Christ, signed by the Angel Gabriel, ninety-eight years after our Savior's birth, to which is added King Agbarrus' letter to our Savior and our Savior's answer; also his miracles.

HERE IS THE ALLEGED LETTER.

Whosoever worketh on the Sabbath day shall be cursed. I command you to go to church and keep the Lord's day holy, without doing any manner of work. You shall not idly spend your time in bedecking yourself with superfluities of costly apparel and vain dresses, for I have ordained it a day of rest. I will have that day kept holy that your sins may be forgiven you.

You shall not break my commandments, but observe and keep them, written with my own hand. Write them in your hearts and steadfastly observe this was written with my own hand and spoken by my own mouth.

You shall not only go to church yourselves, but also your man-servants, and observe my words and learn my commandments. You shall finish your labor every Saturday evening by 6 o'clock, at which time the preparation for the Sabbath begins.

I advise you to fast five Fridays in the year, beginning with Good Friday, and continue for four Fridays immediately following in remembrance of the five Bloody Wounds I received for all mankind.

You shall diligently and peaceably labor in your respective vocations wherein it hath pleased GOD to call you. You shall love one another with brotherly love and cause them that are not baptized to come to church and hear the holy sacraments—namely: Baptism and the Lord's Supper—and be made members thereof. In so doing I will give you long life and many blessings, and your land shall replenish and bring forth abundance.

I will give you many blessings and comfort you in the greatest temptations; and surely he that doth to the contrary shall be cursed and unprofitable. I will also send hardness of heart upon them till I have destroyed them, but especially upon hardened and impenitent unbelievers. He that hath given to the poor shall not be unprofitable.

Remember to keep holy the Sabbath day, for the seventh I have taken to rest myself.

He that hath a copy of this letter, written with my own hand and spoken with my own mouth, and keep it without publishing it to others, shall not prosper, but he that publisheth it to others shall be blessed of me, and though his sins be in numbers as the stars in the sky and he believes in this he shall be pardoned; and if he believe not this writing and my commandments I will send my plagues upon him and consume both him and his children and his cattle: and whoever shall have a copy of this letter and keep it in their houses nothing shall hurt them, neither pestilence or lightning or thunder shall do them any hurt. If a woman be with child and labor and a copy of this letter be about her and she firmly puts her trust in me she shall safely be delivered of her birth.

You shall have no news of me, by the Holy Spirit, until the day of judgment. All goodness and prosperity shall be in the house where a copy of this letter shall be found.

ANOTHER AND POSSIBLY GENUINE LETTER OF CHRIST.

THE KING'S LETTER.

I have heard of thee and the cures wrought by thee without herbs or medicines. It is reported thou restoreth sight to the blind, maketh the lame walk, cleanseth the leprous, raiseth the dead, and healeth those that are tormented with diseases of long continuance.

Having heard this of thee, I was fully persuaded to believe one of those two things, either that thou art the very God and camest down from heaven to do such miracles or else thou art the Son of God and performest them, wherefore I have sent these lines entreating thee to come hither and cure my disease. Besides, having heard that the Jews murmured against and contrived to do thee mischief, I invite thee to come to my city, which is a little one, indeed, but beautiful and sufficient to entertain us both.

THE SAVIOR'S ALLEGED REPLY.

Blessed art thou, Agbarrus, for believing in me, whom thou hath not seen, for it is written of me that they which have seen me should believe on me; that they which have not seen me may believe and be saved.

But concerning the matter thou writest about, these are to acquaint thee that all things for which I am sent hither must be fulfilled, and then I shall be taken up and return to him that sent me; but after my ascension I will send thee one of my disciples, who shall cure thee of thy distemper and give life to thee and them that are with thee.

Chicago Tribune, September 20, 1896. Public domain.

Letter, and with the subtitle "Another and Possibly Genuine Letter of Christ," is printed the Correspondence of Jesus and Abgar. Surrounding the two letters is a journalistic article titled "Did Christ Write These Letters," with a subheading "Theologians admit the probability that Christ corresponded with Abgarus." This is in fact an intensely interesting work of journalism, as it underscores the late nineteenth-century

---

among a group denigrated as unsophisticated or uneducated. Further examples include *The Sun* (Baltimore), January 26, 1889, which reports that both Black and White members of a community near Chestertown, MD, were in an uproar over the letter, emphasizing the "religious enthusiasm" of the Black Christians particularly; this article closes by noting "there are from 500 to 1,000 copies of this letter in circulation, and the superstitious ones are securing them as charms against evil." Other newspapers are more straightforward in their rank racism, as is the *Birmingham Age-Herald* in its June 17, 1895, article with the headline "A Very Strange Letter," which prints the full text of the Letter and describes its use among Black Christians in Montgomery, AL. Elsewhere, the Letter is printed with no reference to the race of those who read and valued it, as in the *National Baptist World* (Wichita, Kansas), November 2, 1894.

sense of possibility, the sense that new works were being discovered all the time by, for example, two unnamed "Englishwomen" from Cambridge. As the article notes, what these women have discovered is *so important* that universities from North America and Europe "sent men" on an "earnest endeavour" to try to find more. While the journalist is happy to leave these women unnamed, we surely cannot: They are, of course, Agnes Smith Lewis and Margaret Dunlop Gibson.[30]

The earliest reference to the Letter in an American newspaper that we have been able to locate thus far is a brief notice in the advertising section of the *Camden Gazette* (published in Camden, South Carolina) on April 11, 1816: "FOR SALE AT THIS OFFICE (Price 12½ cents) COPY OF A LETTER Written by our Saviour Jesus Christ, found eighteen miles from Iconium, 65 years after our blessed Saviour's Crucifixion." Perhaps the most interesting appearance of the letter in an American newspaper—or, indeed, the most predictable in the US American context—is a notice that appeared in the San Francisco *Daily Evening Bulletin* on May 11, 1868. There we find the following news item, titled "A Letter Said to Have Been Written by the Saviour," on page 3:

> F. Wilson has filed in the United States District Court for copyright, the copy of a letter said to have been written by Jesus Christ and found 65 years after his crucifixion, about 80 miles from Iconium. It is said the letter was found under a stone, on the face of which was written, "Blessed is he that shall turn me over." "All people that saw it, prayed to God earnestly, and desired that he would make known to them the meaning of this writing, that they might not attempt in vain to turn it over. In the meantime came a little child and turned it over, without help, to the admiration of all the people that stood by; and under this stone was found a letter written by Jesus Christ, which was carried to Iconium, and there published; and in it was written the Commandments, signed by the Angel Gabriel, 98 years after

30. Biography by Janet Soskice.

> our Saviour's birth, to which is added King Abarus's letter, and our Saviour's answer, and also His miracles, and a full description of His person in Sentulus's epistle to the Senate of Rome."[31]

This otherwise (to us, at least) unknown individual named Wilson clearly has in his possession a copy of the Letter, likely in the form of a broadside containing also the Abgar correspondence and the Letter of Lentulus; we do not know the results of his attempt to copyright it.

What conclusions can we draw about the Letter—what does it tell us about apocryphal literature in particular and Christian literature in general? For Goodspeed, the Letter provided an object lesson in the transmission of texts. He published his synopsis in 1933 in an essay for the *Anglican Theological Review* in an effort to demonstrate, by analogy, how variations entered the New Testament textual tradition, particularly the so-called Western text. He writes as follows:

> There is at present floating about in wholly unsophisticated circles in this country and perhaps also in England a little work of no distinction or worth, which may yet be of great significance for textual study by reason of the glimpse it affords of the extraordinary possibilities of rapid text corruption even today in the case of a pious work circulating quite uncontrolled by scholars or churchmen. It is the so-called Letter of Jesus Christ, written perhaps half a century ago, and probably in England, and never I believe enclosed within the covers of a book until 1931, but obscurely transmitted as a leaflet among ignorant religious individuals.[32]

31. The same report is reprinted also in the *Arizona Miner* (Prescott, AZ), June 6, 1868; *Flake's Weekly Galveston Bulletin* (Galveston, TX), July 1, 1868; *The Daily Austin Republican* (Austin, TX), July 23, 1868.

32. Goodspeed, "Letter of Jesus Christ," 106. With "enclosed within the covers of a book," Goodspeed refers here to his own publication of the work in *Strange New Gospels*.

That he turned out to be quite wrong about the work's origins matters little for the point Goodspeed is making for the readers of *Anglican Theological Review*. Scholars and students of the New Testament often ask how variant readings come about; to many, it seems improbable that scribes creating copies of sacred texts would not be more careful to reproduce precisely the exemplar before them. Or, as Goodspeed states the question (thinking about the Western text in particular): "Why were these numerous changes, most of them apparently purposeless, or nearly so, introduced into a text so highly revered?"[33] For Goodspeed, the Letter provided, if not quite an answer to the question "why," then at least an analogue, suggesting that the introduction of numerous changes is simply inevitable—at least when texts are circulated without the strict oversight of scholarly or ecclesiastical authority.

Goodspeed concludes:

> To us, educated and conventional people, this document seems little better than absurd, and quite unworthy of comparison with the documents of the New Testament, even the least of them. But it is not our estimate of it that matters. It is the estimate of its devotees. They are deeply attached to it and cannot be convinced that it is just a modern invention. On the other hand, greatly as they revere it, in transmitting it they have already made a multitude of changes in it, insomuch that it demands the closest application of the methods of Intrinsic and Transcriptional Probability to determine which form of each sentence was the original.
>
> On the whole, then, it affords a very illuminating modern illustration of the changes that even in an age of printing inevitably overtake a popular religious text, left wholly untrammeled by scholarly or ecclesiastical control. The bearing of this upon the origin of the so-called Western Text seems to be unmistakable and of the highest significance.[34]

33. Goodspeed, "Letter of Jesus Christ," 105.

34. Goodspeed, "Letter of Jesus Christ," 114.

We tend to agree with Goodspeed's conclusion here, even as we are not entirely in agreement as to whether we would prefer to count ourselves among his "us" or his "them." And his analogy is clearly useful. Nevertheless, we think there is much more we can learn from the Letter of Jesus Christ.

The Letter has the potential to provide object lessons on a host of issues pertaining to early Christian textuality. First, as an extreme example of a living or fluid work, the Letter underscores the inadequacy of unidirectional attempts to establish an authorial original. To be sure, an answer to the question of the Letter's origins is well worth pursuing, and the earliest extant versions of the work are the ones that interest us most. But the sheer length and breadth of its life make it absolutely clear that understanding where the Letter goes is at least as important and interesting as understanding where it comes from. Further, the particular fluidity of the Letter demands more attention. The more fluid a liquid (that is, the lower its viscosity), the more quickly and easily it conforms to the shape of its container. The Letter seems to be far more fluid than most Christian works, quickly and easily conforming to the shape of a bewildering variety of linguistic, cultural, literary, and ideological contexts. But are there elements of the Letter that are more viscous than others? Or elements that are more fluid? What can this most fluid of works tell us about the phenomenon of textual fluidity more broadly?

Second, as a wildly popular work explicitly claiming to be written by Jesus himself, the Letter and its reception should surely be included in discussions of Christian pseudepigraphy and forgery, and yet this is rarely the case. When the Letter is treated in discussions of pseudepigraphy, the emphasis is placed exclusively on its rejection by figures such as Licinianus and Boniface, as opposed to its continued and enduring success.[35] In fact, a very consistent aspect of scholarship on the Letter is praise of historical individuals who rejected the letter and open disdain

35. See, e.g., Wolfgang Speyer, *Die literarische Fälschung im heidnischen und christlichen Altertum: Ein Versuch ihrer Deutung*, Handbuch der Altertumswissenschaft 1/2 (Beck, 1971), 60–61.

for those who did not.[36] This attitude is unhelpful, obscuring the fact that the Letter was copied into manuscripts alongside works by John Chrysostom, Basil, Cyril, and others; that it was preached from the pulpit by highly literate clergy; that, for every Licinianus, there was one—or more—Vincentius. Investigations of the positive reception of the Letter, particularly when we have evidence of the use to which it was put, might contribute a great deal to our understanding of pseudepigraphical Christian literature, all the way back to the deutero-Pauline epistles.

Third, while we do not think the Letter was positively received only by the "theologically illiterate" or "simple believers,"[37] we *do* think that apocryphal works like the Letter—like so many other works discussed in this volume—often grant us better access to these individuals (that is, the vast majority of Christians) than do the homilies, treatises, and other highly literate sources that scholars have typically used to construct a history of Christian thought and practice. Within the study of apocryphal Christian literature (but perhaps also within the study of the history of Christianity more broadly), there is a remarkable inverse relationship between the popularity of a given work across Christian history and the likelihood that a contemporary scholar has heard of it, such that a work such as the Gospel of Thomas, with a very limited circulation and exertion of influence, is known by all, while the Letter, which circulated continuously for some fourteen hundred years in more than a dozen languages, remains a work that is most often encountered accidentally.

36. Thus, for example, Haines, *Sunday Observance*, 37, writes: "Fortunately, though the popularity and survival of the Sunday Letter may confirm our worst suspicions about the gullibility and lack of discernment of medieval clergy, we can also derive some comfort from the fact that it was regularly recognized as a fraud."

37. We borrow these phrases from Jack Tannous, *The Making of the Medieval Middle East* (Princeton University Press, 2018), 46–81.

BIBLIOGRAPHY

Aasgaard, Reidar. *The Childhood of Jesus: Decoding the Apocryphal Infancy Gospel of Thomas*. Wipf & Stock, 2009.

Adler, William. "Palaea Historica ('The Old Testament History')." In *Old Testament Pseudepigrapha: More Noncanonical Scriptures*, edited by Richard Bauckham, James Davila, and Alexander Panayotov, vol. 1. Eerdmans, 2013.

Alexander, Paul J. *The Byzantine Apocalyptic Tradition*. University of California Press, 1985.

Alkier, Stefan. "Terminologien kollektiver Identitäten in der Apostelgeschichte des Lukas." In *Juden – Heiden – Christen? Religiöse Inklusion und Exklusion in Kleinasien bis Decius*, edited by Stefan Alkier and Hartmut Leppin. WUNT 400. Mohr Siebeck, 2018.

Allen, Garrick V. *Words Are Not Enough: Paratexts, Manuscripts, and the Real New Testament*. Eerdmans, 2024.

Allen, Garrick V., and Anthony P. Royle. "Paratexts Seeking Understanding: Manuscripts and Aesthetic Cognitivism." *Religions* 11, no. 10 (2020): 1–25.

Andrist, Patrick. "Toward a Definition of Paratexts and Paratextuality: The Case of Ancient Greek Manuscripts." In *Bible as Notepad. Tracing Annotations and Annotation Practices in Late Antique and Medieval Biblical Manuscripts*, edited by Liv Ingeborg Lied and Marilena Maniaci. De Gruyter, 2018.

Assmann, Jan. *Das kulturelle Gedächtnis: Schrift, Erinnerung und politische Identität in frühen Hochkulturen*. 3rd ed. Beck, 2000.

Assmann, Jan. *Religion und kulturelles Gedächtnis*. 3rd ed. Beck, 2008.

Attridge, Harold W. "Acts of John." In *Early New Testament Apocrypha*, edited by J. Christopher Edwards. Ancient Literature for New Testament Study 9. Eerdmans, 2022.

Attridge, Harold W. "Acts of Thomas." In *Early New Testament Apocrypha*, edited by J. Christopher Edwards. Ancient Literature for New Testament Study 9. Eerdmans, 2022.

Barnes, Timothy D. "'Another Shall Gird Thee': Probative Evidence for the Death of Peter." In *Peter in Early Christianity*, edited by Helen K. Bond and Larry W. Hurtado. Eerdmans, 2015.

Barrier, Jeremy W., Jan N. Bremmer, Tobias Nicklas, and Armand Puig i Tàrrech, eds. *Thecla: Paul's Disciple and Saint in the East and West*. Studies on Early Christian Apocrypha 12. Peeters, 2017.

Bartsch, Karl. *Sagen, Märchen und Gebräuche aus Mecklenburg*. Vol. 2. Braumüller, 1880.

Baun, Jane. *Tales from Another Byzantium: Celestial Journey and Local Community in the Medieval Greek Apocrypha*. Cambridge University Press, 2007.

Beck, Eric J. *Justice and Mercy in the Apocalypse of Peter: A New Translation and Analysis of the Purpose of the Text*. WUNT 427. Mohr Siebeck, 2019.

Bejcy, Istvan. *La Lettre du Prêtre Jean: Une Utopie Médiévale*. Imago, 2001.

Bell, H. Idris, and T. C. Skeat, eds. *Fragments of an Unknown Gospel and Other Early Christian Papyri*. Trustees, 1935.

Berger, Albrecht. *Konstantinopel. Geschichte – Topographie – Religion*. Standorte in Antike und Christentum. Anton Hiersemann, 2011.

Bergren, Theodore A. *Fifth Ezra: The Text, Origin and Early History*. SCS 25. Scholars Press, 1990.

Bergren, Theodor A. "Fifth Ezra." In *Old Testament Pseudepigrapha: More Noncanonical Scriptures*, edited by Richard Bauckham, James Davila, and Alexander Panayotov, vol. 1. Eerdmans, 2013.

Bergren, Theodor A. "Sixth Ezra." In *Old Testament Pseudepigrapha: More Noncanonical Scriptures*, edited by Richard Bauckham, James Davila, and Alexander Panayotov. Eerdmans, 2013.

Bockmuehl, Markus. *The Remembered Peter in Ancient Reception and Modern Debate*. WUNT 262. Mohr Siebeck, 2010.

Bockmuehl, Markus. *Simon Peter in Scripture and Memory: The New Testament Apostle in the Early Church*. Eerdmans, 2012.

Bond, Helen K., and Larry W. Hurtado, eds. *Peter in Early Christianity*. Eerdmans, 2015.

Bonnet, Maximilian. "Acta Iohannis." In *Acta Apostolorum Apocrypha*, edited post Constantin Tischendorf by Richard Adalbert Lipsius and Maximilian Bonnet. Hermann Mendelssohn, 1858.

Bonnet, Maximilian. "Martyrium Sancti Apostoli Andreae." *AnBoll* 13 (1894): 353–72.

Bonnet, Maximilian. "Passio Sancti Bartholomaei apostoli." In *Acta apostolorum apocrypha*, edited by Richard Lipsius and Maximilian Bonnet, vol. 2.1. Reprint, Olms, 1959.
Bovon, Francois. "Fragment Oxyrhynchus 840. Fragment of a Lost Gospel. Witness of an Early Christian Controversy over Purity." *JBL* 119 (2000): 705–28.
Bovon, François. "L'enfant Jésus durant la fuite en Égypte: Les récits apocryphes de l'enfance comme légendes profitables à l'âme." In *The Apocryphal Gospels Within the Context of Early Christian Theology*, edited by Jens Schröter. BETL 260. Peeters, 2013.
Brakke, David. *The Gnostics: Myth, Ritual, and Diversity in Early Christianity*. Harvard University Press, 2010.
Brankaer, Johanna, and Bas van Os. *The Gospel of Judas*. OECT. Oxford University Press, 2019.
Brannan, Rick. "John and the Robber: A New Translation and Introduction." In *New Testament Apocrypha: More Noncanonical Scriptures*, edited by Tony Burke and Brent Landau, vol. 1. Eerdmans, 2016.
Bremmer, Jan N. "The Apocalypse of Paul." In *Early New Testament Apocrypha*, edited by J. Christopher Edwards. Ancient Literature for New Testament Study 9. Eerdmans, 2022.
Bremmer, Jan N. "The Apocalypse of Peter: Place, Date and Punishments." In *Maidens, Mmagic and Martyrs in Early Christianity*. WUNT 379. Mohr Siebeck, 2017.
Bremmer, Jan N. "The *Apocryphal Acts*: Authors, Place, Time and Relationship." In *Maidens, Magic and Martyrs in Early Christianity*. WUNT 379. Mohr Siebeck, 2017.
Bremmer, Jan N. "Aspects of the *Acts of Peter*: Women, Magic, Place and Date." In *Maidens, Magic and Martyrs in Early Christianity*. WUNT 379. Mohr Siebeck, 2017.
Bremmer, Jan N. "The Onomastics and Provenance of the *Acts of Paul*." In *Philologie, Herméneutique et Histoire des Textes entre Orient et Occident. Mélanges en Hommage à Sever J. Voicu*, edited by Francesca P. Barone, Caroline Macé, and Pablo A. Ubierna. Brepols, 2017.
Bremmer, Jan N. "The Place, Date and Author of the *Ignatian Letters*. An Onomastic Approach." In *Die Datierung neutestamentlicher Pseudepigraphen: Herausforderungen und neuere Lösungsansätze*, edited by Wolfgang Grünstäudl and Karl Matthias Schmidt. WUNT 470. Mohr Siebeck, 2021.
Bremmer, Jan N. "Timothy, John and Ephesus in the Acts of Timothy." In *The Apostles Peter, Paul, John, Thomas and Philip with Their*

Companions in Late Antiquity, edited by Tobias Nicklas, Janet E. Spittler, and Jan N. Bremmer. Studies on Early Christian Apocrypha 17. Peeters, 2021.

Bremmer, Jan N., J. Andrew Doole, Thomas R. Karmann, Tobias Nicklas, and Boris Repschinski, eds. *The Protevangelium of James*. Studies on Early Christian Apocrypha 16. Peeters, 2020.

Bremmer, Jan N., Veronika Hirschberger, and Tobias Nicklas, eds. *Figures of Ezra*. Studies on Early Christian Apocrypha 13. Peeters, 2018.

Bremmer, Jan N., Thomas R. Karmann, and Tobias Nicklas, eds. *The Ascension of Isaiah*. Studies on Early Christian Apocrypha 11. Peeters, 2016.

Brewer, Keagan. *Prester John: The Legend and Its Sources*. Crusade Texts in Translation 27. Routledge, 2015.

Broadhead, Edwin K. "The Thomas-Jesus Connection." In *Handbook for the Study of the Historical Jesus*, edited by Tom Holmén and Stanley E. Porter. Brill, 2011.

Brodersen, Kai, ed. *Aetheria/Egeria. Reise ins Heilige Land*. De Gruyter, 2016.

Broek, Roeloef van den. *Pseudo-Cyril: On the Life and the Passion of Christ. A Coptic Apocryphon*. VCSup 118. Brill, 2013.

Brown, Peter. *The Rise of Western Christendom. Triumph and Diversity, A.D. 200–1000*. 3rd ed. Wiley Blackwell, 2013.

Brown, Scott G. *Mark's Other Gospel: Rethinking Morton Smith's Controversial Discovery*. Studies in Christianity and Judaism 15. Wilfried Laurier University Press, 2005.

Brox, Norbert, ed. *Irenäus von Lyons, Epideixis. Darlegung der apostolischen Verkündigung. Adversus Haereses. Gegen die Häresien I*. Fontes Christiani 8/1. Herder, 1993.

Brubaker, Leslie, and Mary B. Cunningham, eds. *The Cult of the Mother of God in Byzantium: Texts and Images*. Birmingham Byzantine and Ottoman Studies. 2nd ed. Routledge, 2016.

Brubaker, Leslie, and John Haldon. *Byzantium in the Iconoclast Era, c. 680–850*. 2nd ed. Cambridge University Press, 2015.

Buchinger, Harald. "Liturgy and Early Christian Apocrypha." In *The Oxford Handbook of Early Christian Apocrypha*, edited by Andrew Gregory and Christopher Tuckett. Oxford University Press, 2015.

Buchinger, Harald, with Elisabeth Hernitscheck. "P.Oxy. 840 and the Rites of Christian Initiation. Dating a Piece of Alleged Anti-sacramental Polemic." *EC* 5 (2014): 117–24.

Buchinger, Harald, Andreas Merkt, and Tobias Nicklas, eds. *Extracanonical Traditions and the Holy Land: Texts, Ritual, and*

Material Culture in Late Antique Palestine. Studien und Texte zu Antike und Christentum. Mohr Siebeck, 2025.

Buitenwerf, Rieuwerd. "The Tiburtine Sibyl (Greek)." In *Old Testament Pseudepigrapha: More Noncanonical Scriptures*, edited by Richard Bauckham, James Davila and Alexander Panayotov, vol. 1. Eerdmans, 2013.

Bukovec, Predrag. *Die frühchristliche Eucharistie*. WUNT 499. Mohr Siebeck, 2023.

Burgess, Richard W. *The Chronicle of Hydatius and the consularia Constantinopolitana: Two Contemporary Accounts of the Final Years of the Roman Empire*. OCM. Clarendon, 1993.

Burini, Clara, ed. *Pseudo Cipriano. I Due Monti Sinai et Sion*. Biblia Patristica. Nardini, 1994.

Burke, Tony, ed. *Ancient Gospel or Modern Forgery? The Secret Gospel of Mark in Debate*. Cascade, 2013.

Burke, Tony. *De infantia Iesu Evangelium Thomae graece*. Corpus Christianorum Series Apocryphorum 17. Brepols, 2010.

Burke, Tony. *Secret Scriptures Revealed: A New Introduction to New Testament Apocrypha*. SPCK, 2013.

Burke, Tony. *The Syriac Tradition of the Infancy Gospel of Thomas: A Critical Edition and Syriac Translation*. Gorgias Eastern Christian Studies 48. Gorgias, 2017.

Burns, Dylan M. "A Homily on the Passion and Resurrection." In *New Testament Apocrypha: More Noncanonical Scriptures*, edited by Tony Burke, vol. 2. Eerdmans, 2020.

Burrus, Virginia. *Chastity as Autonomy: Women in the Stories of the Apocryphal Acts*. Studies in Women and Religion 23. Edwin Mellen, 1987.

Busch, Peter. *Das Testament Salomos: Die älteste christliche Dämonologie, kommentiert und in deutscher Erstübersetzung*. TU 153. De Gruyter, 2006.

Butticaz, Simon, and Enrico Norelli, eds. *Memory and Memories in Early Christianity*. WUNT 398. Mohr Siebeck, 2018.

Cain, Andrew. *The Greek Historia Monachorum in Aegypto: Monastic Hagiography in the Late Fourth Century*. OECS. Oxford University Press, 2016.

Calzolari, Valentina. *Apocrypha Armeniaca I: Acta Pauli et Theclae, Prodigia Theclae, Martyrium Pauli. Corpus Christianorum*. Series Apocryphorum 20. Turnhout: Brepols, 2017.

Calzolari, Valentina. "The Legend of St. Thecla in the Armenian Tradition: From Asia Minor to Tarragona Through Armenia." In

The Apocryphal Acts of the Apostles in Armenian. Studies on Early Christian Apocrypha 18. Peeters, 2022.

Calzolari, Valentina. "St. Thecla as a Patroness of Nicean Orthodoxy in the *History of Armenia* by Faustus of Byzantium (*Buzandaran Patmut'iwnk'*)." In *The Apocryphal Acts of the Apostles in Armenian*. Studies on Early Christian Apocrypha 18. Peeters, 2022.

Carlson, Stephen. *The Gospel Hoax: Morton Smith's Invention of Secret Mark*. Baylor University Press, 2005.

Carter, Warren. "Revelation and Roman Rule in First-Century Asia Minor." In *The Oxford Handbook of the Book of Revelation*, edited by Craig R. Koester. Oxford University Press, 2020.

Castelli, Elizabeth. *Martyrdom and Memory: Early Christian Culture Making*. Columbia University Press, 2004.

Chadwick, Henry. *Priscillian of Avila: Occult and Charismatic in the Early Church*. Oxford University Press, 1976.

Charlesworth, James H., ed. *The History of the Rechabites*. Vol. 1, *The Greek Recension*. SBLTT 17. Scholars Press, 1982.

Charlesworth, James H. "History of the Rechabites." *OTP*, vol. 2.

Cobb, L. Stephanie. *Divine Deliverance: Pain and Painlessness in Early Christian Martyr Texts*. University of California Press, 2016.

Concannon, Cavan. "In the Great City of the Ephesians: Contestations over Apostolic Memory and Ecclesial Power in the Acts of Timothy." *JECS* 24 (2016): 419–46.

Connor, Paul, and Jill Roberts for the American Folklife Center. *Pennsylvania German Fraktur and Printed Broadsides: A Guide to the Collections in the Library of Congress*. Library of Congress, 1988.

Copeland, Kirsti. "Mapping the Apocalypse of Paul: Geography, Genre, and History." PhD diss., Princeton University, 2001.

Cosby, Michael R. *Creation of History: The Transformation of Barnabas from Peacemaker to Warrior Saint*. Wipf & Stock, 2017.

Crossan, John Dominic. *Four Other Gospels: Shadows on the Contours of the Canon*. HarperCollins, 1985.

Crossan, John Dominic. *The Historical Jesus: The Life of a Mediterranean Jewish Peasant*. HarperCollins, 1991.

Crossley, James, and Chris Keith, eds. *The Next Quest for the Historical Jesus*. Eerdmans, 2024.

Dabiri, Ghazzal, and Flavia Ruani, eds. *Thecla and Medieval Sainthood: The Acts of Paul and Thecla in Eastern and Western Hagiography*. Cambridge University Press, 2022.

Dam, Raymond van. *Leadership and Community in Late Antique Gaul*. University of California Press, 1985.

Danielou, Jean. *Les origines du christianisme latin*. Histoires des doctrines avaint Nicée 3. Cerf, 1978.

Davies, Stephen L. *The Revolt of the Widows: The Social World of the Apocryphal Acts*. Bardic, 1980.

Davila, James R. *The Provenance of the Pseudepigrapha: Jewish, Christian, or Other?* JSJSup 105. Brill, 2005.

Davis, Stephen J. "An Arabic *Acts of Paul and Thecla*: Text and Translation, with Introduction and Critical Commentary." In *Thecla: Paul's Disciple and Saint in the East and West*, edited by Jeremy W. Barrier, Jan N. Bremmer, Tobias Nicklas, and Armand Puig i Tàrrech. Studies on Early Christian Apocrypha 12. Peeters, 2017.

Davis, Stephen. *Coptic Christology in Practice: Incarnation and Divine Participation in Late Antique and Medieval Egypt*. Oxford University Press, 2008.

Davis, Stephen J. *The Cult of St Thecla: A Tradition of Women's Piety in Late Antiquity*. 2nd ed. OECS. Oxford University Press, 2009.

Davis, Stephen J. *The Early Coptic Papacy 1*. American University in Cairo Press, 2005.

DeConick, April. *Recovering the Original Gospel of Thomas: A History of the Gospel and Its Growth*. LNTS 286. T&T Clark, 2005.

Deletant, Dennis. "The Sunday Legend." *Revue des études sud-est européennes* 15 (1977): 431–51.

Der Nersessian, Sirarpie. "A Psalter and New Testament Manuscript at Dumbarton Oaks." *DOP* 19 (1965): 153–83.

Deun, Peter van. "Sancti Barnabae Laudatio auctore Alexandro Monacho." In *Hagiographica Cypria*. CCSG 26. Brepols, 1993.

Dieterich, Albrecht. "Himmelsbriefe." In *Kleine Schriften*. Teubner, 1911.

Dinzelbacher, Peter. *Die Jenseitsbrücke im Mittelalter*. Dissertationen der Universität Wien 104. Verband der wissenschaftlichen Gesellschaften Österreichs, 1973.

Döhler, Marietheres. *Acta Petri: Text, Übersetzung und Kommentar zu den Actus Vercellenses*. TU 171. De Gruyter, 2018.

Dolbeau, François. *Prophètes, apôtres et disciples dans les traditions chrétiennes d'Occident. Vies brèves et listes en latin*. Subsidia hagiographica 92. Société des Bollandistes, 2012.

Donner, Herbert. *Pilgerfahrt ins Heilige Land. Die ältesten Berichte christlicher Palästinapilger (4.–7. Jh.)*. 3rd ed. Katholisches Bibelwerk, 2011.

Dorfmann-Lazarev, Igor, ed. *Sharing Myths, Texts and Sanctuaries in the South Caucasus: Apocryphal Themes in Literatures, Arts and Cults from Late Antiquity to the Middle Ages*. Studies on Early Christian Apocrypha 19. Peeters, 2022.

Drake, H. A. *A Century of Miracles: Christians, Pagans, Jews, and the Supernatural, 312–410*. Oxford University Press, 2017.

Dresken-Weiland, Jutta. *Bild, Grab und Wort: Untersuchungen zu Jenseitsvorstellungen von Christen des 3. und 4. Jahrhunderts*. Schnell & Steiner, 2010.

Dubois, Jean-Daniel. *Jésus apocryphe*. Mame-Desclée, 2011.

Duensing, Hugo, and Aurelio de Santos Otero. "Apokalypse des Paulus." In *Neutestamentliche Apokryphen*, vol. 2, *Apostolisches, Apokalypsen und Verwandtes*, edited by Wilhelm Schneemelcher. Mohr Siebeck, 1997.

Duncan, Patricia. *Novel Hermeneutics in the Greek Pseudo-Clementine Romance*. WUNT 395. Mohr Siebeck, 2017.

Dunderberg, Ismo. *Beyond Gnosticism: Myth, Lifestyle, and Society in the School of Valentinus*. Columbia University Press, 2008.

Dvornik, Francis. *The Idea of Apostolicity in Byzantium and the Legend of the Apostle Andrew*. Harvard University Press, 1958.

Eastman, David L. *The Ancient Martyrdom Accounts of Peter and Paul*. WGRW 39. SBL Press, 2015.

Eastman, David L. *The Many Deaths of Peter and Paul*. OECS. Oxford University Press, 2019.

Eco, Umberto. *Die Geschichte der legendären Länder und Städte*. 2nd ed. Deutscher Taschenbuchverlag, 2016.

Edwards, J. Christopher, ed., *Early New Testament Apocrypha*. Ancient Literature for New Testament Studies 9. Zondervan Academic, 2022.

Ehlen, Oliver. "Das Pseudo-Matthäusevangelium." In *Antike christliche Apokryphen in deutscher Übersetzung*, vol. 1, *Evangelien und Verwandtes*, edited by Christoph Markschies and Jens Schröter. Mohr Siebeck, 2012.

Ehrman, Bart D. *Journeys to Heaven and Hell: Tours to the Afterlife*. Yale University Press, 2022.

Ehrman, Bart D. *Lost Scriptures: Books That Did Not Make it into the New Testament*. Oxford University Press, 2003.

Ehrman, Bart D. *Truth and Fiction in "The Da Vinci Code": What We Really Know About Jesus, Mary Magdalene, and Constantine*. Oxford University Press, 2006.

Ehrman, Bart D., and Zlatko Pleše. *The Apocryphal Gospels: Texts and Translations*. Oxford University Press, 2011.

Elliott, J. Keith. *The Apocryphal New Testament*. Oxford University Press, 2009.

Elliott, J. Keith. *A Synopsis of the Apocryphal Nativity and Infancy Narratives*. NTTSD 34. Brill, 2006.

Epp, Eldon J. "The Jews and the Jewish Community in Oxyrhynchus: Socio-religious Context for the New Testament Papyri." In *New Testament Manuscripts, Their Texts and Their World*, edited by Thomas J. Kraus and Tobias Nicklas. TENTS 2. Brill, 2006.

Fabricius, Johann Albert. *Codex Apocryphus Novi Testamenti pars tertia*. Schiller & Kisner, 1743.

Feldmeier, Reiner. *Der erste Brief des Petrus*. THKNT 15/I. Evangelische Verlagsanstalt, 2005.

Ferrar, William John. *The Proof of the Gospel: Being the Demonstratio Evangelica*. Wipf & Stock, 2001.

Festugière, André-Jean. *Historia Monachorum in Aegypto. Édition critique du texte grec et traduction annotée*. Subsidia Hagiographica 53. Société des Bollandistes, 1971.

Fiori, Emiliano. "Death and Judgment in the *Apocalypse of Paul*: Old Imagery and Monastic Reinvention." *ZAC* 20 (2016): 92–108.

Foster, Paul. *The Gospel of Peter: Introduction, Critical Edition and Commentary*. TENTS 4. Brill, 2010.

Foster, Paul. "Polymorphic Christology: Its Origins and Development in Early Christianity." *JTS* 58 (2007): 1–34.

Foucault, Michel. "Andere Räume." [1967]. In *Aisthesis. Wahrnehmung heute oder Perspektiven einer anderen Ästhetik. Essais*, edited by Karlheinz Barck. Suhrkamp, 1993.

François, Etienne. "Pierre Nora und die 'Lieux de mémoire.'" In *Erinnerungsorte Frankreichs*, edited by Pierre Nora. Beck, 2005.

François, Etienne, and Hagen Schulze. "Einleitung." In *Deutsche Erinnerungsorte*, edited by Etienne Francois and Hagen Schulze, vol. 1. Beck, 2009.

Frey, Jörg. "Die Fragmente des Ebionäerevangeliums." In *Antike christliche Apokryphen in deutscher Übersetzung*, vol. 1, *Evangelien und Verwandtes*, edited by Christoph Markschies and Jens Schröter. Mohr Siebeck, 2012.

Frey, Jörg. "Die Fragmente judenchristlicher Evangelien." In *Antike christliche Apokryphen in deutscher Übersetzung*, vol. 1, *Evangelien und Verwandtes*, edited by Christoph Markschies and Jens Schröter. Mohr Siebeck, 2012.

Frey, Jörg. "Second Peter in New Perspective." In *2 Peter and the Apocalypse of Peter: Towards a New Perspective*, edited by Jörg Frey, Matthjis den Dulk and Jan G. van der Watt. BIS 174. Brill, 2019.

Friedman, John Block. *The Monstrous Races in Medieval Art and Thought*. Harvard University Press, 2000.

Fürst, Alfons. *Christentum als Intellektuellen-Religion. Die Anfänge des Christentums in Alexandria*. SBS 213. Katholisches Bibelwerk, 2007.

Gabra, Gavdat, ed. *Be Thou There: The Holy Family's Journey in Egypt*. American University in Cairo Press, 2001.

Gabra, Gavdat, and Gertrud J. M. van Loon. *The Churches of Egypt: From the Journey of the Holy Family to the Present Day*. American University in Cairo Press, 2007.

Gathercole, Simon. *The Gospel of Thomas: Introduction and Commentary*. TENTS 11. Brill, 2014.

Gebhardt, Oscar von. *Passio S. Theclae Virginis. Die Lateinischen Übersetzungen der Acta Pauli et Theclae nebst Fragmenten, Auszügen und Beilagen*. TUGAL. Hinrichs, 1902.

Geigenfeind, Matthias. "The Apocalypse of Thomas." In *New Testament Apocrypha: More Noncanonical Scriptures*, edited by Tony Burke, vol. 2. Eerdmans, 2020.

Genequand, Charles. "Vie de Jésus en arabe." in *Écrits apocryphes chrétiens*, edited by François Bovon and Pierre Geoltrain, vol. 1. Bibliotèque de la Pléiade. Gallimard, 1997.

Gero, Stephen. *Byzantine Iconoclasm During the Reign of Constantine V*. CSCO 384. Secrétariat du Corpus SCO, 1977.

Gold, Barbara K. "Hrotswitha Writes Herself: *Clamor Validus Gandeshemensis*." In *Sex and Gender in Medieval and Renaissance Texts: The Latin Tradition*, edited by Barbara K. Gold, Paul Allen Miller, and Charles Platter, 41–70. SUNY Press, 1997.

Goodspeed, Edgar J. *The Curse in the Colophon*. Willett, Clark, 1933.

Goodspeed, Edgar J. "The Letter of Jesus Christ and the Western Text." *AThR* 1, no. 5/2 (1933): 105–14.

Goodspeed, Edgar J. *Modern Apocrypha*. Beacon, 1956.

Goodspeed, Edgar J. *Strange New Gospels*. University of Chicago Press, 1931.

Gottschall, Dagmar. *Das "Elucidarium" des Honorius Augustodonensis: Untersuchungen zu seiner Überlieferungs-und Rezeptionsgeschichte im deutschsprachigen Raum mit Ausgabe der niederdeutschen Übersetzung*. Texte und Textgeschichte 33. De Gruyter, 1993.

Gregory, Andrew. *The Gospel According to the Hebrews and the Gospel of the Ebionites*. Oxford Early Christian Gospel Texts. Oxford University Press, 2017.

Gregory, Timothy E. *A History of Byzantium*. Blackwell History of the Ancient World. 2nd ed. Wiley-Blackwell, 2016.

Gronewald, Matthias. "Unbekanntes Evangelium oder Evangelienharmonie (Fragment aus dem 'Evangelium Egerton')." In *Kölner Papyri (P.Köln) 6*, edited by Klaus Maresch, Michael Gronewald, Bärbel Kramer, Maryline Parca, and Cornelia Römer. Westdeutscher Verlag, 1987.

Grundeken, Mark. "Shepherd of Hermas." In *The Reception of Jesus in the First Three Centuries*, vol. 2, *From Thomas to Tertullian: Christian Literary Receptions of Jesus in the Second and Third Centuries CE*, edited by Jens Schröter and Christine Jacobi. T&T Clark, 2020.

Grünstäudl, Wolfgang. "Enthüllung im Fragment: Notizen zu Überlieferungsgestalt und Figureninventar der Offenbarung des Petrus." In *Shadowy Characters and Fragmentary Evidence: The Search for Early Christian Groups and Movements*, edited by Joseph Verheyden, Tobias Nicklas, and Elisabeth Hernitscheck. WUNT 388. Mohr Siebeck, 2017.

Grünstäudl, Wolfgang. *Petrus Alexandrinus: Studien zum historischen und theologischen Ort des zweiten Petrusbriefes*. WUNT 2/353. Mohr Siebeck, 2013.

Guignard, Christophe. "Greek Lists of the Apostles: New Findings and Open Questions," *ZAC* 20, no. 3 (2016): 469–95.

Guignard, Christophe. "La tradition grecque de la liste d'apôtres 'anonyme I' (BHG 153c), avec un appendice sur la liste BHG 152n*." *Apocrypha* 26 (2015): 171–209.

Hahn, Hans Peter. *Materielle Kultur. Eine Einführung*. 2nd ed. Dietrich Reimer, 2014.

Halbwachs, Maurice. *Das Gedächtnis und seine sozialen Bedingungen*. 6th ed. Suhrkamp Wissenschaft 538. Suhrkamp, 2019.

Halbwachs, Maurice. *Les cadres sociaux de mémoire*. Presses Universitaires de France, 1925.

Hallinger, Stephanie. "Der Raum zwischen 'kanonisch' und 'parabiblisch'. Caravaggios Auferweckung des Lazarus (1609)." *Zeitschrift für Neues Testament* 51 (2023): 107–29.

Hallinger, Stephanie. "Entangled Traditions About Judith. From Heroine to Camp. In *Characters in Mind: The Migration of Characters in Early Jewish, Early Christian and Greco-Roman Literature and Art*, edited by Jan Rüggemeier and Tobias Nicklas. Diegesis in Mind 2. Bonn University Press, forthcoming.

Hallinger, Stephanie, and Tobias Nicklas. "Von der Illustration zum Text: Ein intermediales Spiel mit der Bamberger Apokalypse."

In *Textforschung zur Septuaginta, zum Hebräerbrief und zur Apokalypse*, edited by Georg Gaebel und Matthias Geigenfeind. De Gruyter, 2024.

Halsall, Guy. *Barbarian Migrations and the Roman West 376–568*. 5th ed. Cambridge University Press, 2014.

Hammershaimb, Erling. *Das Martyrium Jesajas*. JSHRZ 2. Gerd Mohn, 1973.

Hand, Wayland D. "A North Carolina Himmelsbrief." In *Middle Ages – Reformation – Volkskunde: Festschrift for John G. Kunstmann*, edited by Frederic E. Coenen. University of North Carolina Press, 1959.

Hartenstein, Judith. *Die zweite Lehre: Erscheinungen des Auferstandenen als Rahmenerzählungen frühchristlicher Dialoge*. TU 146. Akademie, 1999.

Hartl, Martina. *Leichen, Asche und Gebeine: Der frühchristliche Umgang mit dem toten Körper und die Anfänge des Reliquienkults*. Handbuch zur Geschichte des Todes im frühen Christentum und seiner Umwelt 3. Schnell & Steiner, 2018.

Hauler, Édmund. "Zu den lateinischen Bruchstücken der Thomasapokalypse und eines apostolischen Sendschreibens im Codex Vind. Nr. 16." *Wiener Studien* 30 (1908): 308–40.

Häuptli, Bruno, ed. *Jacobus de Voragine, Legenda Aurea. Goldene Legende*. 2nd ed. Fontes Christiani. Herder, 2022.

Hawk, Brandon. *Preaching Apocrypha in Anglo-Saxon England*. University of Toronto Press, 2018.

Henning, Meghan R. *Hell Hath No Fury: Gender, Disability, and the Invention of Damned Bodies in Early Christian Literature*. ABRL. Yale University Press, 2021.

Henning, Meghan, and Tobias Nicklas. "Questions of Self-Designation in the *Ascension of Isaiah*." In *The Ascension of Isaiah*, edited by Jan N. Bremmer and Tobias Nicklas. Studies in Early Christian Apocrypha 11. Peeters, 2016.

Henry, René. *Photius: Bibliothèque*. Société d'édition les Belles lettres, 1959–1977.

Herbert, Máire, and Martin McNamara. *Irish Biblical Apocrypha*. T&T Clark, 1989.

Hernitscheck, Elisabeth. "Im trüben Wasser des 'Davidsteichs' – P.xy. 840 und die Suche nach seiner Provenienz." In *Shadowy Characters and Fragmentary Evidence: The Search for Early Christian Groups and Movements*, edited by Joseph Verheyden, Tobias Nicklas, and Elisabeth Hernitscheck. WUNT 388. Mohr Siebeck, 2017.

Hershkowitz, Isaac. "Asmodeus and Nucleus on Planet Auschwitz. Kazetnik's Theological and Demonological Kabbalah." Unpublished paper. https://www.academia.edu/3316135/Asmodeus_and_Nucleus_on_Planet_Auschwitz_Katzetnik_s_Theological_and_Demonological_Kabbalah.

Hieke, Thomas. "Das Petrusevangelium vom Alten Testament her gelesen. A Profitable Reading of a Non-canonical Text from the Christian Canon." In *Das Evangelium nach Petrus: Text, Kontexte, Intertexte*, edited by Thomas J. Kraus and Tobias Nicklas. TU 158. De Gruyter, 2007.

Hilhorst, Anton. "Tertullian on the Acts of Paul." In *The Apocryphal Acts of Paul and Thecla*, edited by Jan N. Bremmer. Kok Pharos, 1996.

Hirschberger, Veronika. *Ringen um Israel: Intertextuelle Perspektiven auf das 5. Buch Esra*. Studies on Early Christian Apocrypha 14. Peeters, 2018.

Høgel, Christian. *Symeon Metaphrastes: Rewriting and Canonization*. Museum Tusculanum Press, 2002.

Huebenthal, Sandra. "'Frozen Moments' – Early Christianity Through the Lens of Social Memory Theory." In *Memory and Memories in Early Christianity*, edited by Simon Butticaz and Enrico Norelli. WUNT 398. Mohr Siebeck, 2018.

Huebenthal, Sandra. *Gedächtnistheorie und Neues Testament: Eine methodisch-hermeneutische Einführung*. Narr Francke Attempto, 2022.

Jacobi, Christine. "Jesus' Body: Christology and Soteriology in the Body-Metaphors of the *Gospel of Philip*." In *Connecting Gospels: Beyond the Canonical/Non-canonical Divide*, edited by Francis Watson and Sarah Parkhouse. Oxford University Press, 2018.

Jacobs, Andrew S. *The Life of Thecla*. Early Christian Apocrypha 11. Cascade, 2024.

Jeffery, Peter. *The Secret Gospel of Mark Unveiled: Imagined Rituals of Sex, Death and Madness in a Biblical Forgery*. Yale University Press, 2007.

Jenkins, Philip. *The Many Faces of Christ: The Thousand-Year Studies of the Survival and Influence of the Lost Gospels*. Basic Books, 2015.

Jeremias, Joachim. *Unbekannte Jesusworte*. 4th ed. Gerd Mohn, 1965.

Jirouškova, Lenka. *Die Visio Pauli: Wege und Wandlungen einer orientalischen Apokryphe im lateinischen Mittelalter unter Einschluß der alttschechischen und deutschsprachigen Textzeugen*. Brill, 2006.

Jones, F. Stanley "Introduction to the *Pseudo-Clementines*." In *Pseudoclementina Elchesaiticaque inter Judaeochristiana. Collected Studies*. OLA 203. Peeters, 2012.

Josua, Maria, and Friedmann Eißler. "Das arabische Kindheitsevangelium." In *Antike christliche Apokryphen in deutscher Übersetzung*, vol. 1, *Evangelien und Verwandtes*, edited by Christoph Markschies and Jens Schröter. Mohr Siebeck, 2012.

Junod, Éric, and Jean-Daniel Kaestli, eds. *Acta Iohannis*. 2 vols. Corpus Christianorum Series Apocryphorum 1–2. Brepols, 1983.

Junod, Éric, and Jean-Daniel Kaestli. *L'histoire des actes apocryphes des apôtres du IIIe au IXe siècle: le cas des Actes des Jean*. Imprimerie La Concorde, 1982.

Kaestli, Jean-Daniel. "Le rapport entre les deux Vies Latines de l'apôtre Jean." *Apocrypha* 3, no. 1 (1992): 111–23.

Kaiser, U. Ulrike. "Die Geschichte von Joseph dem Zimmermann." in *Antike christliche Apokryphen in deutscher Übersetzung*, vol. 1, *Evangelien und Verwandtes*, edited by Christoph Markschies and Jens Schröter. Mohr Siebeck, 2012.

Kaiser, U. Ulrike, with Josef Tropper. "Die Kindheitserzählung des Thomas." in *Antike christliche Apokryphen in deutscher Übersetzung*, vol. 1, *Evangelien und Verwandtes*, edited by Christoph Markschies and Jens Schröter. Mohr Siebeck, 2012.

Kaldellis, Anthony. *Streams of Gold, Rivers of Blood: The Rise and Fall of Byzantium, 955 A.D. to the First Crusade*. Oxford University Press, 2017.

Karmann, Thomas R. "Apokryph oder doch geradezu kanonisch? Zur Rezeption des *Protevangelium Jacobi* im antiken Christentum." In *The Protevangelium of James*, edited by Jan N. Bremmer, J. Andrew Doole, Thomas R. Karmann, Tobias Nicklas, and Boris Repschinski. Studies on Early Christian Apocrypha 16. Peeters, 2020.

Keith, Chris, Helen K. Bond, Christine Jacobi, and Jens Schröter, eds. *The Reception of Jesus in the First Three Centuries*. 3 vols. T&T Clark, 2020.

Kellas, Carolyn. "The Healing of the Leper: The Accounts in the Synoptic Gospels and Papyrus Egerton 2, Papyrus Köln 255." *IBS* 16 (1994): 161–73.

Kensky, Meira. "Ephesus, Loca Sancta: The Acts of Timothy and Religious Travel in Late Antiquity." In *The Narrative Self in Early Christianity: Essays in Honor of Judith Perkins*, edited by Janet E. Spittler. WGRWSup 15. SBL Press, 2019.

Klauck, Hans-Josef. *The Apocryphal Acts of the Apostles*. Baylor University Press, 2008.
Klauck, Hans-Josef. *Apocryphal Gospels*. Baylor University Press, 2004.
Klijn, Albertus F. J., and G. J. Reinink. *Patristic Evidence for Jewish-Christian Sects*. Brill, 1973.
Klinghardt, Matthias. *Das älteste Evangelium und die Entstehung der kanonischen Evangelien*. Texte und Arbeiten zum neutestamentlichen Zeitalter 60.1–2. Francke, 2015.
Knibb, Michael A. "Martyrdom and Ascension of Isaiah." *OTP*, 2:143–76.
Koester, Helmut. *Ancient Christian Gospels: Their History and Development*. Trinity Press International, 1990.
Kok, Michael J. *The Gospel on the Margins: The Reception of Mark in the Second Century*. Fortress, 2015.
Konradt, Matthias. *Das Evangelium nach Matthäus*. NTD 1. Vandenhoeck & Ruprecht, 2015.
Kötter, Jan-Markus, and Carlo Scardino, eds. *Chronik des Hydatius. Fortführung der Epitome*. Kleine und fragmentarische Historiker der Spätantike G 9–10. Schöningh, 2019.
Kovacs, Judith, and Christopher Rowland. *Revelation*. Blackwell Bible Commentaries. Blackwell, 2004.
Kraus, Thomas J. "Fürbitte für die Toten im frühen Christentum. 'I Will Grant . . . the One They Ask for Out of Punishment.'" in *Das Gebet im Neuen Testament*, edited by Hans Klein, Vasile Mihoc, and Karl-Wilhelm Niebuhr. WUNT 249. Mohr Siebeck, 2009.
Kraus, Thomas J. "Thecla and the *Acts of Thecla*: Searching for Traces in the Manuscript Tradition." in *The Apostles Peter, Paul, John, Thomas and Philip with Their Companions in Late Antiquity*, edited by Tobias Nicklas, Janet E. Spittler, and Jan N. Bremmer. Studies on Early Christian Apocrypha 17. Peeters, 2021.
Kraus, Thomas J., and Tobias Nicklas. *Das Petrusevangelium und die Petrusapokalypse: Die griechischen Fragmente mit deutscher und englischer Übersetzung*. GCS NS 11. De Gruyter, 2004.
Kruger, Michael J. *The Gospel of the Savior: An Analysis of P.Oxy. 840 and Its Place in the Gospel Traditions of Early Christianity*. TENTS 1. Brill, 2005.
Kruger, Michael J. "Papyrus Oxyrhynchus 840." In *Gospel Fragments*, edited by Thomas J. Kraus, Michael J. Kruger, and Tobias Nicklas. Oxford Early Christian Gospel Texts. Oxford University Press, 2009.

Kulpa, Karol P. *The Relevance of the Reception of 2 Thess 2:3–12 for Tyconius: A Theological Reading of Tyconius' Insights*. History of Biblical Exegesis 4. Mohr Siebeck, 2022.

Laato, Anni Maria. *Jews and Christians in De duobus montibus Sina et Sion. An Approach to Early Latin Adversus Iudaeos Literature*. Åbo Akademi University Press, 1998.

Lalleman, Pieter J. *The Acts of John: A Two Stage Initiation into Johannine Gnosticism*. Studies on Early Christian Apocrypha 4. Peeters, 1998.

Lanzillotta, Lautaro Roig, and Jacques van der Vliet. *The Apocalypse of Paul (Visio Pauli) in Sahidic Coptic: Critical Edition, Translation and Commentary*, Vig.Chr.Supp. Brill, 2023.

Lapidge, Michael, and Michael Herren. *Aldhelm: The Prose Works*. D. S. Brewer, 1979.

Lehner, Hans-Christian, and Maximilian Nix. *Marcus von Regensburg, Visio Tnugdali. Vision des Tnugdal*. Fontes Christiani 76. Herder, 2018.

Lenski, Noel. *Failure of Empire: Valens and the Roman State in the Fourth Century*. University of California Press, 2002.

Leppin, Hartmut. *Theodosius der Große: Auf dem Weg zu einem christlichen Imperium*. Gestalten der Antike. Wissenschaftliche Buchgesellschaft, 2003.

Lipsius, Richard Adelbert. *Acta Apostolorum Apocrypha*. Vol. 2.2. Reprint, Wissenschaftliche Buchgesellschaft, 1959.

Lollar, Jacob A. *The History of John the Son of Zebedee: Introduction, Texts and Translations*. Texts from Christian Late Antiquity 56. Gorgias, 2020.

Lona, Horacio E. *Die "wahre Lehre" des Kelsos*. Kommentar zu frühchristlichen Apologeten – Erg. 1. Herder, 2005.

Lundhaug, Hugo. *Images of Rebirth: Cognitive Poetics and Transformational Soteriology in the Gospel of Philip and the Exegesis of the Soul*. Nag Hammadi and Manichaean Studies 73. Brill, 2010.

Luttikhuizen, Gerard. "A Gnostic Reading of the Acts of John." In *The Apocryphal Acts of John,* edited by Jan N. Bremmer. Studies on the Apocryphal Acts of the Apostles 1. Kok Pharos, 1995.

MacDonald, Dennis R. *The Acts of Andrew and Matthias in the City of the Cannibals*. SBLTT 33. Scholars Press, 1990.

MacDonald, Dennis R. *Christianizing Homer: The Odyssey, Plato and the Acts of Andrews*. Oxford University Press, 1994.

Maier, Daniel C., Jörg Frey, and Thomas J. Kraus, eds. *The Apocalypse of Peter in Context*. Studies on Early Christian Apocrypha 21. Peeters, 2024.

Markschies, Christoph. "Haupteinleitung." In *Antike christliche Apokryphen in deutscher Übersetzung*, vol. 1, *Evangelien und Verwandtes*, edited by Christoph Markschies and Jens Schröter. Mohr Siebeck, 2012.

Markschies, Christoph. *Kaiserzeitliche christliche Theologie und ihre Institutionen: Prolegomena zu einer Geschichte der antiken christlichen Theologie*. Mohr Siebeck, 2007.

Markschies, Christoph, and Jens Schröter, eds. *Antike christliche Apokryphen in deutscher Übersetzung*. Vol. 1, *Evangelien und Verwandtes*. Mohr Siebeck, 2012.

Markschies, Christoph, and Hubert Wolf, eds. *Erinnerungsorte des Christentums*. Beck, 2010.

McGinn, Bernard. *Antichrist: Two Thousand Years of the Human Fascination with the Evil*. Columbia University Press, 2000.

McNamara, Martin. *The Apocrypha in the Irish Church*. Dublin Institute for Advanced Studies, 1975.

Meier, Mischa. *Geschichte der Völkerwanderung: Europa, Asien und Afrika vom 3. bis zum 8. Jahrhundert n.Chr.* 2nd ed. Beck, 2020.

Merkt, Andreas. "The Hetero-topography of the Forum Romanum. How Late Antique Peter Traditions Generated an Augmented Reality of Public Space." In *The Apostles Peter, Paul, John, Thomas and Philip with Their Companions in Late Antiquity*, edited by Tobias Nicklas, Janet E. Spittler and Jan N. Bremmer. Studies on Early Christian Apocrypha 17. Peeters, 2021.

Merkt, Andreas, with Tobias Nicklas and Joseph Verheyden. "Das Novum Testamentum Patristicum (NTP): Ein Projekt zu Erforschung und Auslegung des Neuen Testaments in frühchristlicher und spätantiker Zeit." *EC* 6 (2015): 573–95.

Metzger, Paul. *Katechon: II Thess 2,1–12 im Horizont apokalyptischen Denkens*. BZNW 135. De Gruyter, 2005.

Miceli, Calogero A. "The Epistle of Christ from Heaven." In *New Testament Apocrypha: More Noncanonical Scriptures*, ed. Tony Burke and Brent Landau, vol. 1. Eerdmans, 2016.

Milbach-Schirr, Lilia. "Die Rezeption jüdisch-apokalyptischer Traditionen in christlichen Schriften, untersucht anhand des Verhältnisses von 5. und 6. Esra zu 4. Esra." (PhD diss., Humboldt Universität at Berlin, 2020.

Milbach-Schirr, Lillia. "Second Esdras." In *The Reception of Jesus in the First Three Centuries*, vol. 2, *From Thomas to Tertullian: Christian

Literary Receptions of Jesus in the Second and Third Centuries CE, edited by Jens Schröter and Christine Jacobi. T&T Clark, 2020.

Mimouni, Simon C. "Le concept d'apocryphité dans le christianisme ancien et médiéval: réflexions en guise d'introduction." In *Apocryphité. Histoire d'un concept transversal aux religions du livre. En hommage à P. Geoltrain*, edited by Simon C. Mimouni. BEHER 113. Brepols, 2002.

Miroshnikov, Ivan. *The Gospel of Thomas and Plato: A Study of the Impact of Platonism on the "Fifth Gospel."* Nag Hammadi and Manichaean Studies 93. Brill, 2018.

Möhling, Hannes. *Der Weltkaiser der Endzeit: Entstehung, Wandel und Wirkung einer tausendjährigen Weissagung.* Mittelalter-Forschungen 3. Thorbeke, 2000.

Muñoz Gallarte, Israel, and Lautaro Roig Lanzillotta, eds. *New Trends in the Research on the Apocryphal Acts of Thomas.* Studies on Early Christian Apocrypha 20. Peeters, 2024.

Nicklas, Tobias. "Antike Petruserzählungen und der erinnerte Petrus in Rom." In *Petrusliteratur und Petrusarchäologie: Römische Begegnungen*, edited by Jörg Frey and Martin Wallraff. Rom und Protestantismus 4. Mohr Siebeck, 2020.

Nicklas, Tobias. "Apocalypse of Peter." In *The Reception of Jesus in the First Three Centuries*, vol. 2, *From Thomas to Tertullian: Christian Literary Receptions of Jesus in the Second and Third Centuries CE*, edited by Jens Schröter and Christine Jacobi. T&T Clark, 2020.

Nicklas, Tobias. "Apocryphal Jesus Stories in the *Pseudo-Clementine Homilies*: The Syrophoenician Woman (*Hom.* 2.19) and the Dispute with the Sadducees." In *In Search of Truth in the Pseudo-Clementine Homilies*, edited by Benjamin M. J. De Vos and Danny Praet. WUNT 496. Mohr Siebeck, 2022.

Nicklas, Tobias. "An 'Apocryphal' Role Model Allowing for a Different Lifestyle: Olympias as a Late Antique Thecla." *ETL* 96 (2020): 503–19.

Nicklas, Tobias. "'Apokryph gewordene Schriften'? Gedanken zum Apokryphenbegriff bei großkirchlichen Autoren und in einigen 'gnostischen' Texten." in *In Search of Truth: Augustine, Manichaeism and Other Gnosticism: Studies for Johannes van Oort at Sixty*, edited by Jacob Albert van den Berg, Annemaré Kotzé, Tobias Nicklas, and Madeleine Scopello. Nag Hammadi and Manichaean Studies 74. Brill, 2011.

Nicklas, Tobias. "Barnabas Remembered: Apokryphe Barnabastexte und die Kirche Zyperns." In *Religion als Imagination: Phänomene des Menschseins in den Horizonten theologischer Lebensdeutung. Festschrift für Marco Frenschkowski*, edited by Lena Seehausen, Paulus Enke, and Jens Herzer. Evangelische Verlagsanstalt, 2020.

Nicklas, Tobias. "Beyond 'Canon': Christian Apocrypha and Pilgrimage." In *The Other Side: Apocryphal Perspectives on Ancient Christian "Orthodoxies,"* edited by Tobias Nicklas, Candida Moss, Christopher Tuckett, and Joseph Verheyden. NTOA 117. Vandenhoeck & Ruprecht, 2017.

Nicklas, Tobias. "The 'Beyond Canon' Project: Questions, Topics, and Results." In *The Canon and Beyond: Collected Essays on the History and Hermeneutics of Biblical and Parabiblical Traditions*. WUNT 525. Mohr Siebeck, 2024.

Nicklas, Tobias. "Clashing Claims to Apostolicity in Late Antique Apostle Narratives: East and West." In *Apostolicity and Mission in the Early Church*, edited by Tobias Nicklas, Karl-Wilhelm Niebuhr, and Cosmin Pricop. WUNT. Mohr Siebeck, forthcoming.

Nicklas, Tobias. "The Covenant in Christian Apocrypha: Fragmentary Evidence of a Spectrum of Voices." In *Covenant: Concepts of Berit, Diatheke and Testamentum: Proceedings of the Conference at Lanier Theological Library in Houston, Texas, November 2019*, edited by Christian A. Eberhart and Wolfgang Kraus. WUNT 506. Mohr Siebeck, 2023.

Nicklas, Tobias. "Das Petrusevangelium im Rahmen antiker Jesustraditionen." In *Studien zum Petrusevangelium*. WUNT 453. Mohr Siebeck, 2020.

Nicklas, Tobias. "Denk- und Kommunikationsräume jenseits und diesseits des Kanons." In *Kindness, Courage, and Integrity in Biblical Texts and the Politics of Biblical Interpretation. Festschrift Reimund Bieringer*, edited by Marilou S. Ibita, Dominika Kurek-Chomycz, Bénédicte Lemmelijn, and Sarah Whitear. BETL 333. Peeters, 2023.

Nicklas, Tobias. *Der zweite Thessalonicherbrief*. KEK 10/2. Vandenhoeck & Ruprecht, 2019.

Nicklas, Tobias. "Die Akten des Titus; Rezeption 'apostolischer' Schriften und Entwicklung antik-christlicher 'Erinnerungslandschaften.'" *EC* 8 (2017): 458–80.

Nicklas, Tobias. "Die Gottverlassenheit des Gottessohns. Funktionen von Psalm 22/21 LXX in frühchristlichen Auseinandersetzungen mit der Passion Jesu." In *Aneignung durch Transformation: Festschrift für Michael Theobald*, edited by Wilfried Eisele, Christoph Schaefer, and Hans-Ulrich Weidemann. Herders Biblische Studien 74. Herder, 2013.

Nicklas, Tobias. "Die Judasfigur in spätantiken Apokryphen. Pseudo-Cyrill von Jerusalems *Leben und Passion Christi*." In *Bibel und Patristik. Studien zur Exegese und Rezeption von Septuaginta und Neuem Testament*, edited by Siegfried Kreuzer, Wolfgang Kraus, Martin Karrer, and Jörg Persch. BZSup 3. Brill Deutschland, 2022.

Nicklas, Tobias. "'Drink the Cup Which I Promised You!' (*Apocalypse of Peter* 14.4): Peter's Death and the End of Times." In *The Open Mind: Essays in Honour of Christopher Rowland*, edited by Jonathan Knight and Kevin Sullivan. LNTS 522. Bloomsbury, 2015.

Nicklas, Tobias. "Egerton Gospel (P.Egerton 2)." In *The Reception of Jesus in the First Three Centuries*, vol. 2, *From Thomas to Tertullian: Christian Literary Receptions of Jesus in the Second and Third Centuries CE*, edited by Jens Schröter and Christine Jacobi. T&T Clark, 2020.

Nicklas, Tobias. "Eine neue alte Erzählung im Rahmen antiker Jesustraditionen: Reste eines Exorzismus auf P.Oxy. lxxvi 5072." *Annali di storia dell'esegesi* 29 (2012): 13–27.

Nicklas, Tobias. "Eine 'Passionsgeschichte' in Ps-Cyprians De duobus montibus Sina et Sion." *Humanitas* 76, supplement 1 (2021): 74–85.

Nicklas, Tobias. "Elements of a Narratival Plot About the Child Jesus in the *Infancy Gospel of Thomas* (Codex Sabaiticus 259, fols. 66r–77v [H])." In *The Infancy Gospel of Thomas*, edited by David Cielontko and Tobias Nicklas. Peeters, forthcoming.

Nicklas, Tobias. "From Gospel Book to Virtual Reality: A Neglected Aspect of the Gospel of Matthew's Ancient Reception History." In *The Gospel of Matthew in Its Historical and Theological Context*, edited by Karl-Wilhelm Niebuhr, Mikhail Seleznev, and William Loader. WUNT 459. Mohr Siebeck, 2021.

Nicklas, Tobias. "From Heavenly Jerusalem to the City of Christ: Revelation and the Latin *Apocalypse of Paul*." In *Revelation's New Jerusalem in Late Antiquity*, edited by Nathan Betz, Anthony Dupont, and Johan Leemans. History of Biblical Exegesis 6. Mohr Siebeck, 2024.

Nicklas, Tobias. "From Historical Apocalypses to Apocalyptic History: Late Antique Historians and Apocalyptic Writings." In *Dreams, Visions, Imaginations: Jewish, Christian and Gnostic Views of the World to Come*, edited by Jens Schröter, Tobias Nicklas, and Armand Puig i Tàrrech. BZNW 247. De Gruyter, 2021.

Nicklas, Tobias. "Frühchristliche Ansprüche auf die Schriften Israels." In *Scriptural Authority in Early Judaism and Ancient Christianity*. DCLS 16. De Gruyter, 2013.

Nicklas, Tobias. "Gott und Identität: Das Gottesbild der Johannesoffenbarung und ihre Identitätskonstruktion." In *Die Johannesapokalypse: Geschichte – Theologie – Rezeption*, edited by M. Sommer, Uta Poplutz, and Christina Hoegen-Rohls. WUNT 508. Mohr Siebeck, 2023.

Nicklas, Tobias. "History and Theology in the Non-canonical Gospels." In *History and Theology in the Gospels*, edited by Tobias Nicklas, Karl-Wilhelm Niebuhr, and Mikhail Seleznev. WUNT 447. Mohr Siebeck, 2020.

Nicklas, Tobias. "'And I Saw Another Place . . .' (ApcPet 21): The Greek Apocalypse of Peter and Its Otherworldly Landscape of Memories." In *Social Memory Theory and Conceptions of Afterlife in Jewish and Christian Antiquity*, edited by Thomas R. Hatina and Jiří Lukeš. Studies in Cultural Contexts of the Bible 8. Brill and Schöningh, 2023.

Nicklas, Tobias. "The Influence of Jewish Scriptures on Early Christian Apocrypha." In *The Oxford Handbook of Early Christian Apocrypha*, edited by Andrew Gregory and Christopher Tuckett. Oxford University Press, 2015.

Nicklas, Tobias. "'Insider' und 'Outsider': Überlegungen zum historischen Kontext der Darstellung 'jenseitiger' Orte in der Offenbarung des Petrus." In *Topographie des Jenseits: Studien zur Geschichte des Todes in Kaiserzeit und Spätantike*, edited by Walter Ameling. Altertumswissenschaftliches Kolloquium 21. Franz Steiner, 2011.

Nicklas, Tobias. "Inszenierung 'petrinischer Theologie' in den *Acta Petri* (Actus Vercellenses)." In *Peter in the Early Church. Apostle—Missionary—Church Leader*, edited by Judith M. Lieu. BETL 325. Peeters, 2022.

Nicklas, Tobias. *Jews and Christians? Second Century "Christian" Perspectives on the "Parting of the Ways."* Mohr Siebeck, 2014.

Nicklas, Tobias. "The Latin *Apocalypse of Paul*. Images and Ideas of Humanity." In *Stories and Images of Human Beings in the New Testament and Church Tradition*, edited by Karl-Wilhelm Niebuhr, Cosmin Pricop, and Tobias Nicklas. WUNT 521. Mohr Siebeck, 2024.

Nicklas, Tobias. "'Let the Dead Bury Their Own Dead' (Matt 8:22 par. Luke 9:60): A Commandment Without Impact for Christian

Ethos?" In *Biblical Ethics and Application: Purview, Validity, and Relevance of Biblical Texts in Ethical Discourse*, edited by Ruben Zimmermann and Stephen Joubert. WUNT 384. Mohr Siebeck, 2017.

Nicklas, Tobias. "Martyrdom of Mark." In *New Testament Apocrypha: More Noncanonical Scriptures*, vol. 3, edited by Tony Burke. Eerdmans, 2023.

Nicklas, Tobias. "The Martyrdom of Mark in Late Antique Alexandria." In *Alexandria: Hub of the Hellenistic World*, edited by Benjamin Schliesser, Jan Rüggemeier, Thomas J. Kraus, and Jörg Frey. WUNT 460. Mohr Siebeck, 2021.

Nicklas, Tobias. "Neutestamentlicher Kanon, christliche Apokryphen und antik-christliche 'Erinnerungskulturen.'" *NTS* 62 (2016): 588–609.

Nicklas, Tobias. "Neutestamentlicher Kanon und christliche Apokryphen. Trends, Themen und Thesen." *Zeitschrift für Neues Testament* 51 (2023): 5–26.

Nicklas, Tobias. "New Testament Canon and Ancient Christian 'Landscapes of Memory.'" *EC* 7 (2016): 5–23.

Nicklas, Tobias. "'Our Righteous Brethren': Reflections on the Description of the Righteous Ones According to the Greek *Revelation of Peter* (Akhm. 2)." In *Empsychoi Logoi: Religious Innovations in Antiquity: Studies in Honor of Peter Willem van der Horst*, edited by Alberdina Houtman, Albert de Jong, and Magda Misset-van de Weg. AJEC 73. Brill, 2008.

Nicklas, Tobias. "Parting of the Ways? Probleme eines Konzepts." In *Juden – Heiden – Christen? Religiöse Inklusion und Exklusion in Kleinasien bis Decius*, edited by S. Alkier and H. Leppin. WUNT 400. Mohr Siebeck, 2018.

Nicklas, Tobias. "Petrus-Diskurse in Alexandria: Eine Fortführung der Gedanken von Jörg Frey." In *2 Peter and the Apocalypse of Peter: Towards a New Perspective*, edited by Jörg Frey, Matthijs den Dulk, and Jan G. van der Watt. BIS 174. Brill, 2019.

Nicklas, Tobias. "Resurrection—Judgment—Punishment: Apocalypse of Peter 4." In *Resurrection of the Dead. Biblical Traditions in Dialogue*, edited by G. van Oyen and T. Shepherd. BETL 240. Peeters, 2012.

Nicklas, Tobias. "Rezeption und Nicht-Rezeption der Offenbarung des Johannes durch antike christliche Apokalypsen." In *Christian Apocrypha: Receptions of the New Testament in Ancient Christian Apocrypha*, edited by Jean-Michel Roessli and Tobias Nicklas.

Novum Testamentum Patristicum 26. Vandenhoeck & Ruprecht, 2014.

Nicklas, Tobias. "Second Century Apocryphal Acts." In *Second Century Christianity: A Sourcebook*, edited by Michael Bird and Scott Harrower. Baylor University Press, forthcoming.

Nicklas, Tobias. "Second-Century Gospels as 'Re-enactments' of Earlier Writings: Examples from the *Gospel of Peter*." In *Studien zum Petrusevangelium*. WUNT 453. Mohr Siebeck, 2020.

Nicklas, Tobias. "Semiotik – Intertextualität – Apokryphität: Eine Annäherung an den Begriff 'christlicher Apokryphen.'" *Apocrypha* 17 (2006): 55–78.

Nicklas, Tobias. "Signs for the End of the *Saeculum*: Time in the *Apocalypse of Thomas* (Short Version, Codex N)." In *Apocalyptic Time*, edited by Emanuela Grypeou and Stephanie Rabe. Forthcoming.

Nicklas, Tobias. "Spätantike Apostelerzählungen als liturgiegeschichtliche Quellen." In *Ünneplő ember a közösségben. Baráti köszöntő kötet Nóda Mózes tiszteletére*, edited by Korinna Zamfir. Verbum, 2019.

Nicklas, Tobias. "Traditions About Jesus in Apocryphal Gospels (with the Exception of the Gospel of Thomas)." In *Handbook for the Study of the Historical Jesus*, edited by Tom Holmén and Stanley E. Porter. Brill, 2011.

Nicklas, Tobias. "The 'Unknown Gospel' on Papyrus Egerton 2 (+ Papyrus Cologne 255)." In *Gospel Fragments*, edited by Thomas J. Kraus, Michael J. Kruger, and Tobias Nicklas. Oxford Early Christian Gospel Texts. Oxford University Press, 2009.

Nicklas, Tobias. "Zur Problematik der so genannten 'Agrapha.' Eine Thesenreihe." *RB* 113 (2006): 78–93.

Nicklas, Tobias. *Zwischen apokryph und hagiographisch: Spätantike Apostelerzählungen in ihrer Zeit*. Tria Corda Lectures. Mohr Siebeck, forthcoming.

Nicklas, Tobias. "Zwischen Redaktion und 'Neuinszenierung': Vom Umgang erzählender Evangelien des 2. Jahrhunderts mit ihren Vorlagen." In *Gospels and Gospel Traditions in the Second Century. Experiments in Reception*, edited by Jens Schröter, Tobias Nicklas, and Joseph Verheyden. BZNW 235. De Gruyter, 2019.

Nicklas, Tobias, Matthias Geigenfeind, and Johannes Stettner. "Die Deutung der Weltgeschichte in der Langform der Apokalypse des Thomas (Codex Palatinus: §§2–10)." *ETL* 94 (2018): 257–74.

Nicklas, Tobias, and Janet E. Spittler, eds. *Credible, Incredible. The Miraculous in the Ancient Mediterranean*. WUNT 321. Mohr Siebeck, 2013.

Nikolsky, Ronit. "The Adam and Eve Traditions in the Journey of Zosimos." In *Things Revealed. Festschrift Michael E. Stone*, edited by Esther Chazon. JSJSup 89. Brill, 2004.

Nora, Pierre, ed. *Les lieux de mémoire*. 3 vols. Gallimard, 1984–1992.

Nora, Pierre, ed. *Realms of Memory: Rethinking the French Past*. 3 vols. University of Chicago Press, 1998.

North, Richard, and Michael D. J. Bintley. *Andreas: An Edition*. Liverpool University Press, 2016.

Oegema, Gerbern S., ed. *The Oxford Handbook of the Apocrypha*. Oxford University Press, 2021.

O'Leary, Aideen M. "Apostolic Passiones in Early Anglo-Saxon England." In *Apocryphal Texts and Traditions in Anglo-Saxon England*, edited by Kathryn Powell and Donald Scragg. D. S. Brewer, 2003.

Palmer, James T. *The Apocalypse in the Early Middle Ages*. Cambridge University Press, 2014.

Palmer, James T. "The Ordering of Time." In *Abendländische Apokalyptik: Kompendium zu einer Genealogie der Endzeit*, edited by Veronika Wieser, Christian Zolles, Catherine Feik, Martin Zolles, and Leopold Schlöndorff. Kulturgeschichte der Apokalypse 1. Akademie, 2013.

Patterson, Stephen J. "The Gospel of Thomas and Historical Jesus Research." In *Coptica – Gnostica – Manichaica: Mélanges offerts à Wolf-Peter Funk*. Bibliotheque Copte de Nag Hammadi Études 7. Peeters, 2006.

Patterson, Stephen J. "The *Gospel of Thomas* and the Historical Jesus." In *The Oxford Handbook of Early Christian Apocrypha*, edited by Andrew Gregory and Christopher Tuckett. Oxford University Press, 2015.

Patterson, Stephen J. "Jesus Meets Plato: The Theology of the *Gospel of Thomas* and Middle Platonism." In *Das Thomasevangelium: Entstehung – Rezeption – Theologie*, edited by Jörg Frey, Enno Edzard Popkes, and Jens Schröter. BZNW 157. De Gruyter, 2008.

Pellegrini, Silvia. "Das Protevangelium des Jakobus." In *Antike christliche Apokryphen in deutscher Übersetzung*, vol. 1, *Evangelien und Verwandtes*, edited by Christoph Markschies and Jens Schröter. Mohr Siebeck, 2012.

Pervo, "Richard I. The Acts of Titus." In *New Testament Apocrypha: More Noncanonical Scriptures*, vol. 1, edited by Tony Burke and Brent Landau. Eerdmans, 2016.

Pesce, Mauro, *Le parole dimenticate du Gesù*. Arnaldo Mondadori, 2004.
Piay, Augusto Diego. *Priscillian: The Life and Death of a Christian Dissenter in Late Antiquity*. Gorgias, 2024).
Podskalsky, Gerhard. *Byzantinische Reichsideologie: Die Periodisierung der Weltgecshichte in den vier Großreichen (Daniel 2 und 7) und dem tausendjährigen Friedensreiche (Apok. 20), Eine motivgeschichtliche Untersuchung*. Fink, 1972.
Potter, David S. *The Roman Empire at Bay: AD 180–395*. 2nd ed. Routledge History of the Ancient World. Routledge, 2014.
Poupon, Gerard. "Encore un fois: Tertullien, *De baptism* 17.5." In *Nomen Latinum. Mélanges André Schneider*, edited by Den Knoepfler. Université de Neuchâtel, 1997.
Preußler, Otfried. *Die Flucht nach Ägypten: Königlich böhmischer Teil*. Dtv, 1996.
Price, Richard, trans. *The Acts of the Second Council of Nicaea (787)*. Translated Texts for Historians 68. Liverpool University Press, 2020.
Pricop, Cosmin. "Thomas weitererzählt: Rezeption der apokryphen Thomasakten im Synaxarion des Thomas-Festes." in *The Apostles Peter, Paul, John, Thomas and Philip with Their Companions in Late Antiquity*, edited by Tobias Nicklas, Janet E. Spittler, and Jan N. Bremmer. Studies on Early Christian Apocrypha 17. Peeters, 2021.
Rehm, Bernhard. *Die Pseudoklementinen I: Homilien*. 3rd ed. GCS 42. Akademie, 1992.
Röcker, Fritz W. *Belial und Katechon: Eine Untersuchung zu 1 Thess 2,1–12 und 1 Thess 4,13–5,11*. WUNT 2/262. Mohr Siebeck, 2009.
Romm, James S. *The Edges of the Earth in Ancient Thought*. Princeton University Press, 1992.
Roth, Dieter T. "Marcion's Gospel and Luke: A History of Research in Current Debate." *JBL* 177 (2008): 513.
Roukema, Riemer. "Jesus Tradition in Early Patristic Writings." In *Handbook for the Study of the Historical Jesus*, edited by Tom Holmén and Stanley E. Porter. Brill, 2011.
Russell, Norman. *The Lives of the Desert Fathers: The Historia monachorum in Aegypto*. Mowbray, 1980.
Sackur, Ernst. *Sibyllinische Texte und Forschungen. Pseudomethodius, Adso und die tiburtinische Sibylle*. Niemeyer, 1898.
Santos Otero, Aurelio de. "Der apokryphe sogenannte Sonntagsbrief." *StPatr* 3, no. 1 (1961): 290–96.

Schäferdiek, Knut. "The Acts of John." In *New Testament Apocrypha*, edited by Wilhelm Schneemelcher, translated and edited by R. McL. Wilson. Westminster John Knox, 1992.

Schenke, Hans-Martin. "Das Philippusevangelium (NHC II,3)." in *Antike christliche Apokryphen in deutscher Übersetzung*, vol. 1, *Evangelien und Verwandtes*, edited by Christoph Markschies and Jens Schröter. Mohr Siebeck, 2012.

Schneemelcher, Wilhelm. *Neutestamentliche Apokryphen*. Vol. 1. 6th ed. Mohr Siebeck, 1989.

Schneemelcher, Wilhelm. "Apostelgeschichten des 2. und 3. Jahrhunderts: Einleitung." in *Neutestamentliche Apokrypphen*, vol. 2, *Apostolisches, Apokalypsen und Verwandtes*, edited by Wilhelm Schneemelcher. Mohr Siebeck, 1997.

Schneider, Gerhard. *Apokryphe Kindheitsevangelien*. Fontes Christiani 18. Herder, 1995.

Schneider, Paul G. "A Perfect Fit: The Major Interpolation in the Acts of John." in *Society of Biblical Literature 1991 Seminar Papers*. Scholars Press, 1991.

Schreiner, Klaus. "Maria." in *Erinnerungsorte des Christentums*, edited by Christoph Markschies and Hubert Wolf. Beck, 2010.

Schröter, Jens. *Die apokryphen Evangelien*. Beck, 2020.

Schröter, Jens. *Erinnerung an Jesu Worte: Studien zur Rezeption der Logienüberlieferung in Markus, Q und Thomas*. WMANT 76. Neukirchener, 1997.

Schröter, Jens, and Hans-Gebhard Bethge. "Das Evangelium nach Thomas (Thomasevangelium [NHC II,2 p.32,10–51,28]) Oxyrhynchus Papyri I 1, IV 654 und IV 655 (P.Oxy. I 1, IV 654 und IV 655)." In *Antike christliche Apokryphen in deutscher Übersetzung*, vol. 1, *Evangelien und Verwandtes*, edited by Christoph Markschies and Jens Schröter. Mohr Siebeck, 2012.

Schröter, Jens, Benjamin A. Edsall, and Joseph Verheyden, eds. *Jews and Christians—Parting Ways in the First Two Centuries CE? Reflections on the Gains and Losses of a Model*. BZNW 253. De Gruyter, 2021.

Schwarz, Konrad. "Gospel of Thomas." In *The Reception of Jesus in the First Three Centuries*, vol. 2, *From Thomas to Tertullian: Christian Literary Receptions of Jesus in the Second and Third Centuries CE*, edited by Jens Schröter and Christine Jacobi. T&T Clark, 2020.

Shoemaker, Stephen J. *The Ancient Traditions of the Virgin Mary's Dormition and Assumption*. Oxford University Press, 2002.

Shoemaker, Stephen J. *The Dormition and Assumption Apocrypha*. Studies on Early Christian Apocrypha 15. Peeters, 2018.

Shoemaker, Stephen J. *The Life of the Virgin: Maximus the Confessor.* Yale University Press, 2012.

Shoemaker, Stephen J. "The Tiburtine Sibyl." In *New Testament Apocrypha. More Noncanonical Scriptures*, edited by Tony Burke and Brent Landau, vol. 1. Eerdmans, 2016.

Short, Ian. "The Life of St John the Evangelist from Paris, BNF fr. 19525." In *The Trinity Apocalypse (CD-ROM Accompanying)*, edited by David McKitterick. British Library, 2005.

Short, Ian. "The Translation of the Life of St John and the Apocalypse." In *The Trinity Apocalypse (CD-ROM Accompanying)*, edited by David McKitterick. British Library, 2005.

Siegert, Folker. *Einleitung in die hellenistisch-jüdische Literatur. Apocrypha, Pseudepigrapha und Fragmente verlorener Autorenwerke.* De Gruyter, 2016.

Silverstein, Theodore, and Anton Hilhorst, eds. *Apocalypse of Paul: A New Critical Edition of Three Long Latin Versions.* Cahiers d'Orientalisme 21. Patrick Cramer, 1997.

Sivan, Hagith. *Galla Placidia. The Last Roman Empress.* Women in Antiquity. Oxford University Press, 2011.

Skeat, Theodore Cressy. "The Codex Sinaiticus, the Codex Vaticanus and Constantine." In *The Collected Biblical Writings of T. C. Skeat*, edited by J. Keith Elliott. NovTSup 113. Brill, 2004.

Smith, Daniel A. "Marcion's Gospel and the Synoptics: Proposals and Problems." In *Gospels and Gospel Traditions in the Second Century: Experiments in Reception*, edited by Jens Schröter, Tobias Nicklas, and Joseph Verheyden. BZNW 235. de Gruyter, 2020.

Smith, Morton. *Clement of Alexandria and a Secret Gospel of Mark.* Harvard University Press, 1973.

Snyder, Julia. "Acts of John, Acts of Peter, Acts of Thekla, Third Corinthians, and Martyrdom of Paul." In *The Reception of Jesus in the First Three Centuries*, vol. 2, *From Thomas to Tertullian: Christian Literary Receptions of Jesus in the Second and Third Centuries CE*, edited by Jens Schröter and Christine Jacobi. T&T Clark, 2020.

Snyder, Julia. "Relationships Between the Acts of the Apostles and Other Apostle Narratives." In *Between Canonical and Apocryphal Texts: Processes of Reception, Rewriting and Interpretation in Early Judaism and Early Christianity*, edited by Jörg Frey, Claire Clivaz, and Tobias Nicklas. Mohr Siebeck, 2018.

Snyder, Timothy. *Bloodlands: Europe Between Hitler and Stalin.* 7th ed. Beck, 2022.

Sommer, Michael. "The Ethics of Hell: Righteousness in the Apocalypse of Peter and Early Christian Discourses About Ethics." In *The Apocalypse of Peter in Context*, edited by Daniel C. Maier, Jörg Frey, and Thomas J. Kraus. Studies on Early Christian Apocrypha 21. Peeters, 2024.

Sommer, Michael. *Witwen, Recht und Gerechtigkeit: Diskurse über Witwen im frühen Christentum als Rezeptionsorte prophetischer und weisheitlicher Kultkritik gelesen*. WUNT. Mohr Siebeck, forthcoming.

Speyer, Wolfgang. *Die literarische Fälschung im heidnischen und christlichen Altertum: Ein Versuch ihrer Deutung*. Handbuch der Altertumswissenschaft 1/2. Beck.

Spilling, Herrad. *Die Visio Tnugdali: Eigenart und Stellung in der mittelalterlichen Visionsliteratur bis zum Ende des 12. Jahrhunderts*. Münchener Beiträge zur Mediävistik und Renaissance-Forschung 21. Arbeo-Gesellschaft, 1975.

Spittler, Janet E. "The Acts of John by Prochorus." In *New Testament Apocrypha: More Noncanonical Scriptures*, edited by Tony Burke, vol. 3. Eerdmans, 2023.

Spittler, Janet E. "The Acts of John by Prochorus in Patmos Ms. 188: A Test-Case Illustrating the Composition and Development of Later Apocryphal Acts." In *The Apostles Peter, Paul, John, Thomas, and Philip with Their Companions in Late Antiquity*, edited by Tobias Nicklas, Janet E. Spittler, and Jan N. Bremmer. Studies on Early Christian Apocrypha 17. Peeters, 2021.

Spittler, Janet E. "The *Acts of Timothy*, Luke's Prologue, and Gospel Prologues: Accounts of the Composition of Early Christian Narratives." In *Narrative Hermeneutics, History, and Rhetoric. A Festschrift for David P. Moessner*, edited by Robert Matthew Calhoun, Margaret M. Mitchell, Tobias Nicklas, and Janet E. Spittler. NovTSup 194. Brill, 2024.

Spittler, Janet E. *Animals in the Apocryphal Acts of the Apostles: The Wild Kingdom of Early Christian Literature*. WUNT 2/247. Mohr Siebeck, 2008.

Spittler, Janet E. "Apocryphal Epistles: The Curious Case of the *Letter of Jesus Christ That Fell from Heaven*." In *Paul, Christian Textuality, and the Hermeneutics of Late Antiquity*, edited by Robert Matthew Calhoun, Paul Duff, David P. Moessner, and Janet E. Spittler. Brill, 2023.

Spittler, Janet E. "Apokryphe Apostelerzählungen und ihrer Funktion in der Geschichte des Christentums," *Zeitschrift für Neues Testament* 51 (2023): 55–77.

Spittler, Janet E. "Christianity at the Edges: Representations of the Ends of the Earth in the Apocryphal Acts of the Apostles." In *The Rise and Expansion of Christianity in the First Three Centuries CE*, edited by Clare Rothschild and Jens Schröter. WUNT 301. Mohr Siebeck, 2013.

Spittler, Janet E. "John, Acts of." In *Brill Encyclopedia of Early Christianity,* edited by David G. Hunter, Paul J. J. van Geest, and Bert Jan Lietaert Peerbolte. Brill, 2024.

Spittler, Janet E. "Responses to Mark Goodacre, James McGrath, and Caroline Schroeder on the *Gospel of Jesus' Wife*." In *Fakes, Forgeries, and Fictions: Writing Ancient and Modern Apocrypha. Proceedings from the 2015 York University Christian Apocrypha Symposium*, edited by Tony Burke. Cascade, 2017.

Staat, Klazina. "'Useful' Models: The Reception of the Apocryphal *Acts of Paul and Thecla* in Late-Antique Hagiographical Narratives About Female Virgins." in *The Apostles Peter, Paul, John, Thomas and Philip with Their Companions in Late Antiquity*, edited by Tobias Nicklas, Janet E. Spittler, and Jan N. Bremmer. Studies on Early Christian Apocrypha 17. Peeters, 2021.

Stählin, Otto, and Ludwig Früchtel. *Clemens Alexandrinus*. 2nd ed. GCS 17. Akademie, 1970.

Stone, Michael E., and Emanuela Timotin. *The Cheirograph of Adam in Armenian and Romanian Traditions. New Texts and Images.* Brepols, 2023.

Stubbs, William, ed. *Chronica magistri Rogeri de Houedene*. Vol. 4. Her Majesty's Stationary Office, 1871.

Suciu, Alin. *The Berlin-Strasbourg Apocryphon: A Coptic Apostolic Memoire*. WUNT 370. Mohr Siebeck, 2017.

Syroid, Dariya. "The Church Slavonic Redaction of the *Acts of Paul and Thecla* by Dymytrii Tuptalo." in *The Apostles Peter, Paul, John, Thomas and Philip with Their Companions in Late Antiquity*, edited by Tobias Nicklas, Janet E. Spittler, and Jan N. Bremmer. Studies on Early Christian Apocrypha 17. Peeters, 2021.

Talbot, Ann-Mary, and Scott Fitzgerald Johnson, eds. *Miracle Tales from Byzantium*. Dumbarton Oaks Medieval Library. Harvard University Press, 2012.

Tannous, Jack. *The Making of the Medieval Middle East*. Princeton University Press, 2018.

Theobald, Michael. "'Stirb, damit du lebst!' Die Totenauferweckungen des Kallimachos, der Drusiana und des Fortunatus) ActJoh

63–86, bes 74–84." In *Kompendium der frühchristlichen Wundererzählungen*, vol. 2, *Die Wunder der Apostel*, edited by Ruben Zimmermann. Gütersloher Verlagshaus, 2017.

Toepel, Alexander. "The Cave of Treasures." In *Old Testament Pseudepigrapha: More Noncanonical Scriptures*, edited by Richard Bauckham, James Davila, and Alexander Panayotov, vol. 1. Eerdmans, 2013.

Tuckett, Christopher. *The Gospel of Mary*. Oxford Early Christian Gospel Texts. Oxford University Press, 2007.

Vassiliev, A. *Anecdota Graeco-Byzantina, pars prior*. Universitatus Caesareae, 1893.

Verheyden, Joseph, Jens Schröter, and Tobias Nicklas, eds. *Texts in Context: Essays on Dating and Contextualizing Christian Writings from the Second and Early Third Centuries*. BETL 319. Peeters, 2021.

Vinzent, Markus. *Christ's Torah: The Making of the New Testament in the Second Century*. Routledge, 2024.

Wayment, Thomas A. *The Text of the New Testament Apocrypha (100–400 CE)*. Bloomsbury, 2013.

Wehnert, Jürgen. *Pseudoklementinische Homilien. Einführung und Übersetzung*. Kommentare zur apokryphen Literatur 1/1. Vandenhoeck & Ruprecht, 2010.

Weltecke, Dorothea. *Die drei Ringe: Warum die Religionen erst im Mittelalter entstanden sind*. Beck, 2024.

Wieser, Veronika. "Die Weltchronik des Sulpicius Severus. Fragmente einer Sprache der Endzeit im ausgehenden vierten Jahrhundert." In *Abendländische Apokalyptik: Kompendium zu einer Genealogie der Endzeit*, edited by Veronika Wieser, Christian Zolles, Catherine Feik, Martin Zolles, and Leopold Schlöndorff. Kulturgeschichte der Apokalypse 1. Akademie, 2013.

Witetscheck, Stephan. *Thomas und Johannes – Johannes und Thomas: Das Verhältnis der Logien des Thomasevangeliums zum Johannesevangelium*. Herders Biblische Studien 79. Herder, 2015.

Wright, Charles D. "Rewriting (and Re-editing) the *Apocalypse of Thomas*." In *Écritures et réécritures: la reprise interpretative des traditions fondatrices par la littérature biblique et extra-biblique*, edited by Claire Clivaz, Corinna Combet-Galland, Jean-Daniel Macchi, and Christophe Nihan. Peeters, 2012.

Wurst, Gregor. "Das Judasevangelium (CT 3)." In *Antike christliche Apokryphen in deutscher Übersetzung*, vol. 1, *Evangelien und Verwandtes*, edited by Christoph Markschies and Jens Schröter. Mohr Siebeck, 2012.

Zamagni, Claudio. "Passion (Ou Actes) de Timothée. étude des traditions anciennes et edition de la forme BHG 1487." In *Poussières de Christianisme et de Judaïsme Antiques. Études Réunies En l'honneur de Jean-Daniel Kaestli et Éric Junod*, edited by Rémi Gounelle and Albert Frey. Éditions du Zèbre, 2007.
Zarncke, Friedrich. *Der Priester Johannes: Zwei Teile in einem Band.* Reprint, Olms, 1980.
Zelyck, Lorne R. *The Egerton Gospel (Egerton Papyrus 2 + Papyrus Köln VI 255). Introduction, Critical Edition, and Commentary.* TENTS 13. Brill, 2019.
Zelyck, Lorne R. "Elisha Typology in Jesus' Miracle on the Jordan River (Papyrus Egerton 2, 2v.6–14)." *NTS* 62 (2016): 149–56.
Zwierlein, Otto. *Petrus in Rom: Die literarischen Zeugnisse.* 2nd ed. Untersuchungen zur antiken Literatur und Geschichte 96. De Gruyter, 2010.

GENERAL SUBJECT INDEX

ANCIENT SOURCES INDEX

Ancient Christian Literature